MW00850117

"A highly significant contribution to the field of Christology. Aaron Riches argues that the Christology sanctioned by the great ecumenical councils of the first millennium was not about finding some middle line that balanced out excessive and mutually competitive emphases on Jesus' divinity or humanity. Rather, it was animated by an existential and liturgical encounter with the one Lord Jesus Christ, whose integral duality is recognizable only to the extent that his absolute singularity is maintained."

— TRACEY ROWLAND
John Paul II Institute for Marriage and Family, Melbourne

"Pondering the confession of the 'one Lord Jesus Christ' that is the basis of the Nicene faith, Riches demonstrates what is at stake in recognizing that Christianity reaches into the most intimate depths of the human being."

— DAVID L. SCHINDLER
Pontifical John Paul II Institute for Studies on Marriage and Family

INTERVENTIONS

Conor Cunningham

GENERAL EDITOR

It's not a question of whether one believes in God or not. Rather, it's a question of if, in the absence of God, we can have belief, any belief.

"If you live today," wrote Flannery O'Connor, "you breathe in nihilism." Whether "religious" or "secular," it is "the very gas you breathe." Both within and without the academy, there is an air common to both deconstruction and scientism — both might be described as species of *reductionism*. The dominance of these modes of knowledge in popular and professional discourse is quite incontestable, perhaps no more so where questions of theological import are often relegated to the margins of intellectual respectability. Yet it is precisely the proponents and defenders of religious belief in an age of nihilism that are often among those most — unwittingly or not — complicit in this very reduction. In these latter cases, one frequently spies an accommodationist impulse, whereby our concepts must be first submitted to a prior philosophical court of appeal in order for them to render any intellectual value. To cite one particularly salient example, debates over the origins, nature, and ends of human life are routinely partitioned off into categories of "evolutionism" and "creationism," often with little nuance. Where attempts to mediate these arguments are to be found, frequently the strategy is that of a kind of accommodation: How can we adapt our belief in creation to an already established evolutionary metaphysic, or, how can we have our evolutionary cake and eat it too? It is sadly the case that, despite the best intentions of such "intellectual ecumenism," the distinctive voice of theology is the first one to succumb to aphonia — either from impetuous overuse or from a deliberate silencing.

The books in this unique new series propose no such simple accommodation. They rather seek and perform tactical interventions in such debates in a manner that problematizes the accepted terms of such debates.

They propose something altogether more demanding: through a kind of refusal of the disciplinary isolation now standard in modern universities, a genuinely interdisciplinary series of mediations of crucial concepts and key figures in contemporary thought. These volumes will attempt to discuss these topics as they are articulated within their own field, including their historical emergence, and cultural significance, which will provide a way into seemingly abstract discussions. At the same time, they aim to analyze what consequences such thinking may have for theology, both positive and negative, and, in light of these new perspectives, to develop an effective response — one that will better situate students of theology and professional theologians alike within the most vital debates informing Western society, and so increase their understanding of, participation in, and contribution to these.

To a generation brought up on a diet of deconstruction, on the one hand, and scientism, on the other, Interventions offers an alternative that is *otherwise than nihilistic* — doing so by approaching well-worn questions and topics, as well as historical and contemporary figures, from an original and interdisciplinary angle, and so avoid having to steer a course between the aforementioned Scylla and Charybdis.

This series will also seek to navigate not just through these twin dangers, but also through the dangerous "and" that joins them. That is to say, it will attempt to be genuinely interdisciplinary in avoiding the conjunctive approach to such topics that takes as paradigmatic a relationship of "theology and phenomenology" or "religion and science." Instead, the volumes in this series will, in general, attempt to treat such discourses not as discrete disciplines unto themselves, but as moments within a distended theological performance. Above all, they will hopefully contribute to a renewed atmosphere shared by theologians and philosophers (not to mention those in other disciplines) — an air that is not nothing.

CENTRE OF THEOLOGY AND PHILOSOPHY

(www.theologyphilosophycentre.co.uk)

Every doctrine which does not reach the one thing necessary, every separated philosophy, will remain deceived by false appearances. It will be a doctrine, it will not be Philosophy.

Maurice Blondel, 1861-1949

This book series is the product of the work carried out at the Centre of Theology and Philosophy (COTP), at the University of Nottingham.

The COTP is a research-led institution organized at the interstices of theology and philosophy. It is founded on the conviction that these two disciplines cannot be adequately understood or further developed, save with reference to each other. This is true in historical terms, since we cannot comprehend our Western cultural legacy unless we acknowledge the interaction of the Hebraic and Hellenic traditions. It is also true conceptually, since reasoning is not fully separable from faith and hope, or conceptual reflection from revelatory disclosure. The reverse also holds, in either case.

The Centre is concerned with:

- the historical interaction between theology and philosophy.
- the current relation between the two disciplines.
- attempts to overcome the analytic/continental divide in philosophy.
- the question of the status of "metaphysics": Is the term used equivocally? Is it now at an end? Or have twentieth-century attempts to have a postmetaphysical philosophy themselves come to an end?
- the construction of a rich Catholic humanism.

I am very glad to be associated with the endeavours of this extremely important Centre that helps to further work of enormous importance. Among its concerns is the question whether modernity is more an interim than a completion — an interim between a pre-modernity in which the porosity between theology and philosophy was granted, perhaps taken for granted, and a postmodernity where their porosity must be unclogged and enacted anew. Through the work of leading theologians of international stature and philosophers whose writings bear on this porosity, the Centre offers an exciting forum to advance in diverse ways this challenging and entirely needful, and cutting-edge work.

Professor William Desmond, Leuven

ECCE HOMO

On the Divine Unity of Christ

Aaron Riches

WILLIAM B. EERDMANS PUBLISHING COMPANY

GRAND RAPIDS, MICHIGAN

© 2016 Aaron Riches

All rights reserved

Published 2016 by

Wm. B. Eerdmans Publishing Co.

2140 Oak Industrial Drive N.E., Grand Rapids, Michigan

49505

Library of Congress Cataloging-in-Publication Data

Names: Riches, Aaron, 1974-

Title: Ecce Homo: on the divine unity of Christ / Aaron Riches.

Description: Grand Rapids, Michigan: Eerdmans Publishing Company, 2016.

Identifiers: LCCN 2015038500 | ISBN 9780802872319 (pbk.: alk. paper)

Subjects: LCSH: Jesus Christ — Natures. | Hypostatic union.

Classification: LCC BT212 .R53 2016 | DDC 232/.8 — dc23

LC record available at http://lccn.loc.gov/2015038500

Nihil obstat: Reverend Thomas G. Weinandy, O.F.M., Cap.

       Secretariat of Doctrine, United States Conference of Catholic Bishops

       29 July 2013

Imprimatur: The Most Reverend Francisco Javier Martínez Fernández

       Archbishop of Granada

       8 December 2013

In accordance with Canon 824, permission to publish was granted 8 December 2013 by His Excellency Francisco Javier Martínez Fernández, Archbishop of Granada. Permission to publish is an official declaration of ecclesiastical authority that the material is free from doctrinal and moral error. No legal responsibility is assumed by the grant of this permission.

www.eerdmans.com

For Melissa

Contents

CONTENTS

Part Two • The Synergy of Christ

Part Three • The Existence of Christ

Contents

Foreword

Nothing is more fundamental in Christian theology than clarifying what we say and believe about Jesus Christ; if we fail to do this as we should, everything else collapses into confusion — our doctrine of God, our understanding of the church and its sacraments, our commitment to a level of universal human dignity and capacity beyond our imagining, our approach to prayer and contemplation. It is not all that surprising that in a period of general theological transition and diversity in all the churches, some of the depths and subtleties of classical reflection on Christology have been missed. Recent generations have grown up with a vague sense of the inadequacy of this tradition — a sense that it is unhelpfully dominated by "Greek metaphysics" or that it fails to do justice to the humanity of Jesus. The result has been that the close interconnection of classical Christological thinking with all these other areas of our reflective faith has often been missed or understated. The time is ripe for a scholarly survey that pulls these themes back together on the basis of careful and sympathetic study of the tradition and its development, so that the faith of God's people may be more richly resourced.

And this is what Aaron Riches' excellent survey offers. He expounds with clarity the way in which the fifth-century doctrinal formulations took shape, follows through their development in the Middle Ages, and provides a very helpful orientation to some of the debates of the last century. His narrative gently dismisses the clichés that surround the subject and opens up some of the depths implicit in the confession of "*one* Lord Jesus Christ" (not least in some fresh and illuminating thoughts about the implications for what we say concerning Mary the Mother of God). This book is a truly valuable and fresh introduction to the wellspring of all Christian thinking and praying, a witness to the doctrinal foundation that most profoundly unites Christians, and it is a joy to welcome and commend it.

Rowan Williams

Preface

The declaration that Jesus of Nazareth is *verus Deus et verus homo*, true God and true human, lies at the heart of the Christian claim from its origin. The goal of this work is to examine the root of this basic claim in the unity and identity confessed by the apostle Paul: "for us there is . . . one Lord, Jesus Christ" (1 Cor. 8:6).

The apostle's confession of the "one Lord Jesus Christ" is the true starting point of Christology and is the basis of Nicene orthodoxy (*Credo . . . in unum Dominum Iesum Christum*). From this confession is derived the theological meaning of true divinity and true humanity: Jesus Christ is the eternal Son of God, the one who, true God of true God, is eternally begotten of the Father, the one who came down from heaven (*descensus de caelis*), the one who was born of the Virgin Mary, the one who suffered and died for us (*pro nobis*), the one who is the Crucified Lord. All of this is brought together in the traditional doctrine of the hypostatic union, according to which the "union" (*unio, unitas*) of divinity and humanity in Christ occurred in the "one hypostasis" (*unum suppositum*) of the Son of God, such that the one put to death on Calvary can be none other than the Only-begotten Son of the Father. The Logos and the Crucified are "one and the same" (*unus et idem*).

Seen in this light, the Cross is not a mere incident that happened "after" the Incarnation, much less a peripheral aspect of the Christological union. Rather, the Cross is the internal basis of Christology and provides the very meaning of the Incarnation; it is the means by which the Son of God is glorified in his flesh, overcomes sin and death, reconciles humanity to the Father, and obtains for us the new and divine life of the Holy Spirit.

The unity of Christ and the event of the Cross are thus bound together and inseparably constitute the heart of Christology: the meaning of the unity and identity of Jesus Christ lies at once in his eternal filiation from the Father and in his death on the Cross. Only in this light does the real theological meaning of "Ecce homo" come into focus. Pontius Pilate speaks these words as he presents the wounded Lord to the crowd, handing him over to be crucified:

> Jesus came out, wearing the crown of thorns and the purple robe. Pilate said to them, "Here is the man!" (*Ecce homo*). When the chief priests and the officers saw him, they cried out, "Crucify him, crucify him!" Pilate said to them, "Take him yourselves and crucify him." (John 19.5-6)

In the plainest sense "Ecce homo" simply means "behold *this* man," behold this one (*unus*). But there is also a tone of sarcasm in Pilate's mouth: How could you see *this man*, this singularly abject, pathetic, and fragile man, as a dangerous usurper of kingly power? (cf. John 18:33; Luke 23:2). The mocking words of Pilate take on another meaning in the light of faith, by which they are overdetermined to signify an ultimate and unwitting truth: this singular and pathetic being is in fact a king and more than a king, he is the one Lord of Israel, *unus Dominus*. And so to truly behold the man Jesus (which means for the Evangelist much more than simply seeing the physical characteristics of his flesh) is to behold the true God (cf. John 14:9).

The singular and pathetic being Pilate presents to the crowd, then, is much more than *a* human. If to truly behold him is to behold *the* divinity, for the same reason it is also to behold true humanity. Jesus is the one who is *verus homo* by virtue of the fact that he is *verus Deus*. Or better: Jesus is *verus homo*, the truly human "human being," by virtue of the fact that he is *unus Dominus*, the one Lord come down from above. The humanity of Jesus, in its singularity and in its unity, is thus directly rooted in, and constituted by, the divine unity of his person/hypostasis, which is "one" (*unum*) with God the Father (cf. John 10:30). Jesus is the eternally begotten Son, true God of true God, the Crucified One.

The aim of the following pages is to explore this most basic Christological confession of the mystery of Christ's unity. Our task is to free this unity both from dualistic distortions of divinity and humanity that would divide the one Christ, and from an exclusivist *solus Christus* that would remove him from the experience and participative possibilities of everyday life. Our exploration will accordingly focus on two interconnected unions of God and the human: the unique hypostatic union of the Incarnate Son;

and the saving mystical union through which human beings are redeemed and deified in the Son (*filii in Filio*).

Yet to proceed from the unity of Christ, from the "oneness" of his perfect divinity and perfect humanity, is to enter into a paradox of irrepressible tension. In Christ, the absolute difference of the *verus homo* before the *verus Deus* is perfected only in direct proportion to the intimacy of the union between them. Can theology account for the integral difference between the two natures while resisting every temptation to "separation" (*separatio*)? The wager of this book is that theology resists this temptation only to the extent that it upholds and inhabits the scandal at the heart of the Christian faith, namely, the above-mentioned identity of the Only-begotten and the Crucified: "He who was crucified in the flesh, our Lord Jesus Christ, is true God, Lord of glory, and one of the Holy Trinity."[1]

* * *

This book would not have been written without the support and friendship of Msgr. Javier Martínez, Archbishop of Granada; likewise it would not have been written without the friendship and dedication of Conor Cunningham and Melissa Riches, two very different interlocutors who both truly suffered with me the writing of this book, both intellectually and personally. In addition, it would not exist without: John Milbank, who enabled my postgraduate work at the universities of Virginia and Nottingham, in the process becoming a true friend and a tremendous model of intellectual honesty and vitality; Fr. John Behr, whose work has greatly deepened my own thinking and whose recent friendship was a particular help in the last stages of completion of this book; Artur Mrowczynski-Van Allen and Sebastián Montiel, whose intellectual conspirations in the home of Padre Suárez made the writing of this book more thinkable; Josef Seifert, who first suggested that this material (when it formed part of a much larger and unwieldy manuscript) was in fact itself a "book" that should be published on its own; and Thomas Murphy, whose brotherly care ensured that my process of writing and reading came to its end.

Kirsten Pinto Gfroerer, Paula Herwaldt, Matthew Whelan and Fr. Thomas Weinandy, O.F.M., Cap., all read earlier versions of this manuscript. I am deeply grateful to each of them for their generous comments, criticisms and suggestions. In addition, several people read parts of the manuscript;

---

1. *Anathematismi adversus "tria Capitula,"* canon 10 (DS 432; DEC 1.114-122).

to them I am also grateful. They include: Fr. Ricardo Aldana, S.D.J., Peter M. Candler, Jr., Erich Groat, W. Chris Hackett, David Hart, Brad Jersak, Eric Lee, Matthew Levering, Javier Maldonado, Peter McGregor, Fr. John Montag, S.J., Tracey Rowland, Christopher Ben Simpson and Adrian J. Walker.

The seeds of this book were planted through doctoral research undertaken at the University of Nottingham. In addition to John Milbank, I owe another debt to Karen Kilby, who worked with me as a second advisor, making herself always available as a good teacher and rigorous close reader. I also thank Archbishop Rowan Williams and Fr. Simon Oliver, who examined my doctoral thesis, a crucial milestone on the path to writing this book.

Chapter 8, "Theandric Action," incorporates some material from a previously published article, "Theandric Humanism: Constantinople III in the Thought of St. Thomas," *Pro Ecclesia* 23.2 (2014): 195-218. I am grateful to Joseph Mangina, the editor of *Pro Ecclesia*, for originally printing the article and for permission to reuse some of this material. Finally, I would like to thank William B. Eerdmans Jr. for his kindness and support.

I must also thank other friends, colleagues and teachers who have contributed in various other ways; they include: Norberto Arredondo, +Stratford Caldecott, Bill Cavanaugh, +Fr. Georges Chantraine, S.J., Sarah Coakley, Creston Davis, Fr. Andrew Davison, I. Brent Driggers, Louis Dupré, Alessandra Gerolin, Scott Hahn, Stanley Hauerwas, Johannes Hoff, Marcelo López, Michelangelo Mandorlo, Feliciana Merino, Philip McCosker, Alison Milbank, Fr. Miguel Ángel Morell, +Fr. Edward T. Oakes, S.J., Adrian Pabst, Fr. Antonio Jesús Pérez, Guillermo Peris, Fr. Enrique Rico, Eugene F. Rogers, Jr., Rafael Saco, D. C. Schindler, David L. Schindler, Lydia Schumacher, Mátyás Szalay, Keith Starkenburg, Alessandro Rovati, Fr. Augustine Thompson, O.P., Neil Turnbull, Fr. Joseph Vnuk, O.P. and John W. Wright.

I also thank my parents, Bill and Judy, and my sisters and brother, Miriam, Leah and Jacob. I thank my Aunt Judy and Uncle Sigvard von Sicard of Birmingham. I owe a debt of love to the Cunninghams (Conor and Crystal, Rachael, Sara and Murray, Tom and Cath, and Rosie). I also thank the *Memores Domini* of Granada, who looked after me while I was writing this book, and the Schools of Community of Nottingham and Granada, who reminded me what the real subject of this book is. I am grateful to Philip Hunter and Clare Rodger for their encouragement and friendship. Lastly I owe the most profound thanks to my wife, to whom I dedicate this book.

The Feast of St. Agatha, 2015
Granada, Spain

Abbreviations

ACO	*Acta Conciliorum Oecumenicorum*
CCC	Catechism of the Catholic Church
CPG	*Clavis Patrum Graecorum*
CSEL	*Corpus Scriptorum Ecclesiasticorum Latinorum*
CUP	Cambridge University Press
DEC	*Decrees of the Ecumenical Councils* (ed. Norman Tanner, S.J.)
DS	*Enchiridion Symbolorum* (ed. Denzinger-Schönmetzer)
ECF	The Early Church Fathers
GNO	*Gregorii Nysseni Opera* (ed. Jaeger Werner et al.)
LCL	Loeb Classical Library
OUP	Oxford University Press
PG	*Patrologia Graeca* (ed. J.-P. Migne)
PL	*Patrologia Latina* (ed. J.-P. Migne)
PO	*Patrologia Orientalis* (ed. François Nau et al.)
SC	Sources Chrétiennes
ScG	Thomas Aquinas, *Summa contra Gentiles*
ST	Thomas Aquinas, *Summa theologiae*

Author's Note about Sources

All quotations from the Scriptures are from the *Revised Standard Version: Second Catholic Edition* (San Francisco: Ignatius Press, 2006). Texts of the Magisterium of the Church cite the *Enchiridion Symbolorum* where it includes these texts. For ancient texts of the Magisterium not included in the *Enchiridion Symbolorum* I have given alternate citations. For modern texts of the Magisterium not included in the *Enchiridion Symbolorum* (all readily available on the Vatican website), I simply give the document and paragraph or chapter number with no additional bibliographical information. With patristic sources, where two bibliographical sources are given following the citation it is always the former text being used; the other references are given for convenience' sake. Citations of Thomas Aquinas are from the *Corpus Thomisticum S. Thomas de Aquino Opera Omnia* (Universitatis Studiorum Navarrensis, 2009). English quotations from the works of St. Thomas generally follow the following translations (although I have at points altered the translation without noting it): for the *Summa*, the translation is from the Fathers of the English Dominican Province in 5 vols. (Westminster: Christian Classics, 1981); for *Contra Gentiles*, the translation is from the University of Notre Dame Edition in 5 vols. (Notre Dame, IN: University of Notre Dame, 1975); for *Super Ioannem*, the translation is from Fabian Larcher and James Weisheipl, ed. Daniel Keating and Matthew Levering in 3 vols. (Washington, DC: CUA, 2010). All other translations, if not otherwise noted, are my own.

Introduction

In 1951, on the 1500th anniversary of the Council of Chalcedon, Pope Pius XII took the occasion to set a dogmatic limit against those who "make an erroneous use of the authority of the definition of Chalcedon . . . [in order to] emphasize the state and condition of Christ's human nature to such an extent as to make it seem something existing in its own right (*sui iuris*), and not as subsisting in the Word itself (*quasi in ipsius Verbi persona non subsistat*)."[1]

The Pian limit of 1951 was aimed at a modern recurrence of Nestorian heresy.[2] Specifically, the Pian limit aimed at the doctrine of *homo assump-*

---

1. Pope Pius XII, *Sempiternus Rex*, 30-31 (DS 3905).
2. N.B.: "Nestorian" or "*homo assumptus*" logic, as I use the terms in this book (and interchangeably with the term "Theodorian"), may or may not in our own context be directly linked to the figure of Nestorius or to his teacher Theodore of Mopsuestia. What I seek to invoke with this language, broadly, is a logic of *separatio* within Christology that I understand as foreclosed by the standard of traditional orthodoxy. When I use terms like "quasi-Nestorian" or "a Theodorian tendency," I am noting merely a tendency or temptation in this direction and I imply no accusation of heresy. One thing I do not intend to include under the term "Nestorian" — nor should a single page of this book be taken as comment upon it — is the religious and theological life of the modern churches that grew out of the original schism that separated the so-called "Nestorian" churches from the imperial Church after Ephesus (431), including the Assyrian Church of the East and the Chaldean Catholic Church (the latter now in full communion with the Roman Church since 1552). The historical reasons for their separation after Ephesus are deeply complex. It is, however, historically inaccurate to suggest that it was strict fidelity to Nestorius, much less his teaching on the unity of Christ, that led these churches to reject Ephesus; this dogmatic point was stated clearly in 1976 by Patriarch Mar Dinkha IV, the Catholicos-Patriarch of the Assyrian Church of the East. It should be noted, moreover, that these churches, against all odds, preserved a venerable ecclesial and liturgical tradition without the support of the Empire and in very hostile territory across Asia (in Babylon, Persia, and as far as China). Finally, from a Ro-

tus, according to which the Logos is said to have assumed a human being.[3] Against every pretense that the human nature of Jesus did or could subsist *sui iuris*, and against the "erroneous use" of Chalcedonian dyophysitism to underwrite a problematic "dualism"[4] within modern Christology, Pius XII

---

man Catholic point of view, one ought to keep in mind the 1994 "Common Christological Declaration" of Pope John Paul II and Patriarch Mar Dinkha IV, in which the Pope and Patriarch mutually affirmed the orthodoxy of each ecclesial tradition. See Sebastian Brock, "The 'Nestorian' Church: A Lamentable Misnomer," in *Fire from Heaven: Studies in Syriac Theology and Liturgy* (Aldershot: Ashgate, 2006), pp. 1-14; Christoph Cardinal Schönborn, *God Sent His Son: A Contemporary Christology,* trans. Henry Taylor (San Francisco: Ignatius Press, 2004), pp. 147-48.

3. The diagnosis of a perennial Nestorian tendency in modern theology has been recently substantiated by Thomas Joseph White, O.P., in his book *The Incarnate Lord: A Thomistic Study in Christology* (Washington: CUA, 2015), a book I received after this book had gone to press.

4. Some comment needs to be made about the word "dualism" and my use of it. Josef Seifert, in an important contribution to the philosophical discussion of the body-soul relation, cautions about the legion of equivocations too often stuffed into the accusation of "dualism" (*Das Leib-Seele-Problem in der gegenwärtigen philosophischen Diskussion* [Darmstadt: Wissenschaftliche Buchgesellschaft, 1979], pp. 126-39). Seifert identifies no less than eight distinct and wholly incompatible positions that have earned the title of "dualism," some of which are less value-laden than others. The distinctions he has made on this anthropological point are helpful to Christology in that they distinguish with precision the various types of "dualism" there may be in the divine-human relation. At the very least, we can say that within Chalcedonian orthodoxy, a necessary duality (distinction) must be upheld on account of the *inconfusus, immutabilis* side of the *Definitio*. In this way we could speak of a *true dualism in Christ*, since the "dualism" that is *inconfusus, immutabilis* does not, in this case, entail *separatio*. But any duality admitted into Christ that negates the unity and identity of his person (hypostasis) would, on account of the other side of the Chalcedonian formula (*indivisus, inseparabilis*), have to be judged a *false dualism in Christ*, and would need to be rejected outright as Nestorian.

To be clear: *in this book, wherever I use the term "dualism" I am using it in the false sense,* that is, as signifying *separatio*, a negation of the unity and identity of Christ. In the background of my use of the term is the "*Gestalt* logic" of the "philosophies of nothing" outlined by Conor Cunningham (*Genealogy of Nihilism: Philosophies of Nothing and the Difference of Theology* [London: Routledge, 2002]). For Cunningham, the *Gestalt* figure of the Duck/Rabbit opens up the logic of philosophical nihilism, which he understands as oscillating between two monads that never achieve real (true) dualism; in a word we are dealing with dual-monism. This is another way to speak about a duality that negates unity and identity, reducing it in this case to a pure "one." In each philosophical case of the Cunningham analysis, "something" is shown to be grounded in "nothing" in such a way that "nothing" can be thought of *as* "something," and in turn "something" must reduce to "nothing" (as for example Kant grounds the "phenomenal" in the "noumenal," and Lacan the "symbolic" in the "Real"). The dual-monism here of "nothing" and "something" is identical with the *Gestalt*

reaffirmed the standard of orthodoxy bequeathed to the Church by Cyril of Alexandria: the human nature of Jesus only "is" insofar as it is "one" with the divine Logos.

Following the Pian limit, this book understands the human integrity of Jesus Christ as affirmed only in this traditional doctrine: the human nature of Jesus exists only as subsisting in the divine Son such that, in the Son, the human Jesus and the Lord God are "one and the same" (*unus et idem*). This follows the apostle Paul, who proclaims the unity and identity of the "one Lord Jesus Christ" (εἷς κύριος ᾽Ιησοῦς Χριστός [1 Cor. 8:6]). This apostolic proclamation of the "one Lord Jesus Christ" has been at the core of the Church's *credo* from the beginning and has continued throughout the ages.[5] It is the fundamental basis of the Christological confession of Nicaea (*Credo . . . in unum Dominum Iesum Christum*), and forms the basis of every subsequent dogmatic confession of Christology. At the heart of this confession is the conviction that the humanity of Christ is fully communicated (and fully communicates) and is constituted by the Lord God, the Son and Logos of God the Father. The human Jesus thus shares a unity and identity with God (in the person of the Son and Logos) to such an extent that it can be said that he is the one who came down "from above" (*descensus de caelis*).

Therefore, the only tenable starting point for Christology lies in the absolute *unitas* of the human Jesus with the divine Son. This opposes any alternative starting point that would begin from a theoretical or ontological *separatio* of divinity and humanity in Christ in order to proceed discretely "from below."[6] To begin "from below" is to presume that what

---

effect that makes impossible an understanding of real difference, *inconfusus, immutabilis*. Christologically, as we will see, this is similar to how the Nestorian false-dualism betrays, at key points, an uncanny resemblance to the monophysite position.

All of the foregoing about "dualism" could be said about the use of the word "monism" — it too could have both a true and false meaning. It is also the case, as for example in the case of monophysitism, that a false form of anti-dualism (opposed to the *inconfusus, immutabilis* distinction of humanity and divinity in Christ) is as dangerous as a false dualism in itself; hence the need always in Christology to think unity and difference together. In addition to Seifert and Cunningham, cf. the favorable comments on Seifert by Joseph Ratzinger, *Eschatology: Death and Eternal Life*, trans. Michael Waldstein, 2d ed. (Washington, DC: CUA Press, 1988), p. 255.

5. John Behr, *The Case against Diodore and Theodore: Texts and Their Contexts* (Oxford: OUP, 2011), p. 5.

6. Cf. Pope John Paul II, *Redemptoris missio* 6: "To introduce any sort of separation between the Word and Jesus Christ is contrary to the Christian faith. St. John clearly states

homo "is" and what it can "do" in the case of Jesus is something that can be established (with better certitude) apart from the "one Lord" proclaimed in the *Credo*.[7]

---

that the Word, who 'was in the beginning with God', is the very one who 'became flesh' (Jn 1:2, 14). Jesus is the Incarnate Word — a single and indivisible person. One cannot separate Jesus from the Christ or speak of a 'Jesus of history' who would differ from the 'Christ of faith'. The Church acknowledges and confesses Jesus as 'the Christ, the Son of the living God' (Mt 16:16): Christ is none other than Jesus of Nazareth: he is the Word of God made man for the salvation of all. In Christ 'the whole fullness of deity dwells bodily' (Col 2:9) and 'from his fullness have we all received' (Jn 1:16). The 'only Son, who is in the bosom of the Father' (Jn 1:18) is 'the beloved Son, in whom we have redemption. . . . For in him all the fullness of God was pleased to dwell, and through him to reconcile to himself all things, whether on earth or in heaven, making peace by the blood of his Cross' (Col 1:13-14, 19-20). It is precisely this uniqueness of Christ which gives him an absolute and universal significance, whereby, while belonging to history, he remains history's center and goal: 'I am the Alpha and the Omega, the first and the last, the beginning and the end' (Rv 22:13). Thus, although it is legitimate and helpful to consider the various aspects of the mystery of Christ, we must never lose sight of its unity."

7. Within Catholic theology, Roger Haight, S.J. has been a strong proponent of this program of Christology "from below." See Roger Haight, S.J., *Jesus Symbol of God* (Maryknoll: Orbis, 1999), and *The Future of Christology* (London: Continuum, 2005). According to Haight, the Catholic "Tradition must be critically received in today's situation," which means the answer to the question of "who" Jesus is cannot simply be received according to the standard ecclesial proclamation of his divinity, but rather must be rediscovered according to new standards of critical investigation and contemporary human experience. Thus Haight proposes that Christology should proceed "from below." This method consists, for him, in two things: "First, such a christology is one that begins here below on earth: it begins with human experience, with human questioning, with the historical figure Jesus of Nazareth, with disciples who encountered Jesus and interpreted him in various ways. The word 'from' in the phrase 'from below' thus indicates a point of departure in our christological thinking. . . . Second, this beginning epistemologically from below sets up, or constitutes, a structure of thinking and understanding that remains consistent. Epistemologically, christology is always ascending; it is always tied to human experience as to its starting point. And when its conclusions are reached, they must always be explained on the basis of the experience that generated them" (*Future of Christology*, pp. 32-54). Proceeding in this manner, Haight makes a concerted effort to suppress (or cast into suspicion) the Church's proclamation of the divine Christ who "came down from heaven," while at the same time privileging a vague anthropocentric recourse to "experience" determined by some admixture of sociological, historical and/or political insight as essential to a legitimate inquiry into the "real Jesus." Haight's Christology is explicitly cast as an extension of the "ascending Christology" of Karl Rahner, see Karl Rahner, S.J., *Foundations of Christian Faith: An Introduction to the Idea of Christianity*, trans. William V. Dych (New York: Crossroads, 2005), pp. 298-302; Roman A. Siebenrock, "Christology," in Declan Marmion and Mary E. Hines, eds., *The Cambridge Companion to Karl Rahner* (Cambridge: CUP, 2005), pp. 112-27, esp. at pp. 120-22. Cf. The Congre-

To be sure, to begin from the *unio* of humanity with the divine Son is to begin with a paradox. God himself in his divine nature cannot suffer or change; this divine *apatheia* too is axiomatic of orthodox Christianity.[8] Yet, if the reality of the human being "Jesus" is ontologically constituted through union with the Logos, the human birth and real crucifixion of this human being is made possible only in the divine unity of the Logos. The proclamation of the one Lord Jesus Christ, in this way, is animated by an unbearable tension between the incompatible attributes of divinity and humanity. This tension is expressed in the traditional doctrine of *communicatio idiomatum*, the "communication of properties." According to this doctrine, the attributes of the divine Logos can be ascribed to the human Jesus, while those of the human Jesus can likewise be predicated of the Logos.[9] Never directly defined by an ecclesial council, *communicatio idiomatum* articulates the interplay of the incommensurate spheres of existence that are mysteriously "one," yet perfectly "different" in Christ. It concretely concerns the reality of the Cross as the place where the exchange of divine and human properties in Jesus takes on its most radical and important form. Here, on

---

gation for the Doctrine of the Faith, "Notification on the book *Jesus Symbol of God* by Father Roger Haight, S.J.," 13 December 2004 (DS 5099).

8. Cf. Thomas G. Weinandy, O.F.M., Cap., *Does God Suffer?* (Edinburgh: T&T Clark, 2000) and *Does God Change? The Word's Becoming in the Incarnation* (Still River, MA: St. Bede's Publications, 1985).

9. On the doctrine, see Grzegorz Strzelczyk, *Communicatio idiomatum: lo scambio delle proprietà; storia,* status quaestionis *e prospettive* (Rome: Pontifical Università Gregoriana, 2004). The doctrine is fundamentally rooted in the New Testament. Strzelczyk identifies 1 Corinthians 2:8 ("None of the rulers of this age understood this; for if they had, they would not have crucified the Lord of glory") as the central New Testament text, but goes on show how it is perennially evidenced throughout the New Testament. The doctrine is evidenced, moreover, in a surprisingly developed manner already among the apostolic Fathers of the first century, perhaps in a most exemplary form in Ignatius of Antioch (c. 35-c. 117). The letters of Ignatius are animated by the glory of martyrdom (which Ignatius suffered) as the supreme conforming of the follower of Christ to the Cross of Christ. For Ignatius, the heart of Christianity concerns the fact that, in Christ, God united himself perfectly with human flesh and therefore was able to "impassibly suffer." If the Crucified Christ is truly divine and truly human, our language about him and his work will necessarily have to stretch to the breaking point without breaking. Ignatius's way of talking about Christ exemplifies the paradoxical logic of *communicatio idiomatum*: the subjective singularity of the Son necessitates that both divine and human things are attributed and predicated of the one Crucified Son. Ignatius thus famously speaks of "divine blood" (*Letter to the Ephesians* 1 [LCL 24.218]) and "the passion of my God" (*Letter to the Romans* 6 [LCL 24.278]). What he is not saying is that God has "blood" or that God "suffers"; what he is saying is that in the Incarnation, human and divine things are attributed to and are "one" in the person of the Son.

the Cross, the paradox of the Christological *unio* is brought to the ultimate breaking point — the point of *separatio* — but does not break. The *unio* of divinity and humanity is not abrogated even across the uncrossable chasm of death. Here, on the Cross and nowhere else, Christ brings to fulfillment and accomplishes the work *pro nobis* for which he was incarnated; as he himself declares: "consummatum est" (John 19:30). The Cross, in a sense, perfects this *unio* and becomes the synecdotal content of who the Incarnate Son is. As Paul writes to the Corinthians: "I decided to know nothing among you except Jesus Christ and him crucified" (1 Cor. 2:2). The Cross is thus the full revelation of the glory of God (cf. John 12:23-32) and the means by which sin is dealt with (cf. Rom. 3:25). This leads to the agonizing perplexity of the mystery of the apostolic declaration of faith: "we preach Christ crucified, a stumbling block to Jews and folly to Gentiles" (1 Cor. 1:23). *Communicatio idiomatum* is nothing other than the traditional safeguard and expression of the apostolic declaration that the Crucified truly is the one Lord.

Despite its pedigree and precedence, modern theology has characteristically neglected *communicatio idiomatum*. In part, the marginalization of the doctrine in the last century "is due to the twentieth-century's preference for functional over metaphysical / ontological Christologies, and [the] underlying (incorrect) belief that the two can be separated."[10] In other words, modern theology's avoidance of the paradox of *communicatio idiomatum* is internal to its complicity with a Nestorian logic of *separatio*. The starting point of the apostle and of the *Credo* is precisely the opposite: there is "one Lord Jesus Christ," who is "true God from true God," who "came down from heaven," and "for our sake . . . was crucified."

* * *

Jesus is also the realization and prime analogate of what it means to be human; he is *verus homo*. The traditional declaration, then, that *this* Jesus is *verus homo et verus Deus* entails that the fullness and excellence of perfect humanity is constituted by the intimacy of its union with God. This means that the "ever greater dissimilarity," *maior dissimilitudo*, that exists in all cases between created and uncreated being, as it was determined

---

10. Philip McCosker, review of *Communicatio idiomatum: lo scambio delle proprietà; storia*, status quaestionis *e prospettive*, by Grzegorz Strzelczyk, *Modern Theology* 23 (2007): 298-301, at p. 300.

by the Fourth Lateran Council (1215),[11] must be maintained perfectly in Jesus, who is *verus homo et verus Deus*. In other words, if Jesus is the true human, the irreducible difference of the human being in relation to God is perfected in direct (as opposed to inverse) relation to the perfection of the *unio* of his humanity with the divine Logos.[12] In Christ, the relation of divinity and humanity must be, in the first place, and basically, non-contrastive and non-competitive.[13]

In Jesus, because the *verus Deus* establishes and "is" the possibility and reality of *verus homo*, the "et" in the formulation signifies a perfect *unio* of *maior dissimilitudo* wherein *maior dissimilitudo* is internal to the *unitas* of his incarnate being. In the case of the hypostatic union, then, union differentiates and not otherwise.[14] This being the case, only the confession of the "one Lord Jesus Christ" maximally preserves the integrity and difference of *verus homo* before *verus Deus*. Outside of the divine *unio* of Christ,

---

11. Lateran IV, *Constitutions*, 2. *De errore abbatis Iochim* (DS 806; DEC 1.232): "inter creatorem et creaturam non potest similitudo notari, quin inter eos maior sit dissimilitudo notanda."

12. On the "direct" as opposed to "inverse" relation of difference and unity in Christian theology, see David L. Schindler, "The Person: Philosophy, Theology, and Receptivity," *Communio* 21 (1994): 172-90. In light of Schindler's comments, we can say that the essential feature of the God-creature relation (as analogous to the lover-beloved relation) is that they are animated by communion in which the relative opposition of difference and the union of the partners is *directly* related (in the case of the God-creature relation, this holds true only from the side of the creature). This means that the deeper and more perfect the union, the more each is realized in its distinct integrity. Union differentiates. I take this as more or less convertible with Thomas's claim that the more perfect a being is, the more autonomous it is (ST I, q. 18, a. 3, *corpus*). All created being "is" by participation in God (*ipsum esse per se subsistens*). Thus perfection of the creature, which requires *unio* with God, results at the same time in a certain "autonomy" in the sense that it confirms and perfects the *maior dissimilitudo* that nevertheless maintains between the creature and God.

13. On this see, Kathryn Tanner, *God and Creation in Christian Theology: Tyranny or Empowerment?* (Oxford: Blackwell, 1988), and *Jesus, Humanity and the Trinity: A Brief Systematic Theology* (Minneapolis: Fortress Press, 1998).

14. Cf. Henri de Lubac, S.J., *Catholicisme, les aspects sociaux du dogme* (Paris: Cerf, 1947), p. 287: "l'unit n'est aucunement confusion, — pas plus que la distinction n'est séparation. Ce qui s'oppose n'est-il pas pour autant relié, et par le plus vivant des liens, celui d'un mutuel appel ? . . . « Distinguer pour unir, » a-t-on dit, et le conseil est excellent, mais sur le plan ontologique la formule complémentaire ne s'impose pas avec moins de force : « unir pour distinguer » . . . l'union différencie. La solidarité solidifie." De Lubac's confrère and friend, Pierre Teilhard de Chardin, coined the axiom. See Avery Dulles, S.J., *The Catholicity of the Church* (Oxford: OUP, 1987), p. 42.

beginning from an abstract idea of what his humanity might be apart from that *unio*, Christian theology fails before it even begins.

Yet this is theology's perennial temptation: to attempt to proceed from a *separatio* of divinity and humanity in Christ, or from the apparently "separable human existence" of Jesus in relation to the divine Logos. This singular metaphysical a priori animates both of the great post-Nicene heresies of Christological union: Nestorianism and monophysitism. The root error of both is a presumption, as a law of metaphysical truth, that the *apatheia* of God on the one hand, and the fragility of finite human being on the other, requires that a perfect ontological *unio* of the two must compromise *maior dissimilitudo*. This forces a decision between two fraudulent ideas:

1. The monophysite option affirms the full ontological *unio* through a reconfiguration either of the divine *apatheia* of the Logos or the finitude of the human Jesus, such that we must now either conceive divinity in Jesus as passible and/or the humanity of Jesus as that of a "superman." This option requires some kind of recourse to a "tertium quid," a third thing which — while a true *unio* of divinity and humanity — is no longer quite *verus Deus* or *verus homo*, but a blending into something else. While this option seems to begin from *unio* (and indeed affirms a full ontological *unio*), the hidden metaphysical a priori presumes that *separatio* characterizes *maior dissimilitudo*, and therefore *unio* cannot establish or perfect *maior dissimilitudo*.

2. The Nestorian option upholds the *apatheia* of God in Christ and the fragility of his human finitude by "loosening" the *unio*. In this way the "et" of *verus Deus et verus homo* is a caesura; a pause that at best functions as a conjunctive term relating two essentially divisible entities through a "union" determined by a more basic ontological *separatio*, which alone is thought to safeguard *maior dissimilitudo*. The result is to undermine the unity and identity of the human Jesus with the Logos and so undermine the apostolic and Nicene confession of the one Lord Jesus Christ.

The dilemma of these two options makes clear that there is an essential convertibility between the two great post-Nicene Christological heresies. Yet the natural habit of textbook theology is to think of these two options as two heretical poles on either side of orthodoxy.[15] Orthodoxy, however,

---

15. See, for example, Gerald O'Collins, S.J., *Christology: A Biblical, Historical, and Sys-*

entails a revolution in our metaphysical conception of the relationship between God and humanity, and therefore between the uncreated *Unum* and the *maior dissimilitudo* of the creature before the *Unum*. Properly understood, the apostolic confession of the unity of Christ does not stand midway between a "too unitive Christology" on the one hand, and a "too differentiating Christology" on the other; rather, it wholly recapitulates the nature of the difference of man before God. The *maior dissimilitudo* Nestorianism aimed to safeguard is perfected in the absolute ontological *unitas* monophysitism sought to maintain.

* * *

While there have been real instances of monophysitism in the history of the Church (Apollinarian and Eutychian), this book sees the persistent temptation of Christology as leaning in a more or less Nestorian or *homo assumptus* direction. In this regard, I will defend a position that runs counterwise to that of Karl Rahner, who famously lamented the "crypto-monophysitism" of pre–Vatican II Catholicism.[16] Rahner's concern led him to declare later in his life that if "it is possible to be an orthodox Nestorian or an orthodox Monophysite . . . I would prefer to be an orthodox Nestorian."[17]

---

tematic Study of Jesus (Oxford: OUP, 1995), p. 200; Paul Tillich, *Systematic Theology*, vol. 2: *Existence and the Christ* (Chicago: University of Chicago Press, 1957), pp. 142-45; C. Duquoc, *Cristología. Ensayo dogmático sobre Jesús de Nazaret el Mesías*, trans. Alfonso Ortiz (Salamanca: Ediciones Sigueme, 1974), pp. 260-66; Wolfhart Pannenberg, *Jesus – God and Man*, 2d ed., trans. Lewis L. Wilkins and Duane A. Priebe (Louisville: Westminster John Knox Press, 1977), pp. 287-93; J. Liebaert, *L'Incarnation*, vol. 1: *Des origines au concile de Chalcédoine* (Paris: Cerf, 1966), esp. pp. 209-22. While this habit of contemporary textbook theology may be anticipated in some Neo-Scholastic manuals, the more a-historical approach to doctrine offered by the manualist tradition, while it presents problems of its own, guarded against this erroneous tendency. See for example, A. D. Tanquerey, *A Manual of Dogmatic Theology*, vol. 2, trans. John J. Byrnes (New York: Desclee Company, 1959), pp. 2-6; J. Wilhelm and T. B. Scannell, *A Manual of Catholic Theology: Based on Sheeben's "Dogmatik,"* vol. 2 (New York: Benziger Brothers, 1909), pp. 75-82.

16. Karl Rahner, S.J., "Current Problems in Christology," in *Theological Investigations*, vol. 1, trans. Cornelius Ernst, O.P. (Baltimore: Helicon, 1961), pp. 149-200, at pp. 185-200.

17. Karl Rahner, S.J., *Karl Rahner in Dialogue: Conversations and Interviews, 1965-1982*, ed. Paul Imhof and Hubert Biallowons (New York: Crossroad, 1986), pp. 126-27. Cf. Karl Rahner, S.J., "Current Problems in Christology," pp. 149-200; *Foundations of Christian Faith*, pp. 286-88; "Christology Today?" in *Theological Investigations*, vol. 17, trans. Margaret Kohl, pp. 24-38; "Christology Today," in *Theological Investigations*, vol. 21, trans. Hugh M. Riley (London: Darton, Longman & Todd, 1988), pp. 220-27.

Within Catholic theology, it was not only Rahner who sought an "orthodox Nestorian" corrective to the apparent "crypto-monophysitism" of pre-Conciliar popular devotion and magisterial teaching. As Joseph Ratzinger notes, between the World Wars Rahner's judgment was shared by theologians no less eminent, including J. A. Jungmann, Karl Adam and F. X. Arnold.[18] All the preceding, with Rahner, perceived a "factual monophysitism among pious people," and commonly took "monophysitism as the great danger of their epoch."[19] Thus the rehabilitation of a strongly dyophysite Christology — proposed in order to correct the putatively naïve monophysitism of popular piety and the official doctrine of the Church — was complemented by a period of sympathetic flourishing of Nestorius scholarship. This succeeded in raising the question of whether or not Nestorius's doctrine was in fact "Nestorian" (that is, "heretical").[20] A similar movement occurred with regard to Nestorius's teacher, Theodore of Mopsuestia.[21] At the same time, in the realm of biblical scholarship, a *de facto*

18. Joseph Ratzinger, *Un Canto Nuevo Para el Señor: La fe en Jesucristo y la liturgia hoy* (Salamanca: Ediciones Sigueme, 1999), p. 34. The texts to which Ratzinger points are the following: J. A. Jungmann, *Die Frohbotschaft und unsere Glaubensverkündigung* (Regensburg: Pustet, 1936), pp. 76 and 100, n. 2, and *Die Stellung Christi im liturgischen Gebet* (Münster: Aschendorff, 1925), pp. 51 and 200; Karl Rahner, S.J., "Chalkedon - Ende oder Anfang?," in A. Grillmeier and H. Bacht, eds., *Das Konzil von Chalkedon. Geschichte und Gegenwart*, vol. 3 (Würzburg: Echter-Verlag, 1954), pp. 3-49, at 9ff.; F. X. Arnold, "Das gott-menschliche Prinzip der Seelsorge und die Gestaltung der christlichen Frömmigkeit," in A. Grillmeier and H. Bacht, eds., *Das Konzil von Chalkedon. Geschichte und Gegenwart*, vol. 3 (Würzburg: Echter-Verlag, 1954), pp. 287-340; K. Adam, *Christus unser Bruder* (Regensburg: Habbel, 1934), esp. p. 300.

19. Ratzinger, *Un Canto Nuevo Para el Señor*, p. 34.

20. For the emblematic rehabilitations of Nestorius's doctrine, see J. F. Bethune-Baker, *Nestorius and His Teachings: A Fresh Examination of the Evidence* (Cambridge: CUP, 1908); Friedrich Loofs, *Nestorius and His Place in the History of Christian Doctrine* (Whitefish, MT: Kessinger Publishing, [1914] 2004). Cf. Milton V. Anastos, "Nestorius was Orthodox," *Dumbarton Oaks Papers* 16 (1962): 117-40; R. V. Sellers, *Two Ancient Christologies* (London: SPCK, 1940); Aubrey R. Vine, *An Approach to Christology: An Interpretation and Development of Some Elements in the Metaphysic and Christology of Nestorius* (London: Independent Press, 1948); Rowan A. Greer, "The Image of God and the Prosopic Union in Nestorius' Bazaar of Heraclides," in R. A. Norris, ed., *Lux in Lumine: Essays in Honor of W. Norman Pittenger* (New York: Seabury, 1966), pp. 46-61; H. E. W. Turner, "Nestorius Reconsidered," *Studia Patristica* 13 (1975): 306-21; Richard Kyle, "Nestorius: The Partial Rehabilitation of a Heretic," *Journal of the Evangelical Theological Society* 32 (1989): 73-83.

21. On Theodore, see Richard A. Norris, *Manhood and Christ: A Study in the Christology of Theodore of Mopsuestia* (Oxford: OUP, 1963); Rowan A. Greer, *Theodore of Mopsuestia: Exegete and Theologian* (London: Faith Press, 1961). For a full review of the literature on Theodore,

"Nestorianism" set in as a result of the so-called "quest for the historical Jesus," which tended to separate the "Jesus of history" from the glorified "Christ of faith."[22] Whatever the fears of Catholic theologians in the first half of the twentieth century, by the end of it there could be no doubt that the authenticity of the Christian claim was threatened, not by the divinized monism of a super-human Jesus, but by a dualistic dissociation of divinity from the human fact of Christ.

That a theologian no less eminent than Rahner could want to be an "orthodox Nestorian" is significant. On the one hand, it is a sign of the historical resilience of the Nestorian temptation. On the other hand, it signals a deep correspondence between Nestorian logic and some of the constitutive false dualisms of modernity.[23] Indeed, without establishing any direct genealogical link, we can say that modernity is broadly "Nestorian," if we take the term Nestorian as descriptive of the normative mode of conceiving the relation of unity and difference, transcendence and immanence, God and the world. According to David L. Schindler, it has become characteristic of the implied metaphysical vision of modernity since Descartes to presuppose that "if x is truly distinct from y, x must just so far share nothing in common with y."[24] Real difference here "precludes *a priori* any unity between x and y that is inclusive, precisely *qua unity*, of real difference between x and y."[25] Here, "difference" is essentially contrastive and competitive such that an ontological "union" of x and y can only occur if either x is absorbed into y or vice-versa, or a mutual blending of x and y results in z, a *tertium quid*. In other words, as with Nestorian logic, so with modernity, the difference of x and y is only safeguarded by *separatio*, a strict autonomy that ensures that no intimacy crosses the basic parallelism whereby each thing remains distinct from its opposite, the one juxtaposed against the other. In both cases it is impossible to imagine a real unity in

---

see Paul B. Clayton, Jr., *The Christology of Theodoret of Cyrus: Antiochene Christology from the Council of Ephesus (431) to the Council of Chalcedon (451)* (Oxford: OUP, 2007), pp. 53-74; Behr, *The Case against Diodore and Theodore*, pp. 28-47.

22. On the quest for the "historical Jesus," see Luke Timothy Johnson, *The Real Jesus* (San Francisco: Harper, 1997); Ben Witherington III, *The Jesus Quest: The Third Search for the Jew of Nazareth* (Downers Grove: Intervarsity Press, 1995).

23. Cf. Pope Pius X, *Lamentabili Sane Exitu*, prop. 27 (DS 3427).

24. David L. Schindler, "The Embodied Person as Gift and the Cultural Task in America: *Status Quaestionis,*" *Communio: International Catholic Review* 35 (2008): 397-431, at p. 411. Reprinted in David L. Schindler, *Ordering Love: Liberal Societies and the Memory of God* (Grand Rapids: Eerdmans, 2011), pp. 242-76. I have quoted from the *Communio* version.

25. Schindler, "The Embodied Person as Gift," p. 412.

which union perfects difference. Given this basic metaphysical compatibility of modernity and Nestorian logic, it is no coincidence that the broad tendency of Nestorianism to perform a *separatio* of divinity and humanity in Christ was realized afresh in the twentieth century.

But if the modern theological dream of being an "orthodox Nestorian" bears certain markings characteristic of modernity, it is expressive at the same time of a perennial temptation of Latin dogmatic theology itself. While Byzantine theology became resolved in a Cyrillian manner against every trace of the *homo assumptus* theory, Latin theology remained in this regard more dogmatically vague, even at times preferring aspects of *homo assumptus* Christology.[26] This preference is due to at least two factors. In the first place, in the centuries before the Great Schism of 1054, the Latin church tended to receive, only with reticence, the magisterial authority of the post-Chalcedon council of Constantinople II (553). The historical reasons for this are complex, and are treated in part two of this book. Suffice it to say here that while Byzantine theology embraced the council immediately as the "Fifth Ecumenical Council" and allowed the decrees of 553 to shape and determine its doctrine, Latin theology, following the hesitation of key popes from Pelagius I (d. 561) to Gregory the Great (c. 540-604), received the Constantinopolitan decrees at first only with ambiguity.[27] Further, during the mediaeval period in the "largely Greekless West,"[28] the disappearance of the textual evidence of the so-called Christological councils from Ephesus to Constantinople III effectively erased for a time the precise dogmatic formulations and standard by which the *homo assumptus* doctrine was excluded. These two factors made it possible for Peter Lombard in his *Libri quatuor Sententiarum* (c. 1150) to offer the *homo assumptus* doctrine as a legitimate "opinion" of theology, even while the doctrine was in fact rather obviously irreconcilable with the

---

26. Cf. Aidan Nichols, O.P., *Rome and the Eastern Churches: A Study in Schism* (San Francisco: Ignatius Press, 2010), p. 166.

27. See the General Introduction in Richard Price, *The Acts of the Council of Constantinople of 553: With Related Texts on the Three Chapters Controversy, Edited and with an Introduction and Notes*, 2 vols. (Liverpool: Liverpool University Press, 2009), vol. 1, pp. 99-103, esp. p. 103, where Price suggests that the diverse reception of Constantinople II in the east and west in fact anticipates the eventual parting of the ways, formalized in 1054.

28. Joseph Wawrykow, "Wisdom in the Christology of Thomas Aquinas," in Kent Emery, Jr. and Joseph P. Wawrykow, eds., *Christ Among the Medieval Dominicans* (Notre Dame, IN: University of Notre Dame Press, 1998), pp. 175-94, at p. 187.

dogmatic limits set by Ephesus and Constantinople II. And so the *homo assumptus* doctrine and its variants were left to grow roots in the soil of some areas of Latin theology.[29]

Only in the wake of the Modernist crisis, during the pontificate of Pius XII, was the issue of the orthodoxy of *homo assumptus* Christology clarified decisively and negatively by a Bishop of Rome. Yet by this time, quasi-Nestorian modes of thinking had already entrenched themselves and shaped ranges of the Latin theological imagination.

The foregoing may help to explain the suggestive correlation between the logic of *homo assumptus* Christology, which affirms the difference of divinity and humanity through *separatio*, and the basic logic of the modern Latin doctrine of *natura pura*.[30] The integrity of nature, on this latter view, is safeguarded by its natural perfectibility *in se*, and so in a manner essentially "separable" from the order of grace. The convertibility of the doctrine of *natura pura* with a quasi-Nestorian logic of *separatio* lies in the way proponents of *natura pura* insist on deriving the "species" of the human creature wholly from the "proximate, proportionate, natural end" of a "purely natural" human nature, fully divested from the history of salvation.[31] On this view, the human creature is best defined — and with greater precision — when his nature is bracketed (*praescindere*) from everything that "surpasses nature,"[32] including the Christ event and the gift of grace that flows from his Cross. Despite its quasi-Nestorian character, classical proponents of *natura pura* — especially those of a Thomist variety — have nevertheless maintained a robust Cyrillian doctrine

---

29. Cf. Franklin T. Harkins, "*Homo Assumptus* at St. Victor: Reconsidering the Relationship between Victorine Christology and Peter Lombard's First Opinion," *The Thomist* 72 (2008): 595-624.

30. This correlation is not the topic of the work at hand, but it is not extraneous to it. The topic yet awaits a proper treatment, which I hope to give in due course. The classical doctrine of *natura pura*, while it was mostly elided or lightly dismissed in the years following Vatican II, has recently enjoyed a perhaps unlikely renaissance. The two most energetic and persuasive works are: Steven A. Long, *Natura Pura: On the Recovery of Nature in the Doctrine of Grace, Moral Philosophy and Moral Theology* (New York: Fordham University Press, 2010), and Lawrence Feingold, *The Natural Desire to See God According to St. Thomas Aquinas and His Interpreters*, 2d ed. (Naples, FL: Sapientia Press of Ave Maria University, 2010). The latter book, in particular, is a *tour de force* of scholarship that must be reckoned with whatever one's view.

31. Long, *Natura Pura*, p. 8.

32. Francisco Suárez, *De ultimo fine hominis*, dis. 15, sec. 2. On Suárez, see Leopoldo José Prieto López, *Suárez y la metafísica* (Madrid: BAC, 2013).

of the hypostatic union, unencumbered by the dualist logic of the *homo assumptus* doctrine.[33]

But if the doctrine of *natura pura* exhibits a mingled Nestorian residue within Latin theology (beyond the bounds of Christological doctrine), it is indicative at the same time of the distinctive difference between modern and classical variants of Nestorian thinking. Whereas the classical Nestorian *separatio* of divinity and humanity was wholly motivated by a desire to protect the impassibility of God, modern variants of Nestorianism are animated by the opposite concern: to affirm the ontological density of the "humanity" of Christ,[34] as if the real integrity of human nature must be necessarily compromised by the divine union. (In the case of *natura pura*, contemporary theologians similarly prefer to establish the ontological integrity of a "theonomic" principle of nature abstracted from grace, and therefore of the Christian confession.)[35] This modern Nestorian concern is evidenced in Rahner's dedication to refute the "crypto-monophysitism" of classical Cyrillian Christology which he feared had led to "a curious deification of the man [Jesus], in place of a radical acceptance of the bitterly finite character of the person in whom God appeared among us."[36] Rahner sought to emphasize the *inconfusus, immutabilis* side of the Chalcedonian formulation against the *indivisus, inseparabilis* pole of unity in order to free the finitude of the humanity of Christ from the divine unity of the Logos and so give a more authentic account of Jesus's true humanity.

The proposal of this book is precisely the opposite. Theology, I contend, must re-propose the traditional logic of Christological orthodoxy if we are to avoid the fraudulent theological end of a false dualism. The bit-

---

33. The eminent early-twentieth-century Thomist Réginald Garrigou-Lagrange, O.P., is indicative of this. A proponent of *natura pura*, he was at the same time of an impeccably Cyrillian pedigree in matters of Christological doctrine. Compare his account of the relation of grace and nature in *Grace: Commentary on the Summa theologica of St. Thomas, I-II, q. 109-114*, trans. Dominican Nuns of Corpus Christ Monastery (St Louis: B. Herder, 1952) to his account of the doctrine of the hypostatic union in *Christ the Savior — A Commentary on the Third Part of St. Thomas' Theological Summa*, trans. Bede Rose, O.S.B. (New York: B. Herder, 1950).

34. Cf. Weinandy, *Does God Suffer?*, p. 178, n. 10: "Nestorius's christology has grown in stature in recent years, principally because of his defense of the complete humanity of Christ. The irony, an irony that Nestorius would hardly appreciate, is that those theologians who most sing his praises are the same ones who most question the divinity of Jesus and/or the immutability and impassibility of God."

35. Cf. Long, *Natura Pura*, pp. 10-51.

36. Rahner, "Christology Today?" in *Theological Investigations*, vol. 17, trans. Margaret Kohl, pp. 24-38, at p. 28.

terly finite experience of the Incarnation is precisely constituted by — and therefore intensified as a result of — the unbreakable unity of the one Lord Jesus Christ.[37] In Jesus, God does divine things humanly and human things divinely.[38] He divinizes with the frailty of his immanent touch, and in the wounding of his fragile being he reveals the fullness of the divine glory.

Jesus is *verus homo* because he is *verus Deus*.

* * *

The book is divided into four parts. The first part, "The Unity of Christ," recounts the establishment of Cyrillian orthodoxy from the Nestorian cri-

37. In this regard the Christological program of the present work, in terms of dogmatic-theological proposal, is in basic harmony with Christopher Beeley's exceptional book, *The Unity of Christ: Continuity and Conflict in Patristic Tradition* (New Haven: Yale University Press, 2012). As a matter of doctrine, Beeley wants to emphasize the unity of Christ against every dualistic construal of the relation of humanity and divinity in him. On this point the work at hand is in full agreement. Where there is a definite discrepancy between the two books is the more theological-historical question of the dynamic of continuity and discontinuity within the Church's dogmatic tradition, which for Beeley comes to a head in his understanding of the Council of Chalcedon. Leading towards Chalcedon, Beeley offers a compelling and erudite re-reading of the Christological crisis from Apollinarius in which he persuasively elevates Gregory of Nazianzus as the key protagonist of Christological orthodoxy, while demoting Athanasius, construing him as more problematic (i.e. "dualist") than has heretofore been seen. With Gregory now in the position of the new standard bearer of orthodoxy, all that follows is judged by a Gregorian standard, which results, in the first place, with this negative view of Athanasius, in the second place, with an at times ambivalent view of Cyril (at least at the time of his reconciliation with John of Antioch, where Cyril is said to be more "Athanasian" than "Gregorian"), and finally, with a more or less adverse view of the *Definitio fidei* of Chalcedon, as if moving in too much of a "dualist" direction. While I have learned a great deal from Beeley, and have gratefully incorporated some of his elevations (especially of Origen and Gregory of Nazianzus), I think he tends in these elevations to exaggerate discontinuities within the broader tradition of orthodoxy. He does so in a way that forecloses the essential continuity I judge to be maintained between conciliar tradition rightly received and the apostolic proclamation, and this especially with regard to Chalcedon. I rather want to re-read Chalcedon as profoundly in continuity with Cyril (and Cyril with Gregory) on the essential dogmatic question of the unity of Christ (whatever discontinuities of grammar are evident in the *Definitio*), to the effect that the *Definitio* is best understood, not when pitted against the unitive Christology of Gregory and Cyril, but as a formulation that presumes the essential proclamation of the "one Lord Jesus" as it was declared by the apostle and reiterated at Nicaea. However, one point with regard to Chalcedon on which Beeley and I substantially agree is that Chalcedon should not be taken as the great culmination of Christological debate that effectively realizes a perfect Christological synthesis.

38. Denys the Areopagite, *Epistula* 4 (PG 3.1072b-c).

sis (428) to the Council of Chalcedon (451). This examines how the doctrine and legacy of the Alexandrian doctor established the basic standard of orthodox Christology, rooted in the one Lord, proclaimed by the apostolic witness and confessed at Nicaea. In establishing Cyril as the standard of orthodoxy in matters of Christology, I reject outright the modern idea that the Chalcedonian settlement was a theological synthesis resulting from a titanic clash between two "schools" of Christology, one based in Alexandria and the other based in Antioch. This perception, as I will argue, is a distortion of the historical facts and implies (or seeks to encourage) a quasi-Nestorian re-reading of the dogmatic tradition of orthodoxy.

Part Two, "The Synergy of Christ," traces the continuing debate on the unity of Christ after Chalcedon through the Council of Constantinople II (553) to the contribution of Maximus the Confessor and his dyothelite (two will) doctrine of Christ, definitively received as a dogma at the Council of Constantinople III (680-681). Against the modern tendency to either overlook the contribution of Constantinople II or dismiss it as simply an expression of imperial politics, I seek to show the dramatic contribution of the Justinian council and illustrate, moreover, the basic Cyrillian continuity of the two Constantinopolitan councils. The crucial figure here is Maximus the Confessor, rightly understood as "the most determined conqueror of Nestorianism."[39]

Part Three, "The Existence of Christ," presents Thomas Aquinas as the great Latin inheritor of patristic orthodoxy in matters Christological, who resourced the Byzantine conciliar tradition to Latin theology at a crucial juncture. As the first Latin mediaeval theologian to quote directly from the conciliar documents of Ephesus, Chalcedon, Constantinople II and Constantinople III, Thomas's staggeringly important *ressourcement* led him to a decisive judgment against what he perceived as a widespread factual Nestorianism within Latin theology. Positively, Thomas's *ressourcement* of the conciliar tradition contributed to confirm his Cyrillian doctrine of Christ's single divine *esse*, and to a rich theology of theandric synergy.

Part Three closes with a chapter dedicated to the most serious theological resistance to Thomas's *ressourcement* of the Cyrillian standard: the Christology of the thirteenth-century Franciscan John Duns Scotus. While long after Scotus's death the "Scotist" inheritance developed into an open resurgence of *homo assumptus* Christology, it was not originally so with

39. Joseph Ratzinger, *Behold the Pierced One: An Approach to a Spiritual Christology*, trans. Graham Harrison (San Francisco: Ignatius Press, 1986), p. 27.

Scotus. The difficulty he raised, aside from the solution he proposed, was profound and difficult, and concerns the integrity of the human being of Jesus in its very human particularity (*haecceitas*). The difficulty here provokes an urgent return to the dogma of Constantinople II concerning the *persona composita* of Christ, involving recourse to the *ex Maria* fact: how "Mary plays a permanent role in Christ's metaphysical constitution qua 'compound hypostasis.'"[40] The agenda here is twofold. First, it aims to respond to the legitimate perplexity raised by Scotus concerning the status of the individual human Jesus within the traditional doctrine of the divine unity of the one Lord Jesus Christ. Second, it returns to Marian doctrine ("Theotokos") as the essential constituent of a properly non-dualist Christology. Here I claim that the Jesus-Mary relation is so integral to the incarnational fact, and therefore to a coherent Christocentrism, that a Christology without a full Marian account fails to be incarnational in any meaningful way and is reduced to mere abstraction.

The Coda, "The Communion of Jesus and Mary," extends the forgoing in the form of a meditation on co-redemption through the seventeenth-century Dominican spiritual writer Père Louis Chardon. At the foot of the Cross and at the Eucharistic altar, Mary also belongs at the Christological heart of the Church's proclamation: Jesus is the Crucified and Risen Lord.

40. Adrian J. Walker, "*Singulariter in spe constituisti me:* On the Christian Attitude towards Death," *Communio* 39 (2012): 351-63, at p. 359, n. 16.

PART I

The Unity of Christ

CHAPTER I

Against Separation

*If anyone does not confess that the Logos of God suffered in the flesh,
was crucified in the flesh, and tasted death in the flesh, . . . let him
be anathema.*

Cyril of Alexandria

A. The Nestorian Crisis

The dogmatic controversy that ignited the Nestorian crisis concerned
the traditional title of the Blessed Virgin Mary, "Theotokos" (Θεοτόκος),
the Mother of God or God-bearer. While Church Fathers no less eminent
than Athanasius of Alexandria (c. 296-373) had set a precedent of using the
Marian title,[1] it was popular piety that fixed it at the heart of the Church's
proclamation.[2] Devotion to the Theotokos was already considerable and
flourishing in Asia Minor when Nestorius (c. 386-450) was invested as archbishop of Constantinople in 428.[3]

---

1. Athanasius of Alexandria, *Orationes contra Arianos* 3.29 (PG 26.385a): καὶ ὅτι ὕστερον,
δι' ἡμᾶς σάρκα λαβὼν ἐκ Παρθένου τῆς Θεοτόκου Μαρίας.

2. On the extensive pre-Ephesian precedent of the title Theotokos, see Marek Starowieyski, "Le title Θεοτόκος avant le concile d'Ephèse," *Studia Patristica* 19 (1989): 236-42.

3. For Nestorius's extant writings from the time of the controversy, see Friedrich Loofs,
ed., *Nestoriana: Die Fragmente des Nestorius* (Halle: Niemeyer, 1905). For a short history of the
Nestorian Controversy, see Norman Russell, *Cyril of Alexandria*, ECF (London: Routledge,
2000), pp. 31-58; for a more ample account, see John McGuckin, *Saint Cyril of Alexandria
and the Christological Controversy* (Crestwood, NY: Saint Vladimir's Seminary Press, 2004),
pp. 126-74. On Nestorius's Christology, see John McGuckin, "The Christology of Nestorius
of Constantinople," *Patristic and Byzantine Review* 7 (1988): 93-129, revised and reprinted in
McGuckin, *The Christological Controversy*, pp. 126-74; Martin Jugie, *Nestorius et la Controverse*

A pupil of the reputed Antiochene theologian Theodore of Mopsuestia (c. 350-428), Nestorius was installed in the See of Constantinople in the year of his mentor's death,[4] apparently resolved to be vigorous and precise on questions of doctrine and to propagate the standard of "orthodoxy" he had learned at Antioch.[5] As he preached in the presence of Theodosius II: "Give me, O Emperor, the earth purged of heretics, and I will give you heaven in return. Assist me in destroying heretics, and I will assist you in vanquishing the Persians."[6] Convinced that the Christian religion had done away with the "passible" gods of pagan mythology,[7] Nestorius detected a dangerous imprecision in the popular Marian title "Theotokos," an imprecision that to him betrayed a residual pagan confusion of divine and human attributes. A human being, Nestorius reasoned, cannot be the Mother of God, since God can neither be born nor die.[8] "Strictly speaking" (ἀκριβῶς), Mary is

---

nestorienne (Paris: Beauchesne, 1912); Henry Chadwick, "Eucharist and Christology in the Nestorian Controversy," *Journal of Theological Studies* 2 (1951): 145-64; Thomas G. Weinandy, O.F.M., Cap., *Does God Suffer?* (Edinburgh: T&T Clark, 2000), pp. 177-81; Frances M. Young, *From Nicaea to Chalcedon: A Guide to the Literature and Its Background* (London: SCM Press, 1983), pp. 229-40; Aloys Grillmeier, S.J., *Christ in Christian Tradition*, vol. 1, *From the Apostolic Age to Chalcedon (451)*, trans. John Bowden (London: Mowbray, 1975), pp. 488-519; J. N. D. Kelly, *Early Christian Doctrines*, rev. ed. (New York: HarperOne, 1978), pp. 310-23; George A. Bevan, "The Case of Nestorius: Ecclesiastical Politics in the East, 428-451 CE" (Ph.D. diss., University of Toronto, 2005); Susan Wessel, *Cyril of Alexandria and the Nestorian Controversy: The Making of a Saint and of a Heretic* (Oxford: OUP, 2004).

4. Nestorius is said to have stopped in Mopsuestia on his way to Constantinople, staying with Theodore and taking counsel with the great teacher. It is not without a little irony that Theodore died the very year Nestorius became archbishop of the capital, setting off the chain of events that would finally undo Nestorius and bring ecclesial disrepute on the theological legacy of his mentor. On Theodore, see Richard A. Norris, *Manhood and Christ: A Study in the Christology of Theodore of Mopsuestia* (Oxford: OUP, 1963); Rowan A. Greer, *Theodore of Mopsuestia: Exegete and Theologian* (London: Faith Press, 1961); Young, *From Nicaea to Chalcedon*, pp. 199-213; Frederick McLeod, *Theodore of Mopsuestia*, ECF (London: Routledge, 2008); and Francis A. Sullivan, *The Christology of Theodore of Mopsuestia* (Rome: Pontifical Gregorian University Press, 1956). On the so-called Antiochene "school," see D. S. Wallace-Hadrill, *Christian Antioch: A Study of Early Christian Thought in the East* (Cambridge: CUP, 1982); and eminently John Behr, *The Case against Diodore and Theodore: Texts and Their Contexts* (Oxford: OUP, 2011).

5. Within days of his installation, for example, Nestorius began a campaign of severe persecution of heretics, which included the destruction of the last standing Arian chapel in Constantinople.

6. Socrates, *Historia Ecclesiastica* 7.29 (PG 67.804b), trans. Russell.

7. See Nestorius, *Ad Cyrillum II* (ed. Loofs, p. 179); *Über das Nicaenum* (ed. Loofs, pp. 295-97).

8. Cf. Nestorius, *Erster Sermon gegen das* Θεοτόκος, *genannt Anfang des Dogmas* (ed.

neither the Mother of God (Θεοτόκος), nor is she the mother of a mere man (ἀνθρωποτόκος); she is the Mother of Christ (Χριστοτόκος).[9]

By publicly rejecting the traditional Marian title, Nestorius excited a controversy that spiraled out of his control. In his own diocese, clergy began preaching openly against him, admonishing their archbishop for either having revived the heresy of Paul of Samosata (adoptionism), or for maintaining a "two sons" Christology, traceable to Diodore of Tarsus (d. c. 390), the mentor of the young Theodore of Mopsuestia.[10] The local dispute moved beyond Constantinople, meeting with a formidable and intransigent rival in the person of Cyril of Alexandria (c. 376-444), the patriarch of the metropolitan See of Egypt.[11]

Cyril, responding to an influence of Nestorius's teaching among the desert monks under his canonical remit, issued a letter to them in the spring of 429.[12] The letter charged, among other things, that the Marian title "Theotokos" is a truth received from the Fathers and is in accord with Nicene faith.[13] Denial of the Marian title, argued Cyril, amounts to a parsing of the one Lord Jesus[14] that undermines the salvific power of the Incarnation, since to separate divinity and humanity in Christ is to separate God from the Cross.[15] Cyril ensured that copies of his letter found their way

---

Loofs, p. 252): "Paulus ergo mendax, de Christi deitate dicens: ἀπάτωρ, ἀμήτωρ, ἄνευ γενεαλογίας; — οὐκ ἔτεκεν, ὦ βέλτιστε, Μαρία τὴν θεότητα (quod enim de carne natum est, caro est); non peperit creatura eum, qui est increabilis; non recentem de virgine deum verbum genuit pater (in principio erat enim verbum, sicut Joannes ait) non peperit creatura creatorem [. . .] et non est mortuus incarnatus deus."

9. See Nestorius, *Erster Sermon gegen das* Θεοτόκος, *genannt Anfang des Dogmas* (ed. Loofs, pp. 249-64); cf. Nestorius, *Ad Caelestinum I* (ed. Loofs, p. 167); *Ad Caelestinum III* (ed. Loofs, pp. 181-82); *Ad scholasticum quendam eunuchum* (ed. Loofs, p. 191); *Sermo* Τὰς μὲν εἰς ἐμὲ παρά (ed. Loofs, p. 273).

10. McGuckin, *The Christological Controversy*, pp. 31-32. On the link between Paul of Samosata and the doctrinal sensibility engendered by Nestorius, Theodore and Diodore, see Behr, *The Case against Diodore and Theodore*, pp. 5-8. The ascetic community of which Theodore was a part (when he was about twenty years old) included also Maximus (later bishop of Seleucia) and John Chrysostom; see Behr, *The Case against Diodore and Theodore*, pp. 52-53.

11. On Cyril's theology of the Theotokos, see Frances Young, "*Theotokos*: Mary and the Pattern of Fall and Reception in the Theology of Cyril of Alexandria," in Thomas G. Weinandy, O.F.M., Cap., and Daniel A. Keating, eds., *The Theology of Cyril of Alexandria: A Critical Appreciation* (London: T&T Clark, 2003), pp. 55-74.

12. Cyril of Alexandria, *Epistula* 1 (PG 77.9a-40b).

13. Cyril of Alexandria, *Epistula* 1 (PG 77.16a-17d).

14. Cyril of Alexandria, *Epistula* 1 (PG 77.24a-b).

15. Cyril of Alexandria, *Epistula* 1 (PG 77.37a-40b). See McGuckin, *The Christological*

to Nestorius, provoking, at first, only a mild response.[16] Cyril then wrote his famous second letter to Nestorius, in which he argued more forcefully that Nestorius was dividing the one Christ. At the heart of the matter, Cyril argued, lies a concern with fidelity to the *Credo* of Nicaea: "The holy and great Council stated that the only-begotten Son himself . . . [came] down (κατελθεῖν), was incarnate, made man, [and] suffered (παθεῖν)."[17] On this basis, he reasoned, we cannot separate the attributes of the divinity of the Son, eternally born of the Father, from the humanity in which he was born of Mary and through which he died on the Cross. So basic is this unity to a correct doctrine of Christ, Cyril argued, that to depart from it is to depart from Nicene orthodoxy. The "declarations" (λογοίς) and "doctrines" (δόγμασιν) of Nicaea, "we too must follow, in order to realize [by them] what it means for the Logos of God to be made incarnate and made man."[18] For Cyril, therefore, the faith is simple, yet highly paradoxical: the divine Son, the one through whom all things were made, truly came down from above and truly died on the Cross; he is none other than the eternal Logos of the Father, and because he is born of Mary, she is truly Theotokos. Thus to understand the Incarnation aright, we must begin with the one Lord proclaimed at Nicaea, with the unity and identity of the subject who is at the heart of the events of eternal filiation, creation, filiation of Mary, and the death suffered at Calvary. Only by following these precepts do we come to realize what it means to say rightly "the Word became flesh and dwelt among us" (John 1:14).

This second letter raised the ire of Nestorius and provoked a strong response. Furious at the insinuation that he was departing from the standard of Nicaea, Nestorius in turn accused Cyril of misconstruing the *Credo*. To attribute birth and death to the divine Son, wrote Nestorius, is "either the work of a mind that errs in the fashion of the Greeks [i.e. Hellenistic paganism] or that of a mind diseased with the insane heresy of Arius and Apollinarius."[19]

By the summer of 430, news of the crisis had spread to Rome,[20] where

---

Controversy, p. 34. The other key text at the opening of the crisis is Cyril's paschal encyclical of the same year, *Homilia Paschalis* 17 (SC 434.254-294; PG 77.789a-768c).

16. Nestorius, *Ad Cyrillum I* (ed. Loofs, pp. 168-69).

17. Cyril of Alexandria, *Epistula* 4, Second letter to Nestorius (Lionel R. Wickham, ed. and trans., *Cyril of Alexandria: Select Letters* [Oxford: OUP, 1983], p. 5; DEC 1.41).

18. Cyril of Alexandria, *Epistula* 4, Second letter to Nestorius (ed. Wickham, p. 5; DEC 1.41).

19. Nestorius, *Ad Cyrillum II* (ed. Loofs, p. 179).

20. See Cyril of Alexandria, *Epistula* 11 (PG 77.80b-85b).

Pope Celestine I (d. 432) convened a synod of Italian bishops to address the question. The synod ruled against Nestorius.[21] Recognizing the gravity of the situation, Nestorius requested the emperor Theodosius II to convene a council, presuming it would play to his advantage and be held in Constantinople. The emperor was persuaded and convened a general council for the following year. Theodosius, however, called the council to convene in Ephesus, a city with a long history of Marian devotion in which, according to tradition, the Virgin herself had lived her last days. It was unlikely that Nestorius would receive a favorable reception in this place.

Unaware of the emperor's decision, Cyril convened a synod in Alexandria to confirm the Roman synod's pronouncement against Nestorius. Whereas the Roman synodical letter had not made any Christological exposition, this synod did so in the form of Cyril's Twelve Chapters,[22] a list of twelve anathemata directed precisely at the core teaching of Nestorius. A bold statement of the unity of Christ, the anathemata are highly paradoxical and include the famous anathema 12: "If anyone does not confess that the Logos of God suffered in the flesh, was crucified in the flesh, and tasted death in the flesh, . . . let him be anathema."[23] Cyril appended these Twelve Chapters to his third letter to Nestorius.[24] On the eve of the council, the stakes of the dispute were at their highest pitch of intensity.

The Council of Ephesus had been called by Theodosius to open on Pentecost Sunday, 7 June 431.[25] Nestorius and his company arrived first, followed by Cyril and his entourage and a little later by Juvenal, the bishop of Jerusalem. The council was delayed by the Roman delegation of Pope Celestine and a large group of Syrian bishops led by John of Antioch, a childhood friend of Nestorius known to be sympathetic with his cause.[26] On 22 June, after waiting for more than two weeks, Cyril opened the council without either John and the Syrian bishops or the Roman delegation, a right he claimed based on the fact that he was the ranking bishop present.

Nestorius refused to appear before the council when it opened. In his

---

21. For a succinct narration, see Robert Louis Wilken, *The First Thousand Years: A Global History of Christianity* (New Haven: Yale University Press, 2012), pp. 197-200.

22. Cyril of Alexandria, Twelve Chapters (DS 252-263; DEC 1.59-61).

23. Cyril of Alexandria, Twelve Chapters, anathema 12 (DS 263; DEC 1.61).

24. Cyril of Alexandria, *Epistula* 17, Third Letter to Nestorius (ed. Wickham, pp. 12-32; PG 77.105c-121d).

25. For narrations of the events of the Council, see Wessel, *Cyril of Alexandria and the Nestorian Controversy*, pp. 138-80; McGuckin, *The Christological Controversy*, pp. 53-107.

26. See McGuckin, *The Christological Controversy*, p. 20.

absence the *Credo* of Nicaea was solemnly read, as were the second and third letters of Cyril to Nestorius, along with a *florilegium* of earlier Fathers and selections of the writings of Nestorius.[27] The results of the council were quickly determined against Nestorius. He was condemned and his rejection of the doctrine of the Theotokos deemed heretical.

A few days after Cyril's council adjourned, John of Antioch arrived in Ephesus with his company. The Syrian bishops were dumbfounded to discover that the council had been opened and resolved before they had even arrived. Enraged, they convened a second council of Ephesus that condemned Cyril and the council over which he presided.

Having received notice of the parallel "councils" of Ephesus, the emperor attempted to resolve the matter by calling together seven bishops from each faction. The seven bishops met, with Theodoret of Cyrrhus representing the Syrians and Acacius of Melitene representing Cyril's council. The results were inconclusive and did not re-establish communion between the Syrians and those who supported Cyril's council. The Syrians did, however, declare their acceptance of the Marian title "Theotokos," which would in time become the basis of the *Formula unionis* of 433. By late autumn, Nestorius, tired of the fight, gave up the see of Constantinople and petitioned to return to his monastery outside of Antioch.[28]

The final resolution of Cyril's council of Ephesus, and what would finally secure it as "The Third Ecumenical Council," came two years later in response to new pressure from the emperor to resolve the matter.[29] The result was the *Formula unionis* of 433.[30] While not a bold statement of the unity of Christ, the *Formula unionis* unequivocally upholds the doctrine of Mary "Theotokos."[31] Moreover, it crucially reaffirms the *Credo* of Nicaea as the basis of orthodoxy and proceeds from its Christological point of departure:

> We confess, then, our Lord Jesus Christ, the only-begotten Son of God, perfect God and perfect man of a rational soul and a body, begotten

---

27. For the doctrinal texts of the council, see DS 250-251e; for the judgment against Nestorius, see DS 264.

28. Russell speculates that if Nestorius had not abandoned the struggle, Theodosius would have probably continued to support him. Russell, *Cyril of Alexandria*, p. 220, n. 107.

29. See McGuckin, *The Christological Controversy*, pp. 107-25.

30. See the *Formula unionis* (DS 271-273; DEC 1.69-70). For Cyril's letter of accord with the *Formula*, see *Cyrilli epistula ad Ioannem Antiochenum de pace* (DEC 1.70-74).

31. *Formula unionis* (DS 271; DEC 1.69): τῆς θεοτόκου παρθένου . . . φρονοῦμεν καὶ λεγόμεν; and (DS 272; DEC 1.70): ὁμολογοῦμεν τὴν ἁγίαν παρθένον θεοτόκον.

before all ages from the Father in his divinity, the same in the last days, for us and for our salvation, born of Mary the virgin, according to his humanity, one and the same consubstantial with the Father (ὁμοούσιον τῷ πατρὶ τὸν αὐτὸν) in divinity and consubstantial with us in humanity (ὁμοούσιον ἡμῖν κατὰ τὴν ἀνθρωπότητα), for a union of two natures (δύο ... φύσεων ἕνωσις) took place. Therefore we confess one Christ, one Son, one Lord (ἕνα Χριστὸν, ἕνα υἱὸν, ἕνα κύριον).[32]

B. Nestorian Doctrine

The logic of Nestorius is animated in all things by *separatio*; the integral difference of divinity and humanity can only be maintained if the two remain "two." Thus he reasoned:

What was formed in the womb was not itself God, what was created by the Spirit was not itself God, what was buried in the tomb was not itself God — for if that were the case, we would evidently be worshippers of a man and of the dead.[33]

In his Christological program, Nestorius followed his mentor and teacher, Theodore of Mopsuestia.[34] Theodore had attempted to reconcile the Nicene emphasis on the singular reality of the one Lord Jesus Christ with a sense of the Incarnation as an "indwelling" (ἐνοίκησις) of the Logos in the "assumed" (λαμβάνω) human being (viz. *homo assumptus*).[35] For Theodore, the *maior dissimilitudo* of the Logos and the "assumed man" entails a division of labor in the Incarnation between divine things and human things, parsed according to the characteristics of each. According to The-

---

32. *Formula unionis* (DS 272; DEC 1.69-70). For the affirmation of Nicaea, see DS 271 (DEC 1.69).

33. Nestorius, *Erster Sermon gegen das* Θεοτόκος, *genannt Anfang des Dogmas* (ed. Loofs, p. 252).

34. McGuckin, *The Christological Controversy*, p. 126. See John O'Keefe, "Impassible Suffering? Divine Passion and Fifth Century Christology," *Theological Studies* 58 (1997): 39-60. Cf. Nestorius, *The Bazaar of Heracleides*, trans. C. R. Driver and L. Hodgson (Oxford: Clarendon Press, 1925), pp. 332-35.

35. Theodore of Mopsuestia, *De Incarnatione* 7, LT 1 (ed. Behr, p. 282): "Ὥστε ἐνοικήσας ὅλον μὲν ἑαυτῷ τὸν λαμβανόμενον ἥνωσε, παρεσκεύασε δὲ αὐτὸν συμμετασχεῖν αὐτῷ πάσης τῆς ἧς αὐτὸς ὁ ἐνοικῶν.

odore, when Christ dies, the "assumed man" is dying; when Christ heals the sick, the assuming God is healing.[36] Divinity and humanity in Christ are, for Theodore, not merely logical subjects to which different things can be attributed. Rather, divinity and humanity are discrete agents, separate ontological existences. This separation is brought out clearly in Theodore's commentary on the declaration of John the Baptist: "Behold, the Lamb of God, who takes away the sins of the world!" (John 1:29). Theodore wrote:

> [I]n saying, "He saw Jesus coming towards him and said, 'Behold, the Lamb of God,'" it seems to me that he clearly signifies the humanity. For this which John the Baptist saw was that which would accept death, that is to say the body which was offered for the whole world. But that which follows, "who takes away the sins of the world," in no way applies to the flesh. For it was not flesh that takes away the sins of the whole world, but this was certainly the work of divinity.[37]

Only with this basic ontological dualism in the background does Theodore allow the terms of a common predication of two subjects under one formal category. He designates this category with the term *prosopon* (πρόσωπον), a term empty of ontological weight but signifying rather a common "name," a co-signification (*consignificamus*) of two realities that are substantially separable.[38] As such, he was happier to speak of a "conjunction" (συνάφεια) of humanity and divinity in Christ than of a "oneness" (ἕνωσις).[39]

This preference in Theodore for the language of "conjunction" (συνάφεια) over "oneness" (ἕνωσις) is rooted in a polemic against a "mingling" language in Christology. This polemical concern was inherited from his own teacher, Diodore of Tarsus.[40] For both Diodore and Theodore, the designation of the unity of Christ through any recourse to "mingling" or "mixing" (κρᾶσις / μίξις) entails a *tertium quid*, a "third thing" that is, in the

---

36. See Theodore of Mopsuestia, *De Incarnatione* 7, LT 1-4 (ed. Behr, pp. 278-89).

37. Theodore of Mopsuestia, *De Incarnatione* 10.70, FT 20 (ed. Behr, pp. 344-45, trans. Behr).

38. Theodore of Mopsuestia, *De Incarnatione* 5.53, FT 17 (ed. Behr, pp. 340-43).

39. Theodore of Mopsuestia, *De Incarnatione* 8, LT 6 (ed. Behr, p. 290) and LT 20 (ed. Behr, p. 298); *Adversus fraudes Apollinaristarum* 4, LT 35 (ed. Behr, p. 308) and 3, C4T3 (ed. Behr, p. 360).

40. See Diodore of Tarsus, BD 20 (ed. Behr, p. 185) and BD 26 (ed. Behr, p. 189); Theodore of Mopsuestia, *De Incarnatione* 8, LT 6 (ed. Behr, p. 290); *Adversus fraudes Apollinaristarum* LT 33 (ed. Behr, p. 307); *De Incarnatione* [Syriac text] (ed. Behr, p. 441).

case of Christ, no longer truly divine or human, but something else.[41] According to Theodore, "in every respect the concept of 'mixture' (κράσεως) is especially improper and incongruous."[42] Theodore also wanted to resist and rethink what he perceived as an imprecision in the Nicene formulation, the reference to the Lord — who is the Logos — coming down from heaven (*descensus de caelis*). For Theodore, this line clumsily suggested that the Logos moved from place to place, as if the Logos was a Hellenistic god subject to the limits of local motion. In addition, he could not reconcile the biblical language of the Logos "becoming" flesh (cf. John 1:14), which he argued was true only "metaphorically" (κατὰ τὸ δοκεῖν), since impassible divinity simply "is" and so cannot be subject to change.[43] His solution to these two problems was to let the Son stay changelessly in heaven, and to put the emphasis on the Son's assumption of a human being into a union of *prosopon*. Theodore, then, attempted to maintain the full duality of two ontologically discrete entities, the human Jesus and the eternal Son, by assigning each of these two entities their own "nature" (φύσις).[44] Beyond the terminological innovation here (some of which would be nominally endorsed at Chalcedon without retaining Theodore's meaning), the problem of Theodore's use of this terminology is how it is directed to accommodate a fundamental "loosening of the unity in Christ."[45]

Theodore allowed that Christ is a single *prosopon*, but the term *prosopon* did not signify for him a concrete existent (which he reserved for the language of "nature," φύσις). Rather, Theodore took *prosopon* to signify a unified self-manifestation. Importantly, the language of "nature" in Theodore designates both the existential and quidditive makeup of being, while *prosopon* does not signify any meaningful ontological density, but merely an appearance or manifestation. Therefore, to uphold a dyophysite doctrine on Theodorian terms, one must affirm the duality of Christ, not only

41. Cf. Theodore of Mopsuestia, *De Incarnatione* [Syriac text] (ed. Behr, p. 443).

42. Theodore of Mopsuestia, *De Incarnatione* 8, LT 6 (ed. Behr, p. 290).

43. Theodore of Mopsuestia, *De Incarnatione* 8, LT 8 (ed. Behr, p. 292): Ἐνταῦθα τοίνυν τὸ ἐγένετο οὐδαμῶς ἑτέρως λέγεσθαι δυνάμενον εὑρήκαμεν ἢ κατὰ τὸ δοκεῖν [. . .] Τὸ γὰρ δοκεῖν ὁ Λόγος σὰρξ ἐγένετο· τὸ δὲ δοκεῖν, οὐ κατὰ τὸ μὴ εἰληφέναι σάρκα ἀληθῆ, ἀλλὰ κατὰ τὸ μὴ γεγενῆσθαι.

44. Theodore of Mopsuestia, *De Incarnatione* 8, LT6 (ed. Behr, p. 290): Πανταχόθεν ἄρα δῆλον ὡς περιττὸν μὲν τὸ κράσεως καὶ ἀπρεπὲς καὶ ἀφαρμόζον, ἑκάστης τῶν φύσεων ἀδιαλύτως ἐφ' ἑαυτῆς μεινάσης.

Πρόδηλον δὲ ὡς τὸ τῆς ἑνώσεως ἐφαρμόζον· διὰ γὰρ ταύτης συναχθεῖσαι αἱ φύσεις ἓν πρόσωπον κατὰ τὴν ἕνωσιν ἀπετέλεσαν.

45. Grillmeier, *Christ in Christian Tradition*, vol. 1, p. 428.

as quidditive reality but also as an existential fact. To speak of a "prosopic union" after the manner of Theodore is not to insist in any way on a single existent or a single predicative subject, but merely to designate the manifestational unity of two separate ontological entities.

This explains the flexibility with which Theodore could maintain the "union" of Christ with various predications of the *prosopon* of union, at times of the human "nature" and at times of the divine "nature." This allowed, on his view, for a necessary theological precision: as God's nature is impassible and doesn't allow suffering or death, it is strictly wrong, according to Theodore, to predicate the crucifixion of the divine Logos.[46]

* * *

Following Theodore, Nestorius's Christology is rooted above all in the concern to protect the impassibility of God, and does so through the practice of parsing the "passible" and "impassible" attributes of Christ to his humanity and divinity respectively.[47] Whereas the pagan deities were a confusion of anthropomorphic and divine attributes, the constitutive impassibility of the Christian God required a divesting of attributions of passibility from the divine being, even in the case of the Incarnation. Nestorius thus rejected *tout court* those currents within the tradition that had used the language of "mingling" (κρᾶσις / μίξις) to describe the intimacy of the union of divinity and humanity in Christ.[48] Driven by a "fear of mixing,"[49] his ultimate concern was to safeguard against "theopaschism,"

---

46. Theodore of Mopsuestia, *To Those Being Baptized* C4T39 (ed. Behr, pp. 392-94): "Deinde ostendens cuius gratia passus est, diminutionem infert quatenus 'citra Deum pro omnibus gustaret mortem,' quia, diuina natura ita uolunte, separata illa ipse per se pro omnium utilitate gustauit mortem; et ostendens quod deitas separata quidem erat illo qui passus est, secundum mortis experimentum, quia nec possibile erat illam mortis experimentum accipere, non tamen illo qui passus est, afuerat secundum diligentiam."

47. Cf. Nestorius, *Ad Cyrillum II* (ed. Loofs, p. 179); *Über das Nicaenum* (ed. Loofs, pp. 295-97); *Aus Quaternio* 12 (ed. Loofs, p. 278).

48. Nestorius, *Sermo* Τὰς <μὲν εἰς ἐμὲ> παρά (ed. Loofs, p. 273); Frag. 27 (ed. Loofs, p. 339). Also cf. Nestorius, *Bazaar of Heracleides* (ed. Bedjan), trans. Driver and Hodgson, pp. 16, 252.

49. As John McGuckin describes Nestorius, "He was ever on the lookout for the 'mixture' or 'confusion' of divine and human spheres of reality in christological discourse, and regarded this as the most serious deficiency of Cyril's work. He regarded all sense of 'mixture' as inevitably connoting the change, and even annihilation, of the individual elements that were so mixed. For this reason his great concern in all his doctrine was to insist on the

which would suggest that the Incarnation involved a birth of divinity and a suffering of God.[50]

In order to avoid theopaschism and the mingling of divinity and humanity it implied, Nestorius followed Theodore's reallocation of the unity of Christ to the category of *prosopon* (πρόσωπον). Nestorius's doctrine of Christ, accordingly, is rooted in a particular understanding of how *prosopon* links up with the categories of essence (οὐσία), nature (φύσις) and hypostasis (ὑπόστασις).[51] For Nestorius, every existing thing must possess not only an essence/genus and nature, but also a corresponding hypostasis that realizes the actual concrete reality of that being. In addition to its hypostasis, every existing thing has a corresponding *prosopon*, an "observable character" through which the properties of that hypostasis are phenomenally manifested in reality. *Prosopon* thus designates for Nestorius, just as for Theodore, a reality in addition to hypostasis that is not so much an ontological constituent of being as it is the external aspect by which it is subject to outside observation and scrutiny; in a word, *prosopon* designates a category more empirical or phenomenal than ontological.[52]

The implication for Christology is this: to affirm Christ "in two natures" (ἐν δύο φύσεσιν) we must now also affirm him "in two *prosopa*" (ἐν δύο πρόσωπα).[53]

Nestorius's dyophysite doctrine of Christ therefore requires two *prosopa*, which in turn confirms that some of Jesus' acts are "human," while others are "divine."[54] This parallelism is essentially what lies behind Nestorius's formula "in two natures" (ἐν δύο φύσεσιν), by which he hoped to safeguard the ontological autonomy of the divine Logos in relation to the

---

abiding distinctive relationship of the two fully enduring spheres of reality (or 'natures') in the incarnate Lord. For Nestorius all christological language applying the term 'mixis' was irredeemably Apollinarist" (*The Christological Controversy*, p. 131).

50. Cf. Nestorius, *Sermo* Τὰς μὲν εἰς ἐμὲ παρά (ed. Loofs, p. 269).

51. McGuckin, *The Christological Controversy*, p. 138.

52. McGuckin, *The Christological Controversy*, p. 151.

53. McGuckin, *The Christological Controversy*, p. 151: "For Nestorius, there are two distinct genuses in Christ, the two ousiai of divinity and humanity. It follows from this, on his terms, that there must be two natures (physeis) corresponding to the distinct genuses. Accordingly, these two physeis will be apparent to the external observer in their respective prosopa. One can look at the historical figure of Christ in the Gospels and see the clear signs of the two prosopa, divine and human."

54. Nestorius, *Bazaar of Heracleides* (ed. Bedjan), trans. Driver and Hodgson, pp. 131-82.

homo assumptus, ensuring that it is possible to parse certain human attributes (like being born and dying), from the Logos.[55]

The foregoing required Nestorius to understand the union of divinity and humanity in Christ not in terms of "oneness" (ἕνωσις, which follows the Nicene ἕνα), but in terms of Theodore's language of "conjunction" (συνάφεια).[56] Like Theodore, Nestorius wanted to maintain, in the first place, an ontological duality in Christ: there are two grounds of being in the Incarnation with two corresponding *prosopa* that ensure a parallelism of attributes. The Incarnation, then, consists in a secondary "conjunction" of these two prior ontological realities. For Nestorius, the term of union cannot be the term of union of divinity and humanity but is rather the term of the limited sphere of phenomenal manifestation and the shared characteristic of the two *prosopa*, the Logos and the *homo assumptus*.[57] This is the realm of the historical "Christ," which Nestorius terms the "prosopon of union," which is distinct from the *prosopa* of the Logos and that of the *homo assumptus*. As Nestorius clarifies in his *Liber Heraclidis*:[58]

55. Nestorius, *Bazaar of Heracleides* (ed. Bedjan), trans. Driver and Hodgson, pp. 37, 181-82.

56. Cf. Nestorius, *Ad Cyrillum II* (ed. Loofs, p. 176); *Nulla deterior* (ed. Loofs, pp. 248-49); *Sermo* Τὰς μὲν εἰς ἐμὲ παρά (ed. Loofs, pp. 265, 273, 275); Frag. IV (ed. Loofs, p. 254).

57. Cf. McGuckin, *The Christological Controversy*, p. 152: "An accurate scrutiny of the external visible signs and evidence concerning Christ ... clearly tells the observer that there are two separate levels of reality in this figure; two prosopa (or prosopic sets of evidence) signaling to the intelligent exegete the fact that two different *natures* co-exist in this being. Yet it is equally true to say that one encounters unity as well as diversity in the single concrete figure of 'the Christ', only one figure who stands before our scrutiny and somehow combines these two different sets of evidences. This experience our exegetical senses have of the one Christ must signify that Christ himself (that is 'he-who-combines-two-prosopic-realities') is in some sense a single prosopic reality, and this is the prosopon which is known to experience as, and commonly designated, 'Christ.'"

58. The remarkable *Liber Heraclidis* (English Translation: *The Bazaar of Heracleides*) is an apology Nestorius composed after Ephesus and in the time of his banishment. Preserved in a Syriac manuscript and discovered in 1897, the *Liber* is a priceless text, but it does not always clarify the doctrine Nestorius held before and during the controversy. For example, in the *Liber* Nestorius directly misrepresents his own earlier position on the Theotokos, claiming that he always accepted the title with proper qualification (cf. *Bazaar of Heracleides*, pp. 88-95), although the facts seem to be to the contrary. From the few clear and credible texts of Nestorius we have from the time of the controversy there is plain evidence that he believed the pietistic title dogmatically entailed a quasi-"Apollinarian" position. Even accepting the ambivalence of the *Liber* regarding the Theotokos doctrine, the text yet fails to offer a classically orthodox doctrine of Christ: the *Liber* rejects the idea of Christ as *both* Son of God *and* Son of Mary (cf. *Bazaar of Heracleides*,

The natures subsist in their prosôpa and in their natures and in the prosôpon of the union. For in respect to the natural prosôpon of the one the other also makes use of the same on account of the union; and thus [there is] one prosôpon of the two natures.[59]

Attempting to square his dualist Christology with the faith of Nicaea, Nestorius led himself into an ironic cul-de-sac. In maintaining a strict on-tological parallelism of divinity and humanity in Christ (which required that each possess their own proper hypostasis and *prosopon*), Nestorius was forced to designate "Christ" as a quasi-third prosopic reality in addi-tion to the *prosopa* of the *homo assumptus* and of the Logos. While he tidily separated the natures according to a dualism that made impossible the ontological *tertium quid* he so feared, his doctrine nevertheless resulted in a *tertium quid* on the level of manifestation.[60] Hence Nestorius has been called a "phenomenological Monophysite."[61] This strange convertibility of monophysitism and Nestorianism suggests that Christological dualism in fact hides a secret monism (and vice versa).[62]

---

pp. 296-97) and it rejects *tout court* every suggestion that the sufferings of Christ should be attributed to the divine Logos (cf. *Bazaar of Heracleides*, pp. 135-37). Some parts of the *Liber* may, moreover, be composite. See Roberta C. Chestnut, "The Two Prosopa in Nestorius' Bazaar of Heracleides," *Journal of Theological Studies* 29 (1978): 392-409; Young, *From Nicaea to Chalcedon*, p. 231; McGuckin, *The Christological Controversy*, p. 126.

59. Nestorius, *Bazaar of Heracleides* (ed. Bedjan), trans. Driver and Hodgson, p. 305.

60. Cf. McGuckin, *The Christological Controversy*, pp. 158-59: "The problem was that Nestorius was using one and the same technical term to connote the disparate concepts of differentiation and convergence: there are two prosopa (Jesus and Logos) and only one prosopon (Christ). There is, of course, no sensible context whatsoever that would allow one to speak of three prosopa. It may well be that this economy of language in Nestorius led to a fatal weakness in the coherence of his theory, as Cyril argued, but it is clear enough that the caricature of his teaching that described it as no more than a repetition of the old Two Sons theory is an uneven reading of his intent. To this extent Cyril's synopsis of his opponent was inaccurate. But Cyril had nonetheless put his finger on the key matter and his criticism still had force in the way he argued from Nestorius' explicit statements to his necessary implications. In this regard Cyril had posed the essential question and voiced the fears of many others when he asked whether such a theory had done enough to secure a concept of unitive subject in Christ."

61. Weinandy, *Does God Suffer?*, p. 180, n. 12.

62. The heretical fluctuation between dualism and monism noted here in the realm of Christology has been analyzed elsewhere as the basic logic of nihilism. See Conor Cunning-ham, *Genealogy of Nihilism: Philosophies of Nothing and the Difference of Theology* (London: Routledge, 2001).

C. Cyrillian Orthodoxy

Long before the Nestorian crisis thrust him into polemical defense of Nicene orthodoxy, Cyril of Alexandria (made patriarch of the great Egyptian See in 412)[63] had already honed his doctrine of Christ through a series of careful scriptural commentaries. In this Cyril was a faithful disciple of "blessed pope Athanasius," whom he calls the "undistorted rule of the orthodox faith."[64] For Cyril, to say that Athanasius was the "rule of the

---

63. A word about Alexandria is perhaps important here. Cyril was made Patriarch of Alexandria approximately 230 years before the Muslim conquest of Egypt, succeeding his uncle who had ruled for almost thirty years before him. The Egyptian port city was, with its legendary *Bibliotheka* (the first attempt in history to gather together all human knowledge in one place), one of the greatest cultural and educational centers the world has ever known. The city boasted many schools, the largest and most famous of which was the *Museum*, founded by Ptolemy. A cosmopolitan center, Alexandria was home to a large Greek-speaking Jewish population, and it was there that the Septuagint translation of the Hebrew Bible was made in the second century BC. The romantic character of this "universal metropolis" continued into the Christian period, and helped to make it a singularly important locus of theology.

The Church of Alexandria enjoyed the apostolic prestige of Mark the Evangelist, who was said to have founded the Alexandrian Church and to have been its first bishop. The special ecclesial status of Alexandria was noted at the council of Nicaea (325), where its singular prerogative was recognized alongside that of Rome (see Nicaea I, canon 6 [DEC 1.8-9]). To the apostolic eminence of the Alexandrian See should be added the singular position it held in the Christian world of the time as the leading center of theological activity, due to its famous Catechetical School. Jerome records that Mark not only founded the Church of Alexandria but also this celebrated school (*De viris illustribus*, c. 36 [PL 23.683c-686a]), which quickly became to Christian theology what the *Museum* had been to Hellenistic thought.

64. Cyril of Alexandria, *Homilia Paschalis* 8.6 (SC 392.100; PG 572a). Cf. Cyril of Alexandria, *Epistula* 44, "To Eulogius" (ed. Wickham, pp. 62-69; PG 77.224d-228d); *Epistula* 1 (PG 77.13b); Donald Fairbairn, *Grace and Christology in the Early Church* (Oxford: OUP, 2003), pp. 83-85; Robert L. Wilken, *The Spirit of Early Christian Thought* (New York: Yale University Press, 2003), p. 117. Athanasius was, already by the time of Cyril, universally regarded as the great defender of the faith of the apostles, "the true pillar of the Church," whose "conduct [is] the rule of bishops" (Gregory of Nazianzus, *Oratio* 21.26 [SC 270.164; PG 35.1112b] and 21.37 [SC 270.190; PG 35.1128a]). He once wrote that the divine Logos assumed a mortal body for no other reason than to make him capable of the death he died on the Cross (*De Incarnatione Verbi Dei*, 21 [PG 25.132b-c]). Such a formulation suggests that the *descensus de caelis* of Nicaea is rooted in, and does not merely make possible, the crucifixion *pro nobis*. Indeed, for Athanasius, the Cross was not merely a moral exemplar or a narrow remedial punishment for sin (although it is both remedial and exemplary), it is the heart of the mystery of what God accomplishes in Christ; it is how the Son reveals God the Father. And so Calvary is the *pro nobis*, the *ratio* of incarnation, and the site of the ultimate participation of man in God. For a general account of Athanasius, see Thomas G. Weinandy, O.F.M., Cap., *Athanasius:*

orthodox faith" was to say that Athanasius had read the Scripture as the apostles taught; that is, according to the death and resurrection of Jesus.[65] Following this rule of faith, Cyril patiently expounded the Scriptures, writing commentaries on nearly the whole Bible (of which his commentaries on Isaiah, the Minor Prophets, and the Gospels of John and Luke survive in their entirety).[66] His commentary on the Gospel of John is particularly crucial for understanding his views on Nicene orthodoxy.[67]

Before Cyril, Origen of Alexandria (c. 185-c. 254)[68] had been one of the

---

A Theological Introduction (London: Ashgate, 2007). Cf. Peter Leithart, *Athanasius* (Grand Rapids: Baker Academic, 2011); Khaled Anatolios, *Athanasius*, ECF (London: Routledge, 2004). On Athanasius as the architect of "Nicene orthodoxy," see John Behr, *The Nicene Faith*, vol. 2 of *The Formation of Christian Theology* (Crestwood, NY: Saint Vladimir's Seminary Press, 2004), pp. 163-259; Lewis Ayres, *Nicaea and Its Legacy: An Approach to Fourth-Century Trinitarian Theology* (Oxford: OUP, 2006); Rowan Williams, *Arius: Heresy and Tradition*, rev. ed. (London: SCM, 2001).

65. See John Behr, *The Way to Nicaea*, vol. 1 of *The Formation of Christian Theology* (Crestwood, NY: Saint Vladimir's Seminary Press, 2001), pp. 9-70.

66. On Cyril's commentaries on Scripture, see Robert Louis Wilken, "Exegesis and the History of Theology: Reflections on the Adam-Christ Typology in Cyril of Alexandria," *Church History* 35 (1966): 139-56; *Judaism and the Early Christian Mind: Study of Cyril of Alexandria, Exegesis and Theology* (New Haven: Yale University Press, 1971); "St Cyril of Alexandria: The Mystery of Christ in the Bible," *Pro Ecclesia* 4 (1995): 454-78; "St Cyril of Alexandria: Biblical Expositor," *Coptic Church Review* 19 (1998): 30-41; "Cyril of Alexandria as Interpreter of the Old Testament," in Thomas G. Weinandy, O.F.M., Cap., and Daniel A. Keating, eds., *The Theology of Cyril of Alexandria: A Critical Appreciation* (London: T&T Clark, 2003), pp. 1-22.

67. Cyril of Alexandria's *In Ioannis Evangelium* can be found in Philipp E. Pusey, ed., *Sancti patris nostri Cyrilli Archiepiscopi Alexandrini in d. Ioannis Evangelium* (Oxford: Clarendon Press, 1872), and in PG 73 and 74. I did not always have access to the Pusey text; where I had access to it, I quoted from Pusey; otherwise I relied on Migne. For a summary of the essential contours of Cyril's Christology, see J. Liébaert, *La doctrine christologique de S. Cyrille d'Alexandrie avant la querelle nestorienne* (Lille: Facultés Catholiques, 1951); McGuckin, *The Christological Controversy*, pp. 175-226, and Thomas G. Weinandy, O.F.M., Cap., "Cyril and the Mystery of the Incarnation," in Thomas G. Weinandy, O.F.M., Cap., and Daniel A. Keating, eds., *The Theology of Cyril of Alexandria: A Critical Appreciation* (London: T&T Clark, 2003), pp. 23-54.

68. Of all the theologians produced by the Catechetical School, the greatest was Origen. The most significant ante-Nicene theologian of the Church, Origen's singular influence cannot be overstated. For him, the heart of theology is the Cross: the death of Jesus realizes the glory of God and manifests that glory as now divinely possessed by the Son in his incarnate humanity. The best account of Origen and his contribution to Christology is Christopher Beeley, *The Unity of Christ: Continuity and Conflict in Patristic Tradition* (New Haven: Yale University Press, 2012), specifically pp. 3-45, but also *passim*, since a central thesis of the book as a whole concerns the unparalleled influence of Origen on the entirety of Christology from Nicaea onwards. In addition to Beeley, see Wilken, *The First Thousand Years*, pp. 55-64. Also

few exegetes to identify unambiguously the death of Jesus on the Cross with the unity of divinity and humanity in Christ: "the high exaltation of the Son of Man . . . occurred when he glorified God in his own death . . . [whereby] he was no longer different from the Logos, but was the same with him (τὸν αὐτὸν αὐτῷ)."[69] But how exactly this human suffering was to be identified with the divine glory was left more or less underdetermined by Origen. In Cyril this paradoxical identification — declared by Origen but in fact wholly native to the text of the fourth Gospel (cf. John 13:31-32; 14:13; 17:5, 22-24) — yields to a new awareness of the soteriological and divinizing function of the humanity of the Son in the Incarnation.[70] This can be seen in Cyril's exegesis of John 13:31: "Now is the Son of man glorified."

Like Origen, Cyril argues that it is precisely the humanity of Christ that is being glorified in the crucifixion, in such a way that the suffering of Jesus precisely is the realization of this glory: "The perfect fulfillment of his glory and the fullness of his fame clearly lie in this, in his suffering for the life of the world and making a new way through his Resurrection for the resurrection of all."[71] The anguish of the Cross, in this light, is not the unfortunate end, but the scandalous glory towards which Christ's whole being drives. This is the meaning of Christ's declaration that "[t]he hour has come for the Son of man to be glorified" (John 12:23). According to Cyril, by this statement Christ announces that having preached the gospel, he now

see Behr, *The Way to Nicaea*, pp. 163-206; Joseph W. Trigg, *Origen*, ECF (London: Routledge, 1998). Finally, cf. the catecheses on Origen given by Pope Benedict XVI, *Church Fathers: From Clement of Rome to Augustine* (San Francisco: Ignatius Press, 2008), pp. 32-42.

69. Origen, *In Evangelium Ioannis* 32.17 (PG 14.812d-813a). Cf. Beeley, *The Unity of Christ*, pp. 37-38: "Commenting on John 13:31 ('God is glorified in him'), Origen writes that Jesus will 'rise up for the world' and be supremely glorified on the cross. In Jesus' crucifixion 'the Son will reveal the Father by means of the economy, on account of which "God has been glorified in him,"' and here it will be especially true that 'whoever has seen me has seen the Father who sent me' (John 12:45) (*Com. Jn.* 32.359). Earlier in the *Commentary on John*, Origen makes the point quite strongly: 'We must dare to say that the goodness of Christ appeared greater and more divine and truly in accordance with the image of the Father when "he humbled himself and became obedient unto death, even death on a cross," than if he had "considered being equal to God robbery" (Phil. 2:8, 6) and had not been willing to become a servant for the salvation of the world' (*Com. Jn.* 1.231)."

70. Wilken, *The Spirit of Early Christian Thought*, pp. 118-21.

71. Cyril of Alexandria, *In Ioannis Evangelium* 13.31-32 (ed. Pusey 2.376-379), trans. Wilken.

desired to pass to the very crowning point of hope, namely the destruction of death. This could not be brought about in any other way than by life undergoing death for the sake of all men so that in him we all may have life. For this reason Christ says that he is glorified in death.... His cross was the beginning of his being glorified upon earth.[72]

By this glorification, then, Christ transforms death and opens "a way that the human race had not known before."[73] He destroys death through his human death, which alone allows humanity to overcome death and partake in the divine through Christ.[74] It is therefore precisely the fragility of Jesus' human being that accomplishes the salvific vocation.

The Johannine theology of the Cross to which Origen was dedicated was taken up and deepened by Cyril: "If he conquered as God, to us it is nothing; but if he conquered as man we conquered in Him."[75] According to Robert Wilken, this statement is unprecedented in the tradition before Cyril.[76] What Cyril accomplishes by it is to specify that the triumph over death occurs concretely through the Son's mode of being truly human.[77] The *descensus de caelis* of Nicaea is, in this way, not merely attributable to the divine Logos, but to the mode of being human he brings down in bringing himself. As Cyril puts it: "For he is to us the second Adam come from heaven according to the Scriptures."[78] Thus the Son of God is truly *homo factus est*. He is the New Adam, the Son of God Incarnate. If Christ is like us in all things but sin (cf. Heb. 4:15), he is also radically not like us; he is the unique, divine fullness of true humanity because, by not counting divinity "a thing to be grasped" (Phil. 2:6), he receives the divine glory that was the fullness of the human vocation from its origin, the vocation the Old Adam squandered when he succumbed to the satanic temptation to "grasp" by force what he was meant to receive as gift (cf. Gen. 3:6).[79]

---

72. Cyril of Alexandria, *In Ioannis Evangelium* 12.23 (ed. Pusey 2.311), trans. Wilken.

73. Cyril of Alexandria, *In Ioannis Evangelium* 13.36 (ed. Pusey 2.52), trans. Wilken.

74. Cf. John Behr, *Becoming Human: Meditations on Christian Anthropology in Word and Image* (Crestwood, NY: Saint Vladimir's Seminary Press, 2013), pp. 40-48.

75. Cyril of Alexandria, *In Ioannis Evangelium* 16.33 (ed. Pusey, 2.656-57), trans. Wilken.

76. Wilken, *The Spirit of Early Christian Thought*, p. 121.

77. Wilken, *The Spirit of Early Christian Thought*, p. 121.

78. Cyril of Alexandria, *In Ioannis Evangelium* 16.33 (ed. Pusey, 2.656-57), trans. Wilken.

79. Cf. Joseph Ratzinger, *Dogma and Preaching*, trans. Matthew J. O'Connell (Chicago: Franciscan Herald, 1985), p. 25: "the sin of Adam was really not his wanting to be like God; this, after all, is the call the Creator himself has given to human beings [*sic*]. Adam's failure was to have chosen the wrong way of seeking likeness to God and to have excogitated for

* * *

Having thereby formed his Christology through patient exegesis of Scripture, Cyril's Christological polemic in the context of the Nestorian crisis turned on his use of the "mia physis" formula according to which Jesus is conceived as "one incarnate nature of the Word" (μία φύσις τοῦ λόγου σεσαρκωμένη).[80] This formula is linked to Cyril's conception of the union as formed "out of two natures" (ἐκ δύο φύσεσιν) and not "in two natures" (ἐν δύο φύσεσιν). These two formulae were fundamentally declared valid by Cyril in anathema 3 of his Twelve Chapters, where he declared anathema those who divide the one Christ into two hypostases, joining them together by mere "conjunction" (συνάφεια) and thus failing to affirm the real unity of Christ "according to a oneness of nature" (καθ᾽ ἕνωσιν φυσικήν).[81]

At the time of the Nestorian controversy, and even today among some modern theologians, the "mia physis" formula is taken as evidence that Cyril's theology leans in a heterodox direction, towards a problematic "monophysitism."[82] The modern anxiety with the formula is compounded by the fact that Cyril thought, mistakenly, that it was of Athanasian pedigree.[83] It turns out, however, that the formula did not originate with the great defender of Nicene orthodoxy but with the fourth-century heretic

---

himself a very shabby idea of God. Adam imagined that he would be like God if he could subsist solely by his own power and could be self-sufficient in giving life to himself as he saw fit. In reality, such a mistaken quest of an imagined divinization leads to self-destruction, for even God himself, as the Christian faith teaches us, does not exist in isolated self-sufficiency but is fully divine only as infinitely needing and receiving in a dialogue of love and as giving himself freely and without limit. Humans become like God only when they enter into this same movement."

80. On the "mia physis" formula, see V. C. Samuel, "One Incarnate Nature of God the Word," *Greek Orthodox Theological Review* 10 (1964/1965): 37-53.

81. Cyril of Alexandria, Twelve Chapters, anathema 3 (DS 254; DEC 59).

82. For one modern textbook example of this concern, see Roch A. Kereszty, O. Cis., *Jesus Christ, Fundamentals of Christology*, revised and updated (New York: Alba House, 2002), p. 236. But also consider Hans Urs von Balthasar's negative attribution to Karl Barth of being overly Cyrillian: "Barth's Christology, in spite of all the lovely things he has to say about the descent of God's Son, is basically in the manner of Cyril of Alexandria. And of course (even if because of a misunderstanding) behind Cyril stands the figure of Apollinarius. No wonder then that historical justice calls for further elaboration!" (*The Theology of Karl Barth*, trans. Edward T. Oakes, S.J. [San Francisco: Ignatius Press, 1992], p. 401).

83. The "mia physis" formula comes from Apollinarius's *Letter to Jovian*; see Grillmeier, *Christ in Christian Tradition*, vol. 1, p. 334.

Apollinarius of Laodicea (d. 390),[84] the sometime sparring partner of Diodore of Tarsus, condemned precisely for holding a *tertium quid* Christology.[85] To make matters worse, the language of Christology was later refined at Chalcedon (451) to specify that the ontological level of concrete existence was to be henceforth termed "hypostasis" (ὑπόστασις), while the term "nature" (φύσις) came to denote the essence or quiddity of being. While this reallocation of language helped to clarify the nature of the union in Christ, it cast suspicion on the old Cyrillian formula. Only at Constantinople II (553) would it be clarified that the formula, rightly understood, is indeed perfectly orthodox.[86]

Whatever the pedigree of the "mia physis" formula itself, from Cyril's third anathema it is clear that he used it to espouse the singularity of the existence of Jesus and not a blurring of the quiddities of divinity and humanity.[87] The formulation, as Cyril understood it, claims simply that: (1) Jesus is a real existent being (μία φύσις); and (2) he is the one Logos existing as incarnate (τοῦ λόγου σεσαρκωμένη).[88] In other words, in this formulation, "nature" (φύσις) functions to designate not the essence of a being, but precisely its existence, that which is now normatively designated by the term "hypostasis" (ὑπόστασις). Indeed, when Cyril specified what he meant by the union (ἕνωσις) in Christ he rather comfortably shifted between "according to nature" (κατὰ φύσιν) or "according to hypostasis" (καθ᾽ ὑπόστασιν).[89] This signified for him that the two terms can be taken as synonymous and interchangeable in some instances. In this way, the "mia physis" formula in Cyril is basically convertible with the doctrine of the hypostatic union (ἕνωσις καθ᾽ ὑπόστασιν).

Whatever the convertibility of the "mia physis" formula and the formulation of the "hypostatic union," in and of themselves they were important to Cyril only as makeshifts. Cyril was wedded, not to the formulae, but to the expediency with which they served to declare and safeguard the truth that on the Cross it is none other than the divine Son who suffers and

---

84. Cf. Apollinarius, Frag. 9 (ed. Hans Lietzmann, *Apollinarius von Laodicea und seine Schule: Texte und Untersuchungen* [Tübingen: Mohr, 1904], p. 206).

85. Constantinople I, canon 1 (DS 151; DEC 1.31).

86. *Anathematismi adversus "tria Capitula,"* canon 8 (DS 429; DEC 1.117-118).

87. See Thomas G. Weinandy, O.F.M., Cap., *Does God Change?* (New York: Fordham University Press, 2002), pp. 46-48.

88. See Weinandy, "Cyril and the Mystery of the Incarnation," pp. 32-41.

89. Cyril of Alexandria, *Apologeticus contra Theodoretum pro duodecim capitibus* (PG 76.385b-453c).

dies. In this way, the "mia physis" formula and the third anathema are only rightly understood as serving the core declaration of the Twelve Chapters, anathema 12: that the one who is himself the Life (ἡ ζωή [John 14:6]), the one who is impassible to death, nevertheless died (θανάτου γευσάμενον) and in dying transformed death into the womb of true life.[90] This Cyril took as the core of the faith. Because Jesus is the Life, death had no dominion over him (cf. Rom. 6:9), it could not hold him (cf. Acts 2:24), and so his dying became the means of a new birth into new life (cf. John 3:1-26). Thus he is truly the first-born from the dead (cf. Col. 1:18). By dying, he conquers death by death, in order that he might be in truth "the life-giving one" (ὁ ζωοποιός). Only by upholding the absolute *unio* of the impassible and the passible, of life and death, of divinity and humanity in Christ can we call him "Savior." This formulation, despite the fact that it is often suggested to have been aggressively provocative on Cyril's part,[91] is in fact rooted in the *Credo* of Nicaea: for us and for our salvation he came down from heaven, was crucified, suffered death and was buried, and rose again in accordance with the Scriptures.

For Cyril, therefore, the point of Christological doctrine is to declare that the abiding *maior dissimilitudo* of divine and human being is upheld in perfect *unio* in the one Jesus Christ in order to realize the truth of the life-giving Cross. Cyril thus sustains and is wedded to this truth above every linguistic formulation or abstract doctrine.

This need for theological reasoning not to cling to formulations but to the Crucified Lord is clearly seen in the way Cyril maintained his doctrine with perfect consistency, while admitting a variety of different formulae. This is attested to in the flexibility he admitted later in his life to the formula "in two natures."[92] Cyril's concession of the validity of the "in two natures" formula occurred after the condemnation of Nestorius at Ephesus. It is expounded in his second letter to Succensus, in which Cyril was responding to a pointed question concerning whether the "mia physis" formula does not in fact entail a blending of divinity and humanity in a way that compromises the integral preservation of their difference. Cyril responded that the nature of the Logos does not transfer to the nature

---

90. Cyril of Alexandria, Twelve Chapters, anathema 12 (DS 263; DEC 1.61).

91. Cf. Richard Price and Michael Gaddis, *The Acts of the Council of Chalcedon: Translated with an Introduction and Notes*, 3 vols. (Liverpool: Liverpool University Press, 2005), vol. 3, p. 293, n. 89; Russell, *Cyril of Alexandria*, p. 39; Wilken, *The First Thousand Years*, p. 198.

92. See Cyril of Alexandria, *Epistula* 46, Second letter to Succensus (ed. Wickham, pp. 86-88; PG 77.241a-d).

of the flesh, nor does the nature of the flesh transfer to the Logos. To the contrary: after the union "each element . . . persists in its particular natural character," and yet is "mysteriously and inexpressibly unified."[93] According to Cyril, the one existent of Christ (μία φύσις / ὑπόστασις) is a compound existent (σύνθετος). When we call Jesus *unitas* we are referring to this compound fact, an ontological singularity that is nevertheless a composite of two quiddities, divine and human. In this way, Cyril conceded that the formula he originally rejected (ἐν δύο φύσεσιν) is orthodox if it is deployed in terms of his implied distinction between *physis*-as-quiddity and *physis*-as-existent. In other words, the formula is "orthodox" when the term *physis* is taken not in the way it was intended by Theodore and Nestorius, but according to its later reception as always designating quiddity.

With the foregoing stipulation in mind, Cyril allowed that two natures (as in quiddities) do endure "in" (ἐν) the one existent Christ, not "separately" (χωριστῶς) but in perfect "union" (ἕνωσις).[94] According to this standard, the litmus test of orthodoxy regarding the "in two natures" formula lies in the following: when used erroneously, the formula legitimizes an existential duality in Christ that would parse the Logos from the Cross; when used correctly, it is deployed strictly as a speculative distinction, *en theoria mone* (ἐν θεωρίᾳ μόνη), a distinction arising from contemplation of the one Crucified Lord.[95] In the latter, the unity that constitutes the quidditive difference of God and man is maintained in the singular subject of Jesus' compound being. In other words, with regard to the "two natures" in Christ, union differentiates and not otherwise.[96] This means that in terms of the existent concrete subject, there is ever and always only one Lord.

---

93. Cyril of Alexandria, *Epistula* 46, Second letter to Succensus (ed. Wickham, p. 88; PG 77.241b).

94. Cf. McGuckin, *The Christological Controversy*, p. 239.

95. Cyril of Alexandria, *Epistula* 46, Second letter to Succensus (ed. Wickham, p. 92; PG 77.245a).

96. Cf. Cyril of Alexandria, *Epistula* 45, First letter to Succensus (ed. Wickham, pp. 70-83; PG 77.228d-237c); *Epistula* 46, Second letter to Succensus (ed. Wickham, pp. 84-93; PG 77.228d-237c).

CHAPTER 2

The Humanity of Christ

*We proclaim the fleshly death of God's only-begotten Son, Jesus Christ
... when we perform in church the unbloody service.*

Cyril of Alexandria

A. *Communicatio Idiomatum*

It is significant that the Nestorian controversy began over the use of the title of Theotokos for Mary. What was at stake, in technical terms, concerned
the doctrine of *communicatio idiomatum* (ἀντίδοσις τῶν ἰδιωμάτων).[1] The
doctrine holds that, because of the union of divinity and humanity in Jesus,
properties that are properly divine may be predicated of the man Jesus
while properties that are properly human may be predicated of the divine
person of the Son. Rooted in the New Testament,[2] *communicatio idiomatum* is evidenced in the paradoxical terminology of Ignatius of Antioch
(c. 35-c. 117), who writes of the "blood of God" (αἵματι θεοῦ),[3] and of "the
suffering of my God" (τοῦ πάθους τοῦ θεοῦ μου).[4] What he is not saying is

---

1. On *communicatio idiomatum* see Grzegorz Strzelczyk, *Communicatio idiomatum: lo
scambio delle proprietà; storia,* status quaestionis *e prospettive* (Rome: Pontificia Università
Gregoriana, 2004); also see the review of Strzelczyk by Philip McCosker in *Modern Theology*
23 (2007): 298-301. Further, cf. Thomas G. Weinandy, O.F.M., Cap., *Does God Suffer?* (Edinburgh: T&T Clark, 2000), pp. 172-213. Further, cf. Christoph Cardinal Schönborn, *God Sent
His Son: A Contemporary Christology,* trans. Henry Taylor (San Francisco: Ignatius Press,
2004), pp. 151-53.

2. Cf. Strzelczyk, *Communicatio idiomatum,* pp. 11-45.

3. Ignatius of Antioch, *Letter to the Ephesians* 1 (LCL 24.218).

4. Ignatius of Antioch, *Letter to the Romans* 6 (LCL 24.278). Cf. Thomas G. Weinandy,

that God has "blood" or that God "suffers"; what he is saying is that in the Incarnate Son, human and divine things are attributed to the one person of the Son. It is in *communicatio idiomatum* that we find the "hermeneutical key" to Cyril's Christology.[5]

Underpinning Cyril's use of *communicatio idiomatum* is the Christological example of Athanasius for whom the *communicatio idiomatum* functions as a specification by which the Logos's "becoming" flesh does not entail any "change" or "mutation":

> He [the Son] has become flesh not by being changed into flesh, but because he assumed on our behalf living flesh, and has become man. For to say "the Word became flesh" is equivalent to saying "the Word has become man."[6]

For Athanasius this means that the "becoming" in the phrase "the Word became flesh" (John 1:14) entails no change in God, but rather a true communication of eternity and impassibility through the contingencies and fragilities of this first-century Palestinian Jew. The "becoming" in Christ, the drama and history of Jesus of Nazareth, is the "site" of eternal happenings, a pattern of events bound now to the eternal act of God. The "becoming" of "the Word became flesh" is defined by and exists through the terminal incarnational "is," which is the Logos of the Father.[7] This Jesus of Nazareth, a Jew born in the town of Bethlehem in Judah, in the time of King Herod, the son of a carpenter named Joseph and his wife Mary, who was crucified under Pontius Pilate, simply "is" the Logos, the only-begotten Son of God the Father.

Following Athanasius, then, the "becoming" human of the Son means that the Son has taken the frailty and contingency of a concrete human life to himself, and worked through it in such a way that God is truly "one"

O.F.M., Cap., "The Apostolic Christology of Ignatius of Antioch: The Road to Chalcedon," in A. Gregory and C. Tuckett, eds., *Trajectories through the New Testament and the Apostolic Fathers* (Oxford: OUP, 2005), pp. 71-84.

5. Thomas G. Weinandy, O.F.M., Cap., "Cyril and the Mystery of the Incarnation," in Thomas G. Weinandy, O.F.M., Cap., and Daniel A. Keating, eds., *The Theology of Cyril of Alexandria: A Critical Appreciation* (London: T&T Clark, 2003), pp. 23-54, at p. 31.

6. Athanasius of Alexandria, *Epistula ad Epictetum* 8 (PG 26.1064a).

7. See Thomas G. Weinandy, O.F.M., Cap., *Athanasius: A Theological Introduction* (London: Ashgate, 2007), p. 87.

with this human being, with all that he does and with all that befalls him. In Christ the Son "is" human. This allows that, on the Cross,

> when the flesh suffered, the Logos was not external to it, and therefore the passion is said to be his. And when he [the Incarnate] divinely accomplished his Father's works, the flesh was not external to him, but in the body itself did the Lord do them.[8]

Therefore, with regard to the Son who has become incarnate in Jesus, in addition to the predicates we would normally ascribe to divinity (eternity, immutability, aseity, etc.), we must now also ascribe the predicates of his human life (frailty, sorrow, death, etc.). It is not that God suffers or is frail in his divinity, but rather that in the person of the Son, the attributes of human finitude are truly those of the eternal Son through the fragility of his "becoming human."

Rooted thus in the vision of Athanasius, the "undistorted rule of the orthodox faith,"[9] Cyril understood the *communicatio idiomatum* as a fact demanded by both Scripture and Nicaea, which declares that the Son is both of "one substance" with the Father (ὁμοούσιον τῷ Πατρί) and born of the Virgin Mary (σαρκωθέντα ἐκ . . . Μαρίας τῆς Παρθένου). In his *Second Letter to Nestorius*, for example, Cyril argued that the Nicene declaration of the Son as "true God of true God" who "came down" from heaven means that, in the Incarnation, the Son is not "changed and made flesh" but rather "substantially" (καθ᾽ ὑπόστασιν) united with "flesh, endowed with life and reason" and "become man."[10] The unity of Christ is "not merely by way of divine favor or good will," but is rather an ontological union that nevertheless does not imply "that the difference between the natures was abolished through their union."[11] Cyril's doctrine of *communicatio idiomatum* thereby entails a threefold axiom:[12]

1. It is *truly God* the Son who is man. Here, the emphasis is focused upon the full divinity of the Son.

---

8. Athanasius of Alexandria, *Orationes adversus Arianos* 3.32 (PG 26.389c).

9. Cyril of Alexandria, *Homilia Paschalis* 8.6 (SC 392.100; PG 77.572a).

10. Cyril of Alexandria, *Epistula* 4, Second letter to Nestorius 3 (Lionel R. Wickham, ed. and trans., *Cyril of Alexandria: Select Letters* [Oxford: OUP, 1983], p. 6; DEC 1.41).

11. Cyril of Alexandria, *Epistula* 4, Second letter to Nestorius 3 (ed. Wickham, p. 6; DEC 1.41).

12. For this axiom, see Weinandy, "Cyril and the Mystery of the Incarnation," p. 30.

2. It is *truly man* that the Son of God is. Here the emphasis is focused upon the full and complete humanity.

3. The Son of God *truly is* man. Here the emphasis is focused upon the ontological union between the person of the Son and his humanity.

For Cyril, then, following the pattern and rule set down by Nicaea, it is none other than the one Lord Jesus who reveals to us, and "is," true divinity.[13]

B. Pelagianism and Nestorianism

The anthropological meaning of Nestorius's Christology was analyzed at the time of the crisis by the sometime Scythian monk and later abbot of St. Victor in Marseille, John Cassian (c. 360-435).[14] The Scythian monks were a monastic community based in the region where the Danube flows into the Black Sea. In the person of Cassian, they contributed to the Christological critique of Nestorianism. Later, after Chalcedon, their most important doctrinal contribution would be made by advocating the use of the Christological theopaschite formula *unus ex Trinitate passus est*, accepted as a dogma at Constantinople II (553).

In the Latin west, John Cassian was the foremost expert on Greek affairs,[15] and became involved in the matter of the Nestorian crisis in the

13. Cyril of Alexandria, *Epistula* 4, Second letter to Nestorius 3 (ed. Wickham, p. 6; DEC 1.41).

14. Though celebrated as one of the great theologians of the Church in the East, John Cassian has sometimes been tainted in the West with the suspicion of Semi-Pelagianism. Nevertheless, he is considered a saint in both the Roman Catholic Church and the Orthodox Church. By far the most important book on Cassian is Augustine Casiday's *Tradition and Theology in St. John Cassian* (Oxford: OUP, 2007). Casiday does a fine job of clearing Cassian of the smear of his apparent Semi-Pelagianism. Cf. Owen Chadwick, *John Cassian* (Cambridge: CUP, 1950); Columba Stewart, *Cassian the Monk* (Oxford: OUP, 1998). On Cassian's Christology, see Casiday, *Tradition and Theology in St. John Cassian*, pp. 215-58; Donald Fairbairn, *Grace and Christology in the Early Church* (Oxford: OUP, 2003), pp. 169-99.

15. Born, in fact, in the region of Scythia Minor (present day Dobruja), Cassian entered the monastic life in Palestine from whence he traveled to Egypt and encountered the monasticism of the desert. In Egypt Cassian lived among the Desert Fathers. The works he wrote on the Desert Fathers (*De Coenobiorum institutis libri duodecim* [PL 49.53-477] and *Vigintiquatuor collationes* [PL 49.477-1328]) were copied and studied for centuries and became the normative accounts of the Desert Fathers, especially in the Latin West. Around 399 he was forced, along with 300 other "Origenist" monks, to flee the desert on account of the anthropomorphic controversy and thus found himself in Constantinople. Here the monks

summer of 430 after Cyril sent his dossier on the crisis to Pope Celestine I. The Roman Pontiff sent Cyril's dossier via his archdeacon Leo (the future Pope Leo the Great) to the Abbey in Marseille, where the texts were studied by Cassian in order to secure the pope's support for Cyril.

Cassian's theological judgment against Nestorius is recorded in *De Incarnatione Domini contra Nestorium*.[16] The text correlates the error of Nestorius with that of Pelagius, arguing that both make Christ a *solum homo*, an exemplar of achievable human sinlessness, which undermines not only his divine identity but the traditional necessity of his salvific act *pro nobis*. At the heart of this correlation lies Cassian's assessment of Nestorius's construal of the Christological unity of divinity and humanity as a "voluntary union,"[17] and not a substantial union that ontologically constitutes the human existence of Jesus. The implication of a "voluntary union" is Pelagian, so Cassian argues, since the essential work of Christ must now be reconceived no longer as the work of a divine savior who came down from above "to bring redemption to the human race," but of a human "example of good works."[18] In this way, the doctrine of *solum homo* that governs the moral-anthropology of Pelagianism is conceived as the anthropological correlate to the Christological doctrine of *homo assumptus* — the accent in both cases diffusing the Nicene *descensus de caelis*. If Jesus is the exemplar of a human sinlessness, there is no need for the humanity of Christ to be ontologically determined by a constitutive union for which the divine Logos must be the subject of everything Christ did and all that befell him.[19] As Cassian writes:

> If Christ who was born of Mary is not the same one who . . . was born of God, you undoubtedly make two christs, according to the impious

---

appealed to the then-patriarch of Constantinople, John Chrysostom, for protection. Cassian was ordained a deacon in Constantinople and became a member of the clergy associated with the great Byzantine archbishop. When Chrysostom was forced into exile in 404, Cassian went to Rome to plead the Patriarch's cause to Pope Innocent I. While in Rome, Cassian was invited to found a monastery in southern Gaul near Marseille, which he did in 415.

16. John Cassian, *De Incarnatione Domini contra Nestorium* (PL 50.9-272).

17. Cf. Cassian, *De Incarnatione Domini contra Nestorium* 3.2 (PL 50.50c-52a) and 5.3-4 (PL 50.101b-105b); Nestorius, *The Bazaar of Heracleides*, trans. C. R. Driver and L. Hodgson (Oxford: Clarendon Press, 1925), pp. 181-82.

18. Cassian, *De Incarnatione Domini contra Nestorium* 1.3 (PL 50.22a-23a): "Dominum nostrum Jesum Christum hunc in mundum non ad praestandam humano generi redemptionem, sed ad praebenda bonorum actuum exempla venisse."

19. Cf. Cassian, *De Incarnatione Domini contra Nestorium* 1.3 (PL 50.21a-22a).

Pelagian error, which by asserting that a mere man was born of the virgin, said that he was the teacher of the human race rather than the redeemer, for he came to bring to people not redemption of life but [only] an example of how to live.[20]

The Nestorian rejection of the doctrine of the Theotokos, which implies for Cassian that the "Savior was born a mere man (*solitarium hominem natum*)," expresses Christologically the anthropological error of Pelagianism "that asserts that our Lord Jesus Christ lived as a mere man entirely without sin (*sine peccato solitarium hominem*)."[21]

The common error thus involves a wrong idea of human flourishing (perfection and redemption), insufficiently determined by the divine *descensus de caelis*. Christ is not, for Cassian, a perfect instance of human nature, a nature without the defect of sin; he is the Incarnate Son and Lord. This means that human nature, conceived and willed by God, cannot achieve its own perfection; rather, perfection of human nature is achieved by dynamic cooperation of receptivity to God in the synergy of divine grace.

In this light, we clearly see the significance of the fact that the Council of Ephesus not only condemned the error of Nestorianism, but also repeated the condemnation in the synod of Carthage (418) against Pelagianism.[22] "Pelagians" and "Nestorians" were never organized as two internally coherent groups; nor was there any real coordination, theologically or politically, between them. It is, however, a fact of history that these groups had some concrete links.[23] For example, as archbishop of Constantinople, Nestorius welcomed and gave refuge to the prominent followers of Pelagius, Caelestius and Julian. At an earlier stage, the same Julian found a sympathetic ear in Theodore of Mopsuestia. Indeed, before he finally succumbed to doubts over Julian's doctrine, Theodore had already written

---

20. Cassian, *De Incarnatione Domini contra Nestorium* 6.14 (PL 50.171b), trans. Fairbairn.

21. Cassian, *De Incarnatione Domini contra Nestorium* 1.3 (PL 50.23a-b).

22. See Synod of Carthage, canons on nature and grace (DS 222-230); Ephesus, Session 7, canons 1 and 4 (DS 267-268). The ruling of Ephesus was afterwards communicated to Pope Celestine; see *Synodi Relatio ad Caelestinum* 13 (ACO 1.1.3, 9).

23. See Lionel Wickham, "Pelagianism in the East," in Rowan Williams, ed., *The Making of Orthodoxy: Essays in Honour of Henry Chadwick* (Cambridge: CUP, 1989), pp. 200-215; Daniel A. Keating, *The Appropriation of Divine Life in Cyril of Alexandria* (Oxford: OUP, 2004), pp. 227-51; and Geoffrey D. Dunn, "Augustine, Cyril of Alexandria, and the Pelagian Controversy," *Augustinian Studies* 37 (2006): 63-88.

a polemic against those Latin theologians who "say that men sin not by will but by nature."[24]

None other than Augustine of Hippo had kept Cyril abreast of the Latin heresy well before the Nestorian crisis.[25] In *Epistula* 4* (c. 417-421), Augustine gave Cyril an account of the Pelagian heresy, presumably to warn him of Latin-speaking Pelagian sympathizers possibly taking refuge in Alexandria. And it is likely that Augustine included a copy of his *De Gestis Pelagii* with the letter.[26] In the *Epistula*, we learn that it was Cyril who sent Augustine the *Acta* of the 415 Synod of Diospolis that vindicated Pelagius. This gesture suggests some common cause between the great Latin doctor and the Alexandrian pope, especially in light of the condemnation of Pelagianism at Ephesus, which effectively reversed the ruling of Diospolis.

What *Epistula* 4* makes evident beyond a doubt is that Cyril's later condemnation of Pelagianism, far from being a mere "courtesy" to Rome for her support in the case against Nestorius, is rooted in a deeper theological understanding of the heresy and its correlation with Nestorianism.[27] Augustine's doctrine of original sin, clarified in *Epistula* 4* in terms of his claim that not all sinners would suffer eternal punishment,[28] is hardly a doctrine that Cyril would have had trouble affirming.[29]

Whatever doctrinal divergences separated Cyril and Augustine, they were in perfect agreement on the priority and necessity of the grace of Christ in all things.

---

24. Wickham, "Pelagianism in the East," p. 216.

25. See Augustine, *Epistula* 4*, in Johannes Divjak, ed., *Sancti Aureli Augustini opera: Epistolae ex duobus codicibus nuper in lucem prolatae*, CSEL 88 (Vienna: Hoelder-Pichler-Tempsky, 1981), pp. 26-29. This is not the only letter Augustine wrote to Cyril, but it is the only one extant.

26. See Gerald Bonner, "Some Remarks on Letters 4* and 6*," in J. Divjak, ed., *Les Lettres de saint Augustine* (Paris: Études Augustiniennes, 1983), pp. 155-64.

27. This was the old standard view, that Cyril merely condemned Pelagianism as a way of paying Pope Celestine back for his support in condemning Nestorianism. Cf. William Bark, "The Doctrinal Interests of Marius Mercator," *Church History* 12 (1943): 210-16, at p. 215: "Celestine sacrificed Nestorius to Cyril and Cyril agreed to the condemnation of the Pelagians, in whose teaching he had previously shown no interest at all." Also cf. B. R. Rees, *Pelagius: A Reluctant Heretic* (Woodbridge: Boydell Press, 1988), who argues at p. xv that the condemnation of Pelagianism at Ephesus was a mere courtesy.

28. Augustine, *Epistula* 4* 3 (ed. Divjak, p. 27).

29. Cf. Cyril of Alexandria, *The Letter of Cyril of Alexandria to Tiberius the Deacon* 12-13 (ed. Wickham, pp. 169-74).

These concentric circles of ecclesial history illustrate the following correlation of Nestorianism and Pelagianism: if the most basic article of belief of a would-be "Pelagian" concerns the denial of the doctrine of original sin,[30] this denial converges absolutely with the logic of *separatio* of the human Jesus from the one Lord, as if the "man Jesus" and the Cross on which he died could be predicated apart from the Logos of God. The centrality of the Cross, then, as the event of divine salvation apart from which the human being cannot truly find himself, is precisely what eludes the logic of both Pelagianism and Nestorianism and is internal to their convertibility. Hence the truth of the famous dictum: "The Nestorian Christ is a fitting savior of the Pelagian man."[31]

* * *

Nestorian Christology exhibits what Georges Florovsky called an "anthropological maximalism."[32] Hence Nestorius's thought has been recognized as conducive to the anthropocentric agendas of modern "human-centered" Christologies "from below."[33] But the apparent "anthropological maximalism" of Nestorius here organically deflates into an "anthropological minimalism," since by presuming to apprehend all that "fully human" might mean in abstraction from the Incarnation it effectively limits the horizon of authentic humanity. A true Christian "anthropological maximalism," by contrast, must rest in the expansive horizon of Jesus Christ as the content of true humanity.[34] This, in contrast with Nestorius, implies the impossibility of a tidy parallelism of humanity and divinity: humanity must now be directly and symbiotically related to divinity in such a way that only the ground of union with God realizes what the human truly is and what he can do. This is evidenced in the centrality of the doctrine of

---

30. Cf. Gerald Bonner, "Pelagianism and Augustine," *Augustinian Studies* 23 (1992): 33-51.

31. Charles Gore, "Our Lord's Human Example," *Church Quarterly Review* 16 (1883): 282-313, here p. 298.

32. Georges Florovsky, "Christological Dogma and Its Terminology," *The Greek Orthodox Theological Review* 13 (1968): 190-93.

33. Cf. John McGuckin, *Saint Cyril of Alexandria and the Christological Controversy* (Crestwood, NY: Saint Vladimir's Seminary Press, 2004), pp. 134-35: The "resolute acceptance [by Nestorius] of the implications of all that 'fully human' might mean is an aspect of much modern Christological thought too, and in this respect Nestorius's doctrine has taken on a new relevance for contemporary thinkers."

34. Cf. *Gaudium et spes* 22 (DS 4322).

deification for Cyril rooted in 2 Peter 1:4, of human beings becoming "partakers of the divine nature," a verse Cyril invoked more frequently than any previous theologian.[35]

The reality of "full humanity," for Cyril, involves a Christological recovery of the reality for which the human being was created in the first place. This involves two aspects: (1) the human is created according to the image of God, which is the Son (cf. Gen. 1:27); (2) by the inbreathing of the Holy Spirit the human is given "the breath of life" (cf. Gen. 2:7). The fall entails a loss of "full humanity," not in the sense that man loses the divine image, but rather in the sense that he loses his participation in the divine life, the breath of the Spirit, who "'flew away' (ἀπέπτη) from the human race in the first Adam because of sin."[36] Through Christ, this divine participation is recovered through the "Spirit [who] did not merely descend (ἔμεινεν) upon Jesus, but importantly *has remained* (μεμένηκεν) upon him."[37] For Cyril, redemption and deification involve, most especially, a Christological recovery of "the breath of life" in the face of death; a recovery, that is, of the inbreathing of the Spirit. As Cyril writes:

> It was not otherwise possible for man [having lost the Spirit of life] . . . to escape death, unless he recovered that ancient grace, and partook once more of God who holds all things together in being and preserves them in life through the Son in the Spirit. Therefore his Only-begotten Word has become a partaker of flesh and blood (Heb. 2:14), that is, he has become man — though being Life by nature, and begotten of the Life that is by nature, that is, of God the Father — so that, having united himself with the flesh which perishes according to the law of its own nature, . . . he might restore it to his own life and render it through himself a partaker of God the Father. . . . And he wears our nature, refashioning it to his own life. And he himself is also in us, for we have all become partakers of him, and have him in ourselves through the Spirit. For this reason we have become "partakers of the divine nature" (2 Pet. 1:4), and

35. On Cyril's doctrine of deification, see Keating, *The Appropriation of Divine Life in Cyril of Alexandria*, pp. 144-90; "Divinization in Cyril: The Appropriation of Divine Life," in Thomas G. Weinandy, O.F.M., Cap., and Daniel A. Keating, eds., *The Theology of St. Cyril of Alexandria: A Critical Appreciation* (London: T&T Clark, 2003), pp. 149-86; and Norman Russell, *The Doctrine of Deification in the Greek Patristic Tradition* (Oxford: OUP, 2004), pp. 191-204.

36. Keating, "Divinization in Cyril," p. 156.

37. Keating, "Divinization in Cyril," p. 153; emphasis is Keating's.

are reckoned as sons, and so too have in ourselves the Father himself through the Son.[38]

In this light we see that only by becoming "partakers of the divine nature" through Christ do we recover fully the reality for which the human was originally made. The truly "human" is only fully given in Christ: "Man's hominization . . . attains its apex in his divinization."[39]

C. Christology and Eucharist

For Cyril, the divinizing possibilities opened up to humanity through the Cross of the Incarnate Logos are appropriated concretely in the Eucharistic action of the Church. It is in and by the Eucharist that human beings are knit into union with the Crucified Lord, who has destroyed death and accomplished the vocation of humanity in his own life-giving death.[40] Cyril writes:

> [In] the eucharistic reception of the holy flesh and blood, which restores man wholly to incorruption (ἀφθαρσίαν) . . . the holy body of Christ endows those who receive it with life and keeps us incorrupt when it is mingled (ἀνακιρνάμενον) with our bodies. For it is not the body of anyone else, but is thought of as the body of him who is Life by nature, since it has within itself the entire power of the Word that is united with it, and . . . is filled with his energy (ἐνεργείας), through which all things are given life and maintained in being.[41]

It is crucial here that, for Cyril, the salvation of Christ is wholly mediated and participated in through the Eucharist such that the Eucharist must

---

38. Cyril of Alexandria, *In Ioannis Evangelium* 14.20 (in Philipp E. Pusey, ed., *Sancti patris nostri Cyrilli Archiepiscopi Alexandrini in d. Ioannis Evangelium* [Oxford: Clarendon Press, 1872], 2.485-486), trans. by Keating.

39. International Theological Commission, "Theology, Christology, Anthropology," in Michael Sharkey, ed., *International Theological Commission: Texts and Documents 1969-1985* (San Francisco: Ignatius Press, 1989), p. 213.

40. See Keating, *The Appropriation of Divine Life in Cyril of Alexandria*, pp. 54-105; Frances Young, "*Theotokos*: Mary and the Pattern of Fall and Reception in the Theology of Cyril of Alexandria," in Thomas G. Weinandy, O.F.M., Cap., and Daniel A. Keating, eds., *The Theology of Cyril of Alexandria: A Critical Appreciation* (London: T&T Clark, 2003), pp. 55-74, at pp. 72-74.

41. Cyril of Alexandria, *In Ioannis Evangelium* 6.35 (PG 73. 520d-521a), trans. Russell (ECF).

truly be the body of Christ and that body must truly be "one." For Cyril, only an ontological and substantial union (ἕνωσις καθ' ὑπόστασιν) in Christ endows his flesh with that divine power the Church holds to be operative in Eucharist.[42] In this light, we see that Nestorius's doctrine of a mere "conjunction" (συνάφεια) of the humanity and divinity in Christ struck at the very heart of Cyril's sense of the whole meaning and realization of the Christian life, which aims at nothing less than union with God in Christ through the Eucharist.[43] Hence the eleventh anathema of Cyril's Third Letter to Nestorius:

> Whoever does not acknowledge that the Lord's flesh is life-giving (σάρκα ζωοποιόν εἶναι) and belongs to the very Logos of God the Father but says it belongs to somebody different joined to him by way of rank or merely possessing divine indwelling instead of being life-giving, as we said, because it has come to belong to the Word who has power to give life to all things, let him be anathema.[44]

Thus, while the debate between Nestorius and Cyril swirled around the Marian title, another central issue behind Cyril's rejection of Nestorius's Christology lay in how a dualistic rendering of the relation of divinity and humanity in Christ compromised the basic ecclesial meaning of the Eucharist as the means of human participation in the atoning and divinizing Paschal Mystery of Jesus Christ.

Hence for Cyril, the Eucharistic action, a proper doctrine of Mary's maternity, and a correctly articulated theopaschite account of the Cross, are — all three — internal to determine the real meaning of the divine unity of Jesus.[45] This is evidenced in Cyril's second and third letters to Nestorius:

42. Henry Chadwick, "Eucharist and Christology in the Nestorian Controversy," *Journal of Theological Studies* 2 (1951): 145-64, at pp. 155-56. In my remarks on Cyril and the Eucharist I have also benefited from an unpublished essay of W. Chris Hackett, titled "Sacrifice Christology: The Eucharistic 'Reduction' of the Christology of St Cyril of Alexandria."

43. Cf. Nestorius, *Bazaar of Heracleides* (ed. Bedjan), trans. Driver and Hodgson, pp. 144-46.

44. Cyril of Alexandria, *Epistula* 17, Third Letter to Nestorius, anathema 11 (DS 262; ed. Wickham, p. 32; PG 77.121c-d).

45. Chadwick, "Eucharist and Christology," p. 153. Cf. M.-O. Boulnois, "Die Eucharistie, Mysterium der Einigung bei Cyrill von Alexandrien: Die Modelle der trinitarischen und christologischen Einigung," *Theologische Quartalschrift* 4 (1998): 294-310; Lawrence J. Welch, *Christology and Eucharist in the Early Thought of Cyril of Alexandria* (San Francisco: International Scholars Press, 1994); Ezra Gebremedhin, *Life-Giving Blessing: An Inquiry into the Eu-*

1. This is what it means to say that he was also born of woman in the flesh though owning his existence before the ages and begotten of the Father: not that his divine nature originated in the holy Virgin or necessarily required for its own sake a second birth subsequent to that from the Father ... no, it means that he had fleshly birth because he issued from woman for us and for our salvation, having united humanity substantially to himself.[46]

2. This is what we mean when we say he suffered and rose again; not that God the Word suffered blows, nail-piercings or other wounds in his own nature (the divine nature is impassible because it is incorporeal) but what is said is that since his own created body suffered these things he himself "suffered for our sake," the point being that within the suffering body was the Impassable.[47]

3. This too we must add. We proclaim the fleshly death of God's only-begotten Son, Jesus Christ, we confess his return to life from the dead and his ascension into heaven when we perform in church the unbloody service, when we approach the sacramental gifts and are hallowed participants in the holy flesh and precious blood of Christ, savior of us all, by receiving not mere flesh (God forbid!) or flesh of a man hallowed by connection with the Word in some unity of dignity or possessing some divine indwelling, but the personal, truly life-giving flesh of God the Word himself. As God he is by nature Life and because he has become one with his own flesh he rendered it life-giving; and so, though he tells us *"verily I say unto you, unless you eat the flesh of the Son of Man and drink his blood,"* we must not suppose it belongs to one of us men ... but that it was made the truly personal possession of him who for us had become and was called "Son of Man."[48]

In the womb of the Virgin Mother, God "becomes" human, receiving from her the body that makes possible the "passion" of God; while on the Cross, through the Jewish flesh given of Mary, the divine Son is truly cruci-

---

charistic Doctrine of Cyril of Alexandria (Uppsala: Borgstroms, 1977); Ellen Concannon, "The Eucharist as Source of St. Cyril of Alexandria's Christology," *Pro Ecclesia* 18 (2009): 318-36.

46. Cyril of Alexandria, *Epistula* 4, Second Letter to Nestorius 4 (ed. Wickham, p. 6; PG 77.45c-d), trans. Wickham.

47. Cyril of Alexandria, *Epistula* 4, Second Letter to Nestorius 5 (ed. Wickham, p. 6; PG 77.48a), trans. Wickham.

48. Cyril of Alexandria, *Epistula* 17, Third Letter to Nestorius 7 (ed. Wickham, p. 22; PG 77.113c-116a), trans. Wickham.

fied. In the same way, in the Eucharist, Christians receive the very flesh the Logos received of Mary and united to himself, that "truly life-giving flesh of God the Word himself." Only insofar as God receives the possibility of human flesh does he become crucifiable and sacramentally givable.

Whereas the Christological impulse of Theodore and Nestorius issued from a concern to protect the transcendent fact of the divine Logos, the Christological impulse of Cyril issued from his resolve to safeguard the proclamation of the unity of the divine Logos with the one crucified on the Cross, by which the authenticity of the Church's life in the sacramental body is given and received.

CHAPTER 3

Chalcedonian Orthodoxy

The divine Son of God . . . the impassible God did not despise to become a suffering man.

Leo the Great

A. Towards the Council

When the Council of Chalcedon met in 451,[1] Cyril of Alexandria had been dead for less than a decade.[2] Yet his status at the Council was that of

---

1. The indispensable resource on Chalcedon, in English, is Richard Price and Michael Gaddis, *The Acts of the Council of Chalcedon: Translated with an Introduction and Notes,* 3 vols. (Manchester: Liverpool University Press, 2005). See also V. C. Samuel, *The Council of Chalcedon Re-Examined* (New York: Xlibris, 2001); Richard Price and Mary Whitby, eds., *Chalcedon in Context: Church Councils 400-700* (Liverpool: Liverpool University Press, 2009), pp. 70-91; R. V. Sellers, *The Council of Chalcedon: A Historical and Doctrinal Survey* (London: SPCK, 1953); Frances Young, *From Nicaea to Chalcedon: A Guide to the Literature and Its Background* (London: SCM Press, 1983), pp. 178-289; Aloys Grillmeier, S.J., *Christ in Christian Tradition,* vol. 1, *From the Apostolic Age to Chalcedon (451),* trans. John Bowden (London: Mowbray, 1975), pp. 414-519; J. N. D. Kelly, *Early Christian Doctrines,* rev. ed. (New York: HarperOne, 1978), pp. 330-43. On the theology of the *Definitio fidei,* see Sarah Coakley, "What Does Chalcedon Solve and What Does it Not? Some Reflections on the Status and Meaning of the Chalcedonian 'Definition'," in Stephen T. Davis, Daniel Kendall, S.J., and Gerald O'Collins, S.J., eds., *The Incarnation: An Interdisciplinary Symposium on the Incarnation of the Son of God* (Oxford: OUP, 2002), pp. 143-63; Christoph Cardinal Schönborn, *God Sent His Son: A Contemporary Christology,* trans. Henry Taylor (San Francisco: Ignatius Press, 2004), pp. 153-65; André de Halleux, "La Définition christologique à Chalcédoine," *Revue théologique de Louvain* 7 (1976): 3-23, 155-70.

2. On Cyril and Chalcedon, see John McGuckin, *Saint Cyril of Alexandria and the Christological Controversy* (Crestwood, NY: St. Vladimir's Seminary Press, 2004), pp. 233-40; the

---

"our most blessed and holy father Cyril," the doctrinal authority in accordance with which the Council Fathers saw fit to reach their most delicate theological judgments.[3]

The dogmatic pre-eminence of Cyril at Chalcedon is signaled not least in the Council's full ratification of Ephesus (431),[4] and in its insistence on the "fused" (συντρέχω) character of the union of divinity and humanity in Christ.[5] Chalcedon's program of dogmatic continuity with Ephesus was moreover upheld in the *Definitio fidei*'s repeated designation of Christ as "one and the same" (ἕνα καὶ τὸν αὐτόν)[6] and in its insistence on the single substantial/hypostatic reality of his being (μίαν ὑπόστασιν).[7] In this way Chalcedon ensured that its dyophysite affirmation of the two natures in Christ (ἐν δύο φύσεσιν) could not be rightly understood in the Theodorian sense of a "conjunction" (συνάφεια) of two pre-existing realities, but rather needed to be understood in the Cyrillian sense that the Logos himself directly constitutes and is the existence of the human "Jesus."

The overarching presence of Cyril at Chalcedon notwithstanding, a prevalent suspicion that Chalcedon had somehow betrayed the teaching

---

"General Introduction" in Price and Gaddis, *The Acts of the Council of Chalcedon*, vol. 1, pp. 65-75.

3. See the "General Introduction" in Price and Gaddis, *The Acts of the Council of Chalcedon*, vol. 1, pp. 65-75. This is to offer a rather different view than that of Beeley, who takes the Council Fathers at Chalcedon as disingenuously invoking Cyril, while basically proposing a "clear Antiochene bias" (Christopher Beeley, *The Unity of Christ: Continuity and Conflict in Patristic Tradition* [New Haven: Yale University Press, 2012], pp. 276-84, at p. 281). In what follows, moreover, if my account is at odds with Beeley, it is also meant to qualify so as to retract much of what I wrote on Chalcedon and Leo in my article, "After Chalcedon: the Oneness of Christ and the Dyothelite Mediation of his Theandric Unity," *Modern Theology* 24 (2008): 199-224.

4. See *Definitio fidei* (DS 301; DEC 1.85) and *Definitio fidei* (ed. Price and Gaddis, 2.203).

5. *Definitio fidei* (DS 302; DEC 1.86). Against this strong evidence, one might rejoin that the logic of the *Definitio fidei* is nonetheless also based on the *Formula unionis* (which it is), thus apparently suggesting that at the very least the *Definitio fidei* must be a "compromise" between some kind of quasi-Theodorian doctrine and a fully Cyrillian position. The problem with this argument, however, as Price and Gaddis point out, is that while the *Formula unionis* is originally, perhaps, a quasi-Theodorian qualification of Cyril's doctrine, the *Definitio fidei* clearly interprets and paraphrases the *Formula unionis* in conformity with the interpretations given by Cyril himself in his letter *de pace* to John of Antioch following the Council of Ephesus. See Price and Gaddis, *The Acts of the Council of Chalcedon*, vol. 1, p. 69. For the texts of the *Formula unionis*, see DS 271-273 and DEC 1.69; for Cyril's letter to John, see DEC 1.70-74.

6. *Definitio fidei* (DS 301-302; DEC 1.86).

7. *Definitio fidei* (DS 302; DEC 1.86).

of the Alexandrian patriarch followed the Council. The end game of this suspicion led, finally, to ecclesial divisions that persist to this day.[8] The irony, however, is this: while the Council Fathers at Chalcedon formulated a doctrine for which Cyril was the ultimate standard of "orthodoxy," those who rejected the Council did so in the name of upholding Cyril's doctrine.

* * *

The doctrinal crisis that precipitated the Council of Chalcedon concerns the Christological monophysitism of the Constantinopolitan archimandrite, Eutyches (c. 380-c. 456). The Eutychian error is encapsulated in his declaration: "I confess that our Lord was from two natures (ἐκ δύο φύσεσιν) before the union, but after the union I confess one nature (μία φύσις)."[9] Taking the "mia physis" formula of Cyril of Alexandria as axiomatic, Eutyches' error was to apply the Cyrillian formula in a way that implied that the Incarnate Christ is a *tertium quid*, a blending into perfect

---

8. See John Meyendorff, *Christ in Eastern Christian Thought* (Crestwood, NY: Saint Vladimir's Seminary Press, 1975), pp. 29-46.

9. Eutyches was neither a formidable theological figure nor did he enjoy the advantage of Episcopal office. He was, however, respected as a saintly old monk within Constantinople, and possessed significant ecclesial allies, not least in Dioscorus of Alexandria (d. 454), Cyril's nephew and successor to the see his uncle held until his death in 444. The crisis that led to Eutyches' ultimate condemnation at Chalcedon began in 448 when Flavian, the new archbishop of Constantinople, chaired a home synod that charged the old monk of teaching heresy. Clearly with no intent other than to uphold the teaching of Cyril, Eutyches stubbornly defended the "mia physis" formula. What is more, he maintained it with a narrow obstinacy that required that the "in two natures" (ἐν δύο φύσεσιν) formula was, in all cases, evidence of full-blown Nestorian heresy. Eutyches was brought before the second session of the synod, where he was interrogated and made to make a theological defense of his doctrine. The trial centered on whether Jesus was truly "consubstantial with us" (ὁμοούσιν ἡμῖν) and whether he existed "in two natures" (ἐν δύο φύσεσιν). In this way the trial concerned two clarifications of the *Formula unionis* of 433, to which Cyril himself had subscribed (DS 272; DEC 1.69-70). In fact the *Formula* did not quite take up the second formulation ἐν δύο φύσεσιν, though it implies it clearly through the formulation δύο . . . φύσεων ἕνωσις (DS 272), which after the union can yet be distinguished (cf. DS 273). In the course of the trial Eutyches was, for the most part, evasive and showed little theological sophistication. Finally, in response to direct questioning on the two formulae, Eutyches made his famous confession: "I confess that our Lord was from two natures (ἐκ δύο φύσεσιν) before the union, but after the union I confess one nature (μία φύσις)" (ACO 2.1.1, 143). On Eutyches' Christology, see R. Draguet, "La christologie d'Eutyches d'après les actes du synode de Flavien," *Byzantion* 6 (1931): 441-57. On the background to Chalcedon, see Price and Gaddis, General Introduction to *The Acts of the Council of Chalcedon*, vol. 1, pp. 1-85.

unity of divine and human quiddities with the result that, after the union, neither quiddity is integral or whole but rather now only partly so.[10] In other words, Eutyches defended the "mia physis" formula without upholding (or understanding?) the crucial theological distinction Cyril presumed between *physis*-as-quiddity and *physis*-as-existent.[11]

The failure of Eutyches to realize the distinction between *physis*-as-quiddity and *physis*-as-existent meant that, however much his language nominally conformed to that of Cyril, he failed to be truly Cyrillian. He was condemned and deposed in 448 at a local synod presided over by Flavian, archbishop of Constantinople. The result of his condemnation, however, was to plunge the Church afresh into crisis over the doctrine of the unity of Christ. The emperor Theodosius II (who had convened the Council of Ephesus in 431 and forced the *Formula unionis* of 433) was now compelled to call a new council.

The second council at Ephesus, which met in 449, was presided over by Dioscorus of Alexandria, Cyril's nephew and immediate successor.[12] Presuming that the condemnation of Eutyches was a direct attack on the doctrine and legacy of Cyril, Dioscorus moved quickly to exonerate Eutyches and depose Flavian, who was subsequently brutalized by Dioscorus's supporters before dying under suspicious circumstances.[13] Eager to defend and uphold the unequivocal pre-eminence of Cyril and Ephesus I,

10. Cf. V. C. Samuel, "One Incarnate Nature of God the Word," *Greek Orthodox Theological Review* 10 (1964/1965): 37-53.

11. See Thomas G. Weinandy, O.F.M., Cap., "Cyril and the Mystery of the Incarnation," in Thomas G. Weinandy, O.F.M., Cap., and Daniel A. Keating, eds., *The Theology of Cyril of Alexandria: A Critical Appreciation* (London: T&T Clark, 2003), pp. 23-54, at pp. 32-41.

12. On Ephesus II, see Grillmeier, *Christ in Christian Tradition*, vol. 1, pp. 526-30; and Susan Wessel, *Leo the Great and the Spiritual Rebuilding of a Universal Rome* (Leiden: Brill, 2008), pp. 259-83.

13. See Henry Chadwick, "The Exile and Death of Flavian of Constantinople: A Prologue to the Council of Chalcedon," *Journal of Theological Studies* 6 (1955): 17-34. One further example of Dioscorus's conduct, recounted by Price and Gaddis, concerns a moment at Ephesus II in which, in a difficult doctrinal exchange with Domnus II of Antioch, Dioscorus complained that Domnus was tolerating "Nestorian" expression in his diocese. Domnus appealed to the *Formula* and reminded Dioscorus that Cyril had chosen not to press his Twelve Chapters. The response of Dioscorus was to have Domnus immediately condemned by the synod and anathematized for rejecting Cyril's teaching (see the General Introduction to *The Acts of the Council of Chalcedon*, vol. 1, pp. 36-37). On the council's brutality, see Michael Gaddis, "*Non Iudicium sed Latrocinium*: Of Holy Synods and Robber Councils" in *There Is No Crime for Those Who Have Christ: Religious Violence in the Christian Roman Empire* (Berkeley: University of California Press, 2005), pp. 283-322.

Dioscorus moved also to have the bishops Theodoret of Cyrrhus (393-460) and Ibas of Edessa (bishop from 435 to 457) deposed. At Ephesus I, Theodoret and Ibas had followed John of Antioch, and while they had been formally reconciled to Cyril in 433, they were known to be theological disciples of Theodore of Mopsuestia and in principle remained hostile to Cyril's doctrine and especially the Twelve Chapters. Finally, in what was perhaps Dioscorus's most foolish and arrogant act, he refused to allow the Tome of Pope Leo to be read; presumably he feared that reading it would unsettle his retributive defense of what he took as "Cyrillian orthodoxy."

Pope Leo wrote the Tome in 449, sending it to Flavian with the intention of resolving the dispute unleashed by Eutyches' condemnation. At the heart of the letter is Leo's doctrine of the *unitas personae* of Christ, by which he sought to affirm the identity and singularity of Christ on the level of person (*persona*), while affirming the duality of divinity and humanity on the level of nature (*natura*).[14] The doctrine of the *unitas personae* may have struck some, in the Greek context, as dangerously close to the doctrine of Theodore and Nestorius, who had also sought to maintain a strong dyophysitism (ἐν δύο φύσεσιν), while affirming the unity of Christ through recourse to a union on the level of *prosopon* (πρόσωπον).[15] Terminologically, there is a correlation between the Tome and the doctrine of Theodore and Nestorius, at least insofar as the Latin *persona* is understood as convertible with the Greek *prosopon*.[16] However, for Leo the *unitas personae* is in no

14. On Leo's Christology, see Grillmeier, *Christ in Christian Tradition*, vol. 1, pp. 526-39; Wessel, *Leo the Great and the Spiritual Rebuilding of a Universal Rome*, pp. 209-57; and J. M. Armitage, *A Twofold Solidarity: Leo the Great's Theology of Redemption* (Strathfield: St. Pauls, 2005). More generally on Leo, see Bronwen Neil, *Leo the Great*, ECF (London: Routledge, 2009). The onetime archdeacon of Pope Celestine, Leo had played a role in Rome's support for Cyril against Nestorius. While Leo's credentials were accordingly anti-Nestorian, he was astute enough to see that the doctrine of Eutyches threatened the creed of orthodoxy. Cf. *Epistula Papae Leonis ad Flavianum* (DS 290; DEC 1.80): "Nesciens igitur [Eutyches], quid deberet de Verbi Dei incarnatione sentire . . . illam saltem communem et indiscretam confessionem sollicito recepisset auditu, qua fidelium universitas profitetur credere se *in Deum Patrem omnipotentem et in Christum Iesum Filium eius unicum Dominum nostrum, qui natus est de Spiritu Sancto et Maria virgine*."

15. Cf. the concerns raised at Chalcedon, Session II, 29 (ed. Price and Gaddis, 2.26-27).

16. This terminological correlation was not lost on Nestorius, who noted it from his exile in 449 and thought the Tome a subsequent vindication of the doctrine he had maintained. Cf. Nestorius, *The Bazaar of Heracleides*, trans. C. R. Driver and L. Hodgson (Oxford: Clarendon Press, 1925), p. 370:

"Let Nestorius be anathematized, so long as they believe what I believe." Cf. Georges Florovsky, *The Byzantine Fathers of the Sixth to Eighth Century, Collected Works*, vol. 9, trans.

way a conjunction of two heterogeneous *personae* (as it was for Nestorius and Theodore); to the contrary, the Leonian doctrine was precisely a doctrine concerning undivided "oneness." Apparently disconcerted by the nominal similarity of the Tome with one aspect of Theodorian Christology, Dioscorus hindered the papal intervention and provoked the ire of Leo. From this time onwards, Leo referred to the council of 449 as the *Latrocinium* (the "Robber Council") and began calling for a new and legitimate council to overturn Ephesus II and resolve the doctrinal dispute afresh. Only after the death of Theodosius II was Leo's demand realized.

In 451, the new emperor Marcian (396-457) called a new council at Chalcedon. Attended by upwards of six hundred bishops, the Council of Chalcedon reversed the *Latrocinium*, deposed Dioscorus, reaffirmed Flavian's deposition of Eutyches, and reinstated Theodoret and Ibas. Having overturned the basic acts of Ephesus II, the Council Fathers allowed Leo's Tome to be read, which they then proceeded to solemnly confirm.[17] Most significantly, the Council Fathers composed the *Definitio fidei* to surmount the monist reduction of Eutychianism, while at the same time foreclosing the dualistic error of Nestorianism, condemned twenty years earlier at Ephesus I.

If from the one side, by affirming the hypostatic singularity (μίαν ὑπόστασιν) of the one Christ (ἕνα καὶ τὸν αὐτόν), the *Definitio* had refused the possibility of emphasizing duality at the expense of unity, at the same time, by affirming the preservation of two integral natures in this singular hypostatic reality (ἐν δύο φύσεσιν), it overcame the temptation to privilege unity at the expense of difference.[18] This is emphasized above all in the four adverbs the *Definitio* uses to describe the union of divinity and humanity in Christ: *inconfuse, immutabiliter, indivise, inseparabiliter* (ἀσυγχύτως, ἀτρέπτως, ἀδιαιρέτως, ἀχωρίστως). Three of these famous adverbs (ἀσυγχύτως, ἀτρέπτως, ἀδιαιρέτως) were in fact culled directly from Cyril himself;[19] the work they do in both Cyril and the *Definitio* is to specify

---

Raymond Miller and Anne-Marie Döllinger-Labriolle (Vaduz: Büchervertriebsanstalt, 1987), pp. 49-51; Meyendorff, *Christ in Eastern Christian Thought*, p. 37; F. Nau, ed., *Livre d'Héraclide de Damas* (Paris: Letouzy et Ané, 1910), p. 327.

17. The Tome was not confirmed without some debate; see Chalcedon, Session II, 22-31 (ed. Price and Gaddis, 2.14-27), and Session IV, 360 (ed. Price and Gaddis, 2.125-53).

18. *Definitio fidei* (DS 301-302; DEC 1.86; and ed. Price and Gaddis, 2.204), trans. Price and Gaddis with light modification.

19. In Cyril, the adverbs show up in his first letter to Succensus, *Epistula* 45: "We unite the Word from God the Father without confusion (ἀσυγχύτως), without change (ἀτρέπτως),

that, while Jesus is both divine and human, without confusion or mutation (*inconfusus, immutabilis*), nevertheless divinity and humanity only exist in him insofar as they exist without division or separation (*indivisus, insepa-rabilis*). In this way Chalcedon affirms that Christ is perfectly and integrally both divine and human (τέλειον τὸν αὐτὸν ἐν θεότητι, καὶ τέλειον τὸν αὐτὸν ἐν ἀνθρωπότητι). The result of the Chalcedonian formulation was to realize very clearly that "the proximity of the divine" does not threaten or compro-mise "the integrity of the human," but in fact establishes it.[20] The integrity of human difference is now maintained in direct proportion to the extent to which full ontological union with God is affirmed. This means that the *via media* of Chalcedon between Eutychianism and Nestorianism is not so much a careful "balancing" of unity and difference, but rather a return to the original *unitas* of the one Lord Jesus Christ, which is the precondition of the distinction of his human difference (*maior dissimilitudo*). The *via media* of Chalcedon, in this way, entails a radical and paradoxical theology in which the perfect *unio* of Eutychian Christology is fully realized, not in a way that compromises the integral difference of human nature, but in a way that establishes and perfects it. The distinction and difference Nesto-rian Christology failed to safeguard through *separatio* is, at Chalcedon, fully safeguarded and actualized through *unio*.[21]

---

and without alteration (ἀμεταβλήτως) to holy flesh owning mental life in a manner inex-pressible and surpassing understanding, and confess one Son, Christ and Lord, the self-same God and man, not a diverse pair but one and the same being and being seen to be both things (οὐχ ἕτερον καὶ ἕτερον, ἀλλ᾽ ἕνα καὶ τὸν αὐτὸν τοῦτο κἀκεῖνο ὑπάρχοντα καὶ νοούμενον)" (Lionel R. Wickham, ed. and trans., *Cyril of Alexandria: Select Letters* [Oxford: OUP, 1983], p. 74; PG 77.232c-b) — translation is Wickham's, but modified. Cf. McGuckin, *The Christological Controversy*, p. 239: "To have supplied, in substance, three of the four so-called 'Chalcedonian adverbs' already, and with the fourth missing adverb [i.e. ἀχωρίστως] emphasising Cyril's basic point of the inseparability of the natures, is hardly, on anyone's terms, a 'triumph' of western and Antiochene christology. It is surely the complete vindication of Cyril's overall ideas, and shows that the Chalcedonian commission constantly attempts to use his terms. . . In this, Cyril stands out, unarguably, as the primary authority for the Chalcedonian decree, and this, I think, was the deliberate intention of those who framed it."

20. Francis Cardinal George, O.M.I., *The Difference God Makes: A Catholic Vision of Faith, Communion, and Culture* (New York: Crossroad Publishing, 2009), p. 4.

21. This way of formulating the *via media* of Chalcedon runs counter to the standard modern academic reading, which tends to see the *via media* not so much rooted in a return to origins but in a forward-looking synthesis or compromise. In this way, the *Definitio* is cast either as the synthetic "seal of doctrinal development in the early Church" (Norman Tanner, S.J., *The Church in Council: Conciliar Movements, Religious Practice and the Papacy from Nicaea to Vatican II* [London: I. B. Tauris, 2011], pp. 14-15), as if Chalcedon were an es-

At Chalcedon, this truth was nowhere more clearly formulated than in Leo's Tome. In the *unio* of Christ, the pope argues, the divinity of the Logos is in no way diminished, while the integrity of human nature is not merely "preserved," it is enriched (*augens*).[22] Thus "in the whole and perfect nature of true man was true God born . . . complete in what was ours. And by ours we mean what the Creator formed in us from the beginning and what he undertook to restore."[23] In this way, Jesus can truly be the one who "reveals man to himself," as the Second Vatican Council would put it a little more than a millennium and a half later.[24] The only-begotten Son fulfills and over-fulfills our human nature in such a way that he realizes, by his divinity, the graced depth of what it means to be truly human. At this point precisely, the logic of Chalcedon exposes the metaphysical consensus of Nestorian dualism and Eutychian monism.

---

sential (if not *the* essential) milestone on the way to the construction of a systematic edifice of theology; or more modestly the *Definitio* is regarded as a great "compromise document, carefully worded to rule out Apollinarianism, Eutychianism, and extreme Nestorianism, while remaining compatible with a variety of conflicting opinions" (Marilyn McCord Adams, *Christ and Horrors: The Coherence of Christology* [Cambridge: CUP, 2006], p. 54). In both cases, the settlement of Chalcedon is construed as involving a *via media* that achieves something "new," a new "balance between a 'Nestorian' separation [i.e. difference] and a 'Eutychian' blending [i.e. union]" (Gerald O'Collins, S.J., *Christology: A Biblical, Historical, and Systematic Study of Jesus* [Oxford: OUP, 1995], p. 200). On my view, by contrast, the key to the *Definitio* lies in its fundamental act of return to the root of what the Council Fathers took to be the one apostolic faith: the confession preserved in the *Credo* of Nicaea. The essential *novum* of Chalcedon is not a dogmatic "turning point" for Christology; the *novum* of Chalcedon rather lies, fundamentally, in the radicalism of its return to the original proclamation: "for us there is one God, the Father . . . and one Lord Jesus Christ" (1 Cor. 8:6). Cf. Grillmeier, *Christ in Christian Tradition*, vol. 1, p. 550: "the dogma of Chalcedon must always be taken against the background of scripture and the whole patristic tradition. It is not to no purpose that the Definition itself points to the prophets and the sayings of Christ himself (even as the prophets from of old [have spoken of] him, and as the Lord Jesus Christ himself has taught us) and finally to the creed of the Fathers, i.e. to Nicaea, indeed beyond Nicaea to the two succeeding councils and to the letters of Cyril, received with such solemnity, and the Tome of Leo. Few councils have been so rooted in tradition as the Council of Chalcedon. The dogma of Chalcedon is ancient tradition in a formula corresponding to the needs of the hour. So we cannot say that the Chalcedonian Definition marks a great turning point in the christological belief of the early church."

22. *Epistula Papae Leonis ad Flavianum* (DS 293; DEC 1.79). On Leo's doctrine of the humanity of Christ, see Wessel, *Leo the Great and the Spiritual Rebuilding of a Universal Rome*, pp. 231-39.

23. *Epistula Papae Leonis ad Flavianum* (DS 293; DEC 1.79).

24. *Gaudium et spes*, 22 (DS 4322).

What is this shared metaphysical presupposition? As we have noted of these great heresies before, each presumes from the outset that, in the relation of divinity and humanity, *unio* and *maior dissimilitudo* cannot coincide. *Unio* cannot perfect the relation of *maior dissimilitudo* but can only destroy it, while *maior dissimilitudo* requires some degree of *separatio*. Therefore, even though Nestorianism and Eutychianism offer different doctrines of Christ (one dualist, the other monist), both originate from the same metaphysical a priori: the "proximity" of God does not enhance the integrity of human reality but rather weakens it, while the "proximity" of the human to God threatens to corrupt his divine impassibility.

B. Unity and Difference, Cross and Tradition

The dogmatic statement of Chalcedon, formulated in the *Definitio*, was read aloud at the Council's fifth session by the archdeacon of the church of Constantinople. The full content of the *Definitio* is less well known than is the dogmatic *précis* that begins: "Following, therefore, the holy fathers, we all in harmony teach the confession of one and the same Son our Lord Jesus Christ. . . ."[25] The tendency of modern textbooks and commentaries to focus on the *précis* of the *Definitio* to the neglect of the longer text has contributed in no small way to a wrong understanding of what exactly the assembled bishops sought to establish.[26] In the first place, plucking the *précis* from the longer *Definitio* gives the wrong impression that they intended a "statement of faith," some kind of "creed" of Christology, when in fact the opposite is the case. The loss of context also gives the sense that the doctrine of Chalcedon is "abstract," dissociable from the concrete history of the Only-begotten Son of God who came down from above and was crucified and raised in accordance with the Scriptures.[27] Finally, the

25. *Definitio fidei* (DS 301-302; DEC 1.86; and Price and Gaddis, eds., 2.204), trans. Price and Gaddis with light modification.

26. Noted in Coakley, "What Does Chalcedon Solve," p. 145: "What is less commonly remembered in contemporary textbooks and commentaries (given the regrettable tendency to reprint the 'Definition' in isolation from the surrounding text), is that the assembled bishops were deeply reluctant to come up with any new formulae at all, their preference being to reaffirm — as they now did — the faith of Nicaea, itself grounded and founded in the biblical narratives of salvation."

27. This error was unfortunately the judgment of Henry Chadwick; see his Preface to André-Jean Festugière, trans., *Actes du Concile de Chalcédoine* (Geneva: Patrick Cramer, 1983),

self-standing character of the *précis* taken in isolation fails to gesture to the "traditioned" nature of the doctrine of Chalcedon, rooted in what "Jesus Christ himself taught us about him" and handed on through the concrete and sacramental history of the Church. These three points are interconnected.

Only under direct pressure from the emperor Marcian[28] were the Council Fathers moved to compose their *Definitio*. Their resistance was motivated by their resolve not to set out anything that might appear like a new *Credo*, a point made clear by the larger *Definitio*, which stipulated the intention of the Fathers to repel all "doctrines of error" — not through a new synthesis of theology, but through a renewal of "the unerring faith of the fathers, proclaimed to all [in] the creed of the 318 [Fathers of Nicaea]."[29] This reverence for the Nicene *Credo* reflects its earlier sanctification at Constantinople I (381), which prepared the way for the declaration of its fixed status. This happened at Ephesus when, under the presidency of Cyril, it was decreed that "no one is allowed to profess or else to compose or devise a faith other than that defined by the holy Fathers gathered together at Nicaea with the Holy Spirit."[30] The resolve of the Council Fathers at Chalcedon to follow the judgment of Ephesus is unequivocally emphasized by the solemn double-recitation of the *Credo* (in its Nicene and Constantinopolitan forms) immediately before the *précis*.[31] In other words, the more ample text of the *Definitio* includes the *Credo* itself, and more than including it, the larger *Definitio* makes plain that whatever *novum* it contains, this issues from a basic act of return to the proclamation of Nicaea.[32]

After the double-recitation of the *Credo*, still pronouncing the *Definitio*, the archdeacon went on to read aloud the resolve of the Council

---

pp. 7-16, at 15-16. Cf. Coakley, "What Does Chalcedon Solve," p. 145: "attention to the *Acta* . . . gives the lie to the suggestion (associated with a critique of Henry Chadwick) that the 'Definition' lifts away abstractly from the events of salvation and the biblical economy. On the contrary, the 'Definition,' set in context, can be seen precisely to presume and reaffirm those events and then to provide a regulatory *grid* through which to pass them interpretatively."

28. Chalcedon, Session II, 2-3 (ed. Price and Gaddis, 2.9-10), and Session V, 22 (ed. Price and Gaddis, 2.199).

29. *Definitio fidei* (DS 300; DEC 1.84-85; ed. Price and Gaddis, 2.201).

30. Ephesus, canon 7 (DS 265; DEC 65).

31. Chalcedon, Session V, 30-34 (ed. Price and Gaddis, 2.201-25). Cf. Price and Gaddis, General Introduction to *The Acts of the Council of Chalcedon*, vol. 1, pp. 8-9, 56-59.

32. On the importance of the Nicene Creed at Chalcedon and in the controversy leading to the Council, see André de Halleux, "La réception du symbole oecuménique de Nicée à Chalcédoine," *Ephemerides Theologicae Lovanienses* 61 (1985): 5-47.

Fathers to reaffirm the Ephesian dogma of the "Theotokos" and anathematization of Nestorius, while declaring orthodox "the conciliar letters of the blessed Cyril" and "the letter written by the president of the great and senior Rome, the most blessed and holy Archbishop Leo, to Archbishop Flavian."[33] Only then did the archdeacon finally proclaim aloud the specific *novum* of the *Definitio*, what I have here been calling the *précis*:

> Following, therefore, the holy fathers, we all in harmony teach the confession of one and the same (ἕνα καὶ τὸν αὐτόν) Son our Lord Jesus Christ, the same perfect in divinity and the same perfect in humanity (τέλειον τὸν αὐτὸν ἐν θεότητι, καὶ τέλειον τὸν αὐτὸν ἐν ἀνθρωπότητι), truly God and the same truly man, of a rational soul and body, consubstantial (ὁμοούσιος) with the Father in respect of divinity, and the same consubstantial (ὁμοούσιος) with us in respect of humanity, like us in all things apart from sin, begotten from the Father before the ages in respect of divinity, and the same in the last days for us and for our salvation from the Virgin Mary the Theotokos in respect of humanity, one and the same (ἕνα καὶ τὸν αὐτόν) Christ, Son, Lord, only-begotten, acknowledged in two natures (ἐν δύο φύσεσιν) without confusion, change, division, or separation (ἀσυγχύτως, ἀτρέπτως, ἀδιαιρέτως, ἀχωρίστως) — the difference of the natures being in no way destroyed by the union, but rather the distinctive character of each nature being preserved and coming together into one person (ἐν πρόσωπον) and one hypostasis (μίαν ὑπόστασιν) — not parted or divided into two persons (δύο πρόσωπα), but one and the same (ἕνα καὶ τὸν αὐτόν) Son, only-begotten, God, Word, Lord, Jesus Christ, even as the prophets from of old and Jesus Christ himself taught us about him and the symbol [i.e. the *Credo*] of the fathers has handed down to us (ἡμῖν παραδέδωκε).[34]

The *novum* of the *Definitio*, set firmly within what the Council Fathers had received from Nicaea and Cyril, finishes with a resolve to profess only what has been "handed down to us (ἡμῖν παραδέδωκε)," what has been "traditioned" from the apostles to the Fathers, rooted in what "Jesus Christ himself taught us about him."

The handing on of the true faith, the Tradition (*traditio*), according

33. *Definitio fidei* (ed. Price and Gaddis, 2.203).

34. *Definitio fidei* (DS 301-302; DEC 1.86; ed. Price and Gaddis, 2.204), trans. Price and Gaddis with light modification.

to Chalcedon, begins with what "Jesus Christ himself taught us about him." In this way the Council makes clear that the original act of handing on, the origin of *traditio*, is based in — and belongs to — the Lord Jesus himself. Christ is the content of orthodoxy because he is the source and substance of *traditio*.[35] This way of establishing the nature of the orthodox faith means that every subsequent handing on of the faith must be rooted in and serve the original act of self-giving performed by Christ, the mysterious self-gift of the Son that accomplishes salvation, the gift that binds the receiver to the divine "self" of the giver. In his first letter to the Corinthians (11:23-24), the apostle Paul specifies this understanding of the Christian tradition in terms of the Eucharist:

> For I received (παρέλαβον) from the Lord what I also delivered to you (παρέδωκα), that the Lord Jesus on the night when he was betrayed (παρεδίδετο) took bread, and when he had given thanks, he broke it, and said, "This is my body which is for you. Do this in remembrance of me."

The operative word here is the verb *paradidomi* (παραδίδωμι).[36] Paul hands over what was handed down by Jesus in the night when Jesus himself was handed over to the Cross. By this word, *paradidomi*, moreover, Paul clarifies that the true protagonist of the Cross (despite all appearances) is not Judas, Pilate, the mob, or the soldiers, but the Lord Jesus himself, who

---

35. Cf. Hans Urs von Balthasar, *Theo-Drama: Theological Dramatic Theory*, vol. 4, *The Action*, trans. Graham Harrison (San Francisco: Ignatius Press, 1995), pp. 51-56.

36. According to Liddell and Scott (*Greek-English Lexicon*), the word παραδίδωμι signifies to *give, hand over to another, transmit*; it can also signify to *deliver up, surrender*, or to *hand down* by tradition; it can also signify to *betray*. In the Gospel narratives, παραδίδωμι is bound to Judas, and to his betrayal of Jesus; indeed Judas is "the one handing him over" (ὁ παραδιδοὺς αὐτόν [cf. Matt. 10:4, 27:3, John 18:5]). This handing over of Jesus comes to its climax in the "hour" when "the Son of Man is handed over (παραδίδοται) into the hands of sinners" (Matt. 26:45). Once the Passion is set in motion, Jesus, having been handed over by Judas (cf. Matt. 26:47-50), is handed over to Pilate (cf. Matt. 27:2), who in turn hands him over to be crucified (cf. Matt. 27:26). In a sense the tradition of orthodoxy begins here, with the original handing over of Jesus to the Cross. But by the light of Resurrection encounter, the meaning and agent of this handing over of Jesus to the Cross is understood as recapitulated. The disciples now come to see (as is illustrated perfectly on the road to Emmaus, cf. Luke 24:13-35) that Jesus himself is the true protagonist of this act (cf. John 21:15-19): "No one takes it [my life] from me, but I lay it down of my own accord. I have power to lay it down, and I have power to take it again; this charge I have received from my Father" (John 10:18).

gives himself up for the life of the world.[37] For Paul, the handing on of true doctrine, the self-gift of the Cross and the constitutive action of the Church in the Eucharist are here, all three, internal to one another; this internality is designated by his twofold use here of the word *paradidomi*. That *paradidomi* is the very word used by the Council Fathers at Chalcedon to designate the doctrine that has been received and handed on by them is, of course, highly significant.

Paul's theology of the handing on of the true doctrine of Christ is emphasized to similar effect in the Vulgate translation of Paul's text, which uses the verb "tradere"[38] in the two cases of Paul's use of *paradidomi*. It supplements a third use of the verb in the case of Jesus' self-gift of his body: "hoc est corpus meum, quod prò vobis tradetur."[39] So whereas Paul's Greek text reads, "This is my body which is for you," the Vulgate renders it, "this is my body *which will be given up* for you." This Pauline theology of the Eucharist is perfectly articulated in the Liturgy of St. John Chrysostom when the priest, just before he utters the words of consecration, prays:

> On the night when He was delivered up (τῇ νυκτὶ ᾗ παρεδίδοτο), or rather when He gave Himself up for the life of the world (μᾶλλον δὲ παρεδίδου ὑπὲρ τῆς τοῦ κόσμου ζωῆς), He took bread in His holy, pure, and blameless hands. . . .[40]

37. Cf. John Behr, *Becoming Human: Meditations on Christian Anthropology in Word and Image* (Crestwood, NY: Saint Vladimir's Press, 2013), pp. 49-57.

38. *Tradere* evokes in Latin more or less exactly what παραδίδωμι does in Greek. According to Lewis and Short (*Latin Dictionary*), *tradere* signifies to *give up, hand over, deliver, transmit, surrender, consign*; but can also signify to *entrust, confide, to give up*; or to *surrender treacherously, betray*. In the Vulgate Judas is *qui tradidit eum* (cf. Matt. 10:4).

39. The earliest witness of the Vulgate states merely "est corpus meum pro vobis tradetur" (*Codex Amiatinus*, eighth century). A handful of other witnesses add "quod" (as I have quoted the text); this includes the sixteenth century "Clementine" text. Other witnesses simply state "est corpus meum pro vobis." The *pro vobis tradetur*, which finds an echo in the Coptic tradition, may point to an earlier Greek source, which we no longer have, which may have read "τοῦτό μού ἐστιν τὸ σῶμα τὸ ὑπὲρ ὑμῶν διδόμενον." Significantly, the normative Vulgate version is now used in the consecration of the bread in the *Novus Ordo* Mass: "Accipite et manducate ex hoc omnes: hoc est enim Corpus meum, quod pro vobis tradetur." The same consecration in the *Usus Antiquior* did not contain the "quod pro vobis tradetur."

40. Nancy Chalker Takis, ed., *The Divine Liturgy of Our Father Among the Saints. John Chrysostom: For Sunday Worship*, 3rd ed. (Williamston, MI: New Byzantium Publications, 2010), p. 64. Cf. John Behr, *The Mystery of Christ: Life in Death* (Crestwood, NY: Saint Vladimir's Seminary Press, 2006), pp. 31-32: "Here theology proper begins. Christ was put to death, but in the light of God's vindication of the crucified Christ, we affirm that 'he gave himself up for

While the traditional Roman Canon does not contain a formulation like this, in the second Canon of the *Novus Ordo* (culled from the so-called "Canon of Hyppolytus"), the priest prefaces the words of consecration as follows: "At the time he was betrayed and entered willingly into his Passion . . . (*Qui cum Passioni voluntarie traderetur . . .*)."[41] In both cases, that of the second Canon of the *Novus Ordo* and that of the Liturgy of St. John Chrysostom, the logic is fully Pauline and confirms that the core doctrine of the Church concerns very precisely the true meaning and corporal reality of the self-gift of Jesus handing himself over to death for the life of the world. All of this is basically implied in the Chalcedonian invocation of handing on what "Jesus Christ himself taught us about him" through what the Fathers have "handed down to us (ἡμῖν παραδέδωκε)."[42] What Jesus has "handed down" of himself to the Church concerns exactly the question of his free "handing over" of himself to the Paschal Mystery.

The Eucharistic "handing over" of the true faith is bound by Paul, moreover, to how the Crucified Lord opens the Hebrew Scriptures, how his Passion unfolds "in accordance with the Scriptures (κατὰ τὰς γραφάς)" (1 Cor. 15:3-4). This too Paul writes of as a traditioned truth, a doctrine he has received (παραλαμβάνω) and now hands on (παραδίδωμι) to the Church.[43] The determination of the Council Fathers at Chalcedon in this

---

the life of the world.' . . . God's vindication of the crucified Jesus, not letting his holy one see corruption in the grave (Acts 2.25-32; Ps 16.10), does not remove from sight or sideline Jesus' death on the cross, but enables us to see this death as the voluntary self-offering of the innocent servant of the Lord, the conquering of death on the cross by the one born of the virgin."

41. Eucharistic Prayer II. Even if no such formulation appears in the Roman Canon, the traditional Eucharistic Prayer of the Latin Rite has always presumed precisely this recapitulation, a fact signaled in the traditional liturgy for Maundy Thursday according to the *Usus Antiquior*, which is centered on the Epistle lesson from 1 Corinthians. The "pro vobis tradetur" is not used in the consecration formula of the *Usus Antiquior*, but is nevertheless recalled in the Maundy Thursday liturgy — not only in the Epistle lesson, but also in the prayer over the gifts, where the priest prays that Christ himself would render the Sacrifice of this Mass acceptable: "Ipse tibi, quaesumus, Domine sancte, Pater omnipotens, aeterne Deus, sacrificium nostrum reddat acceptum, qui discipulis suis in sui commemorationem hoc fieri hodierna traditione monstravit." This prayer over the gifts, expunged from the *Novus Ordo*, makes clear what the new *Novus Ordo* consecration (see note 39 above) now makes clear: that the prescription of Jesus to his disciples, to do this in remembrance of him, is a prescription demonstrated by his own gesture (*monstrare*), which itself is an act of giving over (*tradere*), in which the tradition (*traditio*) of the Eucharist is itself rooted.

42. *Definitio fidei* (DS 301-302; DEC 1.86; ed. Price and Gaddis, 2.204), trans. Price and Gaddis with light modification.

43. Robert L. Wilken, commenting on this passage of 1 Corinthians (which repeats

light, to teach the truth of the "one and the same" Lord in accord with the "prophets of old," is therefore also rooted in the liturgical *anamnesis* of the Cross, since the un-bloody repetition of the Cross in the Sacrifice of the Mass unlocks, in its evental happening, the mystery of the Hebrew Scriptures: Christ died and was raised according to the Scriptures. The full significance of how Chalcedon reaffirms the Nicene starting point here comes into sharper focus; but it is only fully grasped in the context of Paul's evangelical reconfiguration of the Shema of Israel: "for us there is one God, the Father . . . and one Lord, Jesus Christ" (ἡμῖν εἷς θεὸς ὁ πατήρ . . . καὶ εἷς κύριος Ἰησοῦς Χριστός [1 Cor. 8:6]).

Paul's Christological reconfiguration of the Shema — "Hear, O Israel: The LORD our God is one LORD" (Deut. 6:4) — concerns exactly the divine unity of the "Lord" (κύριος). This word, *"Kyrios,"* bound now by Paul to the "one Lord Jesus" (εἷς κύριος Ἰησοῦς), is the very word used in the Septuagint in place of the unutterable Tetragrammaton, the mysterious name of the God of Israel given to Moses at the burning bush (cf. Exod. 3:1-22). By proclaiming the one Lord Jesus, Paul (and through him Nicaea and Chalcedon) declares that this Jesus is somehow mysteriously internal to the identity of YHWH himself, to the One God of Israel.[44] This identification of Jesus with YHWH is what is accomplished and revealed on the Cross, where Jesus is crucified and raised in accordance with the Scriptures. "When you have lifted up the Son of man, then you will know that I am he (ἐγώ εἰμι)" (John 8:28). The Crucifixion is, in this way, the basic revelation of the divine identity of Jesus, how he truthfully opens the Hebrew Scriptures and reveals the God of Israel. This suggests that the ultimate doctrine traditioned by Jesus, the teaching he most truly hands on, is precisely himself nailed to the Cross. As Thomas Aquinas and Augustine both held, the ultimate teaching of Jesus occurs, not in any discourse or parable, but when he has finally ascended to Calvary, where he teaches *ex cathedra* with his crucified

---

the same formula as 1 Cor. 11), writes: "These words were written down two decades after the death of Jesus, but the formulaic language used by Paul, 'I delivered . . . what I also received . . .' indicates that he is handing on a communal memory that went back to the days immediately after Jesus's death. A personal encounter with the living Christ gave his followers the confidence and the courage to go forth from Jerusalem to proclaim the gospel ('good news'), that the God of Israel had done an extraordinary new thing in Jesus of Nazareth" (*The First Thousand Years: A Global History of Christianity* [New Haven: Yale University Press, 2012], p. 16).

44. John Behr, *The Way to Nicaea*, vol. 1 of *The Formation of Christian Theology* (Crestwood, NY: Saint Vladimir's Seminary Press, 2001), p. 64.

being.[45] The basic presupposition of orthodoxy and of the Council Fathers assembled at Chalcedon concerns, in this way, the fundamental unity of being of the Crucified Lord.

In light of the foregoing, when we return to the specific *nova* of the *précis* of the *Definitio*, to the declaration that Jesus is "consubstantial (ὁμοούσιος) with the Father in respect of divinity, and at the same time consubstantial (ὁμοούσιος) with us in respect of humanity," to the declaration that he is to be "acknowledged in two natures (ἐν δύο φύσεσιν) without confusion, change, division, or separation (ἀσυγχύτως, ἀτρέπτως, ἀδιαιρέτως, ἀχωρίστως)," we see clearly that the possibility of these distinctions — the distinctions that themselves make possible the Eucharistic self-gift of Christ — are rooted in the more fundamental unity of his being the Crucified Lord.

C. Modern Chalcedonianism

The irreducibly Cyrillian character of Chalcedon was duly noted by Pope Pius XII in *Sempiternus Rex* (1951). Not only did the pope reiterate the continuity of Cyril and Chalcedon, he also clarified the properly orthodox manner according to which Cyril's controversial "mia physis" formula could be understood as orthodox,[46] while taking the occasion to reiterate the constitutive theopaschism at the heart of Christian orthodoxy:

> It is indeed the truth that from the earliest times and in the most ancient writings, sermons and liturgical prayers, the Church openly and without qualification professes that our Lord Jesus Christ, the only Begotten Son of the Eternal Father, was born on earth, suffered, [and] was nailed to the cross.[47]

If 1951 prompted a magisterial reaffirmation of the essential Cyrillian character of Chalcedonian Christology properly understood, the same judgment was not celebrated in the most influential currents of academic theology at the time.

---

45. Cf. ST III, q. 46, a. 4, *corpus*: "sicut Augustinus dicit, super Ioan., *lignum in quo fixa erant membra patientis, etiam cathedra fuit magistri docentis.*"

46. Pope Pius XII, *Sempiternus Rex*, 25.

47. Pope Pius XII, *Sempiternus Rex*, 32.

As part of the same commemoration of the 1500th anniversary of Chalcedon marked by *Sempiternus Rex*, Karl Rahner wrote an essay that stands at the source of a major theological renewal of "Chalcedonian Christology" within Catholic theology: "Chalkedon — Ende oder Anfang?"[48] Originally published in 1954, Rahner's essay was revised and published in English in the first volume of his *Theological Investigations* under the title "Current Problems in Christology."[49] Without doubt, "Chalkedon — Ende oder Anfang?" exerted far more influence over the Christological program and mood of late-twentieth-century Catholic theology than did Pius's *Sempiternus Rex.*[50]

In his essay, Rahner programmatically proposed that, in matters Christological, the *Definitio fidei* of Chalcedon (by which he meant the *précis*) must become "not only our end but also our beginning."[51] This was a necessity for Rahner in order to use Chalcedon to correct the said "crypto-

48. Karl Rahner, S.J., "Chalkedon — Ende oder Anfang?" in A. von Grillmeier and H. Bacht, eds., *Das Konzil von Chalkedon,* vol. 3 (Würzburg: Echter Verlag, 1954), pp. 3-49.

49. Karl Rahner, S.J., "Current Problems in Christology," in *Theological Investigations,* vol. 1, trans. Cornelius Ernst, O.P. (Baltimore: Helicon, 1961), pp. 149-200.

50. As Walter Kasper notes: "The first wave of modern Christological thought in the second half of this century began twenty-five years ago — fifteen centuries after the Council of Chalcedon (451-1951). Karl Rahner's article on Chalcedon as end or beginning set the tone" (*Jesus the Christ,* trans. V. Green [London: Burns and Oates, 1976], p. 17). Kasper points to: B. Welte, "'Homoousios hemin.' Gedanken zum Verständnis und zur theologischen Problematik der Kategorien von Chalkedon," in A. von Grillmeier and H. Bacht, eds., *Das Konzil von Chalkedon,* vol. 3 (Würzburg: Echter Verlag, 1954), pp. 51-80; Felix Malmberg, *Über den Gottmenschen* (Basel: Herder, 1960); and perhaps most importantly, Edward Schillebeeckx, O.P., "Die Heiligung des Namens Gottes durch die Menschenliebe Jesu des Christus," in Johann Baptist Metz, ed., *Gott in Welt: Festschrift für Karl Rahner,* vol. 2 (Freiburg-Basel: Wien, 1964), pp. 43-91; "De persoonliike openbaringsgestalte van de Vader," *Tijdschrift voor Theologie* 6 (1966): 274-88; "De toegang tot Jezus van Nazaret," *Tijdschrift voor Theologie* 12 (1972): 28-59; "Ons heil: Jezus' leven of Christus de verrezene?" *Tijdschrift voor Theologie* 13 (1973): 145-66. Significantly more influential within modern Catholic theology than was Pius's commemorative encyclical, Rahner's commemorative essay is still the touch-stone of Chalcedonian renewal, as evidenced in Sarah Coakley's "What Does Chalcedon Solve and What Does It Not?" Coakley admits that her "apophatic" Chalcedonianism is basically a creative extension of Rahner's "pure" Chalcedonianism, animated by a "closeness to (and slight difference from)... Rahner" (p. 144). The basic point is to recast Rahner's "end *and* beginning" into her "*neither* end *nor* beginning, but rather a transitional (though still normative) 'horizon' to which we constantly return, but with equally constant forays backwards and forwards" (p. 162). On Rahner and Coakley, cf. W. Chris Hackett, "A Fragment of Christology: Feminism as a Moment of Chalcedonian Humanism," *Australian Journal of Theology* 20 (2013): 1-17.

51. Rahner, "Current Problems in Christology," p. 151.

monophysite" exaggeration he judged native to the standard pre–Vatican II theology of the hypostatic union. Rahner accordingly understood that the "Council of Chalcedon has still to conquer . . . [within Catholic theology and piety an] existential undercurrent of monophysite tendency."[52] Rahner's rich and important essay proposed much more, but in our own context this suggestion is crucial because in it lies the lineaments of his program for a "'pure' (*reiner*) Chalcedonianism," which he opposed to the Cyrillianism of so-called "neo-Chalcedonianism."[53]

Proposed as a counterpoint to "a piety and a theology . . . tinged with monophysitism,"[54] Rahner's "pure" Chalcedonianism aimed to reaffirm the *inconfusus, immutabilis* side of the *Definitio* that the "average Christian" had let "slip into the background of his consciousness in faith in favor of the ἀδιαιρέτως [*indivise*]."[55] By emphasizing the distinction of divinity and humanity in Christ in this way, Rahner hoped to recover the credibility of Jesus' finite humanity, which he took to be sublated by the "straightforward descending Christology" of the Magisterium.[56] Working now to initiate an "ascending Christology" that would begin, not with the *descensus de caelis* of Nicaea, but with the human experience of Jesus,[57] Rahner hoped he could better affirm the finitude of Jesus, while divesting his death from the impassible divinity of the Logos:

> Death and finiteness belong only to the created reality of Jesus . . . the eternal Logos in its divinity, however, cannot as such take on a historical character and suffer an obedient death.[58]

---

52. Rahner, "Current Problems in Christology," p. 188.

53. Cf. Hans van Loon, *The Dyophysite Christology of Cyril of Alexandria* (Leiden: Brill, 2009), pp. 49-54.

54. Karl Rahner, S.J., *Foundations of Christian Faith: An Introduction to the Idea of Christianity*, trans. William V. Dych (New York: Seabury Press, 1978), p. 287.

55. Rahner, "Current Problems in Christology," p. 179.

56. Rahner, *Foundations of Christian Faith*, p. 286.

57. Rahner, *Foundations of Christian Faith*, pp. 298-302.

58. Karl Rahner, S.J., "Christology Today," in *Theological Investigations*, vol. 21, trans. Hugh M. Riley (London: Darton, Longman & Todd, 1988), pp. 220-27, at p. 213. Cf. Karl Rahner, S.J., *Karl Rahner in Dialogue: Conversations and Interviews, 1965-1982*, ed. Paul Imhof and Hubert Biallowons (New York: Crossroad, 1986), pp. 126-27: "it does not help me to escape from my mess and mix-up and despair if God is in the same predicament . . . From the beginning I am locked into its horribleness while God — if the word continues to have any meaning — is in a true and authentic and consoling sense the God who does not suffer, the immutable, and so on."

That all of this was finally proposed as a critique of the "crypto-monophysitism" of the "official Christology of the church"[59] and animated by a sympathy for an "orthodox Nestorian" position in Christology is not a coincidence.[60] Rahner's Christological program, in no uncertain terms, is driven by the classical concern of Theodore and Nestorius: to protect the impassibility of God and affirm the integrity of the human Jesus by separating the Logos from the crucifixion.

The uniqueness of Chalcedon for Rahner — what allows it to be the "end" and "beginning" of Christology, and what allows for its "purity" — lies in how it is understood as modifying the one-sided Christology that was in ascendency after Ephesus. On this view the *précis* of the *Definitio* is less a recapitulation of the apostolic proclamation and more essentially a "compromise formula" that resolves a great theological clash between two opposing "theological factions." The compromise is achieved, not by a return to the original proclamation, but by a ruling that minimally satisfies each faction by tempering the most egregious heretical tendency each sees in the other.[61] In doing so, the Council is construed as having decided upon a formula without much positive dogmatic content, de facto leaving it to future generations to work out what precisely this formulation might mean. The "pure" Chalcedonianism Rahner sought, then, is based in the presupposition that the aim and key achievement of the *Definitio* was to carefully balance Nestorian "separation" against Cyrillian "union" and thus achieve an unbeknownst balance that negatively avoids the error of each while positively maintaining the truth of each.

The distinguished scholar of conciliar history, Norman Tanner, expresses well the historico-theological premises that underpin the possibility of Rahner's "pure" Chalcedonianism. According to Tanner the *Definitio* is the "seal of doctrinal development" and "the most authoritative and influential statement of the Church outside of the Scriptures."[62] This preeminence of Chalcedon, for Tanner, is rooted in how a balance results in the *Definitio* "between the schools of Antioch and Alexandria regarding Christ's humanity and divinity."[63] In this context, Ephesus represents "a defeat for Asian theology (Antioch) at the hands of Africa (Alexandria),"

---

59. Rahner, *Foundations of Christian Faith*, p. 286.

60. Rahner, *Karl Rahner in Dialogue*, pp. 126-27.

61. Cf. Karen Kilby, *A Brief Introduction to Karl Rahner* (London: The Crossroad Publishing Company, 2007), p. 18.

62. Tanner, *The Church in Council*, p. 14.

63. Tanner, *The Church in Council*, p. 12.

while "Antiochene theology recovered the initiative . . . subsequent[ly at] Chalcedon."[64] Hence Chalcedon is an "endorsement of the Antiochene teaching of two distinct natures in Christ, human and divine, against the monophysitism of Alexandria."[65]

The result of Tanner's construal of the *Definitio*, as if it were an "endorsement of . . . Antiochene teaching" required to correct the one-sided doctrine of Cyril and Ephesus, is that it casts a shadow of monophysite suspicion over at least two Ecumenical Councils (Ephesus and Constantinople II), not to mention the historic judgment of the Church concerning the person and doctrine of Cyril, *Doctor Ecclesiae*.[66] Under the guise of proposing "Chalcedonian Christology," this scheme suggests that it is incumbent on theology to correct the Cyrillianism of the Magisterium by resourcing, in the name of Chalcedon, Theodorian-Nestorian elements in order to balance the overly Cyrillian standard of the "official Christology of the church."

This standard modern point of view, however, presents several problems, of which two are key. The first concerns the grand narrative the scheme presumes, on which the doctrine of Chalcedon resulted from a clash between two internally coherent and disciplined Christological "schools," that of Antioch, associated with Diodore, Theodore and Nestorius, and that of Alexandria, associated with Athanasius, Cyril and Dioscorus. Recent scholarship, however, has questioned the totalizing and "Hegelian" character of this understanding of the two so-called "schools."[67] The second major problem with the standard modern narrative is that the textual evidence of the *Acta* of Chalcedon simply does not support it, and in fact deconstructs it.

D. The "Schools" of Antioch and Alexandria

In the century after the Council of Chalcedon, the towering figures linked to the apostolic see of Antioch were Peter the Fuller, Severus of Antioch

---

64. Tanner, *The Church in Council*, p. 14.

65. Tanner, *The Church in Council*, p. 14. Cf. Schönborn, *God Sent His Son*, p. 153.

66. In 1882 Pope Leo XIII declared Cyril a *Doctor Ecclesiae* of the Roman Catholic Church.

67. Andrew Louth, "Why Did the Syrians Reject the Council of Chalcedon?" in Price and Whitby, eds., *Chalcedon in Context*, pp. 107-16; Donald Fairbairn, *Grace and Christology in the Early Church* (Oxford: OUP, 2003), pp. 3-11; Paul Gavrilyuk, *The Suffering of the Impassible God: The Dialectics of Patristic Thought* (Oxford: OUP, 2004), pp. 137-39; John Behr, *The Case against Diodore and Theodore: Texts and Their Contexts* (Oxford: OUP, 2011), pp. 3-129.

and Philoxenus of Mabbog. Peter and Severus were both patriarchs of the see in 471-488 and 512-518 respectively,[68] while Severus and Philoxenus are widely recognized as two of the most important Cyrillian thinkers of the sixth century.[69] All three also happen to be key protagonists in the non-Chalcedonian cause that rallied against the imperial Church for apparently betraying Cyril at Chalcedon. To the modern student of Christological doctrine this is perplexing. How did Antioch become the seat of such a formidable pro-Cyrillian theology? Was not Antioch the strong-hold of the Antiochene "school" of Christology that resisted in everything the unitive doctrine of Cyril? The truth of the matter of Antioch is in fact more com-

68. Severus was exiled from Antioch in 518, and a pro-Chalcedonian patriarch was installed in his place. From exile until his death in 538, however, he remained recognized by non-Chalcedonians as the lawful patriarch.

69. John McGuckin describes Severus as "one of the great Cyrillian disciples of the 6th century" (*The Christological Controversy*, p. 3). Though condemned by an imperial edict in 536, Severus was never condemned by a council, synod or pope, and has therefore never been condemned by a body with the ecclesial authority to definitively pronounce him a "heretic" (at least nobody recognized with such authority by the Roman Catholic Church). This ambiguity of the Church in relation to Severus is indicative of the whole complex relation of the Church (Greek and Latin) in relation to those churches that broke communion with the imperial Church after Chalcedon. Severus's status is further complicated by the fact that the theological tradition he spawned — a tradition that to this day names him "St. Severus the Great" — seems never to have been characterized by the Latin or Greek Fathers as "heretical." As Georges Florovsky reminds us: "It is important to point out that those who rejected the Council of Chalcedon were not labeled 'heretics' — even St. John of Damascus [who exhaustively enumerated the heresies and heretics of the patristic period in his *De Haeresibus*] considered the Monophysites [i.e. non-Chalcedonian Severan] as 'dissidents' and not 'heretics', and this as late as the eighth century" (*The Byzantine Fathers of the Sixth to Eighth Century, Collected Works*, vol. 9, p. 59). See Pauline Allen and C. T. R. Hayward, *Severus of Antioch*, ECF (London: Routledge, 2004); Roberta C. Chesnut, *Three Monophysite Christologies: Severus of Antioch, Philoxenus of Mabbug, and Jacob of Sarug* (Oxford: OUP, 1985); V. C. Samuel, "The Christology of Severus of Antioch," *Abba Salama* 4 (1973): 126-90 and "Further Studies in the Christology of Severus of Antioch," *Ekklesiastikos Pharos* 58 (1976): 270-301; John Behr, "Severus of Antioch: Eastern and Oriental Perspectives," *St. Nersess Theological Review* 3 (1998): 23-35; Joseph Lebon, *Le monophysisme sévérien. Étude historique, littéraire et théologique sur la résistance monophysite au concile de Chalcédoine jusqu'à la constitution de l'Église jacobite* (Louvain: Excudebat Josephus van Linthout Universitatis Catholicae Typographus, 1909); Aloys Grillmeier, S.J. with Theresia Hainthaler, *Christ in Christian Tradition*, vol. 2, *From the Council of Chalcedon (451) to Gregory the Great (590–604)*, part 2, *The Church of Constantinople in the Sixth Century*, trans. Pauline Allen and John Cawte (Louisville: Westminster John Knox Press, 1995), pp. 256-59; N. Zambolotsky, "The Christology of Severus of Antioch," *Ekklesiastikos Pharos* 58 (1976): 357-86; Iain R. Torrance, *Christology After Chalcedon: Severus of Antioch and Sergius the Monophysite* (Norwich: The Canterbury Press, 1988).

plex, heterogeneous and internally divided than modern accounts have tended to suggest.

In the fourth century, the bishop of Antioch, Leontius, is said to have "stroked his white hairs and remarked, 'When this snow melts, there will be lots of mud.'"[70] Leontius may have had in mind the mixed and difficult theological inheritance of his see; surely he was thinking of its history of divided ecclesial loyalties. Antioch, where followers of Christ were first called "Christians" (Acts 11:19-26), claims a difficult and divided history of Christological doctrine. In 428, the year of the death of Theodore and the installation of Nestorius as Archbishop of Constantinople, Antioch is cast as the locus of the Antiochene "school," hostile to all things "Alexandrian" and "Cyrillian." Less than fifty years later, in 471, the patriarch of the See, Peter the Fuller, is a non-Chalcedonian defender of Cyril who teaches the church under his pastoral care to sing, as a badge of orthodoxy, the theopaschite formula "crucified for us" at the end of the traditional Trisagion prayer ("Holy God, Holy Mighty, Holy Immortal").

The complex Christological situation is confirmed, moreover, by the fact that it was within the remit of the metropolitan See of Antioch that, in the fourth century, the first major "monophysite" crisis occurred through the local polemic between Diodore of Tarsus and Apollinarius of Laodicea (d. 390), the sometime bishop of the Syrian city of Laodicea, 60 miles south of Antioch. That the monophysite heresy of Apollinarianism has indigenous roots in the world of Antioch, and that after Chalcedon, Antioch was host to the most formidable anti-Chalcedonian theology of the day, suggests that the idea of Antioch as dominated by a "school" of Christology led by Diodore, Theodore, and Nestorius is misleading and exaggerated. Given these facts, the standard academic account of the crisis precipitating Chalcedon, which tells of a clash of two coherent "schools" of Christology, one hailing from Antioch, the other from Alexandria, should be called into serious question.[71]

70. Louth, "Why Did the Syrians Reject the Council of Chalcedon?," p. 109.

71. Nevertheless, this style of reading the *Definitio* animates even some of the best scholarship. For example Sarah Coakley writes that "The immediate crisis [leading up to Chalcedon] was an attempt to find a way through the tortured debate between the rival Alexandrian and Antiochene schools of Christology" ("What Does Chalcedon Solve?" p. 145), while the eminent patrologist John Meyendorff opens his celebrated *Christ in Eastern Christian Thought* with the declaration that "Until Chalcedon, the schools of Alexandria and Antioch were the two foci of theological thought" (p. 13). Cf. O'Collins, *Christology*, pp. 184-201; Schönborn, *God Sent His Son*, pp. 131-65. The Alexandrian-Antiochene scheme

While the Antiochene "school" may "correspond to ideas passed on from master to disciple: Diodore to Theodore to Nestorius,"[72] beyond that, the description falls apart. A key piece of evidence here lies in the person of John Chrysostom (c. 349-407), a member of the small ascetic circle linked to Diodore and a close friend of Theodore of Mopsuestia (he is said to have persuaded the young Theodore to return to the ascetic circle when he briefly left it with the intention of marrying). It is highly significant that John's Christology bears none of the characteristic features of his friend Theodore or their mentor Diodore.[73] This suggests that, even among those of the circle of Diodore, we find nothing of the uniformity of what a "school" should imply. This, coupled with the post-Chalcedonian situation in Antioch, indicates that what we are accustomed to call "Antiochene Christology" (that sensibility linked to Diodore, Theodore, and Nestorius), was perhaps much more marginal and idiosyncratic than we have been led to think.

In the case of the so-called Alexandrian school, the situation is precisely the opposite. The Christological vision of Athanasius, represented in *De Incarnatione Verbi Dei* (c. 328), far from being representative of a particular Alexandrian "school," had already by the end of the fourth century been received as the true articulation of the faith of the apostles. Gregory of Nazianzus (who had no territorial allegiance to either Alexandria or Antioch) speaks for the wider tradition when he calls Athanasius "the true pillar of the Church," whose "doctrine is the rule of the orthodox faith."[74]

---

turns up also in the standard narratives of both Kelly and also Grillmeier, whose influence can hardly be overstated.

Grillmeier's hugely influential version of the two "schools" idea is based in the highly problematic characterization that Cyril and Alexandria taught a "Logos-sarx" Christology, while the Antiochenes favored the "Logos-anthropos" model. The most distortive aspect of Grillmeier's version is that it suggests — against all the evidence — that Cyril was not interested in the humanity of Christ but merely his flesh. See the criticism of Grillmeier by McGuckin, *The Christological Controversy*, pp. 206-7.

72. Louth, "Why Did the Syrians Reject the Council of Chalcedon?," p. 111.

73. On this see Behr, *The Case against Diodore and Theodore*, pp. 52-53; and Gavrilyuk, *The Suffering of the Impassible God*, p. 138.

74. Gregory of Nazianzus, *Oratio* 21.26 (SC 270.164; PG 35.1112b), and 37 (SC 207.190; PG 35.1128a). Gregory's comment here would seem to suggest that Christopher Beeley has perhaps exaggerated the complex of discontinuities that do, nevertheless, exist between Gregory and Athanasius on the question of the unity and identity of divinity and humanity in Christ. See Beeley, *The Unity of Christ*, pp. 105-225. According to Beeley, Gregory is the true champion of a properly unitive Christology necessary for orthodoxy, while close study of Athanasius betrays

Indeed, Athanasius's doctrine had already been received as "universal" long before the crisis that led to Chalcedon. Its influence is well evidenced beyond Alexandria, "from the learned theology of the Cappadocians to the simple, though profound, insights of the author of the homilies attributed to St. Macarius."[75] The universal reception of Athanasius's doctrine is attested further by the vastness of the manuscript tradition of *De Incarnatione Verbi Dei*, which seems to have been already translated into Syriac during Athanasius's lifetime.[76] So if an Antiochene "school" misconstrues what amounted to no more than "the influential ideas of one or two theologians associated with Antioch,"[77] to speak of an Alexandrian "school" is to misconstrue what was in fact "something of nearly universal appeal."[78] As Andrew Louth concludes:

> The Christological controversy was not the clash of two more-or-less equipollent "schools," but rather a response to the dangers represented by an eccentric, and rather scholarly approach to Christology, associated with Antioch, by the broad consensus of Christian confession, of which Cyril projected himself as the spokesman.[79]

Only when the Christological controversy is understood in this way can we make sense of how it was possible at Chalcedon for Cyril to be invoked at every session as the standard of orthodoxy.[80] To the Council Fathers, Cyril did not represent one Christological "option," much less a Christology

---

that he in fact held a problematically dualist Christology that threatened to undermine the apostolic confession. While I am happy to allow that discontinuities existed between Gregory and Athanasius, and while I am also persuaded by Beeley of the importance of Gregory and of the crucial role the recovery of his Christology can make to a contemporary reformulation of orthodox Christology, it seems to me an exaggeration to pit the one against the other and to characterize the theological relationship between them as ultimately animated by discontinuity.

75. Louth, "Why Did the Syrians Reject the Council of Chalcedon?," p. 111.

76. Louth, "Why Did the Syrians Reject the Council of Chalcedon?," p. 111.

77. Louth, "Why Did the Syrians Reject the Council of Chalcedon?," p. 111.

78. Louth, "Why Did the Syrians Reject the Council of Chalcedon?," p. 112.

79. Louth, "Why Did the Syrians Reject the Council of Chalcedon?," p. 112.

80. Cf. Price and Gaddis, General Introduction to *The Acts of the Council of Chalcedon*, vol. 1, p. 66: "It is to misconstrue the Council to think of the Definition as attempting a synthesis between Cyril's theology and that of the Antiochene school [*sic*] . . . The fathers [of the Council] only accepted from Antioch what they knew Cyril had not only tolerated but also made his own." Cf. Leontius of Jerusalem, *Contra monophysitas* (PG 86.1769a-1902a).

bound to the style of a particular region; he was for them the representative of Catholic truth, of the Nicene orthodoxy defended by Athanasius, which they understood as the faith handed down from the apostles themselves. The textual evidence of the *Acta* of Chalcedon is overwhelming: the Council Fathers did not see themselves as "Theodorian" in any way, but rather as confirming the doctrine held by "blessed Cyril."

E. The Defenders of Cyrillian Orthodoxy

The evidence of the *Acta* notwithstanding, Chalcedon was received at the time by some as having betrayed Cyril and the standard of orthodoxy he had defended. And thus the Council precipitated ecclesial divisions on a scale never before known in the history of Christianity. For the non-Chalcedonians who rejected the Council there were at least four factors:

1. the sense that the Tome of Leo was marred by a Nestorian tendency;
2. the use in the *Definitio* of the formula "in two natures" (ἐν δύο φύσεσιν);
3. the rehabilitation of Theodoret of Cyrrhus and Ibas of Edessa; and
4. the apparent absence in the *Definitio* of a theopaschite formulation.

These factors were seen as evidence that the great Alexandrian Father had been traduced. We must address these four factors in turn.

1. A statement of the faith of the Roman Church, Leo's Tome is indebted to the Latin tradition of Christology rooted in Tertullian and Augustine, which designates the duality of divinity and humanity in Christ on the level of nature (*natura*) while specifying the unity of Christ on the level of person (*persona*).[81] Whatever the nominal resonance of his language with Theodore and Nestorius, Leo's source was Latin and not Theodorian. What Leo intended by conceiving of the unity of divinity and humanity in Christ as a *unitas personae* was the subjective singularity of the one Lord, the Son of God the Father, specified by Leo with the words of the *Symbolum*

---

81. Cf. Tertullian, *Adversus Praxean* 27 (PL 2.190a-192b). On Augustine's Christology, see Brian E. Daley, S.J., "A Humble Mediator: the Distinctive Elements in St. Augustine's Christology," *Word and Spirit* 9 (1987): 100-117, and "The Giant's Twin Substances: Ambrose and the Christology of Augustine's 'Contra sermonem Arianorum,'" in Joseph T. Lienhard et al., eds., *Augustine: Presbyter factus sum, Collectanea Augustiniana*, vol. 2 (New York: Peter Lang, 1993), pp. 477-95. Also see John McGuckin, "Did Augustine's Christology Depend on Theodore of Mopsuestia?," *Heythrop Journal* 55 (1990): 39-52.

Apostolorum: "Jesus Christ, his only Son, our Lord."[82] This confession of the singular *persona* of the Lord Jesus entails the confession, according to Leo, that "the only-begotten Son of God was crucified and was buried, following what the apostle said, 'if they had known, they would never have crucified the Lord of glory' [1 Cor. 2:8]."[83] This fundamental difference between the Leonian and Theodorian doctrines notwithstanding, certain formulations of the Tome do suggest a parsing of divine and human activity in Christ in terms that allow for a problematic parallelism of predication.

The key passage in this regard occurs where Leo writes of the natures acting in accordance with "what is proper to each (*quod proprium est*)."[84] This means, for Leo, that Jesus does human things humanly and divine things divinely — "the Word performing what is proper to the Word, while the flesh accomplishes what is proper to the flesh."[85]

There is no question that Leo, in this formula, diverges from the style of Cyril's strict deployment of *communicatio idiomatum*, and yet at the same time, this whole clause is qualified under a crucial stipulation: "each form performs the actions which are proper to it in communion with the other (*cum alterius communione*)."[86] In this light, even at its most problematic, the parallelist formulation of the Tome is not straightforwardly dualist, and not so obviously contrary to Cyril *tout court*. It all depends on the qualification. The more the "cum alterius communione" determines the meaning of "quod proprium est," the more the parallelist implication of the Tome is undermined.[87] Despite this qualification, the passage still led sixth-century non-Chalcedonians to hold that the Tome was simply

---

82. *Epistula Papae Leonis ad Flavianum* (DS 290; DEC 1.77).

83. *Epistula Papae Leonis ad Flavianum* (DEC 1.80): "Propter hanc ergo unitatem personae in utraque natura intellegendam et filius hominis legitur descendisse de caelo, cum filius dei carnem de ea virgine de qua est natus, adsumpserit, et rursus filius dei crucifixus dicitur ac sepultus, cum haec non in divinitate ipsa qua unigenitus consempiternus et consubstantialis est patri, sed in naturae humanae sit infirmitate perpessus. Unde unigenitum filium dei crucifixum et sepultum omnes etiam in symbolo confitemur secundum illud apostoli *si enim cognovissent, numquam dominum maiestatis crucifixissent.*"

84. *Epistula Papae Leonis ad Flavianum* (DS 294; DEC 1.79).

85. *Epistula Papae Leonis ad Flavianum* (DS 294; DEC 1.79).

86. *Epistula Papae Leonis ad Flavianum* (DS 294; DEC 1.79): "Agit enim utraque forma cum alterius communione quod proprium est: Verbo scilicet operante quod Verbi est, et carne exsequente quod carnis est. Unum horum coruscat miraculis, aliud succumbit iniuriis."

87. Cf. Adam G. Cooper, *The Body in St. Maximus the Confessor: Holy Flesh, Wholly Deified* (Oxford: OUP, 2005), p. 124.

"Nestorian."[88] Yet even when the "cum alterius communione" is not allowed to determine the "quod proprium est," whatever parallelism Leo's doctrine does permit, it does not apply to two discretely existing entities. This was the error of Theodore's two-subject Christology (taken up by Nestorius); it is not found in Leo's Tome. For Leo, if we can parse what is proper to the Word from what is proper to human nature, this parsing concerns a duality on the level of the "manifestation" of the singular person. Whereas for Theodore and Nestorius the realm of "manifestation" was precisely the realm of union (for which there is no correlate ontological substructure), for Leo it is precisely otherwise: the divine *forma* that shines forth in miracle and the human *forma* that succumbs to suffering may be parsed, but only as different manifestations of the one ontological existent (the *una persona* or *una subsistentia*). The concrete existent in all cases, for Leo, remains and is the one Lord Jesus Christ. This does not mean that all the formulations of the Tome are dogmatically adequate; they are not.[89] But

88. Cf. Severus of Antioch: "[In the Incarnation Christ] mingled [i.e. μίξις] the two [natures], establishing that he is indivisibly one and the same Son and Word, who on our behalf unchangeably became man, speaking as befits God and humanity. Thus too it is often possible to see in his actions what belongs to the character of God and (what is) human mingled together. For how will anyone divide walking upon the water? For to run upon the sea is foreign to the human nature, but it is not proper to the divine nature to use bodily feet. Therefore that action is of the incarnate Word, to whom belong at the same time divine character and humanity indivisibly.

"It is possible to see that those things which are contained in the Tome of Leo go clearly against these things, and I quote them: LEO: 'For each one of the forms does what belongs to it; the Word doing what belongs to the Word, and the body fulfilling those things which belong to the body, and the one of them is radiant with wonders, but the other falls under insults.' For if each form or nature does those things which are its own, those things are of a bastard partnership and of a relationship of friendship, such as a master's taking on himself the things which are performed by a servant, or vice versa, a servant's being glorified with the outstanding possessions of a master, while those things which are not properties of human nature are ascribed to him out of a loving friendship. . . .

"But Jesus is not like that, away with you! For he is seen using his own power as God inhominate, and he confirms this with utterances worthy of God" (First Letter of Severus to Sergius, in Torrance, *Christology after Chalcedon*, pp. 147-63, here at p. 154; cf. Severus, *Ad Nephalium, Oratio* II (ed. Allen and Hayward, pp. 59-66).

89. The biggest problem with Leo's manifestational parallelism is that it tends to presume that we know a priori how God acts and manifests himself and how humans act and manifest themselves. It tends thereby to suggest that the most recognizably "powerful" acts of Jesus' life, like the Transfiguration, walking on water or performing miracles, are somehow more divine than suckling at the breast and dying on the Cross. This would tend to undermine how the Cross itself could be the sight of the revelation of God's glory. To this

it does mean that the Tome was in no way a vindication of Nestorius, and that the Tome supplies in itself the key resource by which any lingering parallelism can be recapitulated.[90]

2. Strong Cyrillians were shocked by the decision of the Council Fathers who drew up the *Definitio fidei* to use the formula "in two natures" (ἐν δύο φύσεσιν), associated with Theodore and used by Nestorius, in place of Cyril's formula "from two natures" (ἐκ δύο φύσεσιν).[91] The formula was added, it seems, only at the last minute in order to exclude Dioscorus, who at the first session (before his deposition at the third session) had declared: "I accept 'from two [natures]'; I do not accept 'two'. I am compelled to speak brashly: my soul is at stake."[92] Whatever the motive, the new formula replaced a formula identified with Cyril with one that had been used by Cyril's chief rival.

Whatever Cyril argued in the earlier phases of the Nestorian crisis, he did acknowledge ultimately that the "in two natures" formula could be understood in a perfectly orthodox sense if the "ἐν" of "in two natures" (ἐν δύο φύσεσιν) was understood *en theoria mone*,[93] that is, within the limits of speculative contemplation. In other words, the confession "in two natures" cannot be taken to correlate with what is in fact the experience of encoun-

---

we need to add a logical absurdity: if God is pure spirit, it is not more like God to walk on water, have his face transfigured, or perform a miracle with the touch of his hand, than it is for him to be crucified. All these acts (whatever the transcendent power they unleash, and certainly the Cross unleashes the greatest transcendent power in the form of salvation) are acts of a finite body performing in time and space. The inadequacy of the Tome in this regard leads John McGuckin to suggest that the Council Fathers at Chalcedon were in part moved to compose the detailed *Definitio* "as a direct corrective of several of the Tome's aspects" (McGuckin, *The Christological Controversy*, p. 236). McGuckin's judgment is harsh; it is likely not without a grain of truth. Cf. Thomas G. Weinandy, O.F.M., Cap., *Does God Suffer?* (Edinburgh: T&T Clark, 2000), p. 178, n. 10.

90. The internal resources of the Tome to overcome dualism notwithstanding, the Nestorian impression of the letter was exacerbated by mistranslations of the text from Latin into Greek (whether accidental or deliberate), which made it sound as if Leo had written of "two persons" in Christ, as Leo himself complained: see Leo the Great, *Epistula* 130 (PL 54.1078a-1080d), and *Epistula* 131 (PL 54.1081a-1082a).

91. Chalcedon, Session V, 13-29 (ed. Price and Gaddis, 2.198-201).

92. Chalcedon, Session I, 332 (ed. Price and Gaddis, 1.194). These words of Dioscorus were used at Session V by the chairman as a basis for removing the expression from the *Definitio*, replacing them with the stronger ἐκ δύο φύσεσιν formula it contains, see Session V, 26 (ed. Price and Gaddis, 2.200).

93. Cyril of Alexandria, *Epistula* 46, Second Letter to Successus (ed. Wickham, p. 92; PG 77.245a): κατὰ μόνην τὴν θεωρίαν.

ter. There is one Jesus, and only one who is perceived and encountered. And so the formula "in two natures" is legitimate within the limits arising upon reflection on the concrete and indivisible Lord Jesus Christ, and not on any other. As Cyril writes:

> insofar as the manner of the only-begotten's becoming human appears as something purely mental (ἔννοιαν), and so only appears to the mind's eye, we would admit that there are two united natures, but only one Christ and Son and Lord, the Word of God made man and made flesh.[94]

Crucially, it is precisely within this Cyrillian limit that the *Definitio fidei* deploys the "in two natures" formula. The proclamation of faith in "one and the same Son" led to a confession (ὁμολογέω / *confiteor*) that this "one" is "in two natures."[95] In this way, the *Definitio* nuances, in a more strictly Cyrillian direction, the doctrine of the *Formula unionis*, which had allowed that certain sayings of the Gospels, precisely "god-befitting" or "lowly," be distinguished and appropriated to one or the other of Jesus' natures.[96] This latter kind of parallelism (resonant with the parallelism of the Tome) was widespread among dyophysites before and after Chalcedon.[97]

Though the *Definitio* has absorbed a language that was not of Cyrillian pedigree, it has nevertheless deployed that language in a mode strictly in accordance with Cyril's *en theoria mone* stipulation. Moreover, it is built concretely on the fundamental Christological distinction that Cyril draws between *physis*-as-quiddity and *physis*-as-existent.

3. For those who feared the Council had compromised the dogmatic legacy of Cyril, the rehabilitation of Theodoret of Cyrrhus[98] and Ibas of Edessa was the most tangible evidence that the Council had traduced Cyril.[99] Both Theodoret and Ibas had been deposed at the *Latrocinium*

---

94. Cyril of Alexandria, *Epistula* 45, First Letter to Succensus (ed. Wickham, p. 76; PG 77.232d-233a).

95. On this point there is perhaps a real discrepancy between the Tome and the *Definitio fidei* — the former does seem to "perceive" the two natures.

96. *Formula unionis* (DS 273; DEC 1.70).

97. Price and Gaddis, *The Acts of the Council of Chalcedon*, vol. 1, p. 70, n. 232.

98. On Theodoret, see Paul B. Clayton, *The Christology of Theodoret of Cyrus: Antiochene Christology from the Council of Ephesus* (Oxford: OUP, 2007); István Pásztori-Kupán, *Theodoret of Cyrus*, ECF (London: Routledge, 2006).

99. The case of the rehabilitation of Ibas was so dramatic that it prolonged the Council for an extra day with various petitions being brought against him (see Session IX [ed. Price and Gaddis, 1.257-64], and Session X [ed. Price and Gaddis, 2.265-309]). In the course of his

of 449 for their writings against Cyril and his doctrine. The decision to rehabilitate them at Chalcedon aroused opposition among many of the Council Fathers. In the end, the decision to rehabilitate them seems to have been taken as necessary in order to realize Chalcedon's perfect overturning of the *Latrocinium*. In any event, there is no evidence that the rehabilitation of Ibas and Theodoret was motivated by any sympathy for their Theodorian doctrine; rather, their rehabilitation was strictly for the expedience which this signaled to a total invalidation of the acts of the *Latrocinium*. This is substantiated by two facts. (1) While Theodoret had been among those followers of John of Antioch who had formally been reconciled with Cyril through the *Formula unionis* in 433, he had then refused to anathematize Nestorius; his rehabilitation at Chalcedon was made contingent on him finally acquiescing to this condemnation.[100] (2) Theodoret himself, in his defense of the orthodoxy of the Tome of Leo, makes direct appeal to Cyril, as the common standard of orthodoxy;[101] this appeal cannot be taken as

---

trial, his Letter to Mari the Persian, composed in 433 and the prime subject of his condemnation in 449, was read out loud (Session X, 138 [ed. Price and Gaddis, 2.295-98]). The letter is Ibas's account of the Council of Ephesus, in which he is somewhat critical of Nestorius's refusal of the Marian title Theotokos, but leaves his sharpest doctrinal criticism for Cyril, whom he accuses of being an Apollinarian, and specifically denounces the Twelve Chapters as heretical. Ibas offers, in addition, a fierce assessment of Cyril's person and conduct, along with a spurious account of the events of 433 in which he describes the *Formula unionis* as a capitulation of Cyril for which he was required to condemn his Twelve Chapters and the "mia physis" formula. In sharp contrast to Cyril, Ibas describes "blessed Theodore" as a "herald of the truth and teacher of the church" (Letter to Mari the Persian, Chalcedon, Session X, 138 [ed. Price and Gaddis, 2.297]). Incredibly, the letter was not only read at Chalcedon, but also after it was read Ibas was restored to his see at Edessa.

Having reversed the fortunes of Ibas, the Council then turned to reinstate Theodoret. Theodoret had been a friend of Nestorius, and after the death of Theodore he emerged as the leading intellectual representative of the theological inheritance of Diodore of Tarsus. He was a prolific writer, who did not hide his contempt for Cyril. The year the Council of Ephesus closed, in 331, Theodoret was commissioned by John of Antioch (still not reconciled with Cyril) to write a refutation of Cyril's Twelve Chapters against Nestorius (Theodoret of Cyrrhus, *Reprehensio XII Anathematismorum* [PG 76.385-452]; cf. Theodoret, *Libri V contra Cyrillum et concilium Ephesinum* [CPG 6215] and *Pro Diodoro et Theodore* [CPG 6215]). On Theodoret's anti-Cyrillian writings, see the General Introduction of Richard Price, *The Acts of the Council of Constantinople of 553: With Related Texts on the Three Chapters Controversy, Edited and with an Introduction and Notes*, 2 vols. (Liverpool: Liverpool University Press, 2009), vol. 1, pp. 84-88.

100. Chalcedon, Session VIII, 5-13 (ed. Price and Gaddis, 2.254-55).

101. Chalcedon, Session II, 26 (ed. Price and Gaddis, 2.26): "Likewise when there was being read from the same letter [the Tome] the part that contains the words, 'Although in-

expressive of Theodoret's personal preference in theology, but rather is evidence that Cyril had become quite simply the universal standard of the Fathers at Chalcedon. Thus it was clear to all present that the will of the Council was in no way aimed to undermine or qualify the legacy of Cyril's teaching.[102] Nevertheless, non-Chalcedonians widely adduced from the double rehabilitation that Chalcedon had indeed maligned the teaching of Cyril and approved (at least tacitly) the teaching of Nestorius and his teacher, Theodore of Mopsuestia.

4. The most dogmatically significant charge brought against Chalcedon was that it demurred on the question of the cruciform identity of the "one and the same" Lord and Christ. This is connected to the question mark of the dogmatic status of Cyril's Twelve Chapters, with its anathematization of those who deny that the Logos truly died in the flesh.[103] That Chalcedon did not pronounce on the Twelve Chapters and that the *précis* of the *Definitio* does not contain in itself a theopaschite formula has been taken as if the Council failed to directly name the subject of the Cross.[104]

---

deed in the Lord Jesus Christ there is one person of God and man, nevertheless that because of which the outrage is common in both is one thing and that because of which the glory is common is another, for he has from us the humanity that is less than the Father, and he has from the Father the Godhead that is equal with the Father,' the most devout Illyrian and Palestinian bishops raised an objection. Theodoret the most devout bishop of Cyrrhus said, 'There is a similar instance in the blessed Cyril which contains the words, "He became man without shedding what was his own, for he remained what he was; he is certainly conceived as one dwelling in another, that is, the divine nature in what is human."'"

102. Cf. Price and Gaddis, *The Acts of the Council of Chalcedon*, vol. 1, p. 66: "Nothing could be more indicative of the mood of the council than the fact that even Theodoret had to defend the Tome [of Pope Leo] by appealing to the authority of Cyril. His own attitude was far more critical: he had strongly attacked Cyril's Twelve Chapters . . . in early 431 and had been very reluctant to accept Nestorius' subsequent condemnation. But he clearly recognized that it would be disastrous to argue that there was something valuable in the Tome of Leo that was lacking in Cyril; instead, he played along with the conviction of the majority that Cyril provided the yardstick of orthodoxy."

103. Cf. Cyril of Alexandria, Twelve Chapters, anathema 12 (DS 263; DEC 1.61).

104. For example, see Jaroslav Pelikan, *The Christian Tradition: A History of the Development of Doctrine*, vol. 1, *The Emergence of the Catholic Tradition 100–600* (Chicago: University of Chicago Press, 1973), p. 265: "It was not clear [at Chalcedon] . . . who the subject of suffering and crucifixion was, for these events in the history of salvation were not so much as mentioned. Presumably, the references to one and the same near the beginning and near the end would indicate that he, in the concreteness of his total person both divine and human, was the subject, but this was not specified." Also see Leo Donald Davis, S.J., *The First Seven Ecumenical Councils (325-787): Their History and Theology* (Collegeville: The Liturgical Press, 1983), p. 188: "Though the Definition insisted on the unity of person in Christ by repeating

While it is true that this lacuna in the *précis* may have contributed to a cer-tain "erroneous use" of Chalcedon by some,[105] it is not true that Chalcedon demurred from the unbearable scandal of the Cross.

There are in fact two concrete and dogmatically ratified theopaschite formulae operative at Chalcedon. The first lies in the *Credo* itself: "for our sake he was crucified . . . suffered death and was buried." Having professed it exactly twice (in both Nicene and Constantinopolitan forms) before the declaration of the *précis* of the *Definitio*, the Council Fathers made abso-lutely clear that the "one and the same Son . . . the Lord Jesus Christ" the *Definitio* confesses cannot be any other but the "one Lord Jesus Christ" confessed in the *Credo*. In this way the *Definitio* makes absolutely clear that it is speaking of none other than the one who died *pro nobis*. The one subject of the *Definitio*, the Son of the Theotokos, is the Logos and Crucified Lord of the *Credo*. If there is any doubt about this, it is because the *précis* has been taken out of the textual context of the wider *Definitio* and read in a "pure" manner.

The other crucial theopaschite formula ratified at Chalcedon is con-tained in Leo's Tome: "The divine Son of God . . . the impassible God did not despise to become a suffering man and, deathless as he is, became [nevertheless] subject to the laws of death."[106] This unequivocal and strong

---

the adjective 'same' eight times, it still left the concept of hypostatic union unclear . . . it did not specify the subject of suffering and crucifixion. Could one say with Cyril that the Word suffered, died and rose?" Cf. Édouard Glotin, S.J., *La Bible du Coeur de Jésus* (Paris: Presse de la Renaissance, 2007), p. 565; Anthony Baxter, "Chalcedon and the Subject in Christ," *Downside Review* 107 (1989): 1-21.

105. This is evidenced not least and famously in the controversy provoked by the inter-polation of the Trisagion by Peter the Fuller. The reaction against Peter's theopaschite gloss betrays a problematic logic within the imperial Church. As John Meyendorff notes: "The Chalcedonian opposition [to Peter's gloss] would have been justified . . . if it had limited its objections to the fact that the hymn was interpreted in a Trinitarian sense . . . and that consequently the interpolated form was dangerously ambiguous. However, if one reads certain Chalcedonian texts relative to this controversy, one finds, against theopaschism in all its forms, objections current in the anti-Cyrillian circles of Antioch before and after the Council of Ephesus" (Meyendorff, *Christ in Eastern Christian Thought*, p. 35). As an example, Meyendorff points to a text attributed to Anteon, the Chalcedonian bishop of Arsinoe, who argued against Peter: "the cross can only be attributed to his human nature" (ACO 3, 217). In this context, the anti-Chalcedonian polemic of Severus of Antioch, the most powerful theo-logical mind of non-Chalcedonian Christology, is somewhat understandable. In particular, Severus was unrelenting in his criticism of Chalcedon's failure to affirm that the Incarnate Word was crucified; see Severus of Antioch, *Homiliae cathedrales*, I.12-25 (PO 38.260-267).

106. *Epistula Papae Leonis ad Flavianum* (DS 294; DEC 1.79): "Filius Dei . . . impassibilis

theopaschite formula gives the final lie to the idea, shared by Nestorius and Severus of Antioch alike, that the pope was dualist in his Christology in a manner more or less convertible with a Theodorian sensibility. To the contrary: by this formulation Leo made bold to profess precisely the theopaschism Theodore and Nestorius had set themselves to oppose.

That the Tome bears a theopaschite formula does not in itself resolve the question of the difficult reception of Chalcedon, neither does it resolve the dogmatic perplexities native to the Tome itself. What the Leonian theopaschite formula does resolve beyond a doubt, however, is the basic unity of Pope Leo with the heart of the Nicene confession: there is one Lord Jesus Christ, who is true God from true God, who came down from heaven, and was crucified for us and for our salvation. The unity of Leo's formula, in turn, evidences the crucial point on which he was absolutely of one accord with Cyril. Cyril declared in anathema 12 of the Twelve Chapters that the Logos, who is the Life and the life-giving one, tasted death in the flesh in order to destroy death by death; whereas Leo in his Tome declares that Jesus, the impassible God, was subjected to the laws of death in order to destroy mortality by the mortality of the immortal one. The core apostolic proclamation of the Crucified Lord, preserved and reaffirmed in the *Credo*, was boldly upheld at Chalcedon in the Tome. Hence the famous acclamation of the Council Fathers: "Peter has uttered this through Leo. The apostles taught accordingly. Leo taught piously and truly. Cyril taught accordingly. Eternal is the memory of Cyril. Leo and Cyril taught the same."[107]

Deus non dedignatus est homo esse passibilis et immortalis mortis legibus subjacere." Cf. *Sermo* 68.1 (March 454) and *Sermo* 57.4 (March 443): "Pendente enim in patibulo creatore, universa creatura congemuit, et crucis clauos omnia simul elementa senserunt. Nihil ab illo supplicio liberum fuit."

107. Chalcedon, Session II, 23 (ed. Price and Gaddis, 2.24).

PART TWO

The Synergy of Christ

CHAPTER 4

Mingling and Inversion

O new mingling; O paradoxical mingling! The one who is has come to be, the Uncreated One is created, the Uncontained One is contained.

Gregory of Nazianzus

A. Christology of "Mingling"

The *Definitio fidei* of Chalcedon led to a revision and specification of traditional Christological language. Most obvious was the refinement of the language of hypostasis (ὑπόστασις) and nature (φύσις). Henceforth, Cyril's distinction within the language of "nature" between *physis*-as-quiddity and *physis*-as-existent would be reallocated, with the former now being attributed to hypostasis/person and the latter to nature. Because the *Definitio* linked together the language of hypostasis and *persona* in a way that tended to equate the more Leonian language of the "oneness of person" (*unitas personae*) with the Cyrillian doctrine of the "hypostatic union" (ἔνωσις καθ᾽ ὑπόστασιν), the category of *persona/prosopon* was now recast as entailing the ontological density of hypostasis/*suppositum*. While these linguistic refinements helped to clarify the notion of the unity and distinction in Christ, and in the long term provided essential paradigms for Christian metaphysis more broadly, they had the unfortunate result of casting a retroactive suspicion over certain pre-Chalcedonian formulations, not least the "mia physis" formula of Cyril.

One Christological discourse that suffered particularly from the linguistic refinement of Chalcedon was that of the pre-Chalcedonian language of "mingling" (μίξις / κρᾶσις). The *Definitio* had been clear that the union of divinity and humanity was "without confusion" (ἀσυγχύτως), which it clarified specifically as meaning without "mingling" (κρᾶσις).[1] Many pre-Chalcedonian Fathers of undoubtedly orthodox pedigree had used this language to account for the intimacy of union, but after Chalcedon it was quietly shunted into the background, together with some of the theological insights of the Fathers who deployed it, for fear that it was proto-monophysite.[2]

The language of "mingling" was a central aspect of the Christological grammar of Gregory of Nyssa (c. 335-c. 394) and Gregory of Nazianzus (330-c. 390). Half a century before Chalcedon, both Gregories used this language as a tool to specify the interpenetration of the union of divinity and humanity in Christ.[3] Their Christologies were written against the backdrop of the Christological debate between Diodore of Tarsus and Apollinarius of Laodicea.[4]

Because Diodore and Apollinarius were both finally condemned and most of their writings destroyed, it is hard to determine the precise contours of their dispute.[5] What we do know is that they were both Nicene

---

1. Cf. *Definitio fidei* (DS 300 [par. 1 and 3]; DEC 1.84 and 86).

2. A modern tradition of *Dogmengeschichte* has reinforced this sidelining of "mingling" Christologies out of a single-minded concern to recount pre-Chalcedonian theology as nothing more than a series of foreshadowings of a later Chalcedonian "orthodoxy." As an example of this tendency, Sarah Coakley points to: Joseph Tixeront, *Histoire des dogmes dans l'antiquité chrétienne*, vol. 2 (Paris: J. Gabalda, 1912), pp. 128-30; Aloys Grillmeier, S.J., *Christ in Christian Tradition*, vol. 2, *From the Council of Chalcedon (451) to Gregory the Great (590–604)*, part 1, trans. Pauline Allen and John Cawte (Louisville: Westminster John Knox Press, 1995), pp. 370-72; and Wolfhart Pannenberg, *Jesus — God and Man*, trans. Lewis L. Wilkins and Duane A. Priebe (London: SCM, 1968), p. 297. See Sarah Coakley, "'Mingling' in Gregory of Nyssa's Christology: A Reconsideration," in Andreas Schuele and Günter Thomas, eds., *Who Is Jesus Christ for Us Today: Pathways to Contemporary Christology* (Louisville: Westminster/John Knox Press, 2009), pp. 72-84. On the Christology of mingling, in addition to Coakley, see Philip McCosker, "Parsing Paradox, Analysing 'And'. Christological Configurations of Theological Paradox in some Mystical Theologies" (Ph.D. Thesis: Cambridge University, 2008).

3. This was not lost on Severus of Antioch, the most elegant and important theological leader of the non-Chalcedonians, who polemically invoked Chalcedon's rejection of the language of "mingling" in order to attack the Council's apparently Nestorian innovation. See Severus of Antioch's Letter II to Sergius the Grammarian, in Iain R. Torrance, *Christology after Chalcedon: Severus of Antioch and Sergius the Monophysite* (Norwich: The Canterbury Press, 1988), pp. 171-202.

4. See Christopher A. Beeley, *The Unity of Christ: Continuity and Conflict in Patristic Tradition* (New Haven: Yale University Press, 2012), pp. 176-82.

5. For the extant fragments of Apollinarius, see Hans Lietzmann, ed., *Apollinarius von Laodicea und seine Schule: Texte und Untersuchungen* (Tübingen: Möhr, 1904). For the extant

in the sense that both purported to uphold and defend the settlement of 325. Apollinarius in particular, who himself had a personal connection to Athanasius,[6] was seen in the 360s and 370s as something of an authoritative defender of Nicaea; indeed Gregory of Nyssa's older brother, Basil of Caesarea (c. 330-379), once consulted him on the proper use of the term "consubstantial" (ὁμοούσια).[7]

Apollinarius became bishop of the Syrian city of Laodicea, a city near Antioch, where Diodore was a respected teacher of the faith and leader of the ascetic school in which he mentored Theodore of Mopsuestia and John Chrysostom.[8] The regional proximity of Apollinarius and Diodore facilitated their debate and ensured that, at the beginning, it was a local polemic. At the heart of their Christological debate, which continued through most of the 370s, lay the question of the predicative unity of Christ.[9] The language of "mingling" played a not superficial role in the controversy. While Apollinarius used the language of "mingling" to emphasize the substantial unity of the Logos and flesh in the one Jesus Christ, Diodore distinguished in Christ two unmixable *prosopa*. These unmixable *prosopa*, according to Diodore, were not merely discrete subjects of predication; they were two divestible subjects of experience: the Son of the Father, born before the ages, is eternal and impassible, while the Son born of Mary, born in history and finite, is the subject of the sufferings of the Cross.[10] On precisely these grounds, Diodore claims that Mary is not "Theotokos" but merely "anthropotokos."[11] In contrast to the dualist Christology of Diodore, Apollinarius put strong emphasis on the unity of Christ and the need for

---

fragments of Diodore, see John Behr, *The Case against Diodore and Theodore: Texts and Their Contexts* (Oxford: OUP, 2011).

6. Beeley, *The Unity of Christ*, p. 176.

7. See Basil of Caesarea, *Epistulae* 361-363 (PG 32.1100c-1105b).

8. On Diodore's dispute with Apollinarius, see Behr, *The Case against Diodore and Theodore*, pp. 59-65.

9. It was during the 370s that Apollinarius wrote his two works against Diodore: Λόγος συλλογιστικός, κατὰ Διοδώρου πρὸς Ἡράκλεον and Πρὸς Διόδωρον ἢ τὸ κατὰ κεφάλιον βιβλίον. The surviving fragments of these texts are collected in Lietzmann, *Apollinarius von Laodicea und seine Schule*. On Apollinarius, cf. Brian Daley, S.J., "'Heavenly Man' and 'Eternal Christ': Apollinarius and Gregory of Nyssa on the Personal Identity of the Savior," *Journal of Early Christian Studies* 10 (2002): 469-88.

10. Diodore of Tarsus, BD 20 (ed. Behr, p. 185), BD 26 (ed. Behr, p. 189), SD 5 (ed. Behr, pp. 238-39), and SD 8 (ed. Behr, pp. 238-41).

11. Diodore of Tarsus, SD 2 (ed. Behr, pp. 236-37), BD 1 (ed. Behr, pp. 168-69), BD 22 (ed. Behr, pp. 186-87).

his flesh and divinity to be predicated of his singular reality.[12] Apollinarius relied heavily on the language of mingling to signify this absolute unity of Christ.[13] Following Jesus's own claim to be "before Abraham" (John 8:58), Apollinarius held that "the man Christ pre-exists (προϋπάρχει ὁ ἄνθρωπος Χριστός)."[14] In this way, in a very radical manner, Apollinarius argues that Christ was the "heavenly man"; that while every other human is "earthly," Jesus is not.[15] The dispute between Diodore and Apollinarius would have likely remained a local dispute had Diodore not been consecrated bishop of Tarsus in 378.

In 379, a year after his episcopal ordination, Diodore attended a synod in Antioch, the aim of which was to marshal support to persuade Emperor Theodosius I to implement a broad pro-Nicene policy throughout the empire. To advance the way for this pro-Nicene settlement, the synod commissioned Gregory of Nazianzus to go to the Byzantine capital in order "to defend the Word" against the "new-fangled heresy" of Apollinarianism, the apparent mistake of which was to claim that in the Incarnation the Logos had replaced the human "mind" (νοῦς) of Jesus.[16] In all likelihood

12. Apollinarius, *De Unione Corporis et Divinitatis in Christo*, 7 (ed. Lietzmann, pp. 185-93).

13. Cf. Apollinarius, *Contra Diodorum*, Frag 134 (ed. Lietzmann, pp. 239-40), *De Unione Corporis et Divinitatis in Christo*, 8 (ed. Lietzmann, pp. 188-243), Frag. 9 (ed. Lietzmann, p. 206), and Frag. 149 (ed. Lietzmann, p. 247).

14. Apollinarius, Frags. 32 and 33 (ed. Lietzmann, pp. 211-12). Cf. Behr, *The Case against Diodore and Theodore*, p. 10.

15. Apollinarius, *Recapitulation* 4 (ed. Lietzmann, pp. 242-46).

16. Gregory of Nazianzus, *De vita sua*, 607-631, in Caroline White, ed., Gregory of Nazianzus, *Autobiographical Poems* (Cambridge: CUP, 1996), pp. 58-59. Despite this traditional judgment against Apollinarius, cf. John Behr's caution: "Although he, more than anyone else, is known for having taught that the Word replaced the human soul or mind of Jesus, it was much more his resolute determination to avoid any suggestion of duality in the one Lord Jesus Christ, and his particular understanding of how Scripture speaks of Christ, that determines the shape of his theology. He takes very seriously one of the most striking aspects of the apostolic account of Christ, that it speaks of him in divine terms where we would most naturally expect to see human ones, and in human terms where we would expect to see divine ones" (Behr, *The Case against Diodore and Theodore*, pp. 9-10). To this we should add (without necessarily sanctioning) the creative re-reading of Apollinarius by the Russian Sophiologist Sergei Bulgakov. In his work *The Lamb of God* (trans. Boris Jakim [Grand Rapids: Eerdmans, 2008]), Bulgakov attempts to free Apollinarius of the heretical caricature made of him, to show that in fact he had a decisive contribution to make to a Christological anthropology. On Bulgakov's view, Apollinarius's opponents misunderstood him to the extent that he was believed to have suggested that certain natural faculties of the human soul were lacking in Jesus. According to Bulgakov, Apollinarius's Christology presupposes a tripartite

it was Diodore himself who informed Gregory of the Antiochene dispute and the error of Apollinarius.[17] It seems, however, that while Gregory was persuaded of the danger of Apollinarius's doctrine, he was at least equally cautious of the Christological doctrine Diodore was proposing.[18]

Remembered as the great defender of orthodoxy against the Apollinarian heresy, Gregory of Nazianzus's Christology is usually summed up by his anti-Apollinarian axiom: "that which is not assumed is not healed."[19] While the axiom was deployed by Gregory against the Apollinarian variant of "monophysitism" condemned at Constantinople I (381),[20] evidence sug-

---

anthropology of "spirit" (πνεῦμα / νοῦς), "soul" (ψυχή) and "body" (σῶμα) and, if it is read with this in mind, it turns out to be much closer to Chalcedonian orthodoxy than is usually allowed. How so? If the trichotomy underpins Apollinarius's account of the Incarnation, then when he suggests that the Logos "took the place" of Christ's human mind-spirit (νοῦς / πνεῦμα) he should be understood as claiming no more than that in Jesus the Logos was the "spirit" of personhood, the hypostatic term Chalcedon designates as the singular divine term of the union of the two natures. On this reading, the density of the traditional composite nature is preserved by the fact that Jesus' humanity is still a full composite of ψυχή and σῶμα with all the human faculties intact (see Bulgakov, *The Lamb of God*, pp. 8-9).

17. John McGuckin, *Gregory of Nazianzus: An Intellectual Biography* (Crestwood, NY: Saint Vladimir's Seminary Press, 2001), pp. 131-32.

18. See Christopher A. Beeley, *Gregory of Nazianzus on the Trinity and the Knowledge of God: In Your Light We Shall See Light* (Oxford: OUP, 2008), pp. 33-34; Beeley, *The Unity of Christ*, pp. 182-91; and Behr, *The Case against Diodore and Theodore*, pp. 55-56 and 86-88.

19. Gregory of Nazianzus, *Epistula* 101 (SC 208.50; PG 37.181c-184a): Εἴ τις εἰς ἄνουν ἄνθρωπον ἤλπικεν, ἀνόητος ὄντως ἐστὶ καὶ οὐκ ἄξιος ὅλως σῴζεσθαι. Τὸ γὰρ ἀπρόσληπτον, ἀθεράπευτον· ὃ δὲ ἥνωται τῷ Θεῷ, τοῦτο καὶ σῴζεται. While *Epistula* 101 was written after Gregory had retired from Constantinople, the logic of the axiom (which originates in the work of Origen of Alexandria) is found fully in the *Oratio* 30.21 (SC 250.270-272; PG 36.132a-c). *Oratio* 30 is one of Gregory's so-called "five theological orations," and according to McGuckin it was written in 381, the year of the condemnation of Apollinarius at Constantinople I (381). Crucially, in *Oratio* 30, Gregory articulates this "assumption" language in terms that foreclose *tout court* every possible *homo assumptus* doctrine. Gregory specifies that when we talk about "the assuming of human nature" we are talking about the Son "who came down from heaven"; the action of "assuming" is that of the Logos, which means that we are not predicating of the human nature assumed (*Oratio* 30.12 [SC 250.248; PG 36.117c]). On the dating of *Oratio* 30, see McGuckin's *Gregory of Nazianzus*, p. 244. On Gregory, see Brian Daley, S.J., *Gregory of Nazianzus*, ECF (London: Routledge, 2006); and John Behr, *The Nicene Faith: The Formation of Christian Theology*, vol. 2 (Crestwood, NY: Saint Vladimir's Seminary Press, 2004), pp. 325-408.

20. Constantinople I, canon 1 (DS 151; DEC 1.31). This condemnation and its background regarding Diodore show the insufficiency of modern construals of Constantinople I, which present it as a "Trinitarian Council" and somehow separable from the Christological crises that led to Ephesus, Chalcedon and the two Constantinopolitan councils. This is noted by

gests that Gregory was even more concerned with the "two sons" doctrine taught by Diodore,[21] which separated the Logos born of God from the man born of Mary.[22] This is confirmed by the fact that, when he was installed as archbishop of Constantinople in 380, Gregory chose not to focus his polemical energies on Apollinarianism but against the dualist separation of the one Christ into "two sons."[23] Indeed, only after he dealt with what was to him the more crippling doctrine of "two sons" did Gregory turn explicitly against those who teach that Christ did not assume a human mind.

Behr in *The Case against Diodore and Theodore* (pp. 3-5) as an example of a modern tendency to parse the so-called "Trinitarian Councils" (Nicaea and Constantinople I) from the so-called "Christological Councils" (Ephesus, Chalcedon, Constantinople II and Constantinople III). As evidence of this parsing Behr points to R. P. C. Hanson, *The Search for the Christian Doctrine of God: The Arian Controversy 318-381* (Edinburgh: T&T Clark, 1988) and Lewis Ayres, *Nicaea and Its Legacy: An Approach to Fourth-Century Trinitarian Theology* (Oxford: OUP, 2004), both of whom cover in detail the decades leading up to Constantinople I with no significant part given to Diodore or his pupil Theodore of Mopsuestia.

21. Gregory's target when he criticizes the "two sons" theory is clearly Diodore. See McGuckin, *Gregory of Nazianzus*, p. 237, n. 33.

22. See Christopher A. Beeley, "The Early Christological Controversy: Apollinarius, Diodore, and Gregory Nazianzen," *Vigiliae Christianae* 65 (2011): 1-32. Elsewhere Beeley shows that the Nazianzen's polemic against Christological dualism was not only greater than his polemic against Apollinarianism, but intensified as he got older; and that he needs to be re-read against the common tendency to exaggerate and misconstrue his anti-Apollinarianism in a "one sided" direction. Beeley shows, moreover, how Gregory's interest to defend the full humanity of Jesus was always internal — even subordinate — to his more fundamental apprehension of the unity of Christ's being. This means that re-construing the Nazianzen's Christology strictly through the lens of his polemic against Apollinarianism turns out to be "positively misleading" (Beeley, *Gregory of Nazianzus on the Trinity and the Knowledge of God*, p. 125). Far from being especially concerned — in a purely proto-Chalcedonian fashion — with the "distinction" of the two natures, the Nazianzen deploys his operative concept of the "assumption" of humanity into the Word in order to articulate a strongly unitive Christology, which notices above all the "full" divinity of Jesus: "the explicit focus of Gregory's Christology is very clearly on the divinity of Christ . . . not on how the two natures are equally combined in one person" (Beeley, *Gregory of Nazianzus on the Trinity and the Knowledge of God*, p. 125). For the Nazianzen, *both* of the natures of Jesus are "divine" — the nature that does not divinize is divinized: "He deigned to be made one thing out of two (οὐ δύο γενόμενος, ἀλλ᾽ ἓν ἐκ τῶν δύο γενέσθαι ἀνασχόμενος). For both are God, that which assumed and that which was assumed, the two natures meeting in one thing (δύο φύσεις εἰς ἓν συνδραμοῦσαι). But not two sons: let us not give a false account of the blending (ἡ σύγκρασις)" (*Oratio* 37.2 [SC 318.274; PG 36.284c-285a]). Cf. McGuckin, *Gregory of Nazianzus*, pp. 390-92.

23. See Gregory of Nazianzus, *Oratio* 22.13 (SC 270.246-248; PG 35.1145b-c). According to John McGuckin, *Oratio* 22 is significantly Gregory's second homily in Constantinople. See McGuckin, *Gregory of Nazianzus*, p. 248.

Gregory is in fact a fully Athanasian thinker for whom the existential unity of Christ is the ground of possibility of his human difference, and this is the Christological program he brought to the capital.[24] Confronting the Apollinarian error, Gregory responded precisely otherwise than Diodore. Gregory does not parse the humanity and divinity of Christ in proto-Nestorian fashion, but rather stresses all the more the perfect unity of Christ as the ground of his full humanity. The integral humanity of Christ is not threatened by the *unio*, but to the contrary: "one nature deifies, the other is deified."[25] This means that there is no aspect of Jesus that does not exist fully within the divine *unio*. All of this is confirmed, moreover, in Gregory's most important Christological axiom, which he inherits from Irenaeus of Lyon and bequeaths, ultimately, to Chalcedon: Christ is *unus et idem*, "one and the same" (ἕνα καὶ τὸν αὐτόν).[26]

Gregory's Christological program and his concern above all to counter the dualism of "two sons" (and thereby "beating Apollinarius at his own game"[27]) is borne out nowhere more clearly than in the ten anathemata of his celebrated *Epistula* 101, a work written a few years after he retired from the capital (and left the Council of Constantinople I to complete its work without him). Of the ten anathemata, remarkably, eight are directed against

---

24. Beeley, *Gregory of Nazianzus on the Trinity and the Knowledge of God*, p. 131: "In Gregory's view, the real danger lies not in compromising the integrity of these two realities [i.e. humanity and divinity], as the Antiochenes would argue, but rather in the opposite direction: the blending should not be misunderstood as being anything less than a real union. If our humanity is not fully united to God in Christ, then he is in fact two different sons and we have not been divinized in the incarnation."

25. Gregory of Nazianzus, *Oratio* 38.13 (SC 358.134; PG 36.325c-d): "God together with what he assumed, one thing made out of two opposites (ἕν ἔκ δύο τῶν ἐναντίων), flesh and Spirit, of which the latter deifies and the former is deified." See Beeley, *Gregory of Nazianzus on the Trinity and the Knowledge of God*, pp. 115-43. My quotations from the Nazianzen here are taken from Beeley (although I have lightly re-translated at some points).

26. Cf. Gregory of Nazianzus, *Epistula* 101 (SC 208.42-46; PG 37.177c-180b). Also cf. Irenaeus of Lyon, *Adversus haereses* 3.16.3 (SC 211.299; PG 7.922a-923a): "Διὰ τοῦτο δὴ καὶ Μάρκος φησίν · « Ἀρχὴ τοῦ εὐαγγελίου Ἰησοῦ Χριστοῦ Υἱοῦ Θεοῦ, καθὼς γέγραπται ἐν τοῖς προφήταις », ἕνα καὶ τὸν αὐτὸν εἰδὼς Υἱὸν τοῦ Θεοῦ Ἰησοῦν Χριστόν, τὸν ὑπὸ τῶν προφητῶν κεκηρυγμένον, τὸν « ἐκ καρποῦ τῆς κοιλίας » τοῦ Δαυίδ, «Ἐμμανουήλ », « μεγάλης βουλῆς » Πατρὸς « ἄγγελον »." See Beeley, *Gregory of Nazianzus on the Trinity and the Knowledge of God*, p. 131. Consequently, as Behr puts it: "There is to be [for Gregory] no separation into different parts of what belongs together in 'one and the same' Christ . . . the divine and the human in Christ must not be conceptualized in term [*sic*] of 'parts', for 'one and the same' is wholly both" (*The Nicene Faith*, p. 402).

27. Beeley, *The Unity of Christ*, p. 217.

the proto-Nestorian doctrine unambiguously taught by Diodore.[28] Among these eight anathemata, the doctrine that God "put on" a fully formed human being (*homo assumptus*) is anathematized,[29] the formula of "one and the same" is reiterated against those who teach "two sons" in Christ,[30] those who do not worship the Crucified are anathematized,[31] and the Christological denial of the doctrine of the Theotokos is condemned.[32] Only after eight anathemata aimed against Christological dualism does Gregory turn in his last two anathemata to condemn the Apollinarian error.

Gregory's program of unitive Christology is based above all in his emphasis on the interpenetration of divinity and humanity in the one Christ, for which he liberally deploys the language of "mingling" (μίξις / κρᾶσις). As he hymns to the marvel of the Incarnation in *Oratio* 38:

> O new mingling (ὢ τῆς καινῆς μίξεως); O paradoxical mingling (ὢ τῆς παραδόξου κράσεως)! The one who is (ὁ ὢν [cf. Exod. 3:14]) has come to be (γίνεται), the Uncreated One is created, the Uncontained One is contained.[33]

The language of "mingling" here emphasizes, for Gregory, the paradoxical fact of divinity and humanity becoming "one and the same" in Christ. Specifically, the language of "mingling" emphasizes how a finite first-century Jew can be truly identified with YHWH, the God of Israel and Creator of all things, who is revealed in the burning bush to Moses as the *Unum* who simply "is" (ἐγώ εἰμι ὁ ὢν [Exod. 3:14]). In Jesus, the *Unum* has come to be (ὁ ὢν γίνεται). It was left to Gregory of Nazianzus's younger Cappadocian counterpart, Gregory of Nyssa, the brother of Basil of Caesarea, to take up and develop this Christological language in a manner that concretely fixes it to the crucifixion.

For Gregory of Nyssa, the "mingling" in Christ concerns how the human nature of Christ is fused into the oneness of the Word through the

---

28. Gregory of Nazianzus, *Epistula* 101 (SC 208.42-50; PG 37.177c-184b). Cf. Behr, *The Case against Diodore and Theodore*, pp. 86-88.

29. Gregory of Nazianzus, *Epistula* 101 (anathema 3) (SC 208.42-48; PG 37.177c-180a).

30. Gregory of Nazianzus, *Epistula* 101 (anathema 4) (SC 208.48; PG 37.180a).

31. Gregory of Nazianzus, *Epistula* 101 (anathema 6) (SC 208.47; PG 37.180b).

32. Gregory of Nazianzus, *Epistula* 101 (anathema 1) (SC 208.42; PG 37.177c).

33. Gregory of Nazianzus, *Oratio* 38.13 (SC 358.134; PG 36.325c). Cf. Severus of Antioch, Letter II to Sergius the Grammarian, in Torrance, *Christology after Chalcedon*, p. 178, where Severus cites Gregory of Nazianzus's *Oratio* 38 in support of his rejection of Chalcedon.

crucifixion of the flesh of the Son on the Cross.[34] In other words, the Nyssen's language of mingling is used to specify the kind of claim made by Cyril in anathema 12, according to which the Logos "crucified in the flesh" becomes truly "the first-born of the dead" and thereby transforms death into Life.[35] The Nyssen writes:

> But death has been swallowed up by life (cf. 1 Cor. 15:54; 2 Cor. 5:4), the Crucified has been restored to life by power from weakness, and the curse has been turned into blessing. And everything that was weak and perishable in our nature, mingled with the divinity (ἐπίκηρον ἀνακραθὲν τῇ θεότητι), has become that which the divinity is. How then would anyone suppose there to be a duality of Sons, when of necessity one is led to such a rejoinder as this by the [Son's] "economy" in the flesh? For he is always in the Father, and always has the Father in him, and is one with him, as it was in the beginning and is now and always will be; and there never was any other Son beside him, nor is there, nor will there be. The first-fruits (1 Cor 15: 20) of the human nature which he has taken up — absorbed, one might say figuratively — by the omnipotent divinity like a drop of vinegar mingled in the boundless sea (οἷόν τις σταγὼν ὄξους ἀπείρῳ πελάγει κατακραθεῖσα), exist in the divinity, but not in their own [i.e. human] distinctive characteristics. For a duality of Sons might consistently be presumed, if a nature of a different kind could be recognized by its own proper signs within the ineffable divinity of the Son — as being weak or small or perishable or temporary, as opposed to powerful and great and imperishable and eternal. But since all the traits we recognize in the mortal [nature] we see transformed by the characteristics of the divinity, and since no difference of any kind can be perceived — for whatever one sees in the Son *is* divinity: wisdom, power, holiness, *apatheia* — how could one divide what is one into double significance, since no difference divides him numerically?[36]

34. See Behr, *The Nicene Faith*, pp. 409-74; Brian E. Daley, S.J., "Divine Transcendence and Human Transformation: Gregory of Nyssa's anti-Apollinarian Christology," *Modern Theology* 18 (2002): 497-506; Coakley, "'Mingling' in Gregory of Nyssa's Christology: A Reconsideration." More generally, see Anthony Meredith, *Gregory of Nyssa*, ECF (London: Routledge, 2009); Hans Urs von Balthasar, *Presence and Thought: Essay on the Religious Philosophy of Gregory of Nyssa*, trans. Mark Sebanc (San Francisco: Ignatius Press, 1995).

35. Cyril of Alexandria, Twelve Chapters, anathema 12 (DS 263; DEC 1.61).

36. Gregory of Nyssa, *Ad Theophilum* (GNO 3.1, pp. 126-27), trans. Daley, adjusted and expanded by Coakley.

In this remarkable passage we see how the conquering of death, the purification of dying whereby the curse of sin is transfigured into blessing, does not occur by an extrinsic operation but works, rather, from within the finitude of Christ's humanity. The fragility of Jesus's flesh becomes the medium of translucency to the glory of God. We might be tempted to think that here, in the most bitterly finite moment, the distinction between divinity and humanity, if ever it could entail *separatio*, would be necessary to protect the impassibility of God. But it is, for Gregory, to the contrary: in the dereliction of the Cross, the frailty of the human is "like a drop of vinegar mingled in the boundless sea of divinity." The overwhelming power of divinity is not identifiable with our usual a priori sense of divine power. On the Cross, the unequalizable power of God is the fragility of a dying man. This means that in Christology, the "proper signs" of humanity and divinity cannot be parsed — "no difference of any kind can be perceived." Because the Crucified Son simply "is" the glory of God, the Cross is the true sign of God's *apatheia* and the death of this Jew is the Life of the world.

A further point here: for Gregory, human flourishing and the appropriation of salvation both occur through a narratological process of intensifying participation in the moral and spiritual characteristics of Christ.[37] This is the same with the Incarnation itself: the transformation through which Jesus purifies the weakness of human nature through the eventual submission of himself to the dereliction of the Cross recapitulates and fulfills the pattern of Jesus's own life. Accordingly, the humanity of Jesus is subjected to a "process" of purification in order that everything that was "weak and perishable" in human nature becomes increasingly "mingled with the divinity" until it has "become that which the divinity is."[38] The Nyssen's "mingling" language specifies the moment of purified transparency as the point at which the flesh of Jesus is fully submitted to the will of God on the one hand, and most horribly subjected to the ravages of the fallen condition on the other. In other words, for the Nyssen, as for Cyril after him, it is precisely the weakness of human nature that is the means of glorification.

The Cross, then, is the concrete center of the Incarnation, because there the contingencies of the fallen world converge perfectly with the eternal will of the Father and are realized in the *pro nobis* the Son ac-

---

37. Cf. Daley, "'Heavenly Man' and 'Eternal Christ.'"
38. Gregory of Nyssa, *Ad Theophilum* (GNO 3.1, p. 127); as quoted by Daley, "Divine Transcendence and Human Transformation," p. 503.

complishes in perfect freedom. Thus Gregory can write that if one considers the mystery of Christ fully, one must see that his death was not a consequence of his being born, but rather that he was born in order to die.[39] This death is the willed mission of the Incarnate Son. On the Cross we cannot really speak in terms of the abstractions of divinity or humanity, *a* "god" or *a* "man"; rather we have to acknowledge that on the Cross hangs the Lord Jesus Christ, without remainder. He is the Crucified Lord, the eternal Son of glory.[40] The Gregorian "mingling" of natures on the Cross is not a "confusion" or a "sublation," but a concretization of language centered on the irreducible singularity of the Cross, the heart of the Son's Incarnation. In its "mingling" of all abstraction, the Cross mystically offers the perfect answer to Jesus's question at Caesarea Philippi, "But who do you say that I am?" (Matt. 16:15; Mark 8:29; Luke 9:20).[41] The total content and consequence of the Petrine reply — "You are the Christ, the Son of the living God" (Matt. 16:16) — is only fully realized at Calvary: "When you have lifted up the Son of man, then you will know that I am he" (John 8:28; cf. 12:33).

B. The Dionysian Contribution

In 519, the great non-Chalcedonian bishop and theologian Severus of Antioch invoked in support of the non-Chalcedonian cause a mysterious and

---

39. Gregory of Nyssa, *Oratio catechetica*, 32 (SC 453.284): Τάχα δ᾽ ἄν τις δι᾽ ἀκριβείας καταμαθὼν τὸ μυστήριον εὐλογώτερον εἴποι μὴ διὰ τὴν γένεσιν συμβεβηκέναι τὸν θάνατον, ἀλλὰ τὸ ἔμπαλιν τοῦ θάνατου χάριν παραληφθῆναι τὴν γένεσιν.

40. See Behr, *The Nicene Faith*, pp. 442-43: "Before the Passion . . . we are obliged to recognize a different set of properties, those pertaining to the flesh in distinction to the Word. But the reason why this does not force us into proclaiming two Christs is because of the transformation wrought through the Passion. It is, then, with respect to the crucified one that we affirm his unity as the one Lord Christ, the very Word of God. As Gregory [of Nyssa] explains: 'We say that he who was highly exalted from the Passion was made Lord and Christ by his union with him who is truly Lord and Christ, knowing from what we have learnt that the divine nature is always one and the same and in the same manner, while the flesh in itself is that which reason and sense apprehend concerning it, yet mixed with the divine it no longer remains in its own limitations and properties, but is taken up to that which prevails and is transcendent' [*Contra Eunomium* (GNO 2, p. 130)]."

41. Cf. John Behr, *The Way to Nicaea*, vol. 1 of *The Formation of Christian Theology* (Crestwood, NY: Saint Vladimir's Seminary Press, 2001), pp. 50-53; John Behr, *The Mystery of Christ: Life in Death* (Crestwood, NY: Saint Vladimir's Seminary Press, 2006), pp. 21-28.

heretofore unknown text of apparently near-apostolic authority: the *Epistula 4* of the *Corpus Areopagiticum*.[42]

Claiming to cite the work of Denys the Areopagite, a convert of the apostle Paul (cf. Acts 17:23), Severus quoted this Denys as formulating "one theandric nature" (μία φύσις θεανδρική) of the Incarnate Logos.[43] In 532, the same Denys was invoked again by non-Chalcedonian bishops in support of their rejection of Chalcedon at a colloquy between Chalcedonians and non-Chalcedonians held at the imperial palace in Constantinople. The specific text of Denys quoted at the colloquy is not known, though we can presume it was the same passage of *Epistula 4* quoted by Severus.[44] The *Epistula* was cited a third time in 633, this time by the Patriarch Cyrus of Alexandria in his *Pact of Union*, which aimed at reconciling Chalcedonians and non-Chalcedonians around the idea of the unity of Christ's energy.[45] This time, Denys was quoted as acknowledging in Christ "one theandric activity" (μία θεανδρικὴ ἐνέργεια).

42. Ronald F. Hathaway, *Hierarchy and the Definition of Order in the Letters of Pseudo-Dionysius: A Study in the Form and Meaning of the Pseudo-Dionysian Writings* (The Hague: Nijhoff, 1969), p. 4. On Denys, see Andrew Louth, *Denys the Areopagite* (London: Continuum, 2001); Alexander Golitzin, "'Suddenly, Christ': The Place of Negative Theology in the Mystagogy of Dionysius Areopagite," in Michael Kessler and Christian Shepherd, eds., *Mystics: Presence and Aporia* (Chicago: University of Chicago Press, 2003), pp. 8-37; Alexander Golitzin, *Mystagogy: A Monastic Reading of Dionysius Areopagita*, ed. Bogdan G. Bucur (Kalamazoo, MI: Cistercian Publications, 2013); William Riordan, *Divine Light: The Theology of Denys the Areopagite* (San Francisco: Ignatius Press, 2008); Charles M. Stang, *Apophasis and Pseudonymity in Dionysius the Areopagite: "No Longer I"* (Oxford: OUP, 2012); and finally, the essays collected in Sarah Coakley and Charles M. Stang, eds., *Re-Thinking Dionysius the Areopagite* (Oxford: Wiley-Blackwell, 2008).

43. Severus of Antioch, *Doctrina patrum de incarnatione Verbi*, 309.15-310.12. For an English translation of the letter, see Pauline Allen and C. T. R. Hayward, *Severus of Antioch*, ECF (London: Routledge, 2004), pp. 152-53.

44. On the colloquy of 532 and the Severan non-Chalcedonian Churches, see Joseph Lebon, *Le monophysisme sévérien: étude historique, littéraire et théologique sur la résistance monophysite au Concile de Chalcédoine jusqu'à la constitution de l'Église jacobite* (Leuven: J. Van Linthout, 1909); W. H. C. Frend, *The Rise of the Monophysite Movement* (Cambridge: CUP, 1972); Elias Tsonievsky, "The Union of the Two Natures in Christ according to the Non-Chalcedonian Churches and Orthodoxy," *The Greek Orthodox Theological Review* 13 (1968): 170-80; V. C. Samuel, *The Council of Chalcedon Re-Examined* (New York: Xlibris, 2001); John Meyendorff, *Christ in Eastern Christian Thought* (Crestwood, NY: Saint Vladimir's Seminary Press, 1975), pp. 47-68; John Meyendorff, *Imperial Unity and Christian Divisions* (Crestwood, NY: Saint Vladimir's Seminary Press, 1989), pp. 221-30.

45. For a partial English translation of this text, see P. Verghese, "The Monothelite Controversy — A Historical Survey," *Greek Orthodox Theological Review* 13 (1968), pp. 198-200.

The Dionysian text, as it has come down to us, says nothing of the Severan "one" (μία), but rather declares in Christ a "new theandric activity" (καινὴ θεανδρικὴ ἐνέργεια).[46] There is debate as to whether Severus and the non-Chalcedonians misquoted the text in order to bolster their own case, or whether John Scythopoli (c. 536-550), the first Chalcedonian defender of Denys, glossed "new" (καινή) in place of "one" (μία), presumably to suppress heretical suspicion from the text. Whatever one concludes, there is near consensus that the mysterious author likely comes from the circle of Severus, that he received a similar education to Severus, that he was likely a monk of the non-Chalcedonian Syrian milieu, and that it may be that Severus well knew who he was.[47] As Andrew Louth notes, one detail of the *Corpus* that fixes the mysterious author firmly in the non-Chalcedonian world of Severan Christianity is his account of the liturgy in *De ecclesiastica hierarchia*.[48] At the beginning of the sixth century when the *Corpus* first came to light, the singing of the *Credo* in the liturgy had not yet been taken up in the Latin or Greek liturgies of the imperial Church. It was a peculiarity of non-Chalcedonian liturgies in which, following Peter the Fuller, the *Credo* was introduced in the Liturgy in 473 as a protest against the supposed "innovation" of *Definitio fidei*.[49] In *De ecclesiastica hierarchia*

---

46. Denys the Areopagite, *Epistula* 4 (PG 3.1072c).

47. Sarah Klitenic Wear and John Dillon, *Dionysius the Areopagite and the Neoplatonist Tradition: Despoiling the Hellenes* (Aldershot: Ashgate, 2007), pp. 1-4. On the Syrian-monastic roots of Denys, see Alexander Golitzin, *Et introibo ad altare dei: The Mystagogy of Dionysius the Areopagite* (Thessalonica: Patriarchal Institute of Patristic Studies, 1994), pp. 349-92, and "Hierarchy versus Anarchy? Dionysius Areopagita, Symeon the New Theologian, Nicetas Stethatos, and Their Common Roots in Ascetical Tradition," *St. Vladimir's Theological Quarterly* 38 (1994): 131-79; Paul Rorem and John C. Lamoreaux, "John of Scythopolis on Apollinarian Christology and the Pseudo-Areopagite's True Identity," *Church History* 62 (1993): 469-82. For the most important dissenting voice to the otherwise consensus view that the mysterious Denys is of Syrian origin, see István Perczel, "The Christology of Pseudo-Dionysius the Areopagite: The Fourth Letter in Its Indirect and Direct Text Traditions," *Le Muséon* 117 (2004): 409-46. Although I disagree with Perczel, he has argued persuasively. In the first place he demonstrates (and on this I fully agree) that even without the specifications of Scythopoli and Maximus there is no hint of heretical "monophysitism" in *Epistula* 4. He then argues (and here I am not persuaded) that the doctrine of *Epistula* 4 is dyophysite without reserve and indebted not to Severan influence but to the influence of Theodore of Mopsuestia.

48. Louth, *Denys the Areopagite*, p. 14.

49. See Hugh Wybrew, *The Orthodox Liturgy: The Development of the Eucharistic Liturgy in the Byzantine Rite* (Crestwood, NY: Saint Vladimir's Seminary Press, 1990), pp. 84-85; Gregory Dix, *The Shape of the Liturgy*, New Edition (London: Continuum, 2005), p. 486.

Denys recounts, after the exit of the catechumens, what can only be the singing of the *Credo* before the celebration of the Eucharistic rite proper.[50]

The Dionysian *Corpus* in itself is not primarily Christological, at least not in a doctrinal sense. In essence, it is concerned with the liturgical order of the cosmos and the Church from a concretely monastic point of view. But in the doctrine of the theandric Christ, the *Corpus* did make a lasting contribution to dogmatic Christology. According to *Epistula* 4:

> [Christ] was not a man, not as though he were not a man at all, but as one come from among men, being beyond men, he has truly become a man in a way that surpasses humanity. And for the rest, he neither does divine things divinely (κατὰ θεόν) nor human things humanly (κατὰ ἄνθροπον), but as God made man, he manifested a certain new theandric energy (καινήν τινα τὴν θεανδρικὴν ἐνέργειαν), as he lived amongst us.[51]

This brief Christological formulation is consonant with the *descensus de caelis* of Nicaea: this one Lord Jesus is not "a man" (*homo assumptus*), he is a "being beyond men" who has "truly become a man" in a way that "surpasses humanity." What "surpasses humanity" is not that he is a superman, a man with noticeably more "human power," but rather lies in the fact of who he is: he is not "from among men." And so, when this human being acts, because who he is "is" divine, he does divine things humanly and human things divinely. As Louth notes, it is hard not to hear in this doctrine an explicit, if subtle, reproof of the Tome of Leo the Great.[52]

According to Leo, as we noted in the previous chapter, the Word performs what is proper to the Word (*verbo scilicet operante quod Verbi est*) while the flesh accomplishes what belongs to the flesh (*carne exequente quod carnis est*).[53] For Denys it is precisely the opposite: the Incarnate

---

50. Denys the Areopagite, *De ecclesiastica hierarchia* 3.2 (PG 3.425c) and 3.3.7 (PG 3.436c-d).

51. Denys the Areopagite, *Epistula* 4 (PG 3.1072b-c). For an English translation of the *Corpus Dionysiacum*, see *Pseudo-Dionysius: The Complete Works*, trans. Colm Luibheid (New York: Paulist Press, 1987). The translation here is Louth's, but slightly modified (*Denys the Areopagite*, p. 75). Elsewhere, unless otherwise noted, I have followed Luibheid's translation.

52. Louth, *Denys the Areopagite*, p. 75.

53. *Epistula Papae Leonis ad Flavianum* (DS 294; DEC 1.79): "Agit enim utraque forma cum alterius communione quod proprium est: Verbo scilicet operante quod Verbi est, et carne exequente quod carnis est. Unum horum coruscat miraculis, aliud succumbit injuriis."

Logos "neither does divine things divinely nor human things humanly."[54] Every tidy parallelism of human and divine action is undermined by the "new theandric energy" of Christ.[55] By this formulation, Denys specifies the traditional doctrine of *communicatio idiomatum* as entailing an ontological inversion.

The significance of the Dionysian formulation should not be underplayed, nor should it be understood as narrowly aimed at Chalcedonian Christology (and especially the Tome). As Adam Cooper has noted, even while Severus of Antioch radically stressed the one subject of Christ and rejected what he took as the Nestorian compromise of Chalcedon; nevertheless, like Leo, he tended to speak of Christ doing miracles "divinely" and suffering "humanly."[56] In other words, the same parallelism that marred some of the formulations in Leo's Tome can also be found in Severan Christology. In this light, the Dionysian doctrine of the theandric Christ makes a contribution across the Chalcedonian–non-Chalcedonian divide. The differentiated-unity of Christ, according to the Dionysian doctrine, entails an inversion of divinity and humanity that plays out on the level of energy (ἐνέργεια), such that we must identify the most human activity of Christ as "divine" at the highest pitch, while his divine action is "human" in its integral fullness. This inversion is precisely what Gregory of Nyssa was moved to articulate a century before in his theology of the mingling of divinity and humanity on the Cross.

But if Denys's doctrine of the theandric Christ is built on a rebuke of the lingering parallelism internal to Leo's Tome, Louth suggests that "Denys's insistence on the newness of Christ's theandric activity could be held to echo Leo's stress on the 'new order' [*novus ordo*], the 'new birth' [*nova nativitas*], of the incarnation."[57] And this seems to be precisely what the *novus ordo* signifies according to Leo: the new mode of being and action that results from the Son's coming down from heaven, by which he enters the weakness and poverty of this world without leaving the Father's

---

54. Denys the Areopagite, *Epistula* 4 (PG 3.1072b-c).

55. Cf. Denys the Areopagite, *Epistula* 4 (PG 3.1072c).

56. Adam G. Cooper, *The Body in St. Maximus the Confessor: Holy Flesh, Wholly Deified* (Oxford; OUP, 2005), p. 48. Cf. Jaroslav Pelikan, *The Christian Tradition: A History of the Development of Doctrine*, vol. 1, *The Emergence of the Catholic Tradition (100-600)* (Chicago: University of Chicago Press, 1975), p. 273.

57. Louth, *Denys the Areopagite*, p. 75. Cf. *Epistula Papae Leonis ad Flavianum* (DS 294; DEC 1.79).

glory.[58] According to Leo, it is from this logic of the Incarnation that the catholicity of the Church lives and grows: by the profession that in the one Jesus Christ, "neither humanity is without true divinity nor divinity without true humanity."[59]

If Louth is right that the "new theandric energy" of Denys gestures to the *novus ordo* of Leo, then the convertibility of the respective doctrines of Leo and Denys lies concretely in the way that, for both, the subjective unity of Christ is rooted in the *descensus de caelis* in a way that forecloses *homo assumptus*. Christ is not a *purus homo*, he is the *novus homo* who unleashes a new mode of being human in which the integrity of human nature is not compromised but enhanced (*augere*). What Christ achieves in the new integrity of human nature discovered in his theandric energy is a crucial inversion: divine things are done humanly and human things are done divinely. All of this finally specifies nothing other than the Christological insight of Cyril, who staked salvation precisely on the theandric inversion of the Cross: "If he conquered as God, to us it is nothing; but if he conquered as man we conquered in him."[60]

58. *Epistula Papae Leonis ad Flavianum* (DS 294; DEC 1.79): "Ingreditur ergo haec mundi infirma [DEC here has *infima*] Filius Dei, de caelesti sede descendens et a paterna gloria non recedens, novo ordine, nova nativitate generatus."

59. *Epistula Papae Leonis ad Flavianum* (DEC 1.81): "quia catholica ecclesia hac fide vivit, hac proficit, ut nec sine vera divinitate humanitas nec sine vera credatur humanitate divinitas."

60. Cyril of Alexandria, *In Ioannis Evangelium*, 16.33, (ed. Pusey, 2.656-57; PG 74.473d).

CHAPTER 5

Theopaschism

[N]either is the human nature of Christ ever spoken of in its own, nor did it possess its own hypostasis or person, but it received the beginning of existence in the hypostasis of the Word.

Justinian

A. The Doctrine of "Enhypostatos"

In Christ, divinity and humanity are "so related" that the humanity of Jesus "is" only insofar as it is "in the mode of existence of the eternal Word of God."[1] This is the way the Swiss Reformed theologian Karl Barth expressed — and resourced to modern theology — the doctrine of "enhypostatos."[2] According to Barth, the substance of the doctrine was "erected into dogma at the Second Council of Constantinople in 553 . . . to guard against the idea of a double existence of Christ as Logos and as Man."[3]

1. Karl Barth, *Church Dogmatics*, I/2, *The Doctrine of the Word of God*, trans. G. T. Thompson and Harold Knight, ed. G. W. Bromiley and T. F. Torrance (Edinburgh: T&T Clark, 1956), pp. 163-65.

2. On Barth's doctrine of "enhypostatos", see Bruce L. McCormack, *Karl Barth's Critically Realistic Dialectical Theology: Its Genesis and Development, 1909-1936* (Oxford: OUP, 1995), pp. 327-74. On the development of the doctrine of "enhypostatos," see Benjamin Gleede, *The Development of the Term* ἐνυπόστατος *from Origen to John of Damascus* (Leiden: Brill, 2012).

3. Barth, *Church Dogmatics*, I/2, p. 163. Cf. CCC 468: "After the Council of Chalcedon, some made of Christ's human nature a kind of personal subject. Against them, the fifth ecumenical council, at Constantinople in 553, confessed that 'there is but one hypostasis, which is our Lord Jesus Christ, one of the Trinity'. Thus *everything in Christ's human nature is to be attributed to his divine person as its proper subject*, not only his miracles but also his sufferings and even his death: 'He who was crucified in the flesh, our Lord Jesus Christ, is

In fact, as Barth well knew, the specific language of "enhypostatos" appears nowhere in the *Acta* of Constantinople II. Nevertheless, the Council's strongly unitive single-subject Christology, which bears to the point of explicit attribution to one of the Holy Trinity the whole scandal of the Cross, upholds what Barth made central to his Christology in the early volumes of the *Kirchliche Dogmatik*. Barth's doctrine specifies Chalcedon in precisely the manner recommended by the Pian limit of 1951, according to which Christ's human nature does not exist in its own right (*sui iuris*), but only as it subsists in the Word itself (*in ipsius Verbi persona subsistat*).[4] To express this Barth exploited the *theologoumenon* of *anhypostasis* — *enhypostasis*, which designated for him the negative and positive sides of one Christological doctrine. As Barth famously articulated the doctrine:

> *Anhypostasis* asserts the negative. Since in virtue of the ἐγένετο, i.e., in virtue of the *assumptio*, Christ's human nature has its existence — the ancients said, its subsistence — in the existence of God, meaning in the mode of being (*hypostasis*, "person") of the Word, it does not possess it in and for itself, *in abstracto*. Apart from the divine mode of being whose existence it acquires it has none of its own; i.e., apart from its concrete existence in God in the event of the *unio*, it had no existence of its own, it is ἀνυπόστατος. *Enhypostasis* asserts the positive. In virtue of the ἐγένετο i.e., in virtue of the *assumptio*, the human nature acquires existence (subsistence) in the existence of God, meaning in the mode of being (*hypostasis*, "person") of the Word. This divine mode of being gives it existence in the event of the *unio*, and in this way it has a concrete existence of its own, it is ἐνυπόστατος.[5]

With precision, Barth renovated to theology the reality of how the human life of Christ simply "is" the human mode of existence of the divine Son's filiation.[6] Crucial here is the function of *anhypostasis*, which

---

true God, Lord of glory, and one of the Holy Trinity' [*Anathematismi adversus "tria Capitula*,"* canon 10 (DS 432; DEC 1.118)]." Emphases are mine.

4. Pope Pius XII, *Sempiternus Rex*, 30-31 (DS 3905).

5. Barth, *Church Dogmatics*, I/2, p. 163.

6. On Barth's contribution and the doctrine generally, see Ivor J. Davidson, "Theologizing the Human Jesus: An Ancient (and Modern) Approach to Christology Reassessed," *International Journal of Systematic Theology* 3 (2001): 129-53, and "Reappropriating Patristic Christology: One Doctrine, Two Styles," *Irish Theological Quarterly* 67 (2002): 225-39. I have relied greatly on these two texts.

dismisses every possibility of Jesus existing as a human being independent of the divine act of the Logos. In his *Unterricht in der christlichen Religion*, where Barth first expounded the doctrine, Barth could declare that those "who want to see revelation in the idea of humanity as such are grasping at something that in itself is not just meaningless but nonexistent."[7] Barth thus wanted, with the negative side of the *theologoumenon*, to close the door decisively on every *homo assumptus* construal of the union: "those who seek revelation in Jesus as a human individual . . . are . . . groping in the void."[8] The only way to grasp who Jesus is is to recognize him as the one who came down "from above." Just as it is not "flesh and blood" that leads Peter to proclaim that Jesus is "the Christ, the Son of the living God" (Matt. 16:16), but rather a revelation descending from the "Father who is in heaven" (Matt. 16:17), so for Barth "anhypostatos" functions to foreclose every *separatio* of the very idea of humanity from its union with the Logos in whom the *verus homo* is constituted.[9]

All this notwithstanding, "enhypostatos" also functions positively, specifying for Barth that the Logos is truly "one" with the fragility and contingency of the human life of Jesus. This means that the most cripplingly finite moments of Jesus's life — the powerlessness of the infant sucking at his mother's breast, the child needing to grow in wisdom and stature, the lost boy found in the Temple, the fear-stricken Jew in prayer at Gethsemane, the wounded king humiliated before Pilate, the abandoned Son pinned to the Cross — the very possibility of all of this finitude, is contingent on the perfect unity of this human nature with the Logos, which constitutes the being and existence of this man.

The importance of Barth's contribution, as Ivor Davidson argues, is to have recalled a way of "speaking of the actuality of the entrance of the divine subject into the conditions of creaturely time and space" in such a way that "the divine Word is present in the frailty and obscurity of human life."[10] When the two sides of the *theologoumenon* are put together (the ἐν- prefix coupled with the privative alpha ἀν-), Barth is able to uphold the "infinite qualitative distinction" between God and man, the *maior dis-*

---

7. Karl Barth, *The Göttingen Dogmatics: Instruction in the Christian Religion*, trans. G. W. Bromiley (Grand Rapids: Eerdmans, 1991), p. 157.

8. Barth, *The Göttingen Dogmatics*, p. 157.

9. On this, see Karl Barth, *The Humanity of God*, trans. John Newton Thomas (Richmond: John Knox Press, 1960). Cf. Stanley Hauerwas, *With the Grain of the Universe: The Church's Witness and Natural Theology* (Grand Rapids: Brazos Press, 2001), pp. 147-72.

10. Davidson, "Theologizing the Human Jesus," p. 142.

similitudo, while nevertheless affirming the utter *unitas* of the man Jesus with the divine Logos: "This *man, this* man (we must emphasize both), is God himself who reveals God himself, who by God himself is revealed as God himself."[11]

Barth proposed his doctrine of "enhypostatos" as "unanimously sponsored by early theology in its entirety."[12] However, the *anhypostasis — enhypostasis* couplet appears nowhere in the Fathers. This, coupled with the fact that the language of "enhypostatos" does not appear at all in the *Acta* of Constantinople II, has cast doubt on the patristic and conciliar pedigrees Barth claims for his doctrine.[13] In addition, while for a long time "enhypostatos" was associated with Leontius of Byzantium, patristic scholarship has now shown that this association was based on a mistaken conflation of Leontius of Byzantium with his contemporary namesake, Leontius of Jerusalem.[14] All of this has contributed to a certain discrediting of the doctrine among patristic scholars.[15] According to these schol-

---

11. Barth, *The Göttingen Dogmatics*, p. 153; emphases are Barth's.

12. Barth, *Church Dogmatics*, I/2, p. 163.

13. See F. LeRon Shults, "A Dubious Christological Formula: from Leontius of Byzantium to Karl Barth," *Theological Studies* 57 (1996): 431-46.

14. The misunderstanding derives from Friedrich Loofs's work, *Leontius von Byzanz und die gleichnamigen Schriftsteller der griechischen Kirche* in *Texte und Untersuchungen* 3, ed. Oskar von Gebhardt and Adolf von Harnack (Leipzig: J.C. Hinrich'sche Buchhandlung, 1887). On Leontius of Byzantium's Christology, see Brian E. Daley, S.J., "Nature and the 'Mode of Union': Late Patristic Models for the Personal Unity of Christ," in Stephen T. Davis, Daniel Kendall, S.J., and Gerald O'Collins, S.J., eds., *The Incarnation: An Interdisciplinary Symposium on the Incarnation of the Son of God* (Oxford: OUP, 2002), pp. 164-96, and Brian E. Daley, S.J., "'A Richer Union': Leontius of Byzantium and the Relationship of Human and Divine in Christ," *Studia Patristica* 24 (1939): 239-65; Aloys Grillmeier, S.J., with Theresia Hainthaler, *Christ in Christian Tradition*, vol. 2, *From the Council of Chalcedon (451) to Gregory the Great (590–604)*, pt. 2, *The Church of Constantinople in the Sixth Century*, trans. Pauline Allen and John Cawte (Louisville: Westminster John Knox Press, 1995), pp. 181-225. On the way Leontius of Byzantium's Christology contributed to the Council of Constantinople II, see Leo Donald Davis, S.J., *The First Seven Ecumenical Councils (325-787): Their History and Theology* (Collegeville: The Liturgical Press, 1983), pp. 230-40. For a rather contrary view of Leontius as an "Origenist," see John Meyendorff, *Christ in Eastern Christian Thought* (Crestwood, NY: Saint Vladimir's Seminary Press, 1975), pp. 51-68; David Evans, *Leontius of Byzantium: An Origenist Christology* (Washington, DC: Dumbarton Oaks, 1970). On Leontius of Jerusalem, see Grillmeier, *Christ in Christian Tradition*, vol. 2, pt. 2, pp. 271-321; Dirk Krausmüller, "Leontius of Jerusalem, A Theologian of the Seventh Century," *The Journal of Theological Studies* 52 (2001): 637-57; Patrick T. R. Gray, ed., *Leontius of Jerusalem: Against the Monophysites: Testimonies of the Saints and Aporiae* (Oxford: OUP, 2006).

15. See Brian E. Daley, S.J., "'A Richer Union'; Anhypostasie," in J.-Y. Lacoste, ed., *Dic-*

ars, when the Fathers use the term "enhypostatos" to describe Christ's human nature, the deployment of the prefix "en" (ἐν-) is not intended as a localizing prefix (to signify *in*-hypostatic), but simply signifies the opposite of the privative alpha (ἀν-) of "anhypostatos." For these scholars, then, "enhypostatos" simply means "real": Christ's human nature really "is." The doctrine of the subsistence of the human nature of Christ *in* the hypostasis of the Son of God (as if "*in*-personed" by the Son), far from having a patristic origin, is said to be a unique contribution of Protestant Scholasticism, where the *anhypostasis — enhypostasis* couplet appears explicitly for the first time.[16]

A number of contemporary theologians have begun resourcing the doctrine of enhypostatos beyond the terminological rigorism of patrology, challenging the coherence of the doctrine's recent dismissal.[17] Even while the *anhypostasis — enhypostasis* couplet cannot be found *verbatim* in the Fathers, and while Leontius of Byzantium is not the author of the doctrine as it was once supposed,[18] the theology implied by the term "enhypostatos," in the sense of the "in-personed" or "in-existent" humanity of the Logos, does have a firm grounding in the paleo-Christian

---

tionnaire critique de Théologie (Paris: PUF, 1998), pp. 50-51; Grillmeier, *Christ in Christian Tradition*, vol. 2, pt. 2, pp. 282-86; Andrew Louth, *St. John Damascene: Tradition and Originality in Byzantine Theology* (Oxford: OUP, 2002), p. 161.

16. Barth found it in the Protestant Scholastic manual of Heinrich Heppe, *Schriften zur Reformierten Theologie* (Elberfeld: Friderichs, 1860).

17. U. M. Lang, "Anhypostatos — Enhypostatos: Church Fathers, Protestant Orthodoxy and Karl Barth," *Journal of Theological Studies* 49 (1998): 630-57; Matthias Gockel, "A Dubious Christological Formula? Leontius of Byzantium and the *Anhypostasis — Enhypostasis* Theory," *Journal of Theological Studies* 51 (2000): 515-32; Dennis Ferrara, "'Hypostatized in the Logos': Leontius of Byzantium, Leontius of Jerusalem and the Unfinished Business of the Council of Chalcedon," *Louvain Studies* 22 (1997): 311-27; Philip McCosker, "Parsing Paradox, Analysing 'And': Christological Configurations of Theological Paradox in Some Mystical Theologies" (PhD Thesis: Cambridge University, 2008), pp. 137-62. Most recently, see Gleede, *The Development of the Term* ἐνυπόστατος, esp. pp. 45-138.

18. Leontius of Byzantium did, however, use the language in the opening of *Contra Nestorianos et Eutychianos* (see 1 [PG 86.1277c-d]). Nevertheless, Gleede argues that the language does not contribute to Leontius's Christology and that Leontius does not advance anything like that which has been received in the form of the doctrine that goes by that name (see Gleede, *The Development of the Term* ἐνυπόστατος, pp. 61-69). Although, cf. Richard Cross, "Individual Natures in the Christology of Leontius of Byzantium," *Journal of Early Christian Studies* 10 (2002): 245-65, where it is persuasively argued that Loofs's conflation of the Leontii notwithstanding, his articulation of the theology of Leontius of Byzantium is not nearly as distorted as many have supposed.

tradition.[19] Moreover, among the Fathers from at least the sixth century, the adjectives *anhypostatos* and *enhypostatos* are widely used (if not in couplet form) to describe how it is that the human nature of Jesus has no reality of its own, but rather subsists exclusively in the hypostasis of the Logos.[20]

The concrete root of the Christological doctrine of "enhypostatos," if not the language, is fully found in Cyril of Alexandria.[21] According to Cyril, the Logos united himself "hypostatically" (καθ᾽ ὑπόστασιν) with the human nature, such that this first-century Palestinian-Jew is the one Lord, Christ and Son, the only-begotten of the Father. This means that the human nature of Jesus does not have its own "hypostasis" and so does not "exist" as a separate human being. The divine Son is himself the singular "existent" of the human Jesus. The Logos is the hypostasis of this human nature, while this human nature is the human nature of the Logos.[22] The doctrine is found, moreover, in John Cassian, who stipulates that the human nature of Christ was at no point instantiated before the Incarnation, "Neither was there any time when that man was without God, since he received from God the very fact that he existed."[23] Cassian and Cyril together confirm the dogmatic legitimacy of all that is intended by the doctrine and language of "enhypostatos." They do so, however, inchoately and without using to Christological effect the language of "enhypostatos."

The first theologian to give Christological prominence to the language of "enhypostatos" is John the Grammarian of Caesarea (early sixth century).[24] The Grammarian developed his use of the language of "enhypostatos" in the context of a Cyrillian defense of Chalcedon against Severus of Antioch. Severus's argument, in opposition to the dyophysitism of Chalcedon, consisted in the claim that there is no nature without hypostasis; therefore to say that Christ is "one" in hypostasis is to say that he is "one nature." Re-

---

19. Gleede, *The Development of the Term* ἐνυπόστατος, pp. 45-138.

20. Davidson, "Reappropriating Patristic Christology," p. 227.

21. Davidson, "Theologizing the Human Jesus," p. 139. Cf. Gleede, *The Development of the Term* ἐνυπόστατος, pp. 38-41.

22. Cf. John McGuckin, *Saint Cyril of Alexandria and the Christological Controversy* (Crestwood, NY: Saint Vladimir's Seminary Press), p. 170, n. 88, and pp. 212-16.

23. John Cassian, *De Incarnatione Christi contra Nestorium* 2.7 (PL 50.49a): "Neque enim umquam sine Deo fuerat homo ille, qui utique, hoc ipsum quod erat, a Deo acceperat."

24. See Lang, "Anhypostatos — Enhypostatos," *passim*; Demetrios Bathrellos, *The Byzantine Christ: Person, Nature, and Will in the Christology of Saint Maximus the Confessor* (Oxford: OUP, 2005), pp. 37-54; Gleede, *The Development of the Term* ἐνυπόστατος, pp. 38-41.

plying to Severus, the Grammarian argued that the human nature of Jesus is united enhypostatically (ἐνυποστάτως) with the hypostasis of the Logos according to the formula "henosis enhypostatos" (ἕνωσις ἐνυπόστατος). According to Uwe Michael Lang, the new terminology of the Grammarian adds little theologically to Cyril's doctrine of the hypostatic union (ἕνωσις καθ' ὑπόστασιν);[25] nevertheless,

> Although the term *enhypostatos* in John's usage primarily means "having a concrete existence," it is implied that a common nature or substance always exists as being individualized *in* a hypostasis. It is the peculiarity of the incarnation that the ensouled flesh is taken up into the hypostasis of the Son of God and is so given individual existence in a unique manner.[26]

After the Grammarian, Leontius of Jerusalem (*c.* 485–c. 543) took up the language of "enhypostatos" with a slight innovation.[27] For Leontius, if the divinity and humanity of Christ are concrete, they must be *enhypostatoi* (ἐνυπόστατοι); that is, each nature must possess an enhypostatic reality of its own. Nevertheless, these two enhypostatic realities must exist in a single hypostasis. As Leontius writes in his *Tractatus contra Nestorianos*:

> For we say that the two natures concretely exist in one and the same hypostasis, not as if one of them could exist without a hypostasis in it, but as if both could subsist in the one common hypostasis; and so each of the two is *enhypostatos* according to one and the same hypostasis.... Thus it is evident that the *enhypostaton* cannot be *heterohypostaton*, but must be thought of in one and the same hypostasis for both of them.[28]

Here to speak specifically of the enhypostatic reality of Christ's human nature is to speak in a certain way of human nature as a reality that only "subsists" or "exists" in the Logos. At the same time, the enhypostatic reality of Christ's humanity remains ambiguous, since it is hard to say how

25. Lang, "Anhypostatos — Enhypostatos," pp. 628-39.

26. Lang, "Anhypostatos — Enhypostatos," p. 640.

27. Cf. A. Michel, "Hypostase: Hypostatique (union)," in A. Vacant et al., eds., *Dictionnaire de théologie catholique*, vol. 7 (Paris: Letouzey et Ané, 1903-1950), pp. 369-568. On Leontius's contribution, see Gleede, *The Development of the Term* ἐνυπόστατος, pp. 123-38.

28. Leontius of Jerusalem [attributed wrongly to Leontius of Byzantium in Minge], *Tractatus contra Nestorianos*, 2.13 (PG 86.1561b), trans. Lang.

an enhypostatic reality is any different from the existence of the divine nature of the Logos in relation to his hypostasis, and the same ambiguity applies to the divine nature. A step beyond the ambiguity of Leontius was necessary, and this occurred in the Chalcedonian patriarch Anastasius I of Antioch (559-598).[29]

For Anastasius, it was clear that the two natures of Christ do not constitute the one hypostasis (ἐνούσιος ὑπόστασις) of the Logos; rather the hypostasis of the Logos constitutes a human nature. Anastasius is anxious, however, to say that Christ's human nature is not *anhypostatos*, which for him would denote that it has no hypostasis at all (in the sense that it would not exist). Nevertheless, for Anastasius, "the humanity of Christ has no hypostasis of its own, but subsists *in* the Logos (ὑποστᾶσα ἐν τῷ λόγῳ) ... the hypostasis of the Logos is the common hypostasis of both divinity and humanity."[30] In this way, Anastasius comes finally to use the language of "enhypostatos" to designate that the humanity of Christ has a concrete existence only insofar as that nature has been taken up into the hypostasis of the Logos. All of this anticipates the decisive contribution of John of Damascus, in whom the *theologoumenon* is maturely explicated: "as a result of the incarnation the ensouled flesh of Christ is taken up by the hypostasis of the Son of God and exists *in* it as *enhypostatos*."[31]

In the contribution of the Damascene, as Lang has shown, the definition of "enhypostatos" does not so much build on earlier Fathers but goes back to the distinction between that which is in something (τὸ ἔν τινι) and that in which it is (τὸ ἐν ᾧ).[32] This "re-starting" of the definition allows the Damascene to make a crucial specification: that which is *enhypostaton* is not identical with its hypostasis; rather it is that which is seen and is real *in* the hypostasis.[33] It is within this logic and with this explicit invocation of the language of "enhypostatos" that the Damascene defines the existence of Christ's human nature: Christ's human nature does not subsist as a proper hypostasis, it has its existence *in* the hypostasis of the Logos.[34]

---

29. Lang, "Anhypostatos — Enhypostatos," pp. 647-48; Gleede, *The Development of the Term* ἐνυπόστατος, pp. 114-22.

30. Lang, "Anhypostatos — Enhypostatos," p. 648.

31. Lang, "Anhypostatos — Enhypostatos," p. 655. Also see Gleede, *The Development of the Term* ἐνυπόστατος, pp. 162-81.

32. Lang, "Anhypostatos — Enhypostatos," p. 651.

33. John of Damascus, *Contra Jacobitas* 11 (PG 94.1441b): Ἐνυπόστατον δὲ, οὐχ ἡ ὑπόστασις, τὸ ἐν ὑποστάσει δὲ καθοπώμενον.

34. John of Damascus, *Contra Jacobitas* 79 (PG 94.1476c).

We thus arrive at the existence of something that is said to "subsist" rather than "exist."[35] And so, two centuries after Constantinople II, in the figure of John of Damascus, the doctrine presumed by Cyril and Cassian finally congealed into the precise language of "enhypostatos." The sensibility that had heretofore functioned inchoately without linguistic precision received mature formulation. As Lang puts it:

> At the heart of John Damascene's Christology there lies the *theologoume-non* that the humanity of Christ has no hypostasis of its own, since it is taken up by the hypostasis of the Logos, the second person of the Trinity, and exists *in* it. In order to denote this in-existence of the human nature, the term ἐνυπόστατος is explicitly used by Damascene.[36]

This mature formulation is stated in *De fide orthodoxa* in various places, but perhaps nowhere as clearly as in the following passage in book 3:

> For the flesh of the divine Logos did not subsist as an independent hypostasis, nor did it become a second hypostasis (ἑτέρα ὑπόστασις) alongside the hypostasis of the divine Logos (τοῦ θεοῦ λόγου ὑπόστασιν); rather it came to be by subsisting (ὑποστᾶσα) in it [the substance of the divine Logos] as an in-existence (ἐνυπόστατος), that is without its own proper hypostasis (ἰδιοσύστατος ὑπόστασις). For this reason it is neither a-hypostatic (ἀνυπόστατος) nor does it introduce another hypostasis into the Trinity.[37]

With this formulation of the Damascene, we come finally to a doctrine of "enhypostatos" that is cogent and broadly convertible with the doctrine expounded in the twentieth century by Barth.[38]

In the Damascene's formulation, the doctrine of "enhypostatos" func-

---

35. Davidson, "Theologizing the Human Jesus," p. 135.

36. Lang, "Anhypostatos — Enhypostatos," p. 654.

37. John of Damascus, *De fide orthodoxa* 3.9 (SC 540.56-58; PG 94.1009ab).

38. The one obvious difference is the way the word ἀνυπόστατος is employed. There is not necessarily any major contradiction, but when Barth uses the word within the distinction of *anhypostasis — enhypostasis,* he is specifying that the human nature of Jesus does not exist apart from its enhypostatic reality. The Damascene, on the other hand, uses the word not as a correlate to ἐνυπόστατος, but simply to designate that this human nature only exists as "enhypostatos," that is, as subsisting in the hypostasis of the Logos (which is what Barth wants to say precisely).

tions not merely as an elaboration of what was always entailed in the doctrine of the hypostatic union, but also as a concrete specification of the Constantinopolitan doctrine of the Incarnate Christ's "compound hypostasis" (ὑπόστασις σύνθετος), a formulation of originally non-Chalcedonian pedigree.[39] The Damascene makes this clear in *De fide orthodoxa* when writing of the Incarnation, as he cites the enhypostatic Wisdom and Power (ἐνυπόστατος σοφία καὶ δύναμις) in the Virgin.[40] Taking flesh and animating spirit in the womb of the Virgin, the Logos did not unite himself with a human nature that had independent preexistence before this enhypostatization, but rather, by taking the flesh of human nature, the Logos himself became flesh (αὐτὸς ὁ λόγος γενόμενος τῇ σαρκὶ ὑπόστασις).[41] The accent of the movement is descending (*descensus de caelis*). This descending union occurs precisely "without confusion or change or division" (ἀσυγχύτως καὶ ἀναλλοιώτως καὶ ἀδιαιρέτως), such that the union does not result in a "compound nature" (φύσιν σύνθετον).[42] To the contrary:

> We affirm the eternal supratemporal preexistence of the hypostasis of the Logos, simple, uncomposite and uncreated (ἀπλῆν καὶ ἀσύνθετον, ἄκτιστον). . . . [And that in the Incarnation] the previously simple hypostasis of the Logos became composite (σύνθετον), composite of two complete natures (σύνθετον δὲ ἐκ δύο τελείων φύσεων), divine and human, while nevertheless keeping the characteristic and distinctive properties of the divine filiation of the Logos, by which he is distinguished from the Father and the Spirit while also, according to the flesh, taking on the characteristic and distinctive properties that distinguish him from his Mother and all other human beings.[43]

In this light, we see that the enhypostatic foundation of the hypostatic union binds and specifies the various grammars the Damascene inherited

---

39. See the General Introduction of Richard Price, *The Acts of the Council of Constantinople of 553: With Related Texts on the Three Chapters Controversy, Edited and with an Introduction and Notes*, 2 vols. (Liverpool: Liverpool University Press, 2009), vol. 1, p. 72.

40. John of Damascus, *De fide orthodoxa* 3.2 (SC 540.14-16; PG 94.985b).

41. John of Damascus, *De fide orthodoxa* 3.2 (SC 540.16; PG 94.985c).

42. John of Damascus, *De fide orthodoxa* 3.9 (SC 540.16-18; PG 94.988a).

43. John of Damascus, *De fide orthodoxa* 3.7 (SC 540.42-44; PG 94.1009ab); as quoted and translated in Jaroslav Pelikan, *The Christian Tradition: A History of the Development of Doctrine*, vol. 2, *The Spirit of Eastern Christendom (600-1700)* (Chicago: University of Chicago Press, 1974), p. 88.

from Cyril, Chalcedon and Constantinople II. It means that Jesus is "one," he is *unus*; and this *unus* is the eternal hypostasis of the Logos, which makes possible and is the source of the difference of his human nature, his complex incarnate hypostatic reality.

If the human Christ is not a human hypostasis (or person), as Cyril, Leontius of Jerusalem, and the Damascene commonly hold, the human Christ is still "personally" human, in the sense that he incarnates "the characteristic and distinctive properties of the divine filiation of the Logos."[44] In this way we see that the doctrine of the "enhypostatos," far from compromising the integrity of the humanity of Jesus, rather "throws into maximum relief the condescension of the divine action: it is this divine Son who lives a fully human life, subject to the contingency and vulnerability of fleshly existence."[45] Here a crucial nuance is brought to bear, wherein we see that an essentially asymmetrical relation animates the Chalcedonian poles of union and difference: the *inconfusus, immutabilis* pole is established ontologically by the *indivisus, inseparabilis* pole since the former only "is" and is "real" by virtue of the latter. Divinity always takes priority in Jesus because it is the *unitas* of his person that establishes the hypostatic union and constitutes his human difference.

Thus articulated, according to the doctrine of "enhypostatos," the human nature of Jesus is derived fully from one of the Trinity in such a way that one can say with Constantinople II that one of the Trinity was crucified. The flesh of the eternal Son is irreducibly concrete: it communicates humanly through the Jewish flesh he receives from Mary the eternal mode of being of divine-filial existence. Jesus is the human "mode" of being the divine Son. In him the Logos took on a particular enfleshed relation in the world in the "mode" of his trinitarian person,[46] while, in turn, all the particularities of this first-century Jewish life are personally "one" with the eternal Son of God. The doctrine of Constantinople II in this way reminds us again that in the hypostatic union we are not dealing with the unification of abstract "natures" so much as we are dealing with the event of a personal fact, that of the Son coming to subsist within a network of enfleshed relations. In this event, the relation of Jesus to his Mother and to Israel is the human-temporal correlate to the divine-

---

44. John of Damascus, *De fide orthodoxa* 3.7 (SC 540.44; PG 94.1009b). Cf. Leontius of Byzantium, *Contra Nestorianos et Eutychianos* 2 (PG 86.1556a).

45. Davidson, "Theologizing the Human Jesus," p. 140.

46. In these comments I am indebted to conversations with Jeremy Ive.

eternal relation of the Son to the Father. The Council specifies this most basically by upholding the doctrine of the double birth of the one Son, *ex Patre* and *ex Maria*.[47]

B. *Unus ex Trinitate crucifixus est*

The *unus ex Trinitate crucifixus est* confession, solemnly declared at Constantinople II, is rooted in the theological insistence of Cyril's Twelve Chapters. The confession's more immediate origin lies with the Scythian monks. In 519, monks led by Joannes Maxentius arrived in Constantinople seeking support in a local dispute with their bishop regarding the orthodoxy of the *unus ex Trinitate crucifixus est* confession they deemed essential to apostolic faith.[48] The *Definitio*, they argued, needed to be clarified in these terms in order to safeguard the true meaning of its doctrine — on the one hand against erroneous and quasi-Nestorian interpretations of the council that purported to be "Chalcedonian," while on the other hand, against Severan and anti-Chalcedonian accusations that Chalcedon had betrayed Cyril. The Christology of the monks can be summarized in five basic points: (1) a differentiated use of the Cyrillian "mia physis" formula coupled with the acknowledgment that it serves to safeguard one-sided interpretations of dyophysitism; (2) simultaneous and interchangeable use of the "in two natures" (ἐν δύο φύσεσιν) and "out of two natures" (ἐκ δύο φύσεσιν) formulae; (3) an insistence on the confession of the Theotokos; (4) a grammar of the Incarnate Christ as *Christos synthetos* or *Christus compositus*; and (5) an insistence on their theopaschite formula: *Christus unus ex Trinitate incarnatus et passus* (or *crucifixus est*).[49]

The program of the Scythian monks was broadly taken on by the emperor Justinian (c. 482-565), whose religious policy aimed to reinforce the dogmatic continuity of Chalcedon with Cyril in order to reunite the non-

---

47. *Anathematismi adversus "tria Capitula*," canon 2 (DS 422; DEC 1.114).

48. For a translation of the text and historical background of the confession, see John A. McGuckin, "The 'Theopaschite Confession' (Text and Historical Context): A Study in the Cyrillian Reinterpretation of Chalcedon," *Journal of Ecclesiastical History* 35 (1984): 239-55. On the Scythian monks' campaign, see Henry Chadwick, *Boethius: The Consolations of Music, Logic, Theology, and Philosophy* (Oxford: Clarendon Press, 1981), pp. 185-90; Grillmeier, *Christ in Christian Tradition*, vol. 2, pt. 2, pp. 317-43.

49. Grillmeier, *Christ in Christian Tradition*, vol. 2, pt. 2, p. 321.

Chalcedonians with the imperial church. The policy of the emperor led, most importantly, to the convening of the Second Council of Constantinople in 553.[50]

Justinian himself was an astute theologian who played a key role in dogmatically defining the Christological program that would be adopted at the council he would call in 553. While he rejected "monophysitism," he was sympathetic with moderate non-Chalcedonian theology.[51] His own Christological view was elucidated in his *Edictum rectae fidei* (c. 551), a considerable work of Cyrillian and Chalcedon Christology in its own right.[52] In the *Edictum*, Justinian carefully retrieved a Cyrillian paradigm as the only valid hermeneutical key to understand the doctrine of Chalcedon. In the first place, he defined hypostatic union as follows:

> Hypostatic union means that God the Word, that is one hypostasis from the three hypostases of the divinity, was not united to a previously existent man (οὐ προϋποστάντι ἀνθρώπῳ ἡνώθη) but in the womb of the holy Virgin fashioned for himself from her in his own hypostasis flesh ensouled by a rational and intelligent soul, which is human nature.[53]

On this formulation, every tendency to a *homo assumptus* position is foreclosed by the claim that this union occurred not with any "previously existent man," but in a way that union with the Logos constituted the human nature from the womb of the Virgin itself. This means that the Incarnate is still "one of the holy Trinity" (καὶ ἔστι καὶ μετὰ τὴν ἐνανθρώπησιν εἷς

---

50. On Justinian and the background leading to Constantinople II, see Price, *Acts of the Council of Constantinople of 553*, vol. 1, pp. 1-108; Davis, *The First Seven Ecumenical Councils*, pp. 225-39; Robert Louis Wilken, *The First Thousand Years: A Global History of Christianity* (New Haven: Yale University Press, 2012), pp. 246-56. On Justinian's Christology, see Kenneth P. Wesche, *On the Person of Christ: The Christology of Emperor Justinian* (Crestwood, NY: Saint Vladimir's Seminary Press, 1991).

51. Justinian's wife, Theodora, was herself a non-Chalcedonian. She advocated in the court on behalf of the non-Chalcedonian cause, founded a non-Chalcedonian monastery in the capital, and provided shelter in the palace for persecuted non-Chalcedonians. See Lynda Garland, *Byzantine Empresses: Women and Power in Byzantium, AD 527–1204* (London: Routledge, 1999); Robert Browning, *Justinian and Theodora* (London: Thames & Hudson, 1987).

52. Justinian, *Confessio rectae fidei* (PG 86.993c-1035b); English Translation: "Edict *On the Orthodox Faith*," in Price, ed., *Acts of the Council of Constantinople of 553*, vol. 1, pp. 129-59. All the translations of Justinian's text are from Price with some light modification.

53. Justinian, *Confessio rectae fidei* (PG 86a.997b).

τῆς ἁγίας τριάδος), yet the Incarnate hypostasis can be recognized, from the point of view of his humanity, as a "composite from both natures" (σύνθετος ἐξ ἑκατέρας φύσεως).[54]

This "compound hypostasis" (ὑπόστασις σύνθετος) of the Incarnate Logos does not change the fact that he is one of the Holy Trinity; it rather specifies that there are now two natures that are constituted by one hypostatic reality. In the unity of this "compound hypostasis," Jesus is both consubstantial with the Father and consubstantial with our fallen humanity. The correct way, then, for Justinian to talk about the union in Christ using the language of "compounded hypostasis" is to talk about two natures united in one hypostasis; this one hypostasis is the Son of God, "different from the Father in hypostasis but identical with him in nature," who constitutes for himself in the Incarnation a human nature.[55] What this entails is clear:

> Neither is the human nature of Christ ever spoken of on its own, nor did it possess its own hypostasis or person, but it received the beginning of its existence in the hypostasis of the Word.[56]

In this way, the doctrine of the hypostatic union entails a "single composite hypostasis of God the Logos" (μίαν ὑπόστασιν τοῦ Θεοῦ λόγου σύνθετον).[57] This means that *this* human being has no existence apart from the hypostatic fact of being one of the Holy Trinity, and so everything in Christ's human nature, including his death on the Cross, must be attributed to his divine hypostasis (the Logos), the unique and proper subject of everything Jesus did and all that befell him. Without using the language of "enhypostatos" (ἐνυπόστατος), the *Edictum* of Justinian fully articulated the doctrine that would be later specified by that language,[58] and in so doing, moreover, he prepared the dogmatic lineaments of the council he would call in 553.

---

54. Justinian, *Confessio rectae fidei* (PG 86a.999b-c).
55. Justinian, *Confessio rectae fidei* (PG 86a.1009d-1011a).
56. Justinian, *Confessio rectae fidei* (PG 86a.1011b): οὔτε γὰρ ἡ ἀνθρωπίνη φύσις τοῦ Χριστοῦ ἁπλῶς ποτε λέγεται, ἀλλ᾽ οὔτε ἰδίαν ὑπόστασιν ἤτοι πρόσωπον ἔσχεν, ἀλλ᾽ ἐν τῇ ὑποστάσει τοῦ λόγου τὴν ἀρχὴν τῆς ὑπάρξεως ἔλαβεν.
57. Justinian, *Confessio rectae fidei* (PG 86a.1011a).
58. See Gleede, *The Development of the Term* ἐνυπόστατος.

C. The Three Chapters

The principal dogmatic issue before the Council Fathers at Constantinople II was to resolve the controversy over the Three Chapters: (1) the anti-Cyrillian writings of Theodore of Cyrrhus; (2) the Letter of Ibas of Edessa to Mari the Persian; and (3) the writings and person of Theodore of Mopsuestia. Justinian hoped that a definitive condemnation of these Three Chapters by an Ecumenical Council that included the participation of the Roman Pontiff would clear the way to the reconciliation of the non-Chalcedonians with the imperial Church.[59]

Underpinning the controversy was the ambivalent dogmatic status of Cyril's Third Letter to Nestorius, and in particular the Twelve Chapters appended to it. Chalcedon had decisively "approved the conciliar letters of the blessed Cyril, then shepherd over the Church of Alexandria, to Nestorius and to the Eastern [bishops]."[60] But what specifically were these "conciliar letters"? Clearly they included Cyril's Second Letter to Nestorius, which had been solemnly read and approved at the first session of Chalcedon.[61] The letter "to the Eastern [bishops]," could be none other than Cyril's *Laetentur caeli,* by which he and John of Antioch were reconciled in the *Formula unionis* of 433; it too had been solemnly read and approved at the Council's first session.[62] But what was the dogmatic status of Cyril's Third Letter to Nestorius and its Twelve Chapters? While it had been approved at Ephesus in 531, its status after the *Formula* of 433 was not clear. In 433, Cyril and John both seem to have judged it a matter of prudence not to raise the question of the Chapters directly. At Chalcedon, the Third Letter was not read, and was referred to only once, when Leo's Tome was being examined and Atticus of Nicopolis urged that the Tome's orthodoxy be measured by

---

59. A key background event was a meeting in 532 in Constantinople between Justinian and a group of non-Chalcedonian leaders. Trying to move beyond the old question of whether Chalcedon had followed Cyril or not, Justinian asked the non-Chalcedonians what they found objectionable besides the formula "in two natures." Their answer was that, while there were many other things to censure, the most disturbing fact of the Council was its reception of Ibas and Theodoret. On this, see Sebastian Brock, "The Conversations with the Syrian Orthodox under Justinian, 523," *Orientalia Christiana Periodica* 47 (1981): 87-121.

60. *Definitio fidei* (DS 300; DEC 85).

61. Chalcedon, Session I, 239-240 (ed. Richard Price and Michael Gaddis, *The Acts of the Council of Chalcedon: Translated with an Introduction and Notes,* 3 vols. [Liverpool: Liverpool University Press, 2005], vol. 1, pp. 173-77).

62. Chalcedon, Session I, 245-246 (ed. Price and Gaddis, 1.178-83). Both letters were read again at Session II, 18-19 (ed. Price and Gaddis, 2.13-14).

"the letter of the blessed Cyril written to Nestorius in which he urged him to assent to the Twelve Chapters."[63] But when, at the fourth session, the Tome was finally examined, only Cyril's Second Letter to Nestorius served as the measure of the Tome's orthodoxy.[64]

The core of the Twelve Chapters, as we have noted, concerns the uncompromising theopaschism declared in its anathema 12. It is this theopaschism that precisely animated the anti-Cyrillian writings of Theodoret and Ibas. Their joint rehabilitation at Chalcedon, then, gave a sense to some that the council was demurring equally on the issue of theopaschism as on the orthodox status of the Twelve Chapters. If there was a sense that Chalcedon had not been bold enough in declaring the one and the same Lord and the Logos the subject of the Cross, the rehabilitation of Theodoret and Ibas was taken as a further equivocation, not only as accommodating a "Theodorian" position, but also as undermining the status of Cyril as the standard of orthodox doctrine. In Justinian's mind, therefore, a condemnation of the Three Chapters would resolve the dogmatic ambiguity that had clung to Cyril's Twelve Chapters since 433.

* * *

The story of the condemnation of the Three Chapters at Constantinople II involves the dramatic and unpleasant history of the relation between the emperor Justinian and Pope Vigilius (d. 555), usually considered the first pope of the Byzantine Papacy.[65] Vigilius came to the Chair of Peter through the machinations of the empress Theodora and the emperor,[66] and was

---

63. Chalcedon, Session II, 29 (ed. Price and Gaddis, 2.26-27).

64. Chalcedon, Session IV, 29 (ed. Price and Gaddis, 2.127-46).

65. The Byzantine Papacy lasted from 537 to 752. In this period popes required the approval of the emperor for their consecration. On Justinian and Vigilius and their relation leading up to the Council of Constantinople, see Price, *Acts of the Council of Constantinople of 553*, vol. 1, pp. 23-31 and 42-58; John Behr, *The Case against Diodore and Theodore: Texts and Their Contexts* (Oxford: OUP, 2011), pp. 119-28; John Meyendorff, *Imperial Unity and Christian Divisions* (Crestwood, NY: Saint Vladimir's Seminary Press, 1989), pp. 237-45.

66. See Liberatus, *Breviarium* 22 (ACO 2.5, 136-138); *Liber Pontificalis*, English Translation: Raymond Davis, *The Book of Pontiffs*, 2d ed. (Liverpool: University of Liverpool Press, 2000), pp. 56-59. According to the *Liber Pontificalis*, it was the empress Theodora who promised and arranged Vigilius's ascension to the papacy in return for Roman support in the cause of non-Chalcedonians. In all events, receiving the see of Rome from the Byzantine court was not a seamless affair. Upon the death of Pope Agapetus in 536, Silverius was elected pope and installed before Vigilius could get back to Rome to receive his Byzantine gift. Only

enthroned at Rome with the support of the Byzantine military. When in 544/5 Justinian issued an edict condemning the Three Chapters, the emperor seems to have presumed the support of the pope who owed his office to the imperial legislator himself.[67] Vigilius, confronted with widespread opposition to the condemnation throughout the West, was forced to prevaricate in his support of the imperial religious policy.

Why was this hostility so acute among the Latins? There are perhaps two reasons, neither of which is due to any sympathy with the theology of Three Chapters.[68] In the first place, a reverential attitude towards Chalcedon had developed in the West that tended to see Chalcedon as the last Council, an attitude that can be traced to the initiative of Pope Leo the Great himself.[69] After Chalcedon, Leo tended more and more to cast Chalcedon as "the immutable and irrevocable Council."[70] The quasi-finality of Chalcedon for Leo in no way reflects the proto-modern sense of Chalcedon as a synthetic advance in Christological doctrine toward a supposed "pure" Chalcedonianism, but rather as a sufficient safeguard of the apostolic faith, a reliable makeshift best left in place and not complicated by new tinkering. Memory of the experience of the 449 *Latrocinium* of Dioscorus seems to have contributed to Leo's sense that any council could too easily make a bigger mess than the one which it might have been called to solve. This

---

with the Byzantine reconquest of Italy from the Goths in 537 was Vigilius able to take possession of the see of Peter promised to him. As the story goes, Silverius, having been promptly deposed and exiled in the Byzantine reconquest, was returned to Rome for an apparent fair trial, only to have the Byzantine general Belisarius hand him over to Pope Vigilius, who banished Silverius to a deserted island where he is said to have starved to death. Pope Silverius is venerated in the Roman Catholic Church as saint, Vigilius is not.

67. The text of the edict does not survive. See Price, General Introduction, *Acts of the Council of Constantinople of 553*, vol. 1, pp. 16-28. On the controversy, see Grillmeier, *Christ in Christian Tradition*, vol. 2, pt. 2, pp. 411-62.

68. This point is corroborated by the fact that most of the Latin bishops did not have a fine sense of the issues at stake, not only for lack of Greek but also because the writings in question seem not to have circulated widely in the West. Cf. Pontianus, *De tribus capitulis ad Iustinianum imperatorem* (PL 97.997a): It "disturbs us not a little, that we are supposed to condemn Theodore, the writings of Theodoret, and the letter of Ibas. Their words have not reached us at all up till now. But if they were indeed to do so and we were to read there some apocrypha contrary to the rule of faith, we could examine the words" (trans. Price).

69. Cf. Leo the Great, *Epistula* 149 (PL 54.119a-120b) and *Epistula* 150 (PL 54.120b-122b). See Aloys Grillmeier, S.J., *Christ in Christian Tradition*, vol. 2, pt. 1, *From the Council of Chalcedon (451) to Gregory the Great (590-604)*, trans. Pauline Allen and John Cawte (Louisville: Westminster John Knox Press, 1995), pp. 136-38.

70. Grillmeier, *Christ in Christian Tradition*, vol. 2, pt. 1, p. 137.

seems to have left Leo with a haunted fear that any new council (or the revision of an old council) risked in fact betraying rather than safeguarding the apostolic faith.[71] The dedication of the Roman Church to Chalcedon was borne out dramatically in a forty-year "Acacian Schism" (484-519), when Rome broke communion with Constantinople over the imposition of the emperor Zeno's *Henotikon* (482), an attempt to bypass the Chalcedonian settlement in order to reconcile non-Chalcedonians with the imperial Church.[72] The Latin bishops accordingly showed their resolve to uphold Chalcedon at all costs.

The second reason regards the person of Theodore of Mopsuestia, but again not for any dogmatic sympathy with his theology (which was not well known in the West). While the condemnation of the Three Chapters concerned certain writings of Theodoret and Ibas, it also concerned the person and writings of Theodore. The idea of retroactively condemning a bishop who had died in good standing with the Church struck many in the West as inappropriate. The Latin African bishop Pontianus makes this plain in a letter to Justinian, where he writes that, if a living person teaches against the true faith, he should be corrected; but if after being corrected he refuses to condemn his error, he is justly condemned.[73] Theodore, however, being already dead for more than a century, would be unable to condemn his own erroneous teaching and would moreover be "in the hands of the true judge, from whom there is no appeal."[74]

In fact, this had also become Cyril's ultimate position in the matter. Withdrawing none of his criticisms of Theodore and his doctrine, Cyril finally judged it too serious a matter to condemn a dead man.[75] Were Theodore alive, it would be another matter, but having faced the judgment of the almighty God, Cyril resigned himself to accept the formal condemnation of Nestorius alone, which doctrinally concerned the errors of Theodore's teaching as well.[76]

---

71. Cf. the comments of Leo in *Epistula* 82.2 (PL 54.918a-b).

72. On the *Henotikon* and the "Acacian Schism," see Jan-Markus Kötter, *Zwischen Kaisern und Aposteln. Das Akakianische Schisma (484-519) als kirchlicher Ordnungskonflikt der Spätantike* (Stuttgart: Franz-Steiner Verlag, 2013).

73. Pontianus, *De tribus capitulis ad Iustinianum imperatorem* (PL 97.997a).

74. Pontianus, *De tribus capitulis ad Iustinianum imperatorem* (PL 97.997b), trans. Price.

75. Cyril of Alexandria, *Epistula* 72 (PG 77.343c).

76. At Constantinople II, Session V, 65-89 (ed. Price, 1.324-40), the Council Fathers, discussing the condemnation of Theodoret, were confronted with Cyril's *Epistula* 72 and

Faced with Latin opposition to the condemnation, Vigilius hesitated on the question of Justinian's edict. He was promptly summoned to Constantinople by the emperor, where he spent the next decade "zigzagging" in the Byzantine capital on the question of the Three Chapters and then on the question of the Second Council of Constantinople.[77] Trapped between the resolve of the emperor on the one hand and the misgivings of Latin bishops on the other, Vigilius appears a stammering pope, whose ambition to ecclesial power was matched only by his lack of political and theological conviction. Under pressure from the emperor, Vigilius publicly and formally condemned the Three Chapters in 548.[78] When his condemnation provoked uproar in the West, Justinian was forced to permit Vigilius to withdraw his public condemnation. In exchange, Vigilius made a secret oath before Theodore Ascidas (the archbishop of Caesarea) and over the nails of the Cross and the four Gospels that he would do all in his power to secure the condemnation of the Three Chapters. At the same time, it seems to have been decided between the emperor and the pope that the issue of the Three Chapters would be best resolved by an ecumenical council.[79] Yet in 551, without waiting for a council, Justinian issued his *Edictum rectae fidei*. To this edict was appended thirteen anathemata, the first eleven of which are dedicated to condemning Theodore and various aspects of his teaching, while the last two deal with the writings of Theodoret and Ibas. Vigilius took the edict as a betrayal and initially threatened anyone who subscribed to it with excommunication. But shortly after the emperor and the pope made some kind of peace; in 552 the edict was in effect withdrawn and the idea of an ecumenical council revived.

The council that would settle the matter of the Three Chapters opened on 5 May 553; it did so without the pope, who had absented himself. After the Council had been in session twenty days, Vigilius sent his first *Constitutum*, which rejects the condemnation of the Three Chapters, while nevertheless offering a detailed condemnation of select writings of Theodore of Mopsuestia.[80] Justinian's reaction was decisive. The day after Vigilius

---

Epistula 91 (containing a similar judgment). With unease and embarrassment, they were finally moved to judge the letters forgeries.

77. This is Price's description of Vigilius's "zigzags"; see Price's General Introduction, *Acts of the Council of Constantinople of 553*, vol. 1, pp. 46 and 54.

78. This was in his *Iudicatum* to Menas of Constantinople, of which only fragments are extant. For the fragments, see Constantinople II, Session I, 7 (11-12) (ed. Price, 1.194), and Vigilius, first *Constitutum* (ed. Price, 2.210-11).

79. See Vigilius, Letter of Excommunication to Ascidas and Menas (ed. Price, 1.161-65).

80. See Vigilius, first *Constitutum* (ed. Price, 2.145-213).

had his text presented to the Council, the emperor returned a dossier to be read out to the assembly of bishops, consisting of texts (some secret) in which Vigilius had given support or solemnly committed himself to the condemnation of the Three Chapters.[81] The pope having been sufficiently discredited by the emperor's revelations, the Council Fathers were left to continue their work in step with the program of Justinian. In June 553, the assembled bishops concluded their proceedings and approved the *Anathematismi adversus "tria Capitula,"* based on the anathemata contained in Justinian's *Edictum rectae fidei.*[82] In February 554, in his second *Constitutum,* Vigilius confirmed the Council's condemnation of the Three Chapters.[83] In 555 he died on his way back to Rome. Vigilius suffered his last humiliation in being the only sixth-century Successor of Peter not to be buried in St. Peter's.

For all of the foregoing reasons, Constantinople II was ambiguously received in the West. Pope Pelagius I, chosen by Justinian as the new Successor of Peter upon the death of Vigilius,[84] makes no mention of the Constantinopolitan council of 553 in his encyclical *Vas electionis* (c. 557), where he writes of only "four holy councils" (Nicaea, Constantinople I, Ephesus and Chalcedon).[85] What gradually became the Latin view of Constantinople II in the sixth century (accommodating the sentiment of Leo the Great concerning the finality of Chalcedon) was to teach the doctrinal sufficiency of the first four councils, while accepting Constantinople II, not so much as an Ecumenical Council concerned with matters of the doctrine of the faith, but as merely a formal pronouncement concerning the theological errors of certain individuals.[86]

Thus the view of Pope Gregory the Great (c. 540-604): Nicaea, Constantinople I, Ephesus, and Chalcedon are "like the four Gospels": they are a "four sided stone" on which the "the holy faith arises and all life and activity exists."[87] Constantinople II is recognized by Gregory as a legitimate

---

81. See Constantinople II, Session VII, 1-17 (ed. Price, 2.74-110).

82. Constantinople II, Session VIII, 5 (ed. Price, 2.120-126).

83. Vigilius, second *Constitutum* (ed. Price, 2.221-269); cf. *Inter innumeras sollicitudines* (DS 416-420).

84. Ironically, Pope Pelagius was one of the main influences on Vigilius's rejection of the condemnation of the Three Chapters, and was furious when Vigilius finally capitulated.

85. Pelagius I, *Vas electionis* (DS 444).

86. Behr, *The Case against Diodore and Theodore,* pp. 128-29.

87. Gregory the Great, *Consideranti mihi* (DS 472).

condemnation of the Three Chapters, but the stone on which the holy faith arises ends with Chalcedon.

In this way, Constantinople II was initially accepted by the Roman Church in a way that minimized its positive dogmatic declarations concerning the single subject of Christ, including the doctrine of Jesus's "compound hypostasis" (ὑπόστασις σύνθετος),[88] the clarification of the orthodoxy of the "mia physis" formula,[89] and the declaration that "he who was crucified in the flesh, our Lord Jesus Christ, is true God, Lord of Glory and one of the Holy Trinity."[90]

The standard Latin policy towards Constantinople II changed only with the Lateran synod of 649. There, under the apostolic authority of Pope Martin I (d. 655), Constantinople II was enumerated by the Roman Church for the first time as one of the Five Ecumenical Councils.[91] The synod took up and endorsed, moreover, the Constantinopolitan doctrine of "compound hypostasis" (ὑπόστασις σύνθετος),[92] along with its own precise theopaschite formula: "one of the holy, consubstantial, and adorable Trinity, descended from heaven and became incarnate... [and] was crucified in the flesh, of his own free will suffered for us and was buried."[93] Finally, the Lateran synod of 649 completed the condemnation of Theodorian Christology by at last condemning, in the name Diodore of Tarsus, the origin of the dualist Christologies of Nestorius and the Three Chapters.[94]

---

88. *Anathematismi adversus "tria Capitula,"* canon 4 (DS 424-425; DEC 1.114-115).

89. *Anathematismi adversus "tria Capitula,"* canon 8 (DS 429-430; DEC 1.117).

90. *Anathematismi adversus "tria Capitula,"* canon 10 (DS 432; DEC 1.118).

91. Lateran synod of 649, canons 19-20 (DS 521-522).

92. Lateran synod of 649, canon 8 (DS 508).

93. Lateran synod of 649, canon 2 (DS 502): "Si quis secundum sanctos Patres non confitetur proprie et secundum veritatem ipsum *unum sanctae et consubstantialis et venerandae Trinitatis Deum Verbum* e caelo descendisse, et incarnatum ex Spiritu Sancto et Maria semper virgine, et hominem factum, *crucifixum carne*, propter nos sponte passum sepultumque, et resurrexisse tertia die, et ascendisse in caelos, atque sedentem in dextera Patris, et venturum iterum cum gloria paterna cum assumpta ab eo atque animata intellectualiter carne eius, judicare vivos et mortuos, condemnatus sit." Also cf. canon 4 (DS 504).

94. Lateran synod of 649, canon 18 (DS 519).

CHAPTER 6

Dyothelite Unity

[W]hen he willingly submitted himself to the condemnation of our nature to passibility . . . [he] made that passibility itself the weapon with which to destroy sin and death.

Maximus the Confessor

A. From "Monenergism" to "Dyothelitism"

The Logos, since he "worked with human hands . . . acted with a human will, and with a human heart he loved," accomplishes the perfect human action in his incarnate self.[1] In this way, he reveals that the human creature is not merely created for God, he is created to be and to act in communion with God. In the words of St. Paul, the human is created for synergy, to become a "fellow worker of God" (συνεργὸν τοῦ Θεοῦ [cf. 1 Cor. 3:9, 1 Thess. 3:2, and Col. 4:11]).[2] This idea of divine-human synergy is simply

---

1. *Gaudium et spes*, 22 (DS 4322).

2. On the Pauline doctrine of synergism, see CCC 307. The internal relativity of synergy and deification is spelled out by Vladimir Lossky in his *The Mystical Theology of the Eastern Church*, trans. Members of the Fellowship of St. Alban and St. Sergius (Crestwood, NY: Saint Vladimir's Seminary Press, 1976), p. 196: "The deification or θέωσις of the creature will be realized in its fullness only in the age to come, after the resurrection of the dead. This deifying union has nevertheless to be fulfilled ever more and more even in this present life, through the transformation of our corruptible and depraved nature and by its adaptation to eternal life. If God has given us in the Church all the objective conditions, all the means that we need for the attainment of this end, we, on our side, must produce the necessary subjective conditions: for it is in this synergy, in this co-operation of man with God, that the union is fulfilled. This subjective aspect of our union with God constitutes the way of union which is the Christian life."

the dynamic and personal aspect of the patristic doctrine of deification, according to which "God became man that man might become God."[3] The apostle Paul himself substantiates this view when he suggests that the presence of God in human life occurs precisely through "synergy"; as, for example, when he gives thanks to the Thessalonians that they have received his word "not as the word of men but as it really is, the word of God, which is at work (ἐνεργεῖται) in you believers" (1 Thess. 2:13).[4] The question of synergy was raised Christologically in the monenergist and monothelite crises. It was resolved in favor of Christological synergism in the form of the dyoenergist and dyothelitist dogmata of the Third Council of Constantinople (680-681).

The monenergist crisis began in the 610s, when the emperor Heraclius (c. 575-641), along with the Patriarch of Constantinople, Sergius (himself of non-Chalcedonian and Syrian parentage), devised a new plan to reunite

---

3. For instances of the patristic axiom, see Irenaeus of Lyon, *Adversus haereses* 5, preface (SC 153.14; PG 7.1120a-b); Athanasius of Alexandria, *Oratio de incarnatione verbi* 54 (PG 25.192b); Gregory of Nazianzus, *Poema dogmatica* 10.5-9 (PG 37.465a); Gregory of Nyssa, *Oratio catechetica magna* 25 (PG 45.65d); Augustine of Hippo, *In Natali Domini, Sermo* 128 (PL 39.1997).

4. This passage underscores the dynamic fact that God works by taking up real human words and actions in order to make them his own. The words Paul speaks are also the word of God, and as such the words of Paul are active in those who receive them in faith (cf. David Bradshaw, *Aristotle East and West: Metaphysics and the Division of Christendom* [Cambridge: CUP, 2004], pp. 121-22). The paradox of this fact — of a human act that is nevertheless also (and more) a divine act — involves the principle that the more the creature is receptive to the gift of God, the more actively the creature responds to the call of God, and the more co-operatively he acts within the constitutive reality that is the condition of the possibility of his action (cf. Kathryn Tanner, *God and Creation in Christian Theology: Tyranny or Empowerment?* [New York: Basil Blackwell, 1988]). This is also highlighted in Paul's letter to the Philippians, where he enjoins the Philippians to "work out your own salvation with fear and trembling; for it is God who is at work in you (ὁ ἐνεργῶν ἐν ὑμῖν), enabling you both to will and to work (ἐνεργεῖν) for his good pleasure" (Phil. 2:12-13). Tanner writes that the Philippians passage "tells Christians that they have to do something: they must not be quietistically complacent, they must not sit on their hands, they must work, they must take responsibility for themselves. On the other hand, they must do so "with fear and trembling": they should not trust in their own accomplishments since everything, including it seems their own power and activity, is given to them by God." See Tanner, *God and Creation in Christian Theology*, p. 19. Commenting on the same passage Bradshaw writes: "Here the exhortation to act is coupled with a reminder that it is God who is acting. Neither negates the other; the Philippians are both the objects of God's working and the conduit by which He works, at least when they obey 'with fear and trembling'" (Bradshaw, *Aristotle East and West*, p. 122). Cf. Augustine of Hippo, *De Natura et Gratia* 27.31 (PL 44.262).

the non-Chalcedonians with the imperial Church.[5] Building on the Cyril-lianism of Justinian, and with one eye fixed on the theandric formulation of Denys's *Epistula* 4, Patriarch Sergius proposed that in Jesus there are two natures, but only one energy (μία ἐνέργεια). The doctrine came to be known as "monenergism." Initially, the monenergist doctrine was moderately successful at winning over non-Chalcedonians to the imperial Church. Non-Chalcedonians in Egypt, for example, boasted that they were being received back into the imperial Church, not because they were accommodating Chalcedon, but rather because "Chalcedon is coming to us!"[6]

Until 633 there seems to have been no opposition from Chalcedonian Christians to the monenergist doctrine. Its fate, however, was quickly to change. In 633, the Patriarch Cyrus of Alexandria organized a mass reconciliation of non-Chalcedonians through a document called *The Nine Chapters* (or *Pact of Union*). Cyrus's document laid out the monenergist doctrine citing both the Cyrillian formula of the "one incarnate nature of God the Word" (μία φύσις τοῦ λόγου σεσαρκωμένη) and the Severan version of the "theandric energy" formula in the form of "one energy" (μία ἐνέργεια). As it happened, a Chalcedonian monk named Sophronius (d. 638) was in Alexandria at the time. Having by chance read *The Nine Chapters*, Sophronius was moved to write against Cyrus's profession of faith, protesting that it was a heretical violation of the doctrine of Chalcedon.[7] Sophronius took his protest to the Patriarch Sergius, who respected Sophronius to the point of issuing an "authoritative statement," a *Psephos*, forbidding further discussion of "one" or "two" energies in Christ. Having issued his *Psephos*, Sergius then wrote to the Bishop of Rome explaining the situation and reiterating his desire to accomplish the reconciliation of the non-Chalcedonians. Pope Honorius (d. 638), in his response to the Patriarch,

---

5. On the background to the "monenergist" and "monothelite" controversies, see J. M. Hussey, *The Orthodox Church in the Byzantine Empire* (Oxford: OUP, 2010), pp. 9-23; Paul Verghese, "The Monothelite Controversy — A Historical Survey," *Greek Orthodox Theological Review* 13 (1968): 196-208; Jaroslav Pelikan, *The Christian Tradition: A History of the Development of Doctrine*, vol. 2, *The Spirit of Eastern Christendom (600-1700)* (Chicago: University of Chicago Press, 1974), pp. 62-75; Christoph Cardinal Schönborn, *God Sent His Son: A Contemporary Christology*, trans. Henry Taylor (San Francisco: Ignatius Press, 2004), pp. 195-96; Andrew Louth, *Maximus the Confessor*, ECF (London: Routledge, 1996), pp. 47-60; Leo D. Davis, S.J., *The First Seven Ecumenical Councils (325-787): Their History and Theology* (Collegeville: Liturgical Press, 1990), pp. 258-89.

6. See Louth, *Maximus the Confessor*, p. 20.

7. On Sophronius, see Christoph von Schönborn, *Sophrone de Jérusalem: vie monastique et confession dogmatique* (Paris: Beauchesne, 1972).

infamously declared that the proper refinement of language required was that of "one will of our Lord Jesus Christ (*unam voluntatem fatemur Domini nostri Iesu Christi*)."[8] Thus the pope proposed to posterity the doctrine of "monothelitism."[9] The Patriarch took up the pope's suggestion and had the doctrine enshrined in an imperial edict of the emperor Heraclius in 638 known as the *Ecthesis*, which reiterated the ban on discussion of the number of energies, while putting forward the doctrine of the single will of Christ as a declaration of faith.

In the meantime, the monk Sophronius was made Patriarch of Jerusalem. He was no more impressed by the doctrine of the *Ecthesis* than he had been by *The Nine Chapters*. As Patriarch, he could now resist the Christological heresies of monenergism and monothelitism from his new position of ecclesial authority. Meanwhile, in the monastery he left behind, Sophronius left a band of monks educated and formed in his style of doctrinal Chalcedonianism. From the ranks of these disciple-monks came Sophronius's most important and precocious pupil, Maximus the Confessor (c. 580-662).

* * *

Maximus took his original monastic vows at a monastery in Chrysopolis, a city not far from Constantinople.[10] By 640, Persian armies had conquered that territory, forcing the monks out of their monastery. Maximus finally ended up in a monastery near Carthage in northern Africa. It was at Carthage that he met Sophronius, and through Sophronius he received his decisive theological education. Although a Greek-speaking easterner, Maximus lived most of his life in the Latin West. It was from the West, and in collaboration with a Roman Pontiff, Pope Martin I, that Maximus

8. Honorius I, *"Scripta fraternitatis" ad Sergium* (DS 487).

9. Pope Honorius was posthumously condemned at Constantinople III (DS 550), but it is noteworthy that Maximus the Confessor in fact defended his orthodoxy. Aidan Nichols writes: "The maligned pope [Honorius], in writing 'We profess one sole will of our Lord Jesus Christ' did not intend to deny the duality of natural wills in Christ, argues Maximus, but only to exclude any inner division in the Saviour produced by human sinfulness." See Aidan Nichols, O.P., *Byzantine Gospel: Maximus the Confessor in Modern Scholarship* (London: Continuum, 1993), p. 53. See Maximus, *Opusculum* 20 (PG 91.240b-c) and *Disputatio cum Pyrrho* (PG 91.353a).

10. My summary of the martyrdoms of Maximus and Martin is based on the account of Robert L. Wilken, *The Spirit of Early Christian Thought* (New Haven: Yale University Press, 2003), pp. 100-135.

waged his battle against the imperial doctrines of monenergism and monothelitism.[11]

In 649, in collaboration with Maximus as his chief theological advisor, Pope Martin presided over a synod intended to be the sixth Ecumenical Council of the Church.[12] Now known as the Lateran Synod of 649,[13] the synod reaffirmed the teaching of the councils of Nicaea, Constantinople I, Ephesus, Chalcedon and Constantinople II, and pronounced the monenergist and monothelite doctrines contrary to the faith of the apostles.[14] The synod, moreover, called into question the authenticity of Cyrus's understanding of Denys as claiming "one energy" (μία ἐνέργεια), and condemned the imperial policy by anathematizing Cyrus along with patriarchs Sergius, Pyrrhus and Paul of Constantinople.

When the Lateran synod adjourned, Martin sent notice of its outcome to Constantinople with a letter urging the emperor, still officially upholding the teaching of the *Ecthesis*, to reject monothelitism in favor of "dyothelitism." The emperor was enraged. He dispatched his chamberlain Olympus as exarch to Rome with instructions to arrest the pope. Initially, the military support of the pope was sufficient to resist. How-

---

11. On the history of Martin and Maximus and relevant primary texts, see Pauline Allen and Bronwen Neil, *Maximus the Confessor and His Companions* (Oxford: OUP, 2003).

12. Martin, though he presided over the synod, did not call it or conceive it. This was the work of his predecessor, Pope Theodore I (d. 649), who, prompted through a correspondence with Maximus, began the Roman campaign to defend the doctrine of Christ's two wills. In the midst of this campaign, in 648, the emperor Constans II issued a *Typos* prohibiting any further discussion of the numbers of wills or energies in Christ. In defiance of the emperor and flouting the Byzantine tradition that gave to the emperor the prerogative to convene an Ecumenical Council, Pope Theodore called the synod which he intended to be the sixth Ecumenical Council. Theodore died in 649, before the synod was convened.

13. For a history of the synod, see F.-X. Murphy and Polycarp Sherwood, *Constantinople II et III*, Histoire des Conciles Oecumeniques 3 (Paris: l'Orante, 1973), pp. 174-88; Andrew J. Ekonomou, *Byzantine Rome and the Greek Popes: Eastern Influences on Rome and the Papacy from Gregory the Great to Zacharias, A.D. 590-752* (Lanham, MD: Lexington Books, 2007), pp. 113-58.

14. Cf. Lateran Synod of 649, canon 10: "Si quis secundum sanctos Patres non confitetur proprie et secundum veritatem duas unius eiusdemque Christi Dei nostri voluntates cohaerenter unitas, divinam et humanam, ex hoc quod per utramque eius naturam voluntarius naturaliter idem consistit nostrae salutis, condemnatus sit" (DS 510); and canon 11: "Si quis secundum sanctos Patres non confitetur proprie et secundum veritatem duas unius eiusdemque Christi Dei nostri operationes cohaerenter unitas, divinam et humanam, ab eo quod per utramque eius naturam operator naturaliter idem exsistit nostrae salutis, condemnatus sit" (DS 511).

ever, in 653, another exarch was sent from Constantinople to arrest Pope Martin along with his monk Maximus. On this occasion Martin was not so fortunate. When the soldiers found him lying ill in the Lateran basilica, where his nursemaids had given him refuge, they handed Martin an imperial order declaring him deposed from the see of Peter. He was then arrested and bound, and taken from Rome by sea to Constantinople. He arrived in the capital in September, having been mistreated and detained for more than three months en route. Having arrived at Constantinople, Martin was charged with treason. To further disgrace the wounded pope, the emperor forced him to stand in a public courtyard while the people of Constantinople jeered at him; his *pallium*, the two strips of lamb's wool marked with six black crosses worn by popes, was then publicly removed from his shoulders as a sign that he had lost the papacy. Pope Martin was then led through the capital in chains on his way to exile in the Crimea. On 16 September 655, Martin died of starvation. He is the last pope to receive from the Church the title of "martyr," and is venerated as such in both Roman Catholic and Eastern Orthodox churches.

Maximus's fate was worse. Imprisoned and exiled for refusing to submit to the emperor, he was brought back from his first exile to be tried a second time. Because he refused again to submit to the imperial doctrine of Christ's singular divine will, his right hand was cut off and his tongue ripped out, that he might never speak or write of the human will of Jesus Christ again. Maximus was then exiled to a remote region of present-day Georgia, where he died on 13 August 662. He too is venerated in both the Latin and Greek churches, remembered as a confessor of the faith.

In 680, twenty-five years after the death of Pope Martin and nearly twenty years after the death of Maximus the Confessor, the Third Council of Constantinople elevated to the status of a dogma of faith the doctrine for which Martin and Maximus had died:

> We . . . proclaim in him, according to the teaching of the holy Fathers, two natural volitions or wills (δύο φυσικὰς θελήσεις ἤτοι θελήματα) and two natural actions (δύο φυσικὰς ἐνεργείας), without division, without change, without separation, without confusion. The two natural wills are not — by no means — opposed to each other as the impious heretics assert; but his human will is compliant, it does not resist or oppose but rather submits to his divine and almighty will. . . . Thus we glory in proclaiming two natural wills (δύο φυσικὰ θελήματα) and energies

(ἐνεργείας) reconciled in correspondence (καταλλήλως συντρέχοντα) for the salvation of the human race.[15]

B. The Dyothelite Christology of Maximus

Maximus the Confessor's dyothelite Christology is rooted in his fundamental distinction between the *logoi* and *tropoi* of being, between "what" things are (λόγος) and the "manner" or "mode" in which they are (τρόπος).[16] This Maximian distinction is, in turn, grounded in the classical Christological distinction between hypostasis (*quis*) and nature (*quid*). As Maximus puts it:

> Each of us works, not insofar as he is a "who," but as a "what": that is, insofar as he is a man. Yet insofar as he is a "who," Peter for instance, or Paul, he gives a shape to the manner (τρόπος) of his work, by easing off of making an effort and by giving his work this or that shape, in accordance with his free will. That is how we recognize the distinction between persons in practice, by the way (τρόπος) they do things; in the

---

15. *Terminus* of Constantinople III (DS 556 and 558; DEC 1.128 and 129-130).

16. The main texts of Maximus's dyothelite reading of Gethsemane are: *Opusculum* 3 (PG 91.45b-56a); *Opusculum* 6 (PG 91.65A-68D); *Opusculum* 7 (PG 91.69b-89b); *Ad Thalassium* 21 (PG 90.312a-317a); and *Disputatio cum Pyrrho* (PG 91.288a-353b). English translations of these texts can be found in the following: *Opusculum* 6 and *Ad Thalassium* 21, in *On the Cosmic Mystery of Jesus Christ*, trans. Paul M. Blowers and Robert L. Wilken (Crestwood, NY: Saint Vladimir's Seminary Press, 2003), pp. 173-76 and pp. 109-113; *Opusculum* 3 and 7 in Louth, *Maximus the Confessor*, pp. 193-98 and pp. 180-191; and *Disputatio cum Pyrrho* in *The Disputation with Pyrrhus of Our Father Among the Saints Maximus the Confessor*, trans. Joseph P. Farrell (South Canaan: St. Tikhon's Seminary Press, 1990). See Marie-Joseph le Guillou, O.P., "Quelques Réflexions sur Constantinople III et la Sotériologie de Maxime," in Félix Heinzer and Christoph Schönborn, O.P., eds., *Maximus Confessor: Actes du Symposium sur Maxime le Confesseur Fribourg, 2-5 septembre 1980* (Fribourg: Éditions Universitaires, 1982), pp. 235-37; International Theological Commission, "Select Questions on Christology," in Michael Sharkey, ed., *International Theological Commission: Texts and Documents 1969-1985* (San Francisco: Ignatius Press, 1989), pp. 185-206. Modern Protestantism especially tended to dismiss the dogma as the *reductio ad absurdum* of patristic doctrine; see John Macquarrie, *Jesus Christ in Modern Thought* (London: SCM Press, 1990), p. 166. Cf. Friedrich Schleiermacher, *The Christian Faith*, trans. H. R. Mackintosh and J. S. Stewart (Edinburgh: T&TClark, 1928), p. 394; Wolfhart Pannenberg, *Jesus — God and Man*, trans. Lewis L. Wilkins and Duane A. Priebe (London: SCM Press, 1968), pp. 293-94.

nature (λόγος) of the work, on the other hand, we recognize the natural operation common to all men.[17]

Natures, then, are defined by their *logos*, a universal and unchangeable principle; but a nature exists always in the concrete reality of a particular "mode of being" (τρόπος ὑπάρξεως).[18] Thus Maximus is able to propose — in a very specific way — that the Incarnate Logos is exactly like any other human being in the *logos* of his human nature, but insofar as he is the eternal Son of God, his "mode of being" is that of the Son. Jesus is, therefore, truly the one who came down from above (*descensus de caelis*) and so cannot be thought of as a "pure man" (ψιλὸς ἄνθρωπος).[19] Nevertheless, in his human nature he is in principle defined like any other human being.[20] Jesus is fully human in the ontological and metaphysical sense, but his mode of being human is uniquely that of the divine Son. In this way, Maximus evidences the deep logic of the doctrine of "enhypostatos": the humanity of the first-century Palestinian-Jew subsists wholly in union with the Son.[21] Jesus is human in the mode of divine filiation.

That Jesus is entirely human in an ontological sense is brought to bear fully in Maximus's reading of the prayer of Jesus at Gethsemane: "My Father, if it be possible, let this chalice pass from me; nevertheless, not as I will, but as thou wilt" (Matt. 26:39).[22] The genius of Maximus's reading of

17. Maximus the Confessor, *Opusculum* 9 (PG 91.137a).

18. Maximus the Confessor, *Ambiguum* 42 (PG 91.1341d). Cf. Ivor J. Davidson, "'Not My Will but Yours Be Done': The Ontological Dynamics of Incarnational Intention," *International Journal of Systematic Theology* 7 (2005): 178-204, at pp. 190-91.

19. Maximus, *Disputatio cum Pyrrho* (PG 91.308d-309a).

20. Maximus, *Ambiguum* 5 (PG 91.1045d-1060d).

21. On Maximus's doctrine of "enhypostatos" and relevant texts, see U. M. Lang, "Anhypostatos — Enhypostatos: Church Fathers, Protestant Orthodoxy and Karl Barth," *Journal of Theological Studies* 49 (1998): 630-57, at p. 643, n. 60 and p. 651, n. 88.

22. Cf. François-Marie Léthel, *Théologie de l'agonie de Christ: La liberté humaine de fils de Dieu et son importance sotériologique mises en lumière par saint Maxime Confesseur*, Théologie Historique, no. 52 (Paris: Éditions Beauchesne, 1979), pp. 29-49, and pp. 86-99; François-Marie Léthel, "La Prière de Jésus a Gethsémani dans la Controverse Monothélite," in Félix Heinzer and Christoph Schönborn, O.P., eds., *Maximus Confessor: Actes du Symposium sur Maxime le Confesseur Fribourg, 2-5 septembre 1980* (Fribourg: Éditions Universitaires, 1982), pp. 207-14; Davidson, "'Not My Will but Yours Be Done,'" pp. 190-97; Marcel Doucet, F.I.C., "La volonté humaine du Christ, spécialement en son agonie: Maxime le Confesseur, interprète de l'Écriture," *Science et Esprit* 37 (1985): 123-59; Paul M. Blowers, "The Passion of Jesus Christ in Maximus the Confessor: A Reconsideration," *Studia Patristica* 37 (2001): 361-77; Lars Thunberg, *Microcosm and Mediator: The Theological Anthropology of Maximus the*

Gethsemane lies in the fresh ontological significance he attributes to both petitions of the prayer: the petition to "let this chalice pass," and the petition for the Father's will to be done. Maximus sought thereby to show the irreducible integrity of the human will of Jesus on the level of his incarnate nature, while at the same time affirming the absolute subjective unity of his act of willing on the level of his divine person (πρόσωπον / ὑπόστασις). In order to articulate this, Maximus was led to argue that the Son must possess a fully operative human will.

Maximus's doctrine of the human will of Christ rests on a careful distinction between what he calls the "gnomic will" (θέλημα γνωμικόν) and "natural will" (θέλημα φυσικόν).[23] While for Maximus Christ possesses a fully human natural will, his humanity lacks a gnomic will. What is this gnomic will? The word *gnome* (γνώμη) signifies a "means of knowing," a "thought" or "judgment," or an "opinion" — connected as it is with its root "γνω-" from "γνῶσις" (*gnosis*). With regard to willing, *gnome* signifies something like a "disposition" or "inclination." Maximus, then, wants to signify with the term gnomic will neither a constituent part of the faculty of the will, nor the concrete *act* of willing, but rather a disposition (or mode) of willing. In particular, he wants to specify the disposition of deliberative willing that results from the Fall.[24]

Whereas prelapsarian humans naturally willed the good, the consequences of the Fall are such that human beings no longer clearly intuit the good that fulfills their nature, and so must therefore deliberate, seek and work out the good they naturally will. Lars Thunberg summarizes Maximus's position:

> What happens through the fall is that a *perversion* of man's capacity for self-determination takes place — not an annihilation of it — a perversion which predisposes man for its constant misuse, and even new misjudgment. That is to say, it forms in man a sinful disposition of will (γνώμη). This, in its turn, affects nature as far as it is misused, and it

---

Confessor, 2d ed. (Chicago: Open Court Publishing, 1995), pp. 208-30; Hans Urs von Balthasar, *Cosmic Liturgy: The Universe According to Maximus the Confessor*, trans. Brian E. Daley, S.J. (San Francisco: Ignatius Press, 2003), pp. 256-71.

23. Maximus the Confessor, *Opuscula* 3 (PG 91.45b-56d). The position of Christ not having a "gnomic will" only arises in Maximus's later thinking during the dyothelite controversy. In his earlier thinking, he had attributed a γνώμη to Christ. For a discussion of this transition in Maximus's theology, see Polycarp Sherwood, O.S.B., *St. Maximus: The Ascetic Life, The Four Centuries on Charity* (Mahwah, NJ: Newman Press, 1955), pp. 58-63.

24. See Thunberg, *Microcosm and Mediator*, pp. 211-19.

is only through Christ's Incarnation that the human . . . is again freed from its slavery, and man's volitional capacities can be freely used in a converted γνώμη.[25]

For Maximus, therefore, "the human will is at the very root of sinful life."[26] The original capacity of the human to "self-determination" (αὐτεξούσιος),[27] the free orientation of the creature before God, is corrupted by the disorientation of original sin, which expresses alienation of the human creature from God.[28] Nevertheless, despite the consequences of sin, "nothing that is natural, and certainly not nature itself, would ever resist the cause of nature."[29] Hence the need to distinguish the natural human will (the will constitutively orientated to God) and the gnomic will (the deliberative manner in which fallen humanity seeks to will what is good in the disorientation of a fallen world).

The gnomic will, because it is deliberative, does not necessarily will the natural will, which is nevertheless its deepest inclination. To admit a gnomic will in Jesus would be to admit a "center" of deliberation that could, in principle, will in opposition (ἀντίπτωσις) to the Father. Moreover, the "gnomic" will occurs on the subjective level of the "mode of being" and thus to admit it in Jesus would be to admit a subjective center in Jesus in addition to the divine filiation of the Son.[30] Therefore, Christ possesses only a natural human will, since by his divine filial constitution he is simply the Son who is wholly orientated to the divine will of the paternal source.[31] This in no way mitigates, however, the truth that Christ fully wills as a human being because he is human, even while all that he wills humanly

---

25. Thunberg, *Microcosm and Mediator*, p. 227.

26. Thunberg, *Microcosm and Mediator*, p. 226.

27. Maximus, *Disputatio cum Pyrrho* (PG 91.324c-325a) and *Opusculum 26* (PG 91.277c).

28. Davidson, "'Not My Will but Yours Be Done,'" p. 192.

29. Maximus, *Opuscula 7* (PG 91.80a).

30. Maximus, *Opuscula 3* (PG 91.53c). Cf. *Disputatio cum Pyrrho* (PG 91.308d-309a). Commenting on this passage, Édouard Glotin writes: "Le *vouloir délibératif* n'est donc pas la volonté comme faculté liée à *l'essence* de la assure humaine, mais sa condition particulière d'exercice dans une *personne*, à savoir l'homme dans son existence contraire actuelle qui est, de fait, une existence de pécheur racheté qui lutte couragement contre la *concupiscence* avec la grâce de Dieu" (*La Bible du Coeur de Jésus* [Paris: Presse de la Renaissance, 2007], p. 572).

31. Maximus, *Opusculum 3* (PG 91.56-d), *Opusculum 7* (PG 91.81c-d), *Opusculum 16* (PG 91.192b-c), *Disputatio cum Pyrrho* (PG 91:308c-309a, and 311a-313c). Cf. Davidson, "'Not My Will but Yours Be Done,'" p. 193.

is willed in hypostatic unity with the Logos of God.[32] Thus what was affirmed in terms of "existence" with the doctrine of "enhypostatos" (that the human nature only "is" as it subsists in unity with the eternal Son) is now affirmed on the level of act and desire: every act and desire of the human nature of Jesus is acted and desired insofar and only insofar as it is constituted by its union with the eternal Son. And since the will of the Logos simply "is" the divine will, and "God our Savior... desires all men be saved" (1 Tim. 2:4), the act and desire of this "will" is what is humanly willed in the Incarnation. Jesus wills the divine will that all might be saved in the filial act of his being "obedient" (ὑπήκοος) to God.[33] There is no act or will in opposition to God in Christ; his human nature is and wills in "perfect harmony and concurrence" (συμφυΐας... ἐντελοῦς καὶ συννεύσεως) with the divine person of the Son.[34] This "perfect harmony and concurrence," however, unfolds in Christ within the agony and discord of fallen nature. Assuming human nature under the consequences of sin, the Son must truly undergo the anguish of death and the natural will to "resist" (συστολή) death.[35] The drama and mystery of the prayer at Gethsemane concerns how the harmony and resistance are drawn together such that Jesus can assume fully the discord of the fallen condition into his divine filiation.

In *Ad Thalassium* 21, Maximus shows how the "slavery" of fallen human nature is rooted specifically in "fear of death."[36] Responding to the question of how the sinless one can put on the passions that result from Adam's sin, Maximus argues that only by putting on these passions has Christ truly "inaugurated a complete restoration."[37] As God, Jesus was under no compulsion to experience the passions of the fallen condition; nevertheless, he willingly took on this condition, descending into the depths of fallen flesh, to assume both the death of Adam and his anguished "fear of death" to redeem human nature from its "lifelong bondage" (Heb. 2:15):

---

32. Maximus, *Opusculum* 6 (PG 91.68b).

33. Maximus, *Opusculum* 6 (PG 91.68d). See Wilken, *The Spirit of Early Christian Thought*, p. 130.

34. Maximus, *Opusculum* 6 (PG 91.65B-68c).

35. Maximus, *Disputatio cum Pyrrho* (PG 91.297d): κατὰ φύσιν μὲν δειλία ἐστὶ, δύναμις κατὰ συστολὴν τοῦ ὄντος ἀνθεκτική· παρὰ φύσιν δὲ, παράλογος συστολή.

36. Maximus, *Ad Thalassium* 21 (PG 90.316a). Cf. Pierre Piret, *Le Christ et la Trinité selon Maxime le Confesseur* (Paris: Les Éditions du Cerf, 1983), pp. 281-83; Blowers, "The Passion of Jesus Christ in Maximus the Confessor," pp. 361-77.

37. Maximus, *Ad Thalassium* 21 (PG 90.313c).

He [the Incarnate Logos] brought to light the equity of his justice through the magnitude of his condescension, when he willingly submitted himself to the condemnation of our nature to passibility, and thereby made that passibility itself the weapon (ὅπλον) with which to destroy sin and death, and the bodily pleasure (ἡδονῆς) and pain (ὀδύνης) that are its consequence.[38]

The possibility of human nature is thus drawn into the person of the Son through his hypostatic union in order to become itself the "weapon" (ὅπλον) of the divine salvation Jesus works.[39] God wills that all men be saved and this divine desire is humanly willed in Jesus' obedience unto death (cf. Phil. 2:5-11).[40] God did not will death nor did he create life to taste death (cf. Wisd. of Sol. 1:13-15; Rom. 5:12, 6:23; 1 Cor. 15), but the Son, absorbing death into his divine filiation, purifies it, submitting it to the pattern of being the Son of the Father, and thus makes it the means of accomplishing the divine will of salvation. Christ "tramples down death by death," as the Paschal troparion states. Without any reference to Maximus, Pope Leo XIII beautifully expressed this principle in the nineteenth century:

38. Maximus, *Ad Thalassium* 61 (PG 90.629c-d). An English translation by Paul Blowers can be found in Blowers and Wilken, *On the Cosmic Mystery of Jesus Christ*, pp. 131-44. The translation here is my own.

39. On the theme of the Son's sinless assumption of sinful human nature, the "stock of Adam," see Thomas G. Weinandy, O.F.M., Cap., *In the Likeness of Sinful Flesh: An Essay on the Humanity of Christ* (Edinburgh: T&T Clark, 1993). Based on the patristic axiom that that which is not assumed is not healed, Weinandy argues persuasively, without mention of Maximus, for the soteriological importance of Jesus' assumption, not just of our human nature, but our human nature lived in fallen human condition. "When the eternal Son of the Father entered into our world, under the then-present conditions, he came to exist as man touched and altered by the reality of sin. He was a son of Adam. He assumed our sinful flesh" (p. 149). Through a survey of patristic sources through the middle ages up to Barth and Balthasar, Weinandy establishes three decisive conclusions: "1. The christological tradition definitively confirms that the eternal Son assumed a humanity which bore the birthmark of Adam. He became man in the likeness of sinful flesh; 2. This truth is of irrefutable soteriological significance. Only if Jesus became as we are, defiled by sin, could he, on our behalf, freely assume our condemnation and lovingly offer (in the Spirit) his holy and innocent life to the Father in reparation for our sin; and 3. In so becoming a son of Adam, Jesus through his cross and resurrection, healed our humanity so that we can now become a new creation in him. Invariably and without deviation, the governing tenet is: what is not assumed (in its entirety) is not saved" (p. 70).

40. Maximus, *Opusculum* 6 (PG 91.68d). Cf. Wilken, *The Spirit of Early Christian Thought*, p. 130.

Jesus Christ, when He redeemed us with plentiful redemption, took not away the pains and sorrows which in such large proportion are woven together in the web of our mortal life. He transformed them into motives of virtue and occasions of merit; and no man can hope for eternal reward unless he follow in the blood-stained footprints of his Savior.[41]

This transformation of suffering, patterned in the blood-stained footprints of our Savior, is, for Maximus, the means by which the Incarnate Son accomplishes "the deification of those being saved by grace."[42] It means that the deification of grace is rooted directly in Christ's "suffering all the infirmities of our nature in the likeness of sinful flesh."[43] And so, at Gethsemane the eternal Son was truly afraid to die:

> He was truly afraid, not as we are, but in a mode surpassing us. Because all things that are natural in Christ are natural both according to our nature's rational principle (τῷ κατ᾽ αὐτὸ λόγῳ) and also as having this rational principle of our nature in accordance with his [Christ's] supernatural mode of existence (τὸν ὑπὲρ φύσιν τρόπον). This was so, in order that both our nature, by means of its rational principle, and the economy [of our nature in Christ], by means of its supernatural mode of existence, might be made trustworthy (πιστωθῇ).[44]

Here we see how Christ turns inside out the weight of human suffering and psychological terror before the fact of death, transforming this most universal human experience — which is also the ultimate experience of inhuman desolation and loneliness — precisely into the decisive act of self-entrusting to the will of God the Father. The Son's anguished "resistance" (συστολή) thus becomes a "trustworthy" (πιστῶς) experience of psychological and ontological fragility before death, because here the anguish of the dying human being is lived wholly within the filial love of the Son for the Father. The Son truly suffers impassibly the wage of Adam's sin, while

---

41. Leo XIII, *Rerum novarum* 21.

42. Maximus, *Ambiguum* 3 (PG 91.1040d). On deification in Maximus and the reality of our *theosis* being entirely correlative with the Logos's *kenosis*, see Norman Russell, *The Doctrine of Deification in the Greek Patristic Tradition* (Oxford: OUP, 2004), pp. 262-95.

43. John Henry Newman, Sermon 3, vol. 2: "The Incarnation," *Parochial and Plain Sermons* (San Francisco: Ignatius Press, 1997), p. 244.

44. Maximus, *Disputatio cum Pyrrho* (PG 91.297d-300a).

maintaining and perfecting, through his divine filiation, the synergy with God for which Adam was originally created.[45]

In the second volume of his *Jesus of Nazareth*, invoking Maximus directly, Pope Benedict expounds this theme of divine-human synergy in the dyothelite prayer of the Son at Gethsemane. Benedict writes:

> Human will, by virtue of creation, tends toward synergy (working together) with the divine will, but through sin, opposition takes the place of synergy: man, whose will attains fulfillment through becoming attuned to God's will, now has the sense that his freedom is compromised by God's will. He regards consenting to God's will, not as his opportunity to become fully himself, but as a threat to his freedom against which he rebels.
>
> The drama of the Mount of Olives lies in the fact that Jesus draws man's natural will away from opposition and back toward synergy, and in so doing he restores man's true greatness. In Jesus' natural human will, the sum total of human nature's resistance to God is . . . present within Jesus Himself. The obstinacy of us all, the whole of our opposition to God is present, and in His struggle, Jesus elevates our recalcitrant nature to become its real self. . . . The prayer "not my will, but yours" (Lk 22:42) is truly the Son's prayer to the Father, through which the natural human will is completely subsumed into the "I" of the Son. Indeed, the Son's whole being is expressed in the "not I, but You" — in the total self-abandonment of the "I" to the "You" of God the Father. This same "I" has subsumed and transformed humanity's resistance, so that we are all now present within the Son's obedience; we are all drawn into sonship.[46]

Benedict helps us to see that Maximus's exegesis of the "drama of the Mount of Olives" realizes a doctrine of theandric synergy in the communion with God in which the "true greatness" of the human being consists, for which the human creature is created and tends by nature. Synergy is

---

45. In this way Maximus's exegesis of Gethsemane presumes an anthropology wherein the more supernatural the *tropos*, the more natural the *telos*. The implication of *Disputatio cum Pyrrho* is shocking because from it Maximus suggests that the temptation of Christ is greater insofar as he immaculately resists sin. Again: the more immaculate, the more truly tempted — "for the moment sin begins, temptation ends" (Joseph Farrell, *The Disputation with Pyrrhus of Our Father among the Saints Maximus the Confessor*, p. 18, n. 29).

46. Joseph Ratzinger — Pope Benedict XVI, *Jesus of Nazareth*, pt. 2, *Holy Week: From the Entrance into Jerusalem to the Resurrection*, trans. provided by the Vatican Secretariat of State (San Francisco: Ignatius Press, 2011), pp. 160-61.

thus internal to the ultimate homonization of the human being, such that being a fellow-worker with God is exactly the truest freedom of the human creature. But the communion of synergy is unraveled by sin, especially by the sense that God's will is somehow contrastively related to human freedom. The more God acts, the less the human acts, to the effect that God's action is seen as compromising the freedom of human action. In this way, human action is misconstrued as flourishing to the extent that it is self-enclosed and autonomous, while the action of God is thought to be a threat to human freedom against which the human ought to rebel.

The drama of the filial prayer of Jesus at Gethsemane undoes the contrast that would pit the will of God against the freedom of man. By representing within himself all of humanity's resistance to God, Jesus "draws man's natural will away from opposition and back toward synergy." In other words, Gethsemane realizes a new pattern of theandric synergy in the obedience of the Son's prayer. In Jesus' "not my will, but Thy will be done," the natural human will, with all of its fear of death and resistance to God, is submitted totally to the Father such that it is "subsumed into the 'I' of the Son." This is unlocked by the traditional profession of the Passion of the Christ as an act freely accepted. In this light, the filial self-abandonment at Gethsemane ("not my will, but thy will be done") articulates the perfect and total "yes" of the Son to the Cross, such that this death cannot be precisely understood as the lynching of an innocent man (although it is that), but rather must be proclaimed as the most perfect sacrifice (self-gift) of the Son who is both priest and victim. The freedom of Jesus' prayer thereby breaks open, as it were, every temptation to self-enclosure, in the consent of the Son to have himself broken open for the salvation of the world. Only therein do we find a human act that is truly free, and so only therein do we find our own sonship. In the human resistance he suffers in the freedom of his "yes," Jesus transforms the sorrow of the fallen condition into his eternal communion with the Father.

C. Christological Synergism

In the one Lord Jesus Christ, the work of salvation is "willed by a divine person through a human will."[47] The achievement of this dogma, ratified at Constantinople III and the Lateran synod of 649, specifies the freedom of

47. International Theological Commission, "Select Questions on Christology," p. 192.

human action in the event of salvation. The basis of this conciliar doctrine is rooted in Maximus's dyoenergist reception of Denys the Areopagite's doctrine of Christ's "theandric energy" (θεανδρικὴν ἐνέργειαν). A key text here is Maximus's fifth *Ambiguum*, which is dedicated to a dyoenergist interpretation of the new theandric energy against the monenergist interpretation of Cyrus of Alexandria. Maximus's aim, accordingly, was to win the doctrine and the figure of Denys for Chalcedonian orthodoxy.[48]

Denys's doctrine had developed in the context of formulating an answer to the mystery of the Incarnation:

> How, you ask, is Jesus, who is beyond everything (πάντων ἐπέκεινα), ranked together with all human beings at the level of being? For here he is not called a man as the cause of humankind but as one who is himself in his whole being truly a man (ἀλλ᾽ ὡς αὐτὸς κατ᾽ οὐσίαν ὅλην ἀληθῶς ἄνθρωπος ὤν).[49]

In the Incarnation, God is human in the fullest sense, "as one who is himself in his whole being truly a man," but yet he remains the one who is "beyond everything." This being the case, for Denys, a special co-inherence must be maintained between this "particular being" and that which is "beyond being." In a word, this co-inherence is the reciprocity which elsewhere Denys, following St. Paul, calls *synergia* (συνέργια), the event of "becoming a co-actor with God" (Θεοῦ συνεργὸν γενέσθαι).[50] The question of how the one who is "beyond being" can become a "human being" moves, in this way, from the question of being as such (οὐσία) to the question of the evental dynamic of action (ἐνέργεια and δύναμις). This new Dionysian focus began a phase of fresh dogmatic possibility in which the Christological question of divine-human synergy in Jesus could be confronted.

More generally, for Denys, synergism occurs within the celestial hierarchy of being, of lower beings with a higher one, reaching all the way up to God himself in such a way that the receptivity of the lower allows for synergy with the higher in terms that nevertheless result in an event of mu-

---

48. If Maximus's interpretation is fully Chalcedonian we should not fail to note that it is, *pace* those modern theologians who characterize the doctrine as swinging in the direction of the so-called Antiochene "school," a Chalcedonian orthodoxy thoroughly Cyrillian in every sense. See Andrew Louth, *Maximus the Confessor*, p. 53.

49. Denys the Areopagite, *Epistula* 4 (PG 3.1072a), trans. Louth (from his translation of Maximus's *Ambiguum* 5).

50. Denys the Areopagite, *De caelesti hierarchia* 3.2 (PG 3.165b).

tual ecstasy.[51] Synergy involves, therefore, a mutual circumincession that catches the hierarchies of being up into communion with each other and ultimately with God. This Dionysian notion of synergy is maximally at work in the Incarnation where, according to Denys, in the happening of Christ, human things are done divinely and divine things are done humanly.[52] The mutual ecstasy of the synergistic event is operative here, and at the highest pitch, in the "new theandric activity" (καινὴ θεανδρικὴ ἐνέργεια) of Jesus in the Incarnation.[53]

Key to Maximus's dyoenergist reading of the Dionysian doctrine is the use he makes of themes indigenous to Proclean Neo-Platonism.[54] Since the time of Plotinus, the language of "energy" (ἐνέργεια) had taken on a new meaning, no longer signifying actuality in contrast to potency (as it had for Aristotle), but rather becoming more or less synonymous with *dynamis* (δύναμις), so that both could be translated "power."[55] Against Plotinus, Proclus proposed that infinity is represented by power (δύναμις) and finitude by being (οὐσία). This Proclean scheme, applied to the Incarnation, understands the event as one that conjoins infinite and finite. This is precisely how Maximus sets up his interpretation of Denys's theandric Christ:

> "And he performs human activities in a way beyond the human": dispassionately instituting afresh the nature of the elements by degrees. For clearly water is unstable, and cannot receive or support material and earthly feet, but by a power beyond nature (ὑπερφυεῖ δυνάμει) it is constituted as unyielding. If then with unmoistened feet, which have bodily bulk and the weight of matter, he traversed the wet and unstable substance, walking on the sea as on a pavement, he shows through this crossing that the natural energy (φύσιν ἐνέργειαν) of his own flesh is inseparable from the power of his divinity (τῇ δυνάμει τῆς ἑαυτοῦ

---

51. Alexander Golitzin, "'Suddenly, Christ': The Place of Negative Theology in the Mystagogy of Dionysius Areopagite," in Michael Kessler and Christian Shepherd, eds., *Mystics: Presence and Aporia* (Chicago: University of Chicago Press, 2003), pp. 8-37, at p. 13.

52. Denys the Areopagite, *Epistula* 4 (PG 3.1072a): Καὶ τὸ λοιπὸν, οὐ κατὰ θεὸν τὰ θεῖα δράσας, οὐ τὰ ἀνθρώπεια κατὰ ἄνθρωπον.

53. Denys the Areopagite, *Epistula* 4 (PG 3.1072c).

54. In what follows I am relying significantly on Frederick Lauritzen, "Pagan Energies in Maximus the Confessor: The Influence of Proclus on *Ad Thomam* 5," *Greek, Roman, and Byzantine Studies* 52 (2012): 226-39.

55. Lauritzen, "Pagan Energies in Maximus the Confessor," p. 232.

θεότητος ἀχωρίστως). For the movement that can make such a crossing is constituted by a nature belonging to no one else than the divinity, that is beyond infinity and being, united to it hypostatically.[56]

The hypostatic singularity of Jesus, who is the Logos, means that the Chalcedonian language of "without separation" (ἀχωρίστως) must apply to the energies of Christ as well, the divine energy (δύναμις) must be synergistically "one" with the natural energy (ἐνέργεια) of this human being. The question of the natures is thus replaced with a concern for Christ's activity, his energies, which are naturally distinct, yet "one" on the level of hypostasis.

Having focused on the energies, Maximus could thus deploy the Proclean distinction of *dynamis* (δύναμις) and being (οὐσία) to the effect that he could attribute *dynamis* to the infinite Logos and action (ἐνέργεια) to the assumed finite nature. This allowed him to account for a unitive synergism, a new theandric energy that does not compromise the *maior dissimilitudo* that must maintain between the power of God and every human act. In the events of Jesus' life, Maximus could now account for how Jesus, in his body in act and in time, realizes "the natural energy of his own flesh is inseparable from the power of his divinity."[57] In this way, in the newness of Denys's theandric action, Maximus found the necessary resources by which to articulate the mode of synergism that would specify the dyothelite fact of Jesus's filial prayer, in which, "as man, being by nature God, he acts humanly, willingly accepting the experience of suffering for our sake . . . [while] as God, who is human by nature, he acts divinely and naturally exhibits the evidence of his divinity."[58] In the Gethsemane event, we are thus given the concrete historical "mystery" of the divine-human inversion in synergy, and this theandric synergy, proper to the Incarnate One, is precisely what is given when Jesus teaches his disciples how to pray: "Our Father . . . thy will be done" (Matt. 6:9-10). The mystery of the Son's prayer is not only a mystery that plunges to the core of his being in act, it is the very basis of the Christian life: "When we cry, 'Abba! Father!' it is the Spirit himself bearing witness with our spirit that we are children of God" (Rom. 8:15-16).

56. Maximus the Confessor, *Ambiguum* 5 (PG 91.1049b-c), trans. Louth (but modified). Cf. Lauritzen, "Pagan Energies in Maximus the Confessor," pp. 233-34.

57. Maximus the Confessor, *Ambiguum* 5 (PG 91.1049c).

58. Maximus the Confessor, *Opusculum* 7 (PG 91.84c).

D. The Most Determined Conqueror of Nestorianism

On the normative and modern account, Constantinople III is described as if the aim of the Council Fathers present was to correct a revanchist return to an imbalanced Cyrillian doctrine, imposed artificially through the imperial machinations of Justinian at Constantinople II.[59] The eminent British scholar of early Christian doctrine, J. N. D. Kelly, decisively proposed this view in his still standard account of the development of patristic doctrine, *Early Christian Doctrines* (1950):

> In spite of all . . . Chalcedon failed to bring permanent peace. . . . [I]f the West remained loyal to the council [Chalcedon], there was an immediate hostile reaction in the East which was to last for centuries. Nestorianism proper had been driven beyond the frontiers of the empire, but monophysitism in its various forms waged incessant war against the Definition [of Chalcedon]. . . . The struggle, as embittered as it was long and closely entangled with politics, resulted in the emergence in the East in the sixth century (cf. the second council of Constantinople, 553) of a "Neo-Chalcedonianism" which subtly shifted the bias of the council, interpreting its teaching in a positive Cyrillian sense. The affirmation at the third council of Constantinople (680) of the existence of two wills in Christ, which settled the monothelite controversy, represented an attempt to restore the Chalcedonian balance.[60]

Yet this account leaves several lingering questions. Was Constantinople III an attempt to recover the "balance" of Chalcedon against the Cyrillianism of Constantinople II? Can we truthfully understand the dyotheletism of

---

59. Commenting on the dogmatic achievement of Constantinople III, Gerald O'Collins, S.J., writes that, while the Council of 553 "represented a return to the Alexandrian triumph at Ephesus," the Council of 680-681 "swung the pendulum in the Antiochene direction" (*Christology: A Biblical, Historical, and Systematic Study of Jesus* (Oxford: OUP, 1995), pp. 184-201, here at p. 195). Norman Tanner, S.J. takes a similar view, writing that, "Constantinople II saw a reversal for the school of Antioch," while subsequently "Constantinople III . . . confirmed Chalcedon and continued further in the Antiochene direction . . . [because it] rejected the monothelite tendency of the Alexandria school" (*The Church in Council: Conciliar Movements, Religious Practice and the Papacy from Nicaea to Vatican II* (London: I. B. Tauris, 2011), pp. 15-16). O'Collins and Tanner are representative of the modern textbook view of the matter. See also Schönborn, *God Sent His Son*, pp. 193-220.

60. J. N. D. Kelly, *Early Christian Doctrines*, rev. ed. (New York: HarperOne, 1978), pp. 342-43.

Maximus the Confessor, received at Constantinople III, as a corrective to a quasi-monophysite tendency indigenous to Cyrillian Christology? Did Constantinople III swing the pendulum in a "Theodorian" direction? Any accounting of the facts leads to an answer in the negative.

The idea that Maximian dyotheletism and the dogma of Constantinople III are best understood as "correcting" the doctrine of Constantinople II distorts the actual history of events and is theologically untenable. The strongest evidence of this lies in the canons of the Lateran synod of 649, which appear to have been composed by Maximus, before the synod met.[61] Contrary to every Theodorian sensibility and any sense of motivation to "correct" Constantinople II, the Lateran synod through Maximus upheld the following canons:

1. canon 20, which affirms Constantinople II as one of five "Ecumenical Councils," thus acknowledging for the first time in the Latin church the Justinian Council as equal in rank with the "Ecumenical Councils" from Nicaea to Chalcedon;[62]
2. canon 16, which declares the doctrine of the two wills of Christ by direct appeal to "blessed Cyril," the sufficient standard of orthodoxy, who is significantly invoked alone and without appeal even to Pope Leo the Great;[63]
3. canon 5, which upholds the orthodoxy of the "mia physis" formula;[64]
4. canon 8, which upholds the Constantinopolitan-Justinian doctrine of the Incarnate Son's "compound hypostasis" (ὑπόστασις σύνθετος);[65]
5. canon 2, an unequivocal theopaschite declaration;[66] and
6. canon 18, which anathematizes, along with Nestorius and Theodore, Diodore of Tarsus; the first such anathematization of Diodore to be made at any synod or council.[67]

---

61. Rudolf Riedinger, "Die Lateransynode von 649 und Maximos der Bekenner," in Félix Heinzer and Christoph Schönborn, O.P., eds., *Maximus Confessor: Actes du Symposium sur Maxime le Confesseur Fribourg, 2-5 septembre 1980* (Fribourg: Éditions Universitaires, 1982), pp. 111-21.

62. Lateran Synod of 649, canon 20 (DS 520).
63. Lateran Synod of 649, canon 16 (DS 516).
64. Lateran Synod of 649, canon 5 (DS 505).
65. Lateran Synod of 649, canon 8 (DS 508).
66. Lateran Synod of 649, canon 2 (DS 502).
67. Lateran Synod of 649, canon 18 (DS 518).

It is not possible to construe the contents of these canons as harboring any sympathy with Theodorian Christology. Decreed at a synod in Rome, moreover, where the persistent reception of Constantinople II had been muted, and in the context of a synod decreed against imperial meddling in ecclesial dogma, the fact that Maximus and Martin endorsed Constantinople II as an Ecumenical Council equal to Nicaea and Chalcedon signals only that they thought its doctrine to be true, and that they understood their own theological program to be in perfect continuity with the decrees of that council. The evidence shows us clearly that, for Maximus and for Martin, the dogmatic issue of monenergism and monothelitism did not involve anything like a failure to "balance" unity and distinction, as the two "schools" narrative implies, but involved rather a misunderstanding of how the full integrity of human difference (*maior dissimilitudo*) is in Christ maintained and constituted by the unity of the Son's hypostasis.

Properly understood, Maximus's doctrine is fully rooted in the Cyrillian vision summed up in the dictum, "if he conquered as God, to us it is nothing; but if he conquered as man we conquered in him."[68] The dyadic fact of natural divinity and humanity in Christ is reaffirmed by Maximus, not in order to establish two grounds of being, not in order to "loosen" the unity of Christ, but rather to affirm more radically the meaning of Christ's *unitas*. As Joseph Ratzinger writes:

> The metaphysical two-ness of a human and divine will is not abrogated, but in the realm of the *person* ... the fusion of both takes place, with the result that they become *one* will, not naturally, but personally. This free unity — a form of unity created by love — is higher and more interior than merely natural unity. It corresponds to the highest unity there is, namely, trinitarian unity.[69]

There is nothing disingenuous or incongruous in Maximus's sense of perfect dogmatic continuity with the strong single-subject Christology of Constantinople II — it is precisely the unity of the single divine subject that makes possible this human difference. Thus, as Ratzinger has it, far from

68. See Wilken, *The Spirit of Early Christian Thought*, pp. 129-30, who links this quote of Cyril to Maximus's theology of Gethsemane.

69. Joseph Ratzinger, *Behold the Pierced One: An Approach to a Spiritual Christology*, trans. Graham Harrison (San Francisco: Ignatius Press, 1986), p. 39. Emphasis is Ratzinger's.

swinging the pendulum in a Theodorian direction, Maximus is, rather, "the most determined conqueror of Nestorianism."[70]

E. Pneumatological Correspondence

The dyothelite doctrine focuses dogmatic speculation on the filial prayer of the Son. As such, it understands Jesus's hypostatic unity as rooted in "Jesus's activity proceeding from the core of his personality . . . his dialogue with the Father."[71] In this dialogue that lies at the core of the Son's person, the role of the Spirit is decisive: the Holy Spirit reveals — and in a certain sense "is" — the will of God the Father.[72] The dyothelite doctrine, in this way, opens the field of Christological speculation to the pneumatological infrastructure of Jesus' incarnate being.[73]

The Holy Spirit incarnates the Logos. This basic fact of the Spirit, as the initiator of the movement of the divine dispensation, is affirmed in both the *Symbolum Apostolorum* and the *Credo* of Nicaea: the Son is conceived by the Holy Spirit and born of the Virgin Mary. The creedal declaration in this way recapitulates precisely the narrative of the Gospel accounts of Jesus' life, where the incarnate action of the Logos, we might say, is a matter "provoked" by the Spirit, who drives and prompts the drama of decision. Jesus lives in the deepest way by the promptings of the Spirit, and from this pneumatological depth he lives his incarnate filiation. In the Gospels Jesus acts and wills in obedient intimacy to the Father, always through the Spirit: "The Spirit of the Lord is upon me, because he has anointed me to preach good news to the poor" (Luke 4:18; cf. Isa. 61:1). This abiding of the Spirit upon Jesus is what it means for him to be the Christ, and it marks him with his incarnate task: "I have come down from heaven, not to do my own will, but the will of him who sent me" (John 6:38).

---

70. Joseph Ratzinger, *A New Song for the Lord: Faith in Christ and Liturgy Today*, trans. Martha M. Matesich (London: Crossroads, 1996), p. 27.

71. Ratzinger, *Behold the Pierced One*, pp. 17-18.

72. Cf. Augustine of Hippo, *De Trinitate* 15.38: "Sed voluntas dei si et proprie dicenda est aliqua in trinitate persona, magis hoc nomen spiritui sancto competit sicut caritas. Nam quid est aliud caritas quam voluntas?" Also see ST I, q. 27, a. 4; q. 28, a. 4; and q. 37, a. 1.

73. On this, see the crucial article of Ivor J. Davidson, "'Not My Will but Yours Be Done.'" In another context, the speculation on Christology in this manner leads to Ratzinger's proposal that the dyothelite doctrine entails the development of "spiritual Christology"; cf. *Behold the Pierced One, passim*, but esp. pp. 13-46.

If in some sense it is the Spirit who ensures the filial communication and unity of Jesus with the Father, the significance of this is not relevant only to Jesus' personal identity. Rather, in the Lord's Prayer, the filial communication of the Son in the Spirit to the Father is precisely what the Son gives his followers as the heart and fundament of their own life of discipleship: "Pray then in this way: Our Father . . ."[74] (Matt. 6:9). For this reason, the "entirety" of the Son's incarnate action — "from his silence in the heart of Mary in Advent, gathering to his passion, from his passion to the darkness of the tomb, from the darkness of the tomb to the daybreak and 'lumen Christi' of Easter morning"[75] — is lived by the Church precisely in *unitate Spiritus Sancti.*[76] Just as the Spirit overshadowed Mary at the Annunciation, so he descends upon the Church at Pentecost (cf. Acts 2:1-13). The Spirit who raised Jesus Christ from the dead gives life to the mortal bodies of the followers of Jesus (cf. Rom. 8:11). The Spirit who anointed the Son at his baptism adopts human beings into the life of divine filiation (cf. Rom. 8:15). The Spirit in whom Jesus conducted his filial dialogue with the Father is the Spirit in whom the Church learns to pray "Abba, Father" (cf. Rom. 8:15 and Gal. 4:6). When the priest prays the Eucharistic prayer of the Mass, he bids the Spirit to come down to effect the transubstantiation of the elements into the body and blood of Christ, that the faithful communicant might be transformed to become truly the mystical body of the Son. The Spirit, the *vinculum amoris* of the Father and Son, who accomplished the *unio* of divinity and humanity in Christ, now constitutes the *communio* of the Church united to Christ by the grace of adoptive filiation.

In all of this, we see that the pneumatological infrastructure of Jesus' life is translated through his bidding to become the same pneumatic in-

---

74. In this light, it is significant that some old manuscripts of the Lord's Prayer in Luke's Gospel, in the place of the petition "Thy kingdom come," have a petition to the Holy Spirit: ἐλθέτω τὸ πνεῦμα σοῦ ("Thy Spirit come") (Luke 11:2; cf. Gregory of Nyssa, *Orationis Dominicae* [PG 44.1157c], and Tertullian, *De Baptismo* [PL 1.1316A]). In his own commentary of the Lord's Prayer, Maximus points to this witness as key to understanding the petition for the Kingdom (*Expositio Orationis Dominicae* [PG 90.884b]).

75. Caryll Houselander, *This War Is the Passion* (Notre Dame, IN: Ave Maria Press, 2008), p. 102. Cf. Pius XII, *Mediator Dei et hominum,* 20 (DS 3841): "The sacred liturgy is . . . the public worship which our Redeemer as Head of the Church renders to the Father, as well as the worship which the community of the faithful renders to its Founder, and through Him to the heavenly Father. It is, in short, the worship rendered by the Mystical Body of Christ in the entirety of its Head and members."

76. "Per ipsum, et cum ipso, et in ipso, est tibi Deo Patri omnipotenti in unitate Spiritus Sancti, omnis honor et gloria per omnia saecula saeculorum."

frastructure of those being adopted into the *communio* of his body. The mode of this pneumatic translation has a wonderful patristic precedent in the *Contra Arianos* of Athanasius. In *Contra Arianos*, written between 356 and 360, Athanasius argues that "what the Word has by nature . . . in the Father . . . He wishes to be given to us in the Spirit."[77] This statement evocatively captures how the adoptive filiation in the Spirit made possible by the Incarnation involves itself as an intra-divine gift, in which the passive voice attributed to the Son is of crucial importance.[78] Becoming *filii in Filio* realizes the divine filial desire of the Son for the Father to give the gift of adoptive filiation in the Spirit. The Incarnation in this light entails for us a concrete interval of gift in the life of God, a moment of bidding and of gratitude, of waiting and receiving. Our adoption is caught up here, in this interval of waiting and receiving. Furthermore, just as the Son asks the Father to be given through the Spirit, this gift of the Son is made in order that the created being can, in turn, be given back to the Father in the filial-likeness of the Son, now adopted by the Spirit. This is confirmed by an earlier passage of the same text in which Athanasius puts a Johannine-like prayer to the Father in the mouth of the Son: "Work thou then in them, O Father, and as thou hast given to me to bear this body, grant to them thy Spirit, that they too in it may become one, and may be perfected in me."[79]

The Son "*bids* the Father *grant* human beings the Spirit, as the Son had bid the Father grant him a body."[80] The Son, humanized by the gift of flesh received from the womb of Mary through the overshadowing of the Spirit, petitions the Father to deify humanity by the gift of the Spirit's *communio* effected through that flesh received of Mary ("that they too in it may become one").[81] The interval of God's gratuitous dealing with humanity is

---

77. Athanasius of Alexandria, *Orationes contra Arianos* 3.25 (PG 26.376b). See Eugene F. Rogers, Jr., "The Eclipse of the Spirit in Karl Barth," in John McDowell and Michael Higton, eds., *Conversing with Barth* (London: Ashgate, 2004), pp. 173-90, at p. 178. Cf. Eugene F. Rogers Jr., *After the Spirit: A Constructive Pneumatology from Resources Outside the Modern West* (Grand Rapids: Eerdmans, 2005), pp. 31-32.

78. Rogers, "The Eclipse of the Spirit," pp. 178-80. On the designation of the Spirit as *Donum*, see John Milbank, "Can a Gift Be Given? Prolegomena to a Future Trinitarian Metaphysic," in *Rethinking Metaphysics*, ed. L. Gregory Jones and Stephen E. Fowl (Oxford: Blackwell, 1995), pp. 119-61, especially pp. 144-54; "The Soul of Reciprocity," *Modern Theology* 17 (2001), part 1, pp. 335-91, and part 2, pp. 485-507.

79. Athanasius, *Orationes contra Arianos* 3.25 (PG 26.376a).

80. Rogers, "The Eclipse of the Spirit," p. 179. Emphases are Rogers's.

81. Cf. Adrienne von Speyr, *The World of Prayer*, trans. Graham Harrison (San Francisco: Ignatius Press, 1985), p. 134.

a variation of difference within the more fundamental communion that constitutes the possibility of synergy of God and man after the pattern of the one Lord Jesus Christ. At the heart of this filial pattern is the Son's abandonment to the Spirit, who incarnates him, drives him into every temptation, and leads him ultimately to Gethsemane and the Cross. The Cross is the ultimate expression of the *unitas* of the Son with the Father. The decision of Gethsemane could not lead anywhere else, only to a total realization of oneness expressed in his freedom to do the Father's will. That the Son "bids" the Father to "grant" the Spirit to human beings is to bid the Father to give human beings the *vinculum amoris* through which the Son accomplished his perfect act of theandric synergy: *Qui cum Passioni voluntarie traderetur.*

PART THREE

The Existence of Christ

CHAPTER 7

The Divine *Esse*

[I]f we should understand existing insofar as one existing belongs to one existing subject, it seems that we should say that there is only one existing in Christ.

Thomas Aquinas

A. Thomas and Constantinople II

Thomas Aquinas's discovery of the conciliar texts of Ephesus, Chalcedon, and Constantinople II confirmed his own highly unitive doctrine of the hypostatic union, which he had already outlined in the *Scriptum super Sententiis,* before coming to know those conciliar texts directly.[1] That he was the first Latin theologian of the high Middle Ages to quote directly from the decrees of those councils,[2] including the *Definitio fidei,* is a remarkable

---

1. Thomas Aquinas, *Scriptum super Sententiis* III, dist. 6, q. 2, a. 2. For a good short treatment of Thomas's doctrine of the hypostatic union, see Frederick Christian Bauerschmidt, *Thomas Aquinas: Faith, Reason, and Following Christ* (Oxford: OUP, 2013), pp. 188-206.

2. Thomas's source for the texts of the first four councils (Nicaea, Constantinople I, Ephesus, and Chalcedon) is the *Collectio Casinensis,* a work unavailable to him until his second stay in Italy (1259-1261). Thus the texts of Chalcedon and Ephesus were yet unfamiliar to Thomas when he wrote his commentary on Lombard's *Libri quatuor Sententiarum.* See Jean-Pierre Torrell, O.P., *Thomas Aquinas,* vol. 1, *The Person and His Work,* trans. Robert Royal (Washington, DC: Catholic University Press, 1996), p. 103. On the theme of Thomas's use of the early conciliar texts, see Martin Morard, "Thomas d'Aquin lecteur des conciles," *Archivum Franciscanum Historicum* 98 (2005): 211-365; H. F. Dondaine, "Note sur la documentation patristique de Saint Thomas à Paris en 1270," *Revue des sciences philosophiques et théologiques* 47 (1963): 403-6; Ignaz Backes, *Die Christologie des heiligen Thomas von Aquin und die griechischen Kirchenväter* (Paderborn: Schöningh, 1931); C. G. Geenen, "En marge du concile de

detail of Latin theological history and a sign of the sad chasm that had come to separate the Latin theological tradition from that of Byzantium.[3] The significance of Thomas's recovery of the conciliar tradition of the first millennium, along with its Byzantine patrimony, is complemented and extended by the bold use he makes of Cyril of Alexandria, and by his privileged reliance on the *De fide orthodoxa* of John of Damascus.[4] Thomas's Christology is truly a Latin work across the Great Schism.

Even more remarkable, given the tentative reception of Constantinople II in the Latin West, is the fact that, among the early councils, it was above all Constantinople II that played a decisive role in shaping Thomas's mature Christology. The *Anathematismi adversus "tria Capitula"* confirmed, in a singular way, Thomas's suspicion of a Nestorian drift within the theology of his own milieu, a drift evidenced, above all, in the first and third so-called *opiniones* of union offered by Peter Lombard in his *Libri quatuor Sententiarum*.[5]

Chalcédoine: Les textes du Quatrième Concile dans les oeuvres de Saint Thomas," *Angelicum* 29 (1952) : 43-59; James Weisheipl, O.P., *Friar Thomas d'Aquino: His Life, Thought and Works* (New York: Doubleday, 1974), pp. 164-65. Cf. Roger E. Reynolds, *Collectio Canonum Casinensis Duodecimi Seculi (Codex Terscriptus): A Derivative of the South-Italian Collection in Five Books: An Implicit Edition with Introductory Study* (Rome: Pontifical Institute of Mediaeval Studies, 2001). On Chalcedon and scholasticism, cf. Ludwig Ott, "Das Konzil von Chalkedon in der Frühscholastik," in A. Grillmeier and H. Bacht, eds., *Das Konzil von Chalkedon: Geschichte und Gegenwart*, vol. 2 (Würzburg: Echter-Verlag, 1953), pp. 873-922.

3. Joseph Wawrykow, "Wisdom in the Christology of Thomas Aquinas," in Kent Emery Jr. and Joseph P. Wawrykow, eds., *Christ Among the Medieval Dominicans* (Notre Dame, IN: University of Notre Dame Press, 1998), pp. 175-94, at p. 187.

4. See Fergus Kerr, O.P., *After Aquinas: Versions of Thomism* (Oxford: Blackwell, 2002), p. 176.

5. So named at the beginning of the twentieth century after the most distinctive feature of each; cf. Bernhard Barth, "Ein neues Dokument zur Geschichte der frühscholastischen Christologie," *Theologische Quartalschrift* 100 (1919): 409-426. On Peter Lombard's Christology, see Philipp W. Rosemann, *Peter Lombard* (Oxford: OUP, 2004), pp. 118-39; Lauge Olaf Nielsen, *Theology and Philosophy in the Twelfth Century: A Study of Gilbert Porreta's Thinking and the Theological Expositions of the Doctrine of the Incarnation during the Period 1130-1180* (Leiden: E. J. Brill, 1982), pp. 243-78; Marcia Colish, *Peter Lombard*, 2 vols. (Leiden: E. J. Brill, 1994), vol. 1, pp. 417-38. Peter's threefold distinction was complicated by the influential commentary of a former pupil, John of Cornwall. In his treatise *Eulogium ad Alexandrum Papam tertium*, John, in the words of Philipp Rosemann, "adduced further authorities in support of each of the theories, identified some of their twelfth-century proponents, expressed his own preference [for the middle position], and urged Pope Alexander III to have the two approaches that he, John, considered heterodox condemned at the upcoming council [the Third Lateran Council of 1179]" (Rosemann, *Peter Lombard*, p. 128). Perhaps most controver-

The first Lombardian theory, the *homo assumptus* theory, traced by John of Cornwall (Lombard's sometime pupil) to Hugh of St. Victor (c. 1096-1141), has roots going back at least as far as Anselm of Laon (d. 1117).[6] More broadly the theory is expressive of the Christology associated with Theodore of Mopsuestia, for whom the Incarnation is an "indwelling" of the Logos in the *homo assumptus*.[7] While Theodore is not named, he would seem to stand in the background of the theory Lombard describes thus:

> In the Incarnation of the Word a certain human being was constituted from a rational soul and human flesh: out of which too every true human being is constituted. And that human being began to be God (*et ille homo coepit esse Deus*) — not, however, the nature of God, but the person of the Word. . . . And although they [those who hold this theory] say that that human being [that is, Christ] subsists from a rational soul and human flesh, nonetheless they do not confess that it is composed of two natures, divine and human; nor [do they confess] that the two natures are parts of that [human being], but only soul and flesh.[8]

On this view, the union of divinity and humanity in Christ is established by a special "identity" of essence between the *Verbum* and the *homo assumptus*, rooted in the assumed human's receptivity to the abiding power of the Word. This human being existed and then began to be God. As with Theodore, so with Lombard: the *homo assumptus* doctrine tends to minimize the ontological unity of Christ to the extent that, while the particular property of *hic homo* is assumed into union with the divine person of the Son, *hic homo* is not necessarily constituted in his existence by the *suppositum* of the Son.[9]

---

sially, John, in chapter 2 of the *Eulogium*, attributes the *habitus* theory to his former Master as the latter's personal opinion on the hypostatic union, and thus to a position John was urging the pope to condemn.

6. See "The *Eulogium ad Alexandrum Papam tertium* of John of Cornwall," trans. Nikolaus M. Häring, *Mediaeval Studies* 13 (1951): 253-300. Cf. Nielsen, *Theology and Philosophy in the Twelfth Century*, p. 362.

7. Theodore of Mopsuestia, *De Incarnatione* 7, LT 1 (ed. John Behr, *The Case against Diodore and Theodore: Texts and Their Contexts* [Oxford: OUP, 2011], p. 282). See chapter 1.

8. Peter Lombard, *Libri quatuor Sententiarum* III, dist. 6, no. 2 (PL 192.768), as translated by Rosemann, *Peter Lombard*, p. 128.

9. This was in fact the implicit teaching of Hugh of St. Victor. Cf. Hugh of St. Victor, *De Sacramentis fidei Christianae* (PL 176.411b). Though Hugh at times alleges that the Incarnate Son in his humanity received all the qualities of divinity — particularly in the case of his

The second theory explicated by Peter, the subsistence theory, is attributed to Gilbert de la Porrée (c. 1075-1154).[10] Those who hold to this theory, according to the Lombard, agree in part with those who hold the *homo assumptus* theory. Beyond the ontological minimalism of the first theory, however, those who hold to the subsistence theory

> say that that human being [Christ] consists not only of a rational soul and flesh, but of a human and of a divine nature, that is of three substances: divinity, flesh, and soul. This [human being] they confess to be Christ, and that He is only one person [i.e., one supposit], who was simple only before the Incarnation, but in the Incarnation came to be composed of divinity and humanity [i.e., *persona composita*].[11]

By contrast to the *homo assumptus* theory, the subsistence theory attributes greater metaphysical weight to the union by establishing that the human element is constituted, not as merely present to the Logos, but in its very existence, by its unity with the Logos.[12] Moreover, as Thomas reads the Porretan theory, it also ensures that, as a composite, Christ himself is one "supposit"[13] in a way that corresponds perfectly with the dogmatic specification Thomas would discover in the texts of Constantinople II (*persona composita*/ὑπόστασις σύνθετος).[14] The Porretan opinion, in this way, secures the relationship of humanity to divinity in Christ, not as an "accident" related to a "substance," but rather as a part related to the whole.

exposition of the Augustinian dictum *Quidquid habuit Filius per naturam, habuit homo ille per gratiam* (cf. Hugh, *De anima Christi* [PL 176.854d, 855a, 385d and 384a]) — nevertheless, as Nielsen has shown, Hugh is not prepared to admit that the person of Christ in time received the qualities which he possessed from eternity (cf. Hugh of St. Victor, *De anima Christi* [PL 176.855c], and *De Sacramentis fidei Christianae* [PL 176.397b]). In this way Hugh shows a reticence to admit the full communication of properties in Christ and evidences a certain parallelism of the natures. See Nielsen, *Theology and Philosophy in the Twelfth Century*, pp. 205-13. For a defense of Hugh and a strong argument that his Christology is not as open to the heretical tendencies of the Lombard's first theory as Nielsen suggests, see Franklin T. Harkins, "*Homo assumptus* and St. Victor: Reconsidering the Relationship between Victorine Christology and Peter Lombard's First Opinion," *The Thomist* 72 (2008): 595-624.

10. Cf. Nikolaus M. Häring, "The Case of Gilbert de la Porrée, Bishop of Poitiers (1142-1154)," *Mediaeval Studies* 13 (1951): 1-40.

11. Peter Lombard, *Libri quatuor Sententiarum* III, dist. 6, no. 5 (PL 192.770), as translated by Rosemann, *Peter Lombard*, p. 129.

12. Rosemann, *Peter Lombard*, p. 129.

13. ST III, q. 2, a. 4, *sed contra*.

14. *Anathematismi adversus "tria Capitula,"* canon 4 (DS 424; DEC 1.114-115).

Finally, as a *persona composita* the Incarnate Christ is composed of two natures, but one of those natures (the human) is itself a composite, which meant that Christ is composed of three different aspects of subsistence (*alia et alia ratio subsistendi*). This, however, should not be allowed to confuse the fact that, being himself personally *composita*, Christ is nevertheless a single whole (*unum subsistens*).[15]

In addition to the *homo assumptus* and subsistence theories, Peter offers the *habitus* theory, whereby the Logos is thought to be "clothed" with the soul and flesh of humanity.[16] John of Cornwall associates the *habitus* theory with Peter Abelard (1079-1142); its origins, however, lie in William of Champeaux (c. 1070-1122) and early scholasticism.[17] Thomas understood the theory to have been condemned by Pope Alexander III,[18] so that even while he believed the theory to be guilty of Nestorian heresy, having been clearly condemned, it did not present itself to him as a serious theological danger. Two *opiniones* remained: *homo assumptus* and subsistence.

In the *Scriptum super Sententiis* (written between 1252 and 1254), Thomas did not yet judge the *homo assumptus* theory heretical, although he already expressed an unfavorable opinion of it. However, when he came to write the *tertia pars* of the *Summa theologiae* nearly twenty years later, Thomas unequivocally pronounced it a species of Nestorian error.[19] The essential impetus behind this hardening verdict results directly from Thomas's recovery of the *Anathematismi adversus "tria Capitula."*[20]

---

15. ST III, q. 2, a. 4, *corpus*.

16. Peter Lombard, *Libri quatuor Sententiarum* III, dist. 6, no. 6 (PL 192.770) as translated by Rosemann, *Peter Lombard*, p. 129.

17. Nielsen, *Theology and Philosophy in the Twelfth Century*, p. 362.

18. ST III, q. 2, a. 6. Cf. Pope Alexander III, *Cum in nostra* (DS 749) and *Cum Christus* (DS 750). In fact, it seems that what Pope Alexander more specifically condemned was the so-called "Christological nihilism" doctrine, which Peter seems to have understood as linked to the *habitus* theory, a position not entirely clear from the Lombard's text (*Libri quatuor Sententiarum* III, dist. 10). Cf. Rosemann, *Peter Lombard*, pp. 131-33; and Paul Glorieux, "L'orthodoxie de III Sentences (d. 6, 7 et 10)," in *Miscellanea lombardiana* (Novara: Istituto geografico de Agostini, 1957), pp. 137-42.

19. Cf. ST III, q. 2, a. 6. Here Thomas states that heretical Christologies either posit union in nature or they posit accidental union; the former is always a variant of monophysitism, while the latter is necessarily a variant of Nestorianism.

20. Martin Morard, "Une source de Saint Thomas d'Aquin: Le deuxième concile de Constantinople (553)," *Revue des sciences philosophiques et théologiques* 81 (1997): 21-56; and R.-A. Gauthier, "Les Articuli in quibus frater Thomas melius in Summa quam in Scriptis," *Recherches de théologie ancienne et médiévale* 19 (1952): 271-326. Drawing on the work of Gauthier, Morard describes how Thomas's Christology became "decisively distanced, in a

Beginning with the *Summa contra Gentiles*, written between 1264 and 1265, Thomas's Christology becomes increasingly determined and informed by the doctrine of Constantinople II.[21] Making his own the Constantinopolitan formula of Christological union, *unio secundum subsistentiam*,[22] the formula became decisive to his rejection of the *homo assumptus* theory.[23] As Constantinople II states, and Thomas is at pains to re-articulate this in the Latin mediaeval context, union *secundum subsistentiam* means that there is in Christ *una subsistentia* and *una persona*.[24] To conceive that the supposit of the Word, in assuming the composite soul-body union, must therefore have assumed a human "supposit" (*hic homo*), is to contradict the dogma of Constantinople II:

---

categorical manner, from every accommodation with the *homo assumptus* theory given by Peter Lombard" (p. 55). In addition, see R.-A. Gauthier, "Introduction historique à S. Thomas d'Aquin," in Thomas Aquinas, *Contra Gentiles*, trans. R. Bernier and M. Corvez, vol. 1 (Paris: P. Lethielleux, 1961), pp. 7-123, esp. pp. 104-5. Cf. Gilles Emery, O.P., "A Note on St. Thomas and the Eastern Fathers," in *Trinity, Church, and the Human Person: Thomistic Essays* (Naples FL: Sapientia Press, 2007), pp. 193-208, here at pp. 202-4.

21. ScG IV.34; IV. 38. Morard shows how, after *Contra Gentiles*, (1) in the form of explicit citations Thomas's Christology is littered word for word with references to the third session and to canons 4, 5, 8, and 9, and (2) in the form of implicit paraphrases, allusions presuppose familiarity with the fourth, eighth and possibly also the fifth, sixth and seventh sessions of Constantinople II. In addition to *Contra Gentiles*, Morard points to: *De potentia Dei*, q. 10, a. 4, ad 13, and q. 10, a. 4, ad 24; *Lectura in Mattheum, cap.* 1, lectio 5; *Super Ioannem* 1, lect. 7, nn. 171-172, and 12, lect. 7; ST III, q. 2, a. 1, ad 1; q. 2, a. 3, *corpus*; q. 2, a. 6, *corpus*, and q. 25, a. 1, *sed contra*; *De unione Verbi incarnati*, a. 1, *corpus*, and a. 2, *corpus*; and the prologue of *Expositio super Psalmos*. On the composition of the *Summa contra Gentiles*, see Torrell, *Thomas Aquinas*, vol. 1, pp. 101-4.

22. The formula is crucially deployed, not only as a refutation of the parallelism of the two natures in Christ, but also at the service of defending and specifying the orthodoxy of Cyril's axiom μία φύσις τοῦ λόγου σεσαρκωμένη. Canon 8 of the *Anathematismi adversus "tria Capitula"* states: "Si quis ex duabus naturis deitatis et humanitatis confitens unitatem factam esse, vel unam naturam Dei Verbi incarnatam (μία φύσις τοῦ θεοῦ λόγου σεσαρκωμένη) dicens, non sic ea excipit, sicut patres docuerunt, quod ex divina natura et humana, unitione secundum subsistentiam (ἐνώσεως καθ᾽ ὑπόστασιν) facta, ... talis a. s." The formula repeats in slight variation ("secundum subsistentiam unitum," "unitate secundum subsistentiam" and "unitione secundum subsistentiam") in the fourth, fifth and seventh anathemas (DEC 1.114-118).

23. Cf. ST III, q. 2, a. 1, *ad* 1, and q. 2, a. 6.

24. Cf. *Anathematismi adversus "tria Capitula*," canon 5 (DS 426; DEC 1.116): "Si quis ... sed non confitetur Dei Verbum carni secundum subsistentiam unitum (καθ᾽ ὑπόστασιν ὑνωθῆναι) esse et propter hoc unam eius subsistentiam seu unam personam, et sic et sanctum Chalcedonense concilium unam subsistentiam domini nostri Iesu Christi confessum esse, talis a. s."

If anyone . . . tries to introduce into the mystery of Christ two supposits (*duas subsistentias*) or two persons (*duas personas*) and then talks of one person only in respect to dignity, honor or adoration, as both Theodore [of Mopsuestia] and Nestorius have written in their madness . . . let him be anathema. For there has been no addition of person or subsistence to the Holy Trinity (*nec enim adiectionem personae vel subsistentiae suscepit sancta Trinitas*) even after the incarnation of one of its members, God the Word.[25]

Making his own the doctrine of Constantinople II, Thomas positively affirms that the union in Christ involves neither a compounded nature out of two (*ex duabus una natura conflata*) nor a parallelism of substances conjoined to something *ad exteriora* (i.e. an accidental relation of one thing to another),[26] but rather a *unio secundum subsistentiam*. This Thomas took as ruling out the metaphysical presupposition that underpins both the Nestorian and Eutychian errors, according to which any *unio* that maintains *in duabus naturis* (that preserves the difference *ex duabus naturis*) cannot occur within a single *suppositum*.[27] Whereas Nestorianism maintains the integral difference *in duabus naturis* at the expense of the integral *unio*, the Eutychian position affirms a maximal union that must result in a *tertium quid* — *una natura ex duabus naturis*.[28] For Thomas, to the contrary, the dogma of the *unio secundum subsistentiam* requires *unio* both *in una persona* and *in duabus naturis*, which requires, in turn, that in Christ the difference of human nature is perfected in direct relation to its union with God. The *mysterium unionis* is thus a mystery of unified differentiation wherein it is precisely the union that differentiates.

---

25. *Anathematismi adversus "tria Capitula,"* canon 5 (DS 426; DEC 1.116); translation modified. Thomas cites this passage against *homo assumptus* Christology in *De unione Verbi incarnati* (a. 2, *corpus*) and in the *Summa* (ST III, q. 2, a. 3, *corpus*). In *Super Ioannem* he refers to Constantinople II when writing against the *homo assumptus* theory (*cap.* 1, *lectio* 7, nn. 171-172).

26. ScG IV.41. In ST III, q. 2, a. 6, *corpus* Thomas lists five modes of "accidental" union proposed by Nestorian-minded thinkers, all of which are *ad exteriora*. First, *secundum inhabitationem*, which proposes union in terms of "dwelling," as in someone dwelling in a temple; second, *secundum unitatem affectus*, a union in terms of a mere agreement of will; third, *secundum operationem*, inasmuch as this humanity was an "instrument" of the Word of God; fourth, *secundum dignitatem honoris*, an honor bestowed to a human, on account of his union with the Son of God; fifth, *secundum aequivocationem* (or *secundum communicationem nominum*), a union of linguistic naming whereby this man is said to be the Son of God.

27. Cf. ST III, q. 2, a. 6, *corpus*.

28. Cf. ScG IV.35.

B. Christ's Single Divine *Esse*

It has been argued that the core objective of Thomas's formulation of the doctrine of the hypostatic union concerns the proper mode of conceiving the incarnational "is."[29] What does it mean to say *Deus est homo*? Thomas responds:

> Supposing the truth of the Catholic belief, that the true divine nature is united with true human nature not only in person, but also in suppositum or hypostasis; we say that this proposition is true and proper; *God is man* — not only by the truth of its terms, i.e., because Christ is true God and true man, but by the truth of the predication.[30]

The union in *suppositum*, then, means that the one who is *ex Patre* is the same one who is *ex Maria*. In this way the Christological unity, the incarnational "is" — the Son's incarnate "being" or "existence" — is the cornerstone of Thomas's doctrine of the hypostatic union.[31] Hence Thomas's doctrine on the singular divine *esse* of Christ:

> We need to profess that things belonging to the existing subject (*suppositum*) or hypostasis are only one thing in Christ (*unum tantum in Christo*). And so, if we should understand existing insofar as one existing belongs to one existing subject (*unum esse est unius suppositi*), it seems that we should say that there is only one existing in Christ (*unum esse*).[32]

Thomas's doctrine of the single divine *esse* of Jesus confirms his wider metaphysics, which itself, in turn, conforms to the basic grammar of Chalcedonian orthodoxy, based in the distinction between *suppositum* / hypostasis and *natura*. Preserving this distinction, Thomas holds that the

---

29. Thomas G. Weinandy, O.F.M., Cap., "Aquinas: God *IS* Man — The Marvel of the Incarnation," in Thomas G. Weinandy, O.F.M., Cap., Daniel A. Keating and John P. Yocum, eds., *Aquinas on Doctrine: A Critical Introduction* (London: T&T Clark International, 2004), pp. 67-89, here at p. 70.

30. ST III, q. 16, a. 1, *corpus*.

31. Weinandy, "Aquinas: God *IS* Man," p. 69.

32. Thomas Aquinas, *Compendium theologiae* I, 212: "Ea vero quae ad suppositum sive hypostasim pertinent, unum tantum in Christo confiteri oportet: unde si esse accipiatur secundum quod unum esse est unius suppositi, videtur dicendum quod in Christo sit tantum unum esse."

"act of being" (*esse*) is constitutive of the real existence (*suppositum*) of the thing in question. The act of being, on this scheme, is neither a formal act (a "form") nor a formal content, but is rather the condition of the possibility of formal action and content.[33] As Cornelio Fabro puts it: "Thomist being expresses the fullness of the act which is possessed by the essence (God) or which rests (*quiescit*) at the base of every being as the primordially participated energy which sustains it above nothingness."[34] To be, then, is to be "in act," which is for creatures to be by participation in the *actus purus* of God, who is *ipsum esse per se subsistens*.[35] Just as "philosophizing" is the act that makes a philosopher philosophize, so existence is the act that makes something have being; it concerns *that* it is (*quis*).

That the essence of something is its nature, by contrast, concerns the nature of the thing; it concerns *what* it is (*quid*). For something to have a nature, for it to have a *quid*, it must be an individuated existent, a *suppositum*; it must be a *quis*.[36] So on the level of *quis*, we are speaking of the reality of a *suppositum*, of an existent, while on the level of *quid* we are speaking of the nature or essence of a being. For Thomas, only *supposita* truly act: "natures," "parts" and "accidents" act only in the sense that by them the *suppositum* acts.[37] A human nature is not a *suppositum* until it has "subsistence," until it is a concrete existent, realized in the act of being through which it comes to exist. Because human nature is rational, when it comes to have its act of being (and to exist through that act) it comes to exist as a "person" according to the Boethian definition (*naturae rationalis individua substantia*).[38] Thus "being" (*esse*), "subsistence" (*suppositum* / hypostasis) and "person" (*persona*) exist on the ontological level of *quis*, while "essence"

---

33. Cf. W. Norris Clarke, S.J., "The Meaning of Participation in St. Thomas," in *Explorations in Metaphysics: Being — God — Person* (London: University of Notre Dame Press, 1994), pp. 89-102; F. Ocáriz, L. F. Mateo Seco and J. A. Riestra, *The Mystery of Jesus Christ*, trans. Michael Adams and James Gavigan (Dublin: Four Courts Press, 2004), pp. 112-13.

34. Cornelio Fabro, C.P.S., *Participation et causalité selon s. Thomas d'Aquin* (Paris: Editions Beatrice-Nauwelaerts, 1961), p. 52.

35. Cf. ST I, q. 4, a. 2.

36. Cf. Thomas Aquinas, *Scriptum super Sententiis* III, dist. 5, q. 1, a. 3; ST I, q. 29, a. 2; ST III, q. 16, a. 12, *ad* 3.

37. Cf. Thomas Aquinas, *De potentia Dei*, q. 9, a. 1, ad 3. On part-whole Christology in Thomas, see Bernard Bro, "La notion métaphysique de tout et son application au problème théologique de l'union hypostatique," *Revue Thomiste* 68 (1968): 181-97 and 357-80.

38. Boethius, *Contra Eutyche et Nestorium* (which also goes by the title *De persona et duabus naturis*), c. 3, ln. 4-5 (in Boethius, *The Theological Tractates and the Consolation of Philosophy* [LCL 74.72-129]). Cf. ST I, q. 29, a. 2, *corpus*.

(*essentia*), "form" (*quidditas*) and "nature" (*natura*) exist on the level of *quid*. These metaphysical distinctions follow from the general reception of the Chalcedonian definition: in Christ there are two natures (both *quid*) in one hypostasis-*suppositum*-person (one *quis*).[39]

In this light, the ground of the *mysterium unionis* lies in the fact that the axis *essentia-natura* does not determine the axis of *esse-persona*.[40] One existence can in principle be two essences, and hence the traditional formulation that in Christ there are two natures in one person / hypostasis. To affirm that in Jesus Christ a human nature inheres the Logos so intimately as to be "one" with the divine person is to affirm that the axis of *esse-persona* is expansive and not determined by quiddity. Thus Thomas proposes that the hypostatic union is a *unio* in the *esse personale* of the Son of God.[41] Jesus is one subject and so possesses a single *suppositum* and a single *persona*, and since the one *suppositum* is that of the Logos, this means that the *ens* of *this* human being is the *ipsum esse per se subsistens* of God insofar as the *esse* of the Incarnate Son must be his divine *esse*.[42]

To understand this more precisely, we must take account of Thomas's doctrine of the "mixed relation" and how the hypostatic union is a species of this relation. According to Thomas there are three types of relation: logical, real and mixed.[43] In a "logical relation," the two terms are related by an intellectual comparison to the effect that the relation does not affect

---

39. Cf. ST III, q. 2, a. 6.

40. Michael Gorman, "The Hypostatic Union According to Thomas Aquinas" (Ph.D. diss., Boston College, 1997), p. 41.

41. Cf. Gorman, "The Hypostatic Union According to Thomas Aquinas," p. 91: "Because the whole supposit of Christ is human by virtue of that nature, Thomas says that that nature is joined to the Word's personal *esse*, in a way that an accident or another supposit never could be. But because that supposit was already existing prior to the advent of its humanity, Thomas does not say that the nature constitutes Christ's personal *esse* but only that it is joined to it. It is drawn to the *esse* of the Word, but it is drawn to it as to something prior, and thus it does not establish or constitute it. Because it is a substantial nature and not an accident, it belongs to the *very heart of Christ's being*, to his personal *esse*."

42. Cf. John Milbank and Catherine Pickstock, *Truth in Aquinas* (London: Routledge, 2001), pp. 84-87.

43. On Thomas's view of the mixed relation I have benefited from Thomas G. Weinandy, O.F.M., Cap., *Does God Change? The Word's Becoming in the Incarnation* (Still River, MA: St. Bede's Publications, 1985), pp. 88-96; Michael Gorman, "Christ as Composite According to Aquinas," *Traditio* 55 (2000): 143-57; Bauerschmidt, *Thomas Aquinas: Faith, Reason, and Following Christ*, pp. 114-19; Conor Cunningham, "Being Recalled: Life as Anamnesis," in Harm Goris, Herwi Rikhof, and Henk Schoot, eds., *Divine Transcendence and Immanence in the Work of Thomas Aquinas* (Leuven: Peeters, 2009), pp. 59-80.

or change either of the terms related, "for instance, when reason compares man to animal as the species to the genus."[44] In a "real relation," the related terms are related such that their relation mutually changes them, such as when a child is born, and his parents become a mother and a father.[45] A mixed relation is a relation that is "real" from one side, but "logical" from the other; it is a relation that effects a change only on one side of the relation. The creator-creature relation is paradigmatic of the mixed relation.[46] As Thomas puts it in the *Summa*:

> Since therefore God is outside the whole order of creation, and all creatures are ordered to him, and not conversely, it is manifest that creatures are really related to God himself; whereas in God there is no real relation to creatures, but a relation only in idea, inasmuch as creatures are referred to him.[47]

In the same way as the mixed relation functions to specify the union of God and creation, so the mixed relation specifies the highest form of relation of God and creation: the hypostatic union in Christ (*per unionem secundum esse*). Thomas writes:

> The union of which we are speaking [the hypostatic union] is a relation which we consider between the divine and the human nature, inasmuch as they come together in one person of the Son of God. Now, as was said above (I, q. 13, a. 7), every relation which we consider between God and the creature is really in the creature, by whose change the relation is brought into being; whereas it is not really in God, but only in our way of thinking, since it does not arise from any change in God. And hence we must say that the union of which we are speaking is not really in God, except only in our way of thinking; but in the human nature, which is a creature, it is really.[48]

The hypostatic union thus, like every relation of created and uncreated being, is mixed in the sense that the human nature of Christ contributes nothing to the existence of the Logos, and is nothing apart from the Lo-

44. ST I, q. 28, a. 1, *corpus*.
45. Cf. ST I, q. 28, a. 1, *corpus*.
46. Thomas Aquinas, *Scriptum super Sententiis*, lib. 1, d. 37, q. 1, a. 2, *corpus*.
47. ST I, q. 13, a. 7.
48. ST III, q. 2, a. 7.

gos. This way of formulating the union in Christ is advantageous because it stipulates on the one hand the mode of the perfect unity of the human nature of Jesus in relation to the Logos, while safeguarding on the other hand the real immutability and impassibility of God.[49]

Thomas grasps the need for this safeguard to reach all the way down. The *apatheia* of God is no less compromised by attributing the normal human experience of walking to the Logos than it is by attributing a moment of human joy, the transfiguration of a human face by divine light or the dereliction of the Cross. God is not a finite being under any circumstance, exceptional or otherwise. There are no degrees between the fact of human finitude (no matter how "supernatural") and the *apatheia* of the divine life. Something is impassible only if it cannot receive anything in addition to itself that would modify it in any way, while something is immutable only if it does not change. Passibility and mutability are internal to every finite experience of being in an essential way, while they must be perfectly excluded from the divine experience in every case. But the Incarnation would seem to require that the Logos receive something (a human life and nature, a history and genealogy), and therefore, from the first moment and in every moment of the Incarnation, the whole problem of theopaschism is always already fully present. Thomas's solution is to think of the relation of the Logos to his incarnate nature as perfectly convertible, in this one respect, with the relation of God and creation generally, that is, as a mixed relation, real on the side of the humanity assumed, logical on the side of the divinity assuming.

If from the one side the mixed relation safeguards the *apatheia* of God, on the other side it forecloses a backward projection from the Incarnate Logos onto, as it were, a "pre-Incarnate life" of the Son, as if the Son experienced a "time" before the hour of his Incarnation. Because the reality of the relation is only maintained on the created side, the Incarnation cannot be reduced to an episode in the longer (eternal) life of the Logos. Rather, the episode of *this* life must express fully the whole immutable reality on which it depends: the person of the eternal Son. What the Logos thus receives *ex Maria*, he receives in a mode that, rather than changing him, recapitulates the reality into which he is incarnated. This means that, if there is no division between the divine and human natures in Christ, neither can there be a division between the eternal life of the Son *ex Patre* and the incarnate life of the Son *ex Maria*. This is a very traditional point, but

49. See ST I, qq. 3 and 9.

it goes against a modern theological tendency to detach Trinitarian speculation from Christology; we can see the traditional view fully operative in Gregory of Nyssa:

> If the divine [element] that came to be (γενόμενον) in the human [element], and the immortal in the mortal, and the strong in the weak, and the unchangeable and incorruptible in the changeable and corruptible, had allowed the mortal [element] to remain in the mortal or the corruptible in the corruptible, and the others likewise, then one might reasonably have contemplated a certain duality in the Son of God, numbered by the opposite properties beheld in each.
>
> If, on the other hand, the mortal [element] that came to be in the immortal became immortality, and the corruptible likewise changed into incorruptibility, and all the other [properties] similarly were transformed into impassible and divine [properties], what argument remains for those who divide the one into a duality?[50]

The Incarnation is not best thought of as another sequence to the pre-existent divine life of the Son, but rather as a transformative becoming that entails most fundamentally that the "human element comes to be in the divine."[51] The asymmetry of the Logos — through whom all things were made — in relation to created being means that the act of incarnation overdetermines every finite becoming; the transformative reality of the Son resides for us wholly in the Incarnate fact of his being *ex Maria*. What the Son receives *ex Maria* does not change the eternal Son; rather it unleashes the transformative power of his divine being into our human world. This is more or less what the mixed relation ensures in Thomas: the whole becoming, the whole drama of the eternal "is" of the Logos resides in the life of Jesus, thus foreclosing (1) every simple transition from the Incarnate Son to the (as if temporally "before") pre-Incarnate Son, while ensuring that (2) it is precisely our human reality that is changed by his divine act.

The logic of the mixed relation in the Incarnation follows from the fact that created being is in all cases supremely subject to its relation to God; it "is" insofar as it is constituted in the basic relation that maintains between it and God. From the other side, because God is immutable and impassible, God himself cannot be subject to this relation: the reality of who God

---

50. Gregory of Nyssa, *Ad Theophilum* (GNO 3.1, pp. 124-25), trans. Behr.
51. Behr, *The Case against Diodore and Theodore*, p. 17.

"is" is not constituted by his relation to anything outside of himself.[52] The relation between God and created being, the unity of this human nature with the Logos, allows God himself to be the foundation of reality on the creaturely side, while on the side of God — precisely because he is this foundation of reality — the relation cannot alter him in any way. If it were otherwise, the Incarnation would involve an accidental relation of being accrued to the Son's person, which would make his divinity contingent on created being in such a way that his human nature could not be "one" with him. Although there is a positive similarity between the relation of all created being to God and that of the human being Jesus to God, there is also a fundamental dissimilarity. This dissimilarity lies in the exceptional nature of the Incarnation: the relation of the *ipsum esse per se subsistens* to this *ens* is uniquely *per unionem secundum esse*. The real relation on the side of created *esse*, in the case of Jesus of Nazareth, constitutes a created nature such that it is truly "one" with the *esse personale* of the Son himself:

> The eternal being of the Son of God (*esse aeternum filii Dei*), which is the divine nature, becomes the being of man (*esse hominis*), inasmuch as the human nature is assumed by the Son of God to unity of person (*in unitate personae*).[53]

C. Christ's *Secundarium Esse*

All but once Thomas consistently upholds with clarity the doctrine of Christ's single divine *esse*.[54] In *De unione Verbi incarnati*, however, Thomas offers an alternative (if cryptic) complication:

> [J]ust as Christ is one simply (*est unum simpliciter*) on account of the unity of the suppositum, and two in a certain respect on account of the two natures, so he has one being simply (*unum esse simpliciter*) on

52. Of course this is not to say that God does not will to be in relation with what God is not; all it is to say is that creation is free, and that by it God does not exercise any necessity. He is free to create something impossibly outside Godself and to love that which he has created, and this expresses something of who God is. It is the gratuitous delight of the God who is Love to create and to be fully present to the creatures he creates.

53. ST III, q. 17, a. 2, *ad* 2.

54. Cf. Thomas Aquinas, *Scriptum Super Sententiis* III, dist. 6, q. 2, a. 2; *Quaestiones de quodlibet* IX, q. 2, a. 2; *Compendium theologiae* I, 212; ST III, q. 17, a. 2.

account of the one eternal being (*unum esse aeternum*) of the eternal suppositum. But, there is also another being of this suppositum, not insofar as it is eternal, but insofar as it became a man in time (*in quantum est temporaliter homo factum*). That being, even if it is not an accidental being, because man is not accidentally predicated of the Son of God . . . nevertheless, it is not the principal being (*esse principale*) of its suppositum, but secondary (*secundarium esse*). Now if there were two supposita in Christ, then each suppositum would have its own principal being. And thus there would be a two-fold being (*duplex esse*) in Christ simply.[55]

What do we make of this passage?

Gilles Emery has called *De unione* "'the most disputed' of St. Thomas's disputed questions."[56] Famously, Cardinal Cajetan dismissed it as an in-

---

55. Thomas Aquinas, *De unione Verbi incarnati*, a. 4, *corpus*.

56. Gilles Emery, O.P., Review of Thomas Aquinas, *Question disputée: l'union du Verbe incarné (De unione Verbi incarnati)*, trans., intro., and ed. Marie-Hélène Deloffre (Paris: J. Vrin, 2000), *Nova et Vetera: Revue trimestrielle* 75 (2001), pp. 98-101, at p. 99. For a more recent edition than that of Deloffre, see Klaus Obenauer, *Thomas von Aquin: Quaestio disputata « De unione Verbi incarnati »* (Stuttgart–Bad Cannstatt: Frommann-Holzboog, 2011). For an overview of recent debate on Thomas's single *esse* Christology, see J.-P. Torrell, O.P., "Le Thomisme dans le débat christologique contemporain," in Serge-Thomas Bonino, ed., *Saint Thomas au XXᵉ siècle: Colloque du centenaire de la "Revue Thomiste"* (Paris: Editions Saint-Paul, 1994), pp. 382-87. On Christ's single divine *esse*, apart from Weinandy's article cited above, see J. L. West, "Aquinas on the Metaphysics of the *Esse* in Christ," *The Thomist* 66 (2002): 231-50; Victor Salas Jr., "Thomas Aquinas on Christ's *Esse*: A Metaphysics of the Incarnation," *The Thomist* 70 (2006): 577-603; A. Patfoort, O.P., *L'unité d'être dans le Christ d'après S. Thomas: A la croisée de l'ontologie et de la christologie* (Paris: Desclée, 1958); A. Patfoort, O.P., "L'enseignement de Saint Thomas sur l'esse du Christ," in H. Bouëssé and J. J. Latour, eds., *Problèmes actuels de christologie* (Paris: Desclée, 1965), pp. 101-28; Weisheipl, *Friar Thomas d'Aquino*, pp. 307-13; Bro, "La notion métaphysique de tout et son application au problème théologique de l'union hypostatique"; Richard Cross, *The Metaphysics of the Incarnation: Thomas Aquinas to Duns Scotus* (Oxford: OUP, 2002), pp. 51-64; Richard Cross, "Aquinas on Nature, Hypostasis, and the Metaphysics of the Incarnation," *The Thomist* 60 (1996): 171-202; J. H. Nicholas, "L'unité d'être dans le Christ d'après St. Thomas," *Revue Thomiste* 65 (1965): 229-60; Étienne Gilson, "L'*esse* du Verbe Incarné selon saint Thomas d'Aquin," *Archives d'Histoire Doctrinale et Littéraire du Moyen Age* 35 (1968): 23-37; M.-V. Leroy, "L'union selon l'hypostase d'après saint Thomas d'Aquin," *Revue Thomiste* 74 (1974): 231-39; Francis Ruello, *La christologie de Thomas d'Aquin* (Paris: Beauchesne, 1987), pp. 115-19 and 317-55; Henk J. M. Schoot, *Christ the "Name" of God: Thomas Aquinas on Naming Christ* (Leuven: Peeters, 1993), pp. 160-64; É.-H. Wéber, *Le Christ selon Saint Thomas d'Aquin* (Paris: Desclée, 1988), pp. 229-35; Martin Bieler, *Befreiung der Freiheit: Zur Theologie der stellvertretenden Sühne* (Freiburg: Herder, 1996), pp. 303-4; Hans Urs

consequential work of juvenilia that "must be understood as retracted."[57] More radically, Ludovico Billot simply declared the work inauthentic.[58] Committed as they were to the single *esse* Christology of the *Summa*, Cajetan and Billot were baffled by the *secundarium esse* of *De unione*, which they understood as skirting disconcertingly close to the Scotist position; this they sought to refuse for its apparently quasi-Nestorian implications.[59] Since the work of the Leonine Commission, however, it is no longer possible to relegate the text to the status of a spurious work.[60] Moreover, recent scholarship has shown that the Cajetanian dismissal of the text as a work of juvenilia is unfounded; in fact the work was composed much later than previously thought, and just before (or in tandem with) the beginning of the *tertia pars*.[61] This has led to an aporia, complicated by the fact that *De unione* is likely, by a matter of mere months, the penultimate statement of Thomas on the *esse* of Christ, after which he seems to have returned, in the *tertia pars*, to the consistency of his earlier view.

There are several ways to confront this perplexity. One recent and paradoxical position[62] offers that *De unione* from the point of view of his-

---

von Balthasar, *Theo-Drama: Theological Dramatic Theory*, vol. 3, *Dramatis Personae: Persons in Christ*, trans. Graham Harrison (San Francisco: Ignatius Press, 1992), pp. 222-30.

57. Cajetan, *Commentaria in Summam theologiae*, Leonine edition, n. 6, p. 224; as quoted by Marie-Hélène Deloffre, "Introduction to Thomas Aquinas," in Thomas Aquinas, *Question disputée: l'union du Verbe incarné (De unione Verbi incarnati)*, trans., intro., and ed. Marie-Hélène Deloffre (Paris: J. Vrin, 2000), pp. 13-78, at p. 13.

58. Ludovico Billot, *De Verbo Incarnato: Commentarius in Tertiam Partem S. Thomae* (Prati: Libraria Giachetti, 1912). Cf. Torrell, *Thomas Aquinas*, vol. 1, p. 206.

59. Cf. Deloffre, "Introduction to Thomas Aquinas," pp. 15-17; Aaron Riches, "Christology and the 'Scotist Rupture'," *Theological Research* 1 (2013): 31-63.

60. Cf. Torrell, *Thomas Aquinas*, vol. 1, p. 206: "The Leonine Commission's labors no longer leave any doubt about its [*De unione*] authenticity, since the text of this Question was already transmitted in manuscripts from the end of the thirteenth century and it is included in the works announced by the booksellers in the taxation lists of the most ancient catalogues" (citing the Preface to the Leonine edition, vol. 24).

61. In agreement with Weisheipl and Glorieux, Torrell offers spring 1272 as the date of the composition of *De unione Verbi incarnati*, "when the *Tertia Pars* was nearly ready to be written if not already begun" (Torrell, *Saint Thomas Aquinas*, vol. 1, pp. 206-7). Every indication points to the fact of *De unione Verbi incarnati* being composed before Easter 1272, after which time Thomas left Paris for Naples (p. 24), where he is said to have finished composing questions 1-20 of the *Tertia Pars* by the autumn of 1272 (p. 260). Cf. Palémon Glorieux, "Les Questions Disputées de S. Thomas et leur suite chronologique," *Recherches de théologie ancienne et médiévale* 4 (1939): 5-33, at pp. 30-31; and Weisheipl, *Friar Thomas d'Aquino*, pp. 307-312.

62. See Obenauer, *Thomas von Aquin: Quaestio disputata « De unione Verbi incarnati »*, and Klaus Obenauer, "Aquinas's De unione verbi incarnati: An Interview with Klaus

tory and Thomas's own doctrine is indeed a "deviation" within his wider Christology. On this view, Billot and those who understood *De unione* as irreconcilable with the single *esse* doctrine of the *tertia pars* were, in fact, correct in their interpretation. On the other hand, still on this same proposal, from the point of view of the contemporary practice of "systematic theology," the theologian ought, despite the deviation, to look for a synthetic reconciliation of *De unione* with the doctrine of the *tertia pars*. The key to this synthetic reconciliation is to conceive of the "unio secundum subsistentiam" as fixing the mode by which we understand how the "esse personale Verbi," the subsistence of the divine Son, applies to the human nature.[63] The *unio secundum subsistentiam* must therefore fix the way we apply the divine *esse* to Christ's human nature, which means that there cannot be, even conceptually, any distinction between the subsistence of Christ's human nature and the act of its substantial existence. Within these limits, a second, human *esse* of Christ, in the form of a "formal secumferential" of the *esse personale*, can be admitted in such a way that it performs merely the function of "formal efficiency," and crucially it does not then differ numerically from the divine *esse*.

Other scholars are more interested in proposing the native internal consistency of *De unione* and the *tertia pars*, while at the same time seeking something denser than merely "formal efficiency" for the *secundarium esse*. On this view, "Aquinas implicitly held two *esses* from the start . . . but only explicitly stated this position on the one occasion."[64] According to this view, the second *esse* in *De unione* in no way compromises the oneness of Christ or the oneness of his divine *esse* since the created *esse* belongs to the human nature and not to the person of the Son.[65] A correct understanding of the doctrine of *De unione*, on this view, thus involves grasping how *secundarium* functions in that text in reference to the created *esse* relative

---

Obenauer," online at http://thomistica.net/news/2011/9/6/aquinas-de-unione-verbi -incarnati-an-interview-with-dr-klaus.html.

63. Obenauer, "Aquinas's De unione verbi incarnati: An Interview with Klaus Obenauer," pt. 2.

64. Weinandy, "Aquinas: God *IS* Man," p. 80.

65. Cf. Weinandy, "Aquinas: God *IS* Man," p. 81: "Aquinas categorically stated: 'The being of the human nature is not the being of the divine nature (*esse humanae non est esse divinae*)' [*De unione* a. 4, ad 1]. If the *esse* of the humanity's existence were the divine uncreated *esse* of the Son [i.e. the *esse personale* and *principale*], then the humanity would be divinised in an entirely unacceptable and wholly inappropriate manner. The humanity would not be divinised in the sense of it becoming perfectly human within its relationship with the Son and so acquiring divine qualities and virtues in a human manner."

to the single *esse personale*. What the *secundarium esse* names is neither accidental nor principal / personal, but rather "a substantial *esse* that is such only in that it is in ontological union with the Son."[66] In this way the two lines of thinking on the issue begin to converge in a Christology in which the *unio secundum subsistentiam* "fixes" how we apply the *esse personale* of the Son to his human mode of existence.

It is important to note here, however, that it is not the view of Thomas that to subsist as human God must have assumed a *substantial* being.[67] If we closely follow the text of Thomas, we see that he in fact insists that Christ's human nature is not a substance (i.e. its own *suppositum* or hypostasis):

> Since the human nature in Christ does not subsist in itself separately but exists in another, that is, in the hypostasis of the Word of God (not as some accident in a subject, nor properly as a part of a whole, but through an ineffable assumption), therefore the human nature of Christ can be said to be some individual, particular, or singular; however, it cannot be a hypostasis or *suppositum*, as it cannot be called a person.[68]

The created *esse* in *De unione* cannot be "substantial" in the normal sense; if it were, the human nature would introduce into Christ the very parallelism Thomas sought to foreclose. Christ's human nature is not a "substance," but rather possesses "a substantial *esse* that is such only in that it is in ontological union with the Son."[69]

A third interpretation of the *secundarium esse* offers the view that the latter doctrine, far from being a "deviation" from the single divine *esse*, rather indicates how the Incarnation recapitulates the manner according to which the created *esse*'s "coming into being" can be thought of as a "created supposit" at the moment of creation.[70] Here the "mixed relation" designates the real becoming of the incarnational event on the side of created being — *in quantum est temporaliter homo factum*. Since created *esse* does not subsist of itself, being most fundamentally a participation in

66. Weinandy, "Aquinas: God *IS* Man," p. 82.

67. Salas, "Thomas Aquinas on Christ's *Esse*," p. 594.

68. Thomas Aquinas, *De unione Verbi incarnati*, a. 2; as quoted in Salas, "Thomas Aquinas on Christ's *Esse*," p. 594.

69. Weinandy, "Aquinas: God *IS* Man," p. 82.

70. Bieler, *Befreiung der Freiheit*, pp. 303-4. I am indebted in these remarks to conversations with Adrian Walker.

the *ipsum esse per se subsistens* of God, to speak of "created *esse*" is in the first place to speak of the manner or mode by which a supposit *receives* its act of existence (*esse*) within the limits of *essentia*.[71] The *esse-essentia* distinction entails that for creatures *essentia* must specify how the finite supposit participates in *esse*, such that *esse* is related to *essentia* as act to potency.[72] Nature is thus the proper receiving principle of created being; it is the "finitization" of being.[73]

In this light, on this third view, the Incarnation of the Logos is a recapitulation of the "finitization" of *esse* as a way of now being "himself," receiving himself precisely from human nature. Hence the necessity for the doctrine of the Theotokos and hence the fittingness of the Incarnation of the divine Son as opposed to the Father or Spirit.[74] In the filial receptivity of his Incarnate person, the Son reveals the dynamism of the first aspect of created being as "being received," as always already animated by an anterior receptivity.[75]

71. See John F. Wippel, *The Metaphysical Thought of Thomas Aquinas: From Finite Being to Uncreated Being* (Washington, DC: The Catholic University of America Press, 2000), pp. 94-131.

72. Wippel, *The Metaphysical Thought of Thomas Aquinas*, pp. 153-54.

73. Thomas Aquinas, *De spiritualibus creaturis*, a. 1, *corpus*: "Unde dicimus, quod Deus est ipsum suum esse. Hoc autem non potest dici de aliquo alio: sicut enim impossibile est intelligere quod sint plures albedines separatae; sed si esset albedo separata ab omni subiecto et recipiente, esset una tantum; ita impossibile est quod sit ipsum esse subsistens nisi unum tantum. Omne igitur quod est post primum ens, cum non sit suum esse, habet esse in aliquo receptum, per quod ipsum esse contrahitur; et sic in quolibet creato aliud est natura rei quae participat esse, et aliud ipsum esse participatum. Et cum quaelibet res participet per assimilationem primum actum in quantum habet esse, necesse est quod esse participatum in unoquoque comparetur ad naturam participantem ipsum, sicut actus ad potentiam. In natura igitur rerum corporearum materia non per se participat ipsum esse, sed per formam; forma enim adveniens materiae facit ipsam esse actu, sicut anima corpori." This is crucial. For Thomas, *composition* (that *esse* in created being is diverse from *essentia*) is what both allows created being "to be" and entails that created being is "limited," that *esse* is received under the form of *essentia* (which is different from *esse*). *Esse* in and of itself cannot be either limited or divided, and hence is infinite; the process, then, of rendering *esse* diverse, of ensuring that the act of being of one supposit is different from that of another, occurs on account of a diversity of *essentiae*, such that each finite *esse* is different based on its mode of receiving *esse*, that is, based on the receiving principle of its being, which is a "finitization" of being. Cf. ScG II.5.

74. Cf. ST III, q. 3, a. 8.

75. See David L. Schindler, "'Thomism' and the Human Person: The Question of Receptivity and the Philosophy-Theology Distinction," in *Heart of the World, Center of the Church: Communio Ecclesiology, Liberalism, and Liberation* (Grand Rapids: Eerdmans, 1996), pp. 275-311.

Noting the specifically filial character of the hypostatic union (of the Son *ex Patre* coming to be *ex Maria*) helps to establish more deeply the dogmatic continuity between Thomas's single *esse* doctrine and his doctrine of the *secundarium esse*. The mode of divine filiation itself is here the concrete term "fixing" the application of the divine *esse* to the incarnate nature, such that now there cannot be any distinction between the filial subsistence of the incarnate nature and the divine filial fact of substantial existence.

Moreover, following the suggestion that the *secundarium esse* signifies the recapitulation of the "finitization" of *esse* into the incarnational receptivity of the Son through human nature helps us to avoid at the same time any substantialist temptation (viz. that for God to subsist as human he must have assumed a substantial being). In this way a fundamental consistency between the *Summa* and *De unione* opens: the oneness of the *esse personale* of Christ, which simply "is" the relation of divine filiation, is itself the concrete term of unity of the twofold nature.

We are now in a position to clarify more concretely the internal theological continuity of the *Summa* and *De unione Verbi* on the question of Christ's *esse,* as confirmed by a concrete textual witness. In both the *Summa* and *De unione* the *esse personale* is affirmed in two ways: (1) in itself (*in se*), and (2) according to the different aspects of subsistence (*alia ratio subsistendi*). In the first case, affirming the singular *esse personale* ensures the absolute *unitas* of Christ; in the second case, it safeguards the differentiated-unity of the Incarnate Son subsisting in a manner eternal and simple on the one hand, and in a manner temporal and compound on the other. As Thomas writes in the *Summa*:

> The person or hypostasis of Christ may be viewed in two ways. First as it is in itself (*in se*), and thus it is altogether simple (*simplex*), even as the nature of the Word. Secondly, in the aspect of person or hypostasis to which it belongs to subsist in a nature; and thus the person of Christ subsists in two natures. Hence though there is one subsisting being in him, yet there are different aspects of subsistence, and hence he is said to be a composite person, insomuch as one being subsists in two.[76]

76. ST III, q. 2, a. 4, *corpus*: "Respondeo dicendum quod persona sive hypostasis Christi dupliciter considerari potest. Uno modo, secundum id quod est in se. Et sic est omnino simplex, sicut et natura verbi. Alio modo, secundum rationem personae vel hypostasis, ad quam pertinet subsistere in aliqua natura. Et secundum hoc, persona Christi subsistit in duabus naturis. Unde, licet sit ibi unum subsistens, est tamen ibi alia et alia ratio subsistendi. Et sic dicitur persona composita, inquantum unum duobus subsistit."

The unity of Christ's *esse* is in this way formulated in terms convertible with *De unione*. Though Thomas does not in the *Summa* use the language of *esse principale* or *secundarium esse*, as he does in *De unione*, what those terms designate is fully expounded. In *De unione* Thomas had stated that Jesus possesses one *esse* on account of the singular *esse* of his eternal *suppositum*,[77] and then went on to argue that there is another *esse* (*autem et aliud esse*), but only insofar as the eternal Son became a man in time (*inquantum est temporaliter homo factum*).[78] There are consistently, then, two ways of talking of the *esse* of Christ: simply and as subsisting. In the first manner, to speak simply (*simpliciter*, as *De unione* puts it, or *omnino simplex*, as the *Summa* puts it), there will always and only ever be *unum esse*. Jesus simply is the Logos. But in addition to this, both the *Summa* and *De unione* allow that there is another way to talk about *esse* in the Incarnate Son; that is, with regards to the nature in which it subsists (*secundum naturam quod subsistit*). In the case of the *esse* of Christ, which subsists in two natures, there is more than one way to talk about his being. We can talk about the divine Logos *in se* or we can talk about him according to the *alia ratio subsistendi* of his Incarnation. On this point there is no real discrepancy between the *Summa* and *De unione*.

The discrepancy between the *Summa* and *De unione* comes in the manner in which we talk about the *unitas* of the Logos according to the *alia ratio subsistendi*, the human nature in which he subsists in his Incarnation. The divergence consists, it seems, in this: whereas the *Summa* talks of the different aspects in terms of the Constantinopolitan dogma of *persona composita* (ὑπόστασις σύνθετος),[79] *De unione* talks of a *secundarium esse*. This suggests that the doctrine of the *secundarium esse*, curious as it sounds, signifies nothing other than the complex subsistent fact of Christ's Incarnation and implies nothing other than that doctrine elevated to a dogma of faith at Constantinople II. The Logos *in se*, in his *esse* and in his *persona*, is *unus* because he is simple. Therefore he is *unitas subsistens* in all cases. And yet, because the Incarnate Logos is a complex of natures, his *unum subsistens* can be contemplated in terms of different aspects of subsistence (*aliter subsistens*): he can either be contemplated in himself (*in se*) or from the point of view of his assuming of human nature (*aliter subsistens*). In the

---

77. Thomas Aquinas, *De unione Verbi incarnati*, a. 4, *corpus*: "ita habet unum esse simpliciter propter unum esse aeternum aeterni suppositi."

78. Thomas Aquinas, *De unione Verbi incarnati*, a. 4, *corpus*.

79. *Anathematismi adversus "tria Capitula*," canon 4 (DS 424; DEC 1.114-115).

latter case, if we are talking about the *esse* of Christ, we will have to make a distinction between his *esse principale* and his *secundarium esse*, while if we are talking about his person or hypostasis we will talk of his *persona composita*, neither of which implies any kind of existential dualism in Christ.

The function in Thomas of the distinction between the *esse personale* of Christ in itself (*in se*) and that according to its other aspect of subsistence (*alia ratio subsistendi*) works more or less along the same lines Cyril stipulates for the orthodox function of the "in two natures" formula.[80] There are two natures in Christ, but this duality in Christ is a truth perceived only *en theoria mone* (ἐν θεωρίᾳ μόνῃ).[81] Everything that is apprehended of Jesus and everything predicated of him, finally, is apprehended and predicated of "only one Christ and Son and Lord, the Word of God made man and made flesh," even while we must allow the speculative distinction that there are two natures "in" him, divine and human.[82] The same rule, it would seem, must apply to Thomas's doctrine of the *secundarium esse*, and herein consists the final continuity of this doctrine with the standard Thomist doctrine of the single divine *esse* of Christ.

In this light, the *esse principale*, while it may be thought of as correlate to the *secundarium esse* of Christ when the being of Christ is considered *en theoria mone* (that is, as *subsistens in duabus naturis*), is nevertheless the singular *esse* of Christ in the sense that it is the principle of his being. The *esse principale*, in other words, "fixes" the *secundarium esse* in the *unio secundum subsistentiam* such that the *secundarium esse* only exists as "one" with the *esse personale* of the Logos through the *unio secundum subsistentiam*. If *aliud esse* is accrued by the person of the Logos insofar as he becomes "this man" (*hic homo*),[83] this occurs only within the one existence of Christ. In this way, *De unione* helps us to specify how, in the mystery of Christ's oneness, the Logos is nevertheless truly "finitized" and receives his being through human nature *ex Maria*. It is as if Jesus really were a human hypostasis, constituted in substantial being by human nature, yet without ceasing to be the eternal Son of God.

---

80. Cyril of Alexandria, *Epistula* 45, First Letter to Succensus (Lionel R. Wickham, ed. and trans., *Cyril of Alexandria: Select Letters* [Oxford, OUP, 1983], pp. 70-83; PG 77.228d-237c), and *Epistula* 46, Second Letter to Succensus (ed. Wickham, p. 84-93; PG 77.228d-237c).

81. Cyril of Alexandria, *Epistula* 46, Second Letter to Succensus (ed. Wickham, p. 92; PG 77.245a).

82. Cyril of Alexandria, *Epistula* 45, First Letter to Succensus (ed. Wickham, p. 76; PG 77.232d-233a).

83. Here my comments are indebted to personal conversations with Adrian Walker.

CHAPTER 8

Theandric Action

Christ's meritorious and satisfactory acts were theandric in this sense, that they proceeded both from His human will and from His divine personality. And herein consists the essence of the very mystery of Redemption.

Réginald Garrigou-Lagrange

A. Thomas and Constantinople III

While Thomas likely discovered the *Acta* of Constantinople III (680-681) as early as the 1260s during his second stay at Rome, he only fully integrated the doctrine of the council in the Christology he wrote in the early 1270s,[1] first in *De unione Verbi incarnati* and then especially in the *tertia pars* of the *Summa*.[2] By this last act of Christological *ressourcement*,

1. Ignaz Backes, *Die Christologie des hl. Thomas v. Aquin und die griechischen Kirchenväter* (Paderborn: Schöningh, 1931), p. 25. On Thomas's dyothelitism, see Corey L. Barnes, *Christ's Two Wills in Scholastic Thought: The Christology of Aquinas and Its Historical Contexts* (Toronto: PIMS, 2012). On Thomas's recovery of Constantinople III, see Martin Morard, "Thomas d'Aquin lecteur des conciles," *Archivum Franciscanum Historicum* 98 (2005): 211-365, at pp. 305-16. Also cf. Thomas Joseph White, O.P., "Dyotheletism and the Instrumental Human Consciousness of Jesus," *Pro Ecclesia* 17 (2008): 369-422.

2. Cf. Barnes, *Christ's Two Wills in Scholastic Thought*, p. 117, n. 11: "Thomas' discussion of Christ's two wills and operations in the *Summa contra Gentiles* demonstrates no knowledge of Constantinople III. Thomas seems to refer to Constantinople III first in *Quodlibet* IV, q. 5, a. 8 [*sic* — he means the *corpus*, there is no "a. 8"], but the first substantial use comes in the *De unione Verbi Incarnati* or ST III, q. 9, a. 1." In this light, a trace of the influence of Constantinople III may lie in Thomas's *secundarium esse*, proposed in precisely the text, *De unione*, in which Thomas first discusses Constantinople III at length. The impetus to clarify

Thomas became the first Latin scholastic to demonstrate direct knowledge of Constantinople III.

Unlike his recovery of Constantinople II, Constantinople III did not compel Thomas to rethink the standard of "orthodoxy" of mediaeval Latin Christology. Nevertheless, the doctrine of the council allowed Thomas to clarify, in a way none of his immediate predecessors could, specifically how the principle of non-contrariety is internal to an orthodox understanding of Christ's dyophysite reality and action, and so how the integral duality in Christ does not in anyway threaten — but rather confirms — the unity and identity of the one Lord Jesus Christ.[3]

---

the *secundarium esse* in *De unione, quaestio* 4 would be explained by what immediately follows in *quaestio* 5, in which Thomas quotes directly from the *Terminus* of Constantinople III. I am following Torrell's dating and presuming *De unione* was written shortly before the first questions of *tertia pars*. See Jean-Pierre Torrell, O.P., *Thomas Aquinas*, vol. 1, *The Person and His Work*, trans. Robert Royal (Washington, DC: Catholic University Press, 1996), pp. 206-7 and 347.

3. Without recourse to the foundational texts of the orthodox doctrine of dyotheletism, both the theologically formative texts of Maximus the Confessor (who remained unknown even to Thomas except as mediated through the *De fide orthodoxa* of John of Damascus) and the magisterial formulation of the doctrine at Constantinople III, thirteenth-century Latin dyotheletism relied on Peter Lombard's *Libri quatuor Sententiarum*, which *de facto* set the standard of the thirteenth-century doctrine of Christ's two wills. Key to Lombard's theology of the human will of Christ is the distinction he draws between the *affectus* of "reason" and the *affectus* of "sensuality." From this distinction, Peter argues that Christ willed his own Passion according to "reason" while nevertheless his natural "sensuality" recoiled from death (*Libri quatuor Sententiarum* III, dist. 17). The Lombardian position is extended in the early thirteenth century by William of Auxerre, who supplements Lombard's defense of non-contrariety by arguing that contrary things willed only determine contrary wills when the wills are in the same genus or in the same part of the soul (*Summa aurea* III, *tr.* 4, c. 1, *solutio*). William could show how Christ both willed his Passion and willed not to die. In this way, William could achieve a non-contrariety of wills by specifying a distinction within the genus of the human will according to which the lower and higher aspects could in principle contradict each other without entailing contrariety with the will of God. This line of thinking is continued in the *Summa fratris Alexandri* (sometimes attributed to Alexander of Hales).

More informed by John of Damascus's *De fide orthodoxa*, the *Summa fratris* advances on William by distinguishing diversity from contrariety, arguing that the former does not entail the latter. There is non-contrariety in Christ because the distinction of things willed are being willed from different "parts" of the will: "contraries must be identified through the same (*circa idem*); because, therefore, the will was not for dying and for living through the same (*circa idem*) nor according to the same (*secundum idem*) in Christ, since one through (*circa*) sensuality, another through (*circa*) reason, there was no contrariety of the will of sensuality and the will of reason" (*Summa fratris Alexandri* III, *tr.* 4, q. 1, c. 2). Furthermore, the *Summa fratris* invokes the Damascene's distinction between θέλησις and βούλησις (*Summa fratris Alexandri* III, *tr.* 4,

According to Thomas, "contrariety can exist only where there is opposition in the same and as regards the same (*in eodem et secundum idem*)."[4] For there to be contrariety of wills, then, it is necessary that this contrariety should be with regards to the same thing. The example Thomas gives is that of a judge who wills a criminal to execution for the sake of the common good and a relative of the criminal who wishes he would not be killed for private love. Thomas explains that there is no necessary contrariety of wills here between the judge and the relative, unless the private love of the relative went so far as to will to hinder the public good for the sake of his private love.

Regarding the agony of Jesus, it is clear that whatever the recoil of the human will of Jesus to the death he would presently suffer, this recoil issues from his natural desire not to suffer death and so does not contradict the free resolve of his filial obedience to accomplish the Father's will.[5] Thomas also argues that for there to be contrariety it is necessary for this contrariety to be in the same will (*quod sit circa eandem voluntatem*). There is, therefore, no contrariety of wills when someone wills one thing according to intellective appetite (*secundum appetitum intellectus*) and another according to sensitive appetite (*secundum appetitum sensitivum*), so long as what is willed intellectually determines the act performed. In order to specify this, Thomas draws on the distinction of John of Damascus between

---

q.1; *De fide orthodoxa* 2.22 [SC 535.328-340; PG 94.940b-949a]). This distinction ensures that it is now possible to affirm Christ's fear of death in a manner that is not limited merely to the sensual recoil from death that every animal possesses, but his recoil can now be considered fully human. In this way, the *Summa fratris* gestures towards the Maximian paradox of realizing the full ontological depth of both petitions of the filial prayer at Gethsemane: (1) "let this chalice pass from me"; (2) "not as I will, but as thou wilt" (Matt. 26:39).

Albert the Great (1193/1206-1280) and Bonaventure (1221-1274) both found fault with the logic of non-contrariety. Against non-contrariety, Albert argued that a contrariety of wills in Christ is paradoxically required in order to preserve the more fundamental conformity of the two wills in Christ to God: God willed Jesus to recoil from the Cross sensually and through his natural will, which means that Jesus obeyed the divine will by willing something contrary (*De incarnatione*, q. 2, and *Commentarii in III Sententiarum*, d. 17). Bonaventure too rejects non-contrariety, but does so by parsing the "will of piety" from the "rational will," thus signaling a return to the basic position of the Lombard that in Christ there was no rational movement of the will not to die. Thomas rejects the position of Albert and Bonaventure and follows the line of argument of William of Auxerre and the *Summa fratris Alexandri*, which is substantiated and deepened through his encounter with the *Terminus* of Constantinople III and Pope Agatho's *Epistula* I. The foregoing is nothing more than a simplification of the ample and sophisticated account given by Barnes in his *Christ's Two Wills in Scholastic Thought*, pp. 1-112.

4. ST III, q. 18, a. 6, *corpus*.

5. ST III, q. 18, a. 6, *corpus*.

voluntas ut natura (θέλησις) and *voluntas ut ratio* (βούλησις), the former being "the act of the will, inasmuch as it is drawn to anything desired of itself," while the latter designates the act of will as it is "drawn to anything that is desired only in order to something else."[6] From this, Thomas is able to affirm, following the doctrine of Constantinople III, that, in assuming the integrity of human nature, the Logos allowed the powers of his human soul to function in accordance with what naturally belonged to them. Not only, then, does the sensual impulse of Christ's humanity recoil from sensible pain, but more profoundly: "the will as nature (*voluntas ut natura*) recoils from what is against nature (*repudiat ea quae naturae sunt contraria*) and what is evil in itself, such as death and the like."[7] For Thomas, thus, as for Maximus the Confessor before him (of whom Thomas had only mediated knowledge through the Damascene), Christ truly suffered the fear of dying.

Constantinople III allowed Thomas to affirm this resistance of the human nature of Jesus to death in a way that was ontologically profound, while at the same time holding that this recoil from death is not in fact a sign of contrariety but rather suffered within the more fundamental synergy of the human will of Christ to accomplish the will of the Father.[8] The dogmatic consequences of Constantinopolitan doctrine for Thomas are worth quoting at length:

> It must be said that although the natural will (*voluntas naturalis*) and the sensitive will (*voluntas sensualitatis*) in Christ wished what the divine will (*voluntas divina*) did not wish, yet there was no contrariety of wills in Him. First, because neither the natural will nor the will of sensuality rejected the reason for which the divine will and the will of the human reason (*voluntas rationis humanae*) in Christ wished the passion. For the absolute will (*voluntas absoluta*) of Christ wished the salvation of the human race . . . while the movement of sensuality could nowise extend so far. Secondly, because neither the divine will nor the will of reason (*voluntas rationis*) in Christ was impeded or retarded by the natural will or the appetite of sensuality. So, too, on the other hand, neither the divine will nor the will of reason in Christ shrank from or retarded the movement of the natural human will and the movement of the sensuality in Christ. For it pleased Christ, in his divine will, and in his will

---

6. ST III, q. 18. a. 3, *corpus*.

7. ST III, q. 18, a. 5, *corpus*.

8. *Terminus* of Constantinople III (DS 558; DEC 1.230).

of reason, that his natural will and will of sensuality should be moved according to the order of their nature. Hence it is clear that in Christ there was no opposition or contrariety of wills.[9]

The logic of Constantinople III thus clarifies that the existence of an integrally functioning natural will in Christ is, paradoxically, made possible by the more fundamental synergy of divine and human willing. In this synergy, the non-resistance of the *voluntas rationis* to the *voluntas divina* makes possible the freedom of ascent (*liberum arbitrium*) whereby the natural resistances of the *voluntas sensualitatis* and *voluntas naturalis* are subjected to the *voluntas divina* through the medium of human freedom (*voluntas rationis*).[10] This means that the most fundamental aspect of willing in Christ involves drawing into divine union every natural inclination of the fallen state through the *liberum arbitrium* of human ascent now perfectly united with the "I" of the divine Son.

B. Dyoenergism and *Instrumentum Divinitatus*

Thomas specifies his account of the synergy of divine and human action in Christ through his doctrine of *instrumentum Divinitatis*.[11] Absorbed from

---

9. ST III, q. 18, a. 6, *corpus*: "Sic igitur dicendum est quod, licet voluntas naturalis et voluntas sensualitatis in Christo aliquid aliud voluerit quam divina voluntas et voluntas rationis ipsius, non tamen fuit ibi aliqua contrarietas voluntatum. Primo quidem, quia neque voluntas eius naturalis, neque voluntas sensualitatis, repudiabat illam rationem secundum quam divina voluntas, et voluntas rationis humanae in Christo, passionem volebant. Volebat enim voluntas absoluta in Christo salutem humani generis, sed eius non erat velle hoc in ordine ad aliud. Motus autem sensualitatis ad hoc se extendere non valebat. Secundo, quia neque voluntas divina, neque voluntas rationis in Christo, impediebatur aut retardabatur per voluntatem naturalem, aut per appetitum sensualitatis. Similiter autem nec e converso voluntas divina, vel voluntas rationis in Christo, refugiebat aut retardabat motum voluntatis naturalis humanae, et motum sensualitatis in Christo. Placebat enim Christo secundum voluntatem divinam, et secundum voluntatem rationis, ut voluntas naturalis in ipso et voluntas sensualitatis secundum ordinem suae naturae moverentur. Unde patet quod in Christo nulla fuerit repugnantia vel contrarietas voluntatum."

10. ST III, q. 18, a. 4, *ad* 3: "quod voluntas Christi, licet sit determinata ad bonum, non tamen est determinata ad hoc vel illud bonum. Et ideo pertinebat ad Christum eligere per liberum arbitrium confirmatum in bono, sicut ad beatos."

11. For the doctrine of Christ's human nature as *instrumentum Divinitatis*, see ST III, q. 19, a. 1, and for the definition of instrumental causality, see ST I, q. 45. a. 5. Further, cf. Theophil Tschipke, *L'humanité du Christ comme instrument de salut de la divinité*, trans. Philibert

John of Damascus, the language of *instrumentum Divinitatis* (ὄργανον τῆς θεότητος)[12] carefully signifies the absolute *unio* of operation of divinity and humanity in the Incarnate Son by stipulating that the integral human nature only "acts" insofar as it acts as "one" with the divine Logos. Thomas writes: "The humanity of Christ is the instrument of the divinity — not, indeed, an inanimate instrument, which nowise acts but is merely acted upon; but an animate instrument of rational soul, which is so acted upon as to act."[13] Accordingly, the language of *instrumentum* signifies no limitation of human flourishing or freedom (*liberum arbitrium*), but rather the action of God in Christ fulfills and realizes the integrity of "an instrument animated by a rational soul," such that being the *instrumentum Divinitatis* ensures that, in this human being, human nature and freedom flourish to the fullest extent.[14] In other words, the divine action of the Logos in the humanity of Christ is non-competitive with regard to the action of his human nature; it is acted upon so as to act (*ita agit quod etiam agitur*).[15] This means that the more God acts in the human nature of Christ, the more this humanity in turn realizes an action that is integrally human. This entails, in the context of Gethsemane, that Jesus must truly recoil from the inhumanity of the Cross: "if it be possible, let this chalice pass from me" (Matt. 26:39); while on the other hand, being the *instrumentum Divinitatis*, Jesus can do nothing other than submit the whole of his humanity to the will of the Father: "nevertheless, not as I will, but as thou wilt" (Matt. 26:39). In his prayer Christ also displays the real synergy of his human will (*voluntas*

Secrétan (Fribourg: Academic Press Fribourg, 2003); Jean-Pierre Torrell, O.P., "La causalité salvifique de la résurrection du Christ selon saint Thomas," *Revue thomiste* 96 (1996): 179-208; and Paul G. Crowley, S.J., "*Instrumentum divinitatis* in Thomas Aquinas: Recovering the Divinity of Christ," *Theological Studies* 52 (1991): 451-75.

12. Cf. John of Damascus, *De fide orthodoxa* 3.15 (SC 540.94; PG 94.1060a).

13. ST III, q. 7, a. 1, *ad* 3: "humanitas Christi est instrumentum divinitatis, non quidem sicut instrumentum inanimatum, quod nullo modo agit sed solum agitur, sed tanquam instrumentum animatum anima rationali, quod ita agit quod etiam agitur."

14. Cf. Rowan Williams, "Jesus Christus III: Mittelalter," *Theologische Realenzyklopädie*, vol. 16 (New York: Walter de Gruyter, 1987), pp. 745-59, at p. 751: "Obwohl die Menschheit Christi nach der Terminologie des Damasceners ein ὄργανον oder *instrumentum* ist, entfaltet sie doch ein tätiges und volles menschliches Leben, das auch fähig ist, menschliches *Verdienst* zu erwerben."

15. Hence Thomas's conviction that God is able to move with free will interiorly in all cases; see ST I, qq. 80-83, I-II, qq. 6-21, and I-II, qq. 109-14. On Christology and the language of non-competitive relation of God and creation, see Kathryn Tanner, *Jesus, Humanity and the Trinity: A Brief Systematic Theology* (Edinburgh: T&T Clark, 2001).

rationis) with the will of God (*voluntas divina*), revealing the *liberum arbitrium* of human nature perfected in a fully graced actualization of accord with God the Father.

The doctrine of the *instrumentum Divinitatis*, in this light, designates for the "action" of Christ precisely what the language of "enhypostatos" designates with regard to the "existence" of his human nature. In both cases, the Son is the subject of this human nature, the one who directly constitutes the reality of this nature and its action insofar as it is "one" with him, apart from whom it neither acts nor exists.

To recognize the essential interrelation between the language of *instrumentum Divinitatis* and that of "enhypostatos" is to see how the former doctrine ensures the absolute difference of human action and freedom within the *unitas* of the divine filiation. This is internal to the function of the mystery of salvation according to Thomas:

> the operation of Christ's human nature, as the instrument of the divinity, is not distinct from the operation of the divinity; for the salvation wherewith the manhood of Christ saves us and that wherewith his divinity saves us are not distinct; nevertheless, the human nature in Christ, inasmuch as it is a certain nature, has a proper operation distinct from the divine.[16]

There is no "equality" therefore between the divine and human natures in Christ because there is no "division" in what they achieve. The activity of the natures is distinguished by the fact that one is wholly dominant, because this nature simply is the divine person of the Son who alone is responsible for all that is done, said and willed by Jesus. In Christ, whatever distinction we must make in order not to confuse the natures, in all cases it is "one and the same" subject, the one Lord Jesus Christ, who acts and wills in the perfect unity of his being.

* * *

Thomas's most sustained treatment of the instrumentality of Christ's human nature is in the *tertia pars, quaestio* 19, on Christ's unity of activity (*operatio*), directly following the dyothelite *quaestio* 18 on the human and divine wills of Jesus. These two questions are logically intertwined by the

16. ST III, q. 19, a. 1, *ad* 2.

doctrine of Constantinople III, which condemned both the monophysite doctrine of "one will" in Christ and the monenergist doctrine of "one energy" or "activity" (ἐνέργυα / *operatio*). Thomas does not treat the questions symmetrically, but rather dedicates *quaestio* 18 to affirming the distinctive will of each nature while turning in *quaestio* 19 to affirm the theandric unity of action of the two natural principles.[17] In this way, we see how, for Thomas, the doctrine of Constantinople III concerns not only the distinction of the natural activities in Christ but also their fundamental and existential *unio*.

The unitive accent of Thomas's dyoenergist doctrine is bound to his reception of Denys the Areopagite's notion of Christ's "new theandric energy." For Thomas, the Dionysian doctrine specifies what the language of *instrumentum Divinitatis* is invoked to safeguard: the meritorious value of all that Jesus does. Replying to the monenergist construal of Denys's doctrine (as if it concerned the possession in Christ of only one operation), Thomas states the contrary: the Dionysian doctrine does not entail in Christ "any confusion of the [human and divine] operations or powers" but rather indicates that "his divine operation uses his human operation, and his human operation participates in the power of the divine operation."[18] The logic here is fully that of *instrumentum Divinitatis*: God uses an operation / activity proper to human nature, while insofar as the operation of this human nature is "one" with the operation / activity / power of God (because it is constituted fully by the divine Logos), it is not an operation apart from God; to the contrary, it is constituted by the divine operation but integrally human. Concretely, this entails that the humanity of Christ must operate beyond what is human according to the inversion of Denys by which divine things are done humanly (*divina operabatur humanitus*) because "being God made man, his was a new operation of both God and man."[19]

To illustrate the nature of this theandric reciprocity, Thomas invokes, as an example, the physical touch of Jesus's hand: "he wrought divine things humanly, as when he healed the leper with a touch."[20] The touch of a human being is not in itself miraculous, and even in Jesus this human

17. See Coleman E. O'Neill, O.P., Appendix 3: "The Problem of Christ's human autonomy" in St. Thomas Aquinas, *Summa Theologiae*, vol. 50 (III, 16-26), *The One Mediator* (Cambridge: CUP, 2006), pp. 229-37.

18. ST III, q. 19, a. 1, *ad* 1: "divina operatio eius utitur humana eius operatione, et humana operatio participat virtutem divinae operationis."

19. Denys the Areopagite, *Epistula* 4 (PG 3.1072c).

20. ST III, q. 19, a. 1, *ad* 1.

action is not humanly healing. The miraculous fact of the healing power of this human touch, rather, as Réginald Garrigou-Lagrange puts it, "proceeds from God as the principal cause and from Christ's human nature as the instrumental cause."[21] Jesus works divine things humanly. More ultimately, Jesus wills the divine will of salvation humanly. And so he wills theandrically in the sense that what he wills has an "infinite value" that "derives from the divine suppositum that is the agent which operates."[22] The deifying effects of the Incarnation are thus contingent on the theandric fact of the interpenetrating unity of divine-human operations. As Garrigou-Lagrange summarizes:

> Christ's meritorious and satisfactory acts were theandric in this sense, that they proceeded both from His human will and from His divine personality. And herein consists the essence of the very mystery of Redemption, in the infinite value of these theandric acts of Christ, which are called theandric because of the suppositum or divine person of the Word incarnate, who operates through Christ's most holy soul.[23]

All of this implies that, if there is a divine-human synergy distinguishable on the abstract level of nature, this synergy is substantiated by the simple oneness of Jesus on the existential level of *suppositum*. Dyoenergism, in this way, while it concerns the distinctive integrity of two fully operative and integral natures, also concerns the *unitas* of the theandric Christ, which is the condition and possibility of the integral difference of the distinct energies. In this way, dyoenergism eminently confirms that the *suppositum* or agent of the double action (divine and human) is in fact "one," that there is in Christ, as Constantinople II put it, a *unio secundum subsistentiam*. The human action of Christ participates fully in the divine act that constitutes its reality and possibility, ensuring that the theandric action is the work of a single agent.[24] The doctrine maintains, therefore, a *simplex unio* of operation in Christ, even while, on the metaphysical level of natures, we affirm a *maior dissimilitudo* by which we speculatively (*en theoria mone*)

---

21. Réginald Garrigou-Lagrange, O.P., *Christ the Savior: A Commentary on the Third Part of St. Thomas' Theological Summa*, trans. Bede Rose, O.S.B. (St. Louis: B. Herder, 1950), p. 474.

22. Garrigou-Lagrange, *Christ the Savior*, p. 474.

23. Garrigou-Lagrange, *Christ the Savior*, p. 474.

24. Cf. Francis Ruello, *La christologie de Thomas d'Aquin* (Paris: Beauchesne, 1987), pp. 202-3.

differentiate the actions of two different and integral natures, one human and created, the other divine and uncreated.[25]

C. Apostolic "Sending"

Thomas further specifies the numerical singularity of the divine and human reality of Christ and the theandric synergy that entails from this unity in his doctrine of the incarnate *missio*.[26] The *missio* of Christ, according to Thomas, "includes the eternal procession, with the addition of a temporal effect."[27] Thus Thomas speaks of a "twin procession" while clarifying: "not that there is a double relation to the principle, but a double term, temporal and eternal."[28]

Hans Urs von Balthasar developed this Thomist doctrine of Christ's *missio* further, showing how the *missio* of the Son can be deployed as the

---

25. Cf. Andrew Hofer, O.P., "Dionysian Elements in Thomas Aquinas's Christology: A Case of the Authority and Ambiguity of Pseudo-Dionysius," *The Thomist* 72 (2008): 409-42. Hofer argues this point cogently with regard to Thomas's use of Denys. Pointing specifically to Thomas's refutation of Macarius's heresy in *Contra Gentiles*, Hofer argues that "While upholding the Church's teaching of two operations and two wills, Aquinas concedes that one must speak of a kind of oneness when discussing Christ's activities" (pp. 433-34). He points to the following passage of *Contra Gentiles*: "It seems that this position [monotheletism and monenergism] arose because its authors did not know how to distinguish between that which is one simply and that which is one in order [*simpliciter unum et ordine unum*]. For they saw the human will in Christ to be completely ordered under the divine will so that Christ willed nothing by his human will except that which the divine will disposed him to want. Similarly, also, Christ did nothing according to his human nature, either by acting or by undergoing, except what the divine will disposed, according to John 8:29: 'I always do the things pleasing to him.' For the human operation of Christ conveys a certain divine efficacy from the union of the divinity, just as an action of a secondary agent conveys a certain efficacy from a primary agent. On this account, it happens that his every action or undergoing was saving. For this reason, Dionysius calls the human operation of Christ 'theandric,' i.e. 'deivirile,' and also because it is of God and of a human. Therefore seeing the human will and operation of Christ to be ordained under the divine infallible order, they judged there to be only one will and operation in Christ. However, as was said, one of order and one simply are not the same thing [*quamvis non sit idem, ut dictum est, ordinis unum et simpliciter unum*]" (ScG 4.36). Hofer concludes: "Aquinas thus affirms a certain 'oneness' in Christ's action, while making a vital distinction. Moreover, he is clear that the term 'theandric' applies to what he calls the human operation of Christ" (p. 434).

26. ST I, q. 43, a. 2.

27. ST I, q. 43, a. 2, *ad* 3.

28. ST I, q. 43, a. 2, *ad* 3.

essential term by which to root Christology firmly in the filial *relatio* in a way that ensures that Christology cannot be discretely parsed from Trinitarian theology.[29] For Balthasar, the key to a meaningful mediation of the Christological and Trinitarian reality of the Incarnate Son's *persona* lies in the conception of his "person" as constituted by a conscious response to a unique mission (*Sendung*), and the recognition of himself as uniquely sent (*der Gesendete*). Hebrews 3:1 is here an important text: "consider Jesus, the apostle and high priest (*apostolum et pontificem*) of our confession." Jesus is *apostolus*.

Sent by the Father, the Son's *missio* is rooted in the primordial *processio* of divine filiation, which for Thomas defines his person (*relatio subsistens*). This allows, according to Balthasar, that "Jesus' existence-in-mission manifests a paradoxical unity of *being* (and *being that has always been*) and *becoming*."[30] In this way, Balthasar offers a way of thinking through the Thomist doctrine of the *secundarium esse* of the Incarnate Son in a manner that upholds the doctrine of *unum esse simpliciter* in Christ by specifying the *processio* of the Son as the term that fixes in all things the act of the filial *missio*, the temporal effect of Christ's incarnate being (the reality of his *secundarium esse*). The incarnate *missio*, then, is none other than the *relatio subsistens* of the eternal Son, the absolute relativity of the "I" of Jesus in relation to the Father, a reality perfectly enacted in Jesus's prayer on the Mount of Olives: "not as I will, but as thou wilt" (Matt. 26:39). On this view, the paradoxical unity of the eternal-*being* and being-*becoming* of Christ is distinguished only in terms of the dynamic relation of the *missio* to the eternal *processio* — which are "one" because there is only one Christ. Yet the *missio* and *processio* are distinguishable *en theoria mone*, since we affirm a *secundarium esse* (being-*becoming*) within the *missio* of incarnate filiation. The caveat is that this *secundarium esse* is metaphysically "real" only in virtue of the unity of the *missio* "in" the primordial *processio* of the Son from the Father, his *unum esse simpliciter* (eternal-*being*).

The dynamic relation of Jesus to his origin (the Father) is the whole content of who he is. This means that "both elements — both *being* and *becoming* in the Incarnate One — express a single *being*, which, while we may

---

29. Hans Urs von Balthasar, *Theo-Drama: Theological Dramatic Theory*, vol. 3, *Dramatis Personae: Persons in Christ*, trans. Graham Harrison (San Francisco: Ignatius Press, 1992), pp. 149-259. Cf. Nicholas J. Healy, *The Eschatology of Hans Urs von Balthasar: Being as Communion* (Oxford: OUP, 2005), pp. 118-37.

30. Balthasar, *Theo-Drama*, vol. 3, *Dramatis Personae: Persons in Christ*, p. 157.

not call it *becoming*, is the streaming-forth of eternal life, superevent."[31] The divine filiation of Jesus in his *missio*, then, precisely "is" the *unitas* of eternal-being and human-becoming. The filial unity of Jesus with the Father and the hypostatic unity of divinity and humanity in Christ are thus internal to one another. This correspondence is confirmed in Thomas's reading of the "I am" statement of Jesus in the Gospel of John.

Beginning from Jesus's declaration "I am the light of the world" (John 8:12), in what follows in chapter 8 of John's Gospel, the Evangelist carefully balances the "I am" statements (cf. vv. 16, 18, 23, 24, 28) with declarations of the Son's being "sent" (cf. vv. 14, 16, 18, 21, 26, 29). The filial unity and distinction of Jesus's relation to the Father is, in this way, highlighted since (1) the "I am" statements are declarative of Jesus' unity of being as God, and (2) the statements of being "sent" from the Father declare his filial relation to God the Father. As Thomas notes, the "I am" statements recall especially the burning bush where God revealed himself as *Ego sum qui sum* (Exod. 3:14), and Moses learned that "existence itself (*ipsum esse*) is proper to God," such that God simply is the one who is.[32] In this light, Jesus' proclamation "Ego sum" indicates his eternal unity with the Father, which, in turn, safeguards against every parallelism of divinity and humanity in Christ such that, according to Thomas, it "eliminates the heresy of Nestorius, who said that the Son of God was united to human nature by mere indwelling."[33] Jesus' declaration "Ego sum" specifies that the created being of this man is the being of God:

> [I]n any other nature but the divine nature existence (*esse*) and what exists are not the same: because any created nature participates in its existence (*esse*) from that which is being by its essence (*ens per essentiam*), that is, from God who is his own existence (*ipsum suum esse*), so that his existence (*suum esse*) is his essence (*essentia*). Thus, this designates God. And so he [Jesus] says, "For if you do not believe that I am," that is that I am truly God, who has existence by his essence, "you will die in your sin" [John 8:24].[34]

Belief in Jesus means belief in the one who sent him, God the Father. The Son's *missio* proceeds perfectly from and communicates the *processio* of

---

31. Balthasar, *Theo-Drama*, vol. 3, *Dramatis Personae: Persons in Christ*, p. 159.
32. Thomas Aquinas, *Super Ioannem* 8 lect. 3, no. 1179.
33. Thomas Aquinas, *Super Ioannem* 8, lect. 3, no. 1143.
34. Thomas Aquinas, *Super Ioannem* 8, lect. 3, no. 1179.

his eternal filiation, and as such is the condition of the possibility of a theandric *communio* of created and uncreated being in the Love the Son eternally lives with the Father.[35]

* * *

In the obedience of his prayer and in his submission to the Father's will, Jesus reveals the whole content of who he is: he is *ex Patre*. The absolute relativity of the Son entails, according to Pope Benedict XVI, a paradoxical "divine filial submission" mysteriously internal to his non-subordinate divine identity: "While Jesus subordinates himself as Son entirely to the Father, it is this that makes him fully equal with the Father, truly equal to and truly one with the Father." [36] When this dynamic of the "filial will" is applied to the conviction of Thomas — of the manner according to which Jesus identifies himself with the name of God given at the burning bush — we begin to see that the oneness of Jesus is rooted in the revelation that "Jesus is wholly 'relational', that his whole being is nothing other than relation to the Father."[37] The "I am" of Jesus and the single *esse* of Christ are therefore rooted in the filial paradox of relation, which is expressed and lived in the Son's *missio* to reveal the Father and his Love through obedient submission. In an ultimate sense, then, all the "I am" sayings gather into the "Ego sum" of the Cross: "When you have lifted up the Son of man, then you will know that I am he" (John 8:28). Here the "Ego sum" of the God of Israel fuses with the *relatio subsistens* of the Crucified Lord, and the two are beheld as "one."[38]

What does it mean to speak of the inseparability of the Cross and the "Ego sum"? The Cross is the "turning of God against himself in which he gives himself in order to raise man up and save him."[39] This "turning of

---

35. Cf. Thomas Aquinas, *Super Ioannem* 8, lect. 3, no. 1192.

36. Joseph Ratzinger — Pope Benedict XVI, *Jesus of Nazareth*, pt. 1, *From the Baptism in the Jordan to the Transfiguration*, trans. Adrian Walker (London: Bloomsbury, 2007), p. 343.

37. Ratzinger — Benedict XVI, *Jesus of Nazareth*, pt. 1, p. 348.

38. Ratzinger — Benedict XVI, *Jesus of Nazareth*, pt. 1, p. 349. Cf. p. 348: "When Jesus says 'I am he' [cf. John 8:24], he is taking up this story [i.e. of the name given at the burning bush as it is developed in the Hebrew Bible] and referring it to himself. He is indicating his oneness. In him the mystery of the one God is personally present: 'I and the Father are one'." And cf. p. xiv, where Benedict describes the prayer of Jesus as "the true center of his personality." On this theme Ratzinger cites Heinrich Zimmerman, "Das absolute 'Ich bin' in der Redeweise Jesu," *Trierer Theologische Zeitschrift* 69 (1960): 1-20.

39. Benedict XVI, *Deus caritas est* 12.

God against himself," in the context of Thomas's theology, resonates with his use of the Dionysian idea of creation as the inversion of the divine Lover's self-externalization in realization of a reality "other" than himself.[40] Thomas writes:

> A lover is placed outside himself (*sic fit extra se*), and made to pass into (*translatus*) the object of his love, inasmuch as he wills good to the beloved (*vult amato bonum*); and works for that good by his providence even as he works for his own. Hence Dionysius says (*Div. Nom.* iv, 1): "On behalf of the truth we must make bold to say even this, that He Himself, the cause of all things (*ipse omnium causa*), by His abounding love and goodness, is placed outside Himself (*extra seipsum fit*) by His providence for all existing things."[41]

In both the case of creation and that of the Cross, a seemingly impossible inversion of the divine *Unum* realizes the freedom of the *Unum* to be related to what is other. This is made possible only by virtue of a paradoxically free act of the *Unum* to give away its oneness, to create an other from the primordial *nihil* (in creation) or from the *nihil* of sin (in redemption).[42] The freedom of the *Unum* in this way grounds the reality of the other through a self-gift in which the *Unum* turns inside-out to constitute (or save) what is impossibly — but truly — other. What does this mean? It means that the distinguishing regard of relativity (being-for) in God accomplishes *maior dissimilitudo* through a more fundamental *unio*. This means that neither in the act of creation nor in the act of salvation is the *Unum* abrogated, but the *Unum* constitutes (or saves) the mysterious relation to what is not-the-*Unum* but only "is" by the freedom of the *Unum*. On the Cross this impossible logic allows that the integrity of Jesus' "self" is not broken even by his act of freely handing himself over to death. The cruciform "turning of God against himself" does not sever the hypostatic

---

40. On this use of Denys by Thomas, see John Milbank and Catherine Pickstock, *Truth in Aquinas* (New York: Routledge, 2001), pp. 84-87, especially at p. 85: "[I]f what creation discloses of *esse* is that it somehow can exist outside of itself, what the ontological revision that is the hypostatic union discloses is that *esse* is in itself this ecstatic going outside itself. For divine *esse* is now shown to be such that a new thing can inhere in it, to be such that it can become entirely the *suppositum* of a creature outside itself, yet without real addition to itself."

41. ST I, q. 20, a. 2, *ad* 1.

42. Cf. the comments of Ephraim Radner on creation *ex nihilo* in his *A Brutal Unity: The Spiritual Politics of the Christian Church* (Waco, TX: Baylor University Press, 2012), pp. 9-13.

unity of the Incarnate Son, but rather draws created being into the salvific communion of divine Love. Thus the logic of *exitus et reditus*, in this light, is specified by a cruciform center. Pope Benedict writes:

> His death on the Cross is the culmination of that turning of God against himself in which he gives himself in order to raise man up and save him. This is love in its most radical form. By contemplating the pierced side of Christ (cf. [John] 19:37), we can understand the starting-point . . . "God is love" (*1 Jn* 4:8). It is there that this truth can be contemplated. It is from there that our definition of love must begin. In this contemplation the Christian discovers the path along which his life and love must move.[43]

Contemplation of the wounded heart of Christ directs us to the path of love, the paradoxical inversion that makes possible creaturely being and saves it. This paradox of love is the perfection of being, because it is the deepest reality of God himself:

> Love embraces the whole of existence in each of its dimensions, including the dimension of time. It could hardly be otherwise, since its promise looks towards its definitive goal: love looks to the eternal. Love is indeed "ecstasy" . . . a journey, an ongoing exodus out of the closed inward-looking self towards its liberation through self-giving, and thus towards authentic self-discovery and indeed the discovery of God: "Whoever seeks to gain his life will lose it, but whoever loses his life will preserve it" (*Lk* 17:33), as Jesus says throughout the Gospels (cf. *Mt* 10:39; 16:25; *Mk* 8:35; *Lk* 9:24; *Jn* 12:25). In these words, Jesus portrays his own path, which leads through the Cross to the Resurrection: the path of the grain of wheat that falls to the ground and dies, and in this way bears much fruit. Starting from the depths of his own sacrifice and of the love that reaches fulfillment therein, he also portrays in these words the essence of love and indeed of human life itself.[44]

In this light, the divine *missio* is perfected in the pierced side of the crucified while it unlocks the filial fact of Jesus's divine *esse*. He is the only-begotten Son of the Father.

---

43. Benedict XVI, *Deus caritas est* 12.
44. Benedict XVI, *Deus caritas est* 6.

CHAPTER 9

Union and Abandon

He alone, who sees the Father and rejoices fully in him, can under-
stand completely what it means to resist the Father's love by sin.

Pope John Paul II

A. The Sufferings of Christ

Following the traditional ascription of Lamentations 1:12 — "Look and
see if there is any sorrow like my sorrow" — Thomas Aquinas holds that
in the Passion, "there was a true and sensible pain in the suffering Christ
... [and] also, there was internal pain, which is caused from the apprehension of something hurtful, and this is termed 'sadness.'"[1] Christ is understood to have suffered both psychologically and physically. This *via*
crucis of sorrow and pain is rightly described as "liturgical" in the sense
that Thomas specifies that the Passion begins at the Lord's Supper, the
institution of the Eucharist,[2] and ends on the Cross with his declaration,
consummatum est (cf. John 19:30). The Crucified Lord has accomplished
in himself the perfect sacrifice, which fulfills all the juridical, moral and
ceremonial precepts of the Mosaic Law.[3] The key to this fulfillment, however, does not lie in the suffering and sorrow in itself, but in the charity

---

1. ST III, q. 46, a. 6, *corpus*.
2. Cf. Thomas Aquinas, *Super Ioannem* 13, lect. 6.
3. ST III, q. 47, a. 2, *ad* 1. On this topic, see Matthew Levering, "Israel and the Shape of
Thomas Aquinas's Soteriology," *The Thomist* 63 (1999): 65-82; *Christ's Fulfillment of Torah*
and Temple: Salvation According to Thomas Aquinas (Notre Dame, IN: University of Notre
Dame Press, 2002).

with which the Son freely enters into the suffering and sorrow that leads him to this death.[4]

According to Thomas, in the internal and sensible sufferings of the Passion and Cross, Jesus both (1) suffers all the human sufferings of the world, and (2) he suffers a depth of suffering exceeding in magnitude every other human suffering. The latter is rooted in the former; both are made possible by the hypostatic union.

Thomas contemplates the magnitude of Christ's sufferings from four different aspects:

1. The phenomenal extent of the crucified body: "the death of the crucified is most bitter," the body is "pierced in nervous and highly sensitive parts . . . the weight of the suspended body intensifies the agony. And besides this there is the duration of the suffering" because one who is crucified does "not die at once like those slain by the sword."[5] To this sensible pain is added the "interior pain" of Jesus' sorrow for "all the sins of the human race, for which He made satisfaction by suffering," which he ascribes to himself; for the fall of those who "sinned in his death chiefly of the apostles"; and for "the loss of his bodily life, which is naturally horrible to human nature."

2. The "susceptibility of the sufferer as to both soul and body": Christ's humanity is perfectly constituted, having been "fashioned miraculously by the operation of the Holy Ghost," and "consequently, Christ's sense of touch, the sensitiveness of which is the reason for our feeling pain, was most acute. His soul likewise, from its interior powers, apprehended most vehemently all the causes of sadness."[6]

3. The singleness of his pain and sadness: invoking to significant effect an axiom of John of Damascus, that Christ "permitted each one of his powers to exercise its proper function (*unicuique enim virium permisit agere quod est sibi proprium*),"[7] Thomas argues that "the magnitude of Christ's suffering can be estimated from the singleness of his pain and sadness." What does this mean? Thomas goes on: in "other sufferers

---

4. Cf. Romanus Cessario, O.P., *The Godly Image: Christ and Salvation in Catholic Thought from Anselm to Aquinas* (Petersham, MA: St. Bede's Publications, 1989), pp. 149-66.

5. ST III, q. 46, a. 6, *corpus*.

6. ST III, q. 46, a. 6, *corpus*.

7. ST III, q. 46, a. 6, *corpus*. Cf. John of Damascus, *De fide orthodoxa* 3.14 (SC 540.80-82, 90-92; PG 94.1037a and 1045a), 3.15 (SC 540.95-97; PG 94.1048a-c), and 3.19 (SC 540.130; PG 94.1080a-b).

the interior sadness is mitigated, and even the exterior suffering, from some consideration of reason, by some derivation or redundance from the higher powers into the lower; but it was not so with the suffering Christ, because 'He permitted each one of His powers to exercise its proper function.'" In other words, by virtue of the hypostatic union with the Logos, the natural operations of Christ's human being function at a superlative pitch of perfection in all their capacities, with the result that he sorrowed and suffered to the fullest human extent.

4. The filial freedom of the obedience of Jesus to accomplish the Father's will *pro nobis*. This death and this suffering — unlike all other human examples of death and suffering — is uniquely and freely willed in order to destroy humanity's servitude to sin. In order to effect this exchange, Jesus freely "embraced the amount of pain proportionate to the magnitude of the fruit which resulted therefrom."[8]

In the second and third cases, the perfection of Jesus' human being, perfect on account of the hypostatic union, is decisive to constitute the unparalleled magnitude of his sufferings. The natural human horror of death, the innocence of the one abandoned and betrayed, the heightened sensitivity of his immaculate body, the functioning of his human operations without mitigation — all of this is more or less directly rooted in the perfect and sinless fact of his human nature. The first and fourth cases are somewhat different. In the first case, the objective horror of crucifixion as a "most bitter" way of dying contributes to the magnitude of Jesus' physical suffering, while the objective sins of the world and the abandonment of the apostles contribute to the unbearable psychological pain of his sorrow. The emphasis here is on the objective facts that stand in a sense over and against Jesus, which are certainly exceptional (even if we could still think of parallel objective circumstances). In the fourth case, the focus returns to the concrete fact of Jesus' Passion, but now from the subjective side of the human freedom of the Son's decision to suffer and die in obedience to the Father's will *pro nobis*.

The bondage to sin that results from the disobedience of Adam and leads to his suffering and death is unwound by the *via crucis* of the Son, by the absolute and unique freedom with which Jesus resolves and submits himself to the wage of Adam's sin (cf. Rom. 6:23).[9] Jesus alone dies in freedom: *Qui cum Passioni voluntarie traderetur.* As Thomas writes:

---

8. ST III, q. 46, a. 6, *corpus.*
9. ST III, q. 47, a. 2.

according to the pleasure of his will, [Christ] could lay down his life when he willed, and he could take it up again [cf. John 10:18]; no mere human being can do this. . . . This explains why the centurion, seeing that Christ did not die by a natural necessity, but by his own [will], . . . recognized a divine power in him, and said: "Truly, this was the Son of God" (Mt 27:54).[10]

The unique freedom of the Son's gesture of handing himself over to death is concretely rooted, for Thomas, in his submission to the will of the Father, and so in the prior freedom of the Father to hand over his Son.[11] "God so loved the world that he gave his only-begotten Son" (John 3:16). The Father hands over the Son in three ways: (1) by the eternal will whereby he ordains the Lord's sufferings for the sake of the world; (2) by filling the Incarnate Son with the charity that would inspire him to suffer for the world; and (3) by refusing to shield him from his persecutors and so abandoning him to death.[12] The Son in turn responds in three ways: (1) he willfully carries out the task given him; (2) he fulfills the precepts of charity out of obedience and is obedient out of love; and (3) he suffers the violence that leads to his death while at the same time wills it because he had the power to prevent it.[13] This is the merit of his suffering and death, rooted in his love of the Father.

At the core, then, of the freedom of the Son to willingly enter into his Passion — and therefore of the meaning of the sorrow and agony he suffers — is the perfect charity with which he realizes his *via crucis*. On one level, this is bound to the hypostatic union, since Christ was incarnated precisely to accomplish this task. Out of this love Christ willingly enters into the depth of human suffering precisely in order that his suffering might correspond to the redemption he makes real, that the universality of redemption would be accomplished through a likewise inclusive and universal experience of human anguish. Accordingly, the fittingness of the Cross for Thomas lies in the fact that it is a universal sign: "the shape of the Cross extending out into four extremes from their central point of contact denotes the power and the providence diffused everywhere of him who hung upon it."[14] Specifically, this universal sign of suffering

---

10. Thomas Aquinas, *Super Ioannem* 10, lect. 4, no. 1425.

11. See Cessario, *The Godly Image*, pp. 156-58.

12. Cf. ST III, q. 47, a. 3.

13. Cf. ST III, q. 47, aa. 2-3.

14. ST III, q. 46, a. 4 quoting Gregory of Nyssa, *In Christi Resurrectionem* 1 (PG 46.624).

is a sign of love: by it Jesus is the "teacher of that breadth, and height, and length, and depth," of which the apostle wrote (cf. Eph. 3:18).[15] The Passion in this way recapitulates the meaning of suffering to reveal the love of God and thereby set an example of the sanctity that corresponds to the objective end of the human being.[16] Linked to this is the question of the magnitude of Christ's sufferings, which are greater than all the other sufferings of the world. Thomas is not hereby trying to equate Christ's sufferings in a quantitative way with salvation: "The very least one of Christ's sufferings was sufficient of itself to redeem the human race from all sins."[17] The specific sufferings of Jesus do not amount to redemption; rather, redemption is wrought through the uniqueness of the person who suffered and the perfect charity for which, in which and by which he suffered. The uniqueness of the suffering of Christ, then, lies in the *pro nobis*, which is bound to the freedom through which the Son endures "every human suffering" on account of love.[18] To say that Jesus endured "every human suffering" does not mean that he specifically suffered every thing that every person ever did or could suffer, but that he "sums up" in his Passion the sufferings of the world, mystically including them in his own suffering and recapitulating them in the form of perfect love.[19] The whole weight of the psychological and physical dereliction of humanity is, in Christ, suffered and sorrowed now within God himself, in the sense that the human sufferings of Christ are "one" with the divine filial relation that constitutes his unity with the Father.

---

15. ST III, q. 46, a. 4, quoting Augustine, *Epistula* 140 (PL 33.566).

16. Levering, "Israel and the Shape of Thomas Aquinas's Soteriology," p. 77.

17. ST III, q. 46, a. 5, *ad* 3.

18. ST III, q. 46, a. 5, *corpus.*

19. ST III, q. 46, a. 5, *corpus*: "quantum ad speciem . . . non oportuit Christum omnem humanam passionem pati . . . Sed secundum genus, passus est omnem passionem humanam." The mystical inclusion of all the suffering of the world involves for Thomas a threefold acceptance: (1) *ex parte hominum*, suffering at the hands of Jews and Gentiles, women and men, the rulers of the world and the lowly, and friends and acquaintances; (2) *ex parte eorum in quibus homo potest pati*, suffering from the abandonment of friends, in his reputation, in his honor, in loss of possessions, in his soul, and in his body; and (3) *ad corporis membra*, suffering over his entire body from his head crowned with thorns to his pierced hands and feet, and suffering in all his bodily senses: "in touch, by being scourged and nailed; in taste, by being given vinegar and gall to drink; in smell, by being fastened to the gibbet in a place reeking with the stench of corpses, 'which is called Calvary'; in hearing, by being tormented with the cries of blasphemers and scorners; in sight, by beholding the tears of His Mother and of the disciple whom He loved."

B. *Simul Viator et Comprehensor*

In Thomas Aquinas's theology of the sufferings of Christ, the Christological union sounds another note in the form of the doctrine of Christ *simul viator et comprehensor*. According to this doctrine, not only did Christ endure all human suffering and suffer in a manner surpassing every other suffering in intensity, he did so while humanly enjoying the bliss of vision of God.[20]

Thomas's understanding of Jesus' simultaneous experience of the *fruitio beata* and *maximos dolores* in the Passion developed significantly over his career.[21] While the young Thomas held that the bodily pain suffered by Christ did not exceed his body, that the sufferings of the Cross affected Christ physically but not psychologically, the mature Thomas held quite another view: "there was a true and sensible pain in the suffering Christ . . . [and] also, there was internal pain . . . termed 'sadness.'"[22]

Thomas's development on this issue is animated by a fundamental tension that grows from his attempt to synthesize two apparently irreconcilable trends in mediaeval theology: a concerted resolve to uphold the doctrine of Jesus's enjoyment of *visio Dei* on the one hand, while on the other hand overcoming the quasi-docetic implication of Hilary of Poitier's denial of the psychological or affective reality of suffering and pain in Christ's soul.[23] Against Hilary, Thomas comes to hold that the human soul assumed by the Logos did indeed undergo affective and psychological suffering as a result of the Passion, while at the same time enjoying the *fruitio beata*.

Why would Thomas want to uphold such a seemingly contradictory doctrine? And what does it mean to say that Jesus simultaneously experienced *fruitio beata* while suffering *maximos dolores*? Without seeking rote answers, the questions themselves merit a fuller contemplation of the Cross in which the "simultaneous presence of . . . two seemingly irreconcilable aspects is rooted in the fathomless depths of the hypostatic union."[24]

Visio Dei is the constituent effect of supernatural union with God in ev-

---

20. Cf. ST III, q. 15, a. 10, *corpus*.
21. Paul Gondreau, *The Passions of Christ's Soul in the Theology of St. Thomas Aquinas* (Münster: Aschendorff, 2002). Cf. Fergus Kerr, O.P., "Thomistica III," *New Blackfriars* (2004): 628-41, at pp. 638-41, where Kerr offers a helpful summary of Gondreau's book.
22. ST III, q. 46, a. 6, *corpus*.
23. Gondreau, *The Passions of Christ's Soul*, p. 25.
24. John Paul II, *Novo Millennio Ineunte* 26.

ery case.[25] And so with Christ, in whom the highest union of God and man takes place, the beatific vision proceeds from the hypostatic unity of his human nature with the person of the Logos.[26] This being the case, "there can be [for Thomas] no suspension or cessation of the divine nature's being without breaking up the union altogether."[27] But to uphold this position would seem immediately to commit Thomas to something like the position of Hilary, since the *fruitio beata* implies precisely the deification of the soul. Even worse: with the soul deified, Christ's body should have been rendered impassible and immortal by a redounding of glory from the soul onto the body.[28] Thomas's solution is to reserve the *visio Dei* to Jesus' *apex animae*, allowing the *anima sensitiva* to plunge into the sorrow of the Passion and the body into its tortures.

Citing John the Damascene's doctrine of the functioning of the divine and human natures in Christ, whereby each was "permitted each one of his powers to exercise its proper function," Thomas appropriates the doctrine to the upper and lower parts of Jesus' soul in order to justify how "the higher part of his soul enjoyed fruition perfectly while Christ was suffering."[29] Yet this poses a problem for Thomas, since the position fully contradicts the hylomorphic notion of *redundantia* (overflow) he upholds as basic to his general anthropology.[30]

According to the doctrine of *redundantia*, the upper and lower parts of the soul function in terms of a quasi–*communicatio idiomatum* according to which the experiences of each redound to the other and to the body and vice-versa. Consequently, if Christ truly enjoyed the *fruitio beata* in his *apex animae*, it follows that he did not suffer in his *anima sensitiva*:

---

25. Cf. ST I-II, q. 3, a. 8, *corpus*: "Ad perfectam igitur beatitudinem requiritur quod intellectus pertingat ad ipsam essentiam primae causae. Et sic perfectionem suam habebit per unionem ad Deum sicut ad obiectum, in quo solo beatitudo hominis consistit, ut supra dictum est."

26. ST III, q. 9, a. 2, *ad 2*: "ex ipsa unione homo ille est beatus beatitudine increata, sicut ex unione est Deus. Sed praeter beatitudinem increatam, oportuit in natura humana Christi esse quandam beatitudinem creatam, per quam anima eius in ultimo fine humanae naturae constitueretur." Cf. ST III, q. 10; q. 2, a. 1, *ad 2*; q. 9, a. 2.

27. Fergus Kerr, O.P., *After Aquinas: Versions of Thomism* (Oxford: Blackwell, 2002), pp. 176-77.

28. Thomas Aquinas, *Compendium theologiae* 231; see ST III, q. 14, a. 1, *ad 2*. Cf. Gondreau, *The Passions of Christ's Soul*, p. 448.

29. ST III, q. 46, a. 8, *corpus*.

30. On the whole topic, see Gondreau, *The Passions of Christ's Soul*, pp. 441-52.

Given the glory of the beatific vision that occurred in the higher part of Christ's soul, and its "normal" redounding effects onto the lower powers of the soul and even onto the body, it would seem nonsensical to affirm the reality of psychosomatic suffering.[31]

The solution for Thomas is to argue that uniquely and exceptionally in Christ, there is, in this regard, a suspension of the normal basis of human nature's operation. By a divine *dispensatio*, Jesus enjoys in his *apex animae* the full extent of divine presence and bliss, while the lower part of his soul suffers in its apparently usual and undivinized mode. The divine *dispensatio* that suspends the *redundantia* of bliss from the *apex animae* to the *anima sensitiva* is pressed radically to the breaking point in Christ's "fourth word" from the Cross: "My God, my God, why hast thou forsaken me?" (Matt. 27:46 and Mark 15:34). How can Jesus both enjoy the light of the vision of God and experience the darkness of Godforsakenness? Without directly invoking Thomas, Pope John Paul II sums up what can be taken as the essence of Thomas's doctrine:

> Truly, if Jesus experiences the sense of being abandoned by the Father he knows, nevertheless, that that is absolutely not the case. He himself said: "I and the Father are one" (John 10:30). And talking of his future passion he said: "I am not alone, because the Father is with me" (John 16:32). At the loftiest point of his spirit [i.e *apex animae*], Jesus has a perfectly clear vision of God and certainty of union with his Father. But in those areas bordering on the sensitive [i.e. *anima sensitiva*] (and therefore more subject to impressions, emotions and repercussions of painful internal and external experiences), the human soul of Jesus is reduced to a desert, and he no longer feels the presence of the Father, but rather suffers the tragic experience of the most complete desolation.[32]

Even confined to the *apex animae*, it has struck most modern theologians as impossibly disingenuous to affirm that Jesus in the moment of dereliction yet enjoyed the *fruitio beata*.[33] Countless questions arise here.

---

31. Gondreau, *The Passions of Christ's Soul*, p. 443.

32. John Paul II, "Audiencia general del 30 de noviembre de 1988," no. 4. Quoted from the Spanish, online at http://www.vatican.va/holy_father/john_paul_ii/audiences/1988/documents/hf_jp-ii_aud_19881130_sp.html.

33. For three of the best (and orthodox) critiques of the position upheld by Thomas, see Hans Urs von Balthasar, *Theo-Drama: Theological Dramatic Theory*, vol. 3, *Dramatis Personae:*

How can the Father be both present and absent to Jesus? How can Jesus have a "perfectly clear vision of God and certainty of his union with his Father" and yet experience his soul "reduced to a desert" such that "he no longer feels the presence of the Father"? How do these seemingly dichotomous subjective experiences remain authentic realities of one and the same subject? And how are they held together in the identity of the one person who simultaneously dies on the Cross and lives in infinite bliss?

We seemingly find ourselves at the point of total contradiction. If the divine *dispensatio* simply negates the normal *redundantia* in a way that leaves the upper and lower parts of the soul to operate strictly in terms of a parallelism, then Jesus's human experience of the *fruitio beata* and *maximos dolores* would seem dangerously bifurcated, as if the one were wholly extrinsic to the other, indeed as if there were in Jesus two discrete subjective experiences.[34] But there is another way of approaching the conundrum. Beyond parallelism and reduction (whether by synthesis or by elimination), Thomas's doctrine of the simultaneous *fruitio beata* and *maximos dolores* of the Suffering Christ can be read as leading us to the frontier of an unfathomable mystery at the heart of the incarnate fact. In matters of the most profound reality, wrote Cardinal John Henry Newman,[35] it is normal to come upon two seemingly opposed truths, while knowing that

---

Persons in Christ, trans. Graham Harrison (San Francisco: Ignatius Press, 1992), pp. 222-30; Thomas G. Weinandy, O.F.M., Cap., "Jesus' Filial Vision of the Father," *Pro Ecclesia* 13 (2004): 189-201; Jean Galot, S.J., "Le Christ terrestre et la vision," *Gregorianum* 67 (1986): 429-50. Even the eminent French Thomist and scholar of Thomas's life, Jean-Pierre Torrell, O.P., has expressed unease with Thomas's doctrine; see his "S. Thomas d'Aquin et la science du Christ: une relecture des Questions 9-12 de la *tertia pars* de la *Somme de théologie*," in S.-T. Bonino, ed., *Saint Thomas au XXe siècle* (Paris: Editions St. Paul 1994), pp. 394-409. For what I take to be the best apologia of Thomas in light of Balthasar, see Matthew Levering, *Scripture and Metaphysics: Aquinas and the Renewal of Trinitarian Theology* (Oxford: Blackwell, 2004), pp. 120-43. For the most compelling contemporary defense of Thomas's doctrine, see Edward T. Oakes, S.J., *Infinity Dwindled to Infancy: A Catholic and Evangelical Christology* (Grand Rapids: Eerdmans, 2011), pp. 210-21.

34. See Weinandy, "Jesus' Filial Vision of the Father," pp. 189-201, and Thomas G. Weinandy, O.F.M., Cap., "The Beatific Vision and the Incarnate Son: Furthering the Discussion," *The Thomist* 70 (2006): 605-615. Responding to Weinandy's charge, Thomas Joseph White, O.P. has championed a defense of the traditional position; see "The Voluntary Action of the Earthly Christ and the Necessity of the Beatific Vision," *The Thomist* 69 (2005): 497-534, and "Dyotheletism and the Instrumental Human Consciousness of Jesus," *Pro Ecclesia* 17 (2008): 369-422.

35. John Henry Newman, Sermon 19, vol. 4: "The Mysteriousness of Our Present Being," *Parochial and Plain Sermons* (San Francisco: Ignatius Press, 1997), pp. 914-21. On this point I am indebted to conversations with Josef Seifert.

of course, if they are both "true," they cannot be opposed: "the state of the case is a contradiction *when put into words*; we cannot so express it as not to involve an apparent contradiction."[36] The experience of aporia here tempts us to "discriminate our terms, and make distinctions, and balance phrases, and so on."[37] But the problem with the systematic and rigorist pursuit of a synthesis, Newman worries, is that it finally ends in a "technical, artificial and speculative" use of words, which are ultimately "without meaning."[38] Keeping this warning in mind, and seeking to maintain the tension and drama of the paradox that entails from Thomas's doctrine, we pursue a hint in Thomas that may take us deeper into this ultimate mystery his doctrine provokes.

We have seen how the magnitude of the sufferings of Christ is rooted in his *pro nobis*, in the love with which he carries out the mission given him by the Father. But another aspect also grounds his sufferings: the fact of his uniquely perfect humanity. "Christ's sense of touch . . . was most acute."[39] He literally felt at a higher pitch of human feeling. And this "sensitiveness . . . is the reason for our feeling pain."[40] Jesus' soul, as well, "from its interior powers, apprehended most vehemently all the causes of sadness."[41] He sorrowed with an exceptional sensitivity and feeling of human emotion. His humanity did not operate in the normal way but rather in a transcendently flourishing way: Christ's sense of physical touch and psychological tenderness were that of the *verus homo.*

Nothing else but *unio* with God himself could be the cause of Christ's being *verus homo* and therefore of his uniquely heightened human experience, and this heightened experience was precisely one of finitude, of the fragility and sensitivity of created being. This same *unio*, moreover, is the key to Thomas's doctrine of Christ *simul viator et comprehensor:* Jesus' enjoyment of the *visio Dei* is the effective evidence of union with God such that to fail to have *visio* is to fail to be in union.[42] In other words, the hypostatic union ensures both the *fruitio beata* and the *maximos dolores* in Jesus insofar as the former is the direct effect of union and the latter results

---

36. Newman, Sermon 19, vol. 4: "The Mysteriousness of Our Present Being," p. 916. Italics are Newman's.

37. Newman, Sermon 19, vol. 4: "The Mysteriousness of Our Present Being," p. 916.

38. Newman, Sermon 19, vol. 4: "The Mysteriousness of Our Present Being," p. 916.

39. ST III, q. 46, a. 6, *corpus.*

40. ST III, q. 46, a. 6, *corpus.*

41. ST III, q. 46, a. 6, *corpus.*

42. Cf. ST I-II, q. 3, a. 8, *corpus*, and III, q. 9, a. 2, *ad* 2.

from the perfect functioning of human nature, which is also an effect of the hypostatic union. This suggests that, whatever the suspension of *redundantia* accomplishes in Christ, the function is not straightforward in the sense of leaving the upper and lower parts of the soul to operate in terms wholly extrinsic to each other. We may deduce that perhaps there is still a circumincessive relation of the upper and lower parts of the soul by which the *fruitio beata* and the *maximos dolores* are yet somehow internally related in Christ and even, mysteriously, in communication. John Paul II has suggested something luminous along these lines:

> Precisely because of the knowledge and experience of the Father which *he alone has*, even at the moment of darkness he sees clearly the gravity of sin and suffers *because* of it. He alone, who sees the Father and rejoices fully in him, can understand completely what it means to resist the Father's love by sin.[43]

In this light it would seem that, almost impossibly, the *maximos dolores* of Christ occur precisely "because of the knowledge and experience of the Father," and are therefore mysteriously rooted in the *fruitio beata*.

If the *maximos dolores* suffered by Jesus are internal to the *fruitio beata* he nevertheless enjoys, then the function of the *dispensatio* that secures the simultaneity of the *fruitio beata* and *maximos dolores* might be more enigmatic and paradoxical than we have previously imagined. It cannot be, in light of the foregoing, that the *dispensatio* simply suspends *redundantia*, but neither can there be here anything like a normal operation of *redundantia* (since this would imply moreover the deification of his body and the lack even of physical pain). Could it be, rather, that in the case of the Incarnate Son the *redundantia* is radically overdetermined by the *fruitio beata* in a wholly unique way?

A hint seems to lie in Thomas's insistence that the Logos did not simply assume human nature, but rather assumed fallen nature, that is, human nature under the historical reality of the fallen condition; he came in the "likeness of sinful flesh" (Rom. 8:3).[44] Taking this into account we can per-

---

43. John Paul II, *Novo Millennio Ineunte* 26. Oakes highlights this text of John Paul II as fully illustrative of Thomas's doctrine in *Infinity Dwindled to Infancy*, p. 215. The italics here are Oakes's.

44. ST III, q. 15, a. 1, *ad* 4; ScG IV. 29. Cf. Thomas G. Weinandy, O.M.F., Cap., *In the Likeness of Sinful Flesh: An Essay on the Humanity of Christ* (Edinburgh: T&T Clark, 1993), p. 51, and *passim*.

haps say that the *redundantia* of *fruitio beata* in the lower parts of the soul, far from being cut off by the *dispensatio*, now paradoxically saturates the normal functioning of human nature, not to the effect of deification, but to the effect of a most intimate participation in the conditions of fallen nature, that is, in the likeness of sinful flesh. Could it be, then, that woven into the fabric of the fallen world, of which affective and psychological suffering is basic, the joy of the *fruitio beata* redounds to a mysterious capacity to suffer the sorrow of the fallen condition at a higher pitch of intensity? Could the *maximos dolores* of Jesus thus be rooted in the inscrutable mystery of the *fruitio beata* he enjoyed?

Raising these questions brings us beyond the customary parallelism: without ceasing to acknowledge the unfathomable mystery, we may now contemplate Jesus as suffering the Father's absence in his *anima sensitiva* (and so suffering "the tragic experience of the most complete desolation"), in a manner impossibly internal to how he nevertheless enjoys at the same time the Father's presence in his *apex animae* (and so knowing "a perfectly clear vision of God and certainty of union with his Father").[45] At the same time, this would suggest that Thomas's unprecedented attention to the affectivity of Christ should be read as paradoxically rooted in his resolve to uphold the traditional mediaeval view that Christ enjoyed the beatific vision, even in his moment of dereliction. This is implied by Thomas's insistence that in Christ the two states are not simply contradictory: the "joy of fruition is not opposed directly to the grief of the Passion."[46] Another way of saying this is to say that the darkness of grief in the moment of the Son's dereliction is rooted in the luminous experience of his perfect charity.

In this light, the love of Christ for the Father, as well as his resolve to accomplish the paternal will, unites in itself — and is the most profound source of — his sorrow and his joy. In this sense, Jesus's sorrow is governed by the "rule of reason,"[47] a reason deeper than we can know, but nevertheless entailed by a grief that could never be despairing or outside knowledge of the truth of his mission. It means concretely that

> this grief in Christ surpassed all grief of every contrite heart, both because it flowed from a greater wisdom and charity, by which the pang

---

45. Cf. John Paul II, "Audiencia general del 30 de noviembre de 1988," no. 4.

46. ST III, q. 46, a. 8, *ad* 1.

47. ST III, q. 46, a. 6, *ad* 2: "ut satisfaceret pro peccatis omnium hominum, assumpsit tristitiam maximam quantitate absoluta, non tamen excedentem regulam rationis."

of contrition is intensified, and because He grieved at the one time for all sins, according to Isaiah 53:4: "Surely He hath carried our sorrows."[48]

To suggest that the grief of Christ issues from his perfect wisdom and charity would confirm that true sorrow is human and therefore cannot correspond to despair, since the hopelessness of despair would yield nothing about which to sorrow. If life is meaningless, there is no reason to mourn. Truth is what makes grief authentic and real, and so it follows that Truth Incarnate, come down from heaven to our vale of tears, would grieve at the highest pitch. The "tragic experience of the most complete desolation"[49] depends on "the knowledge and experience of the Father."[50] Or as Adrienne von Speyr puts it: "The Father is never more present than in this absence on the Cross."[51]

The unimaginable weight of Jesus's "feeling of being abandoned by the Father" is, in light of the foregoing, seen to result from the impossible paradox of a "perfectly clear vision of God and certainty of . . . union with that Father."[52] The intensity of suffering, which reaches deeper into the transcendent depth of suffering than any other human experience of suffering, is thus supremely borne on account of Christ's eternal filial knowledge of the Father.

C. The Body of Christ in the Tomb

The burden of this chapter has been to verify Thomas's doctrine of the unity of Christ in the depths of the Son's Passion. In this sense it is a witness to how the Cross is internal to the doctrine of the hypostatic union and Christ's single divine *esse*. Nowhere does Thomas more radically uphold the depth

---

48. ST III, q. 46, a. 6, *ad* 4. Commenting on this passage, Levering notes that guilt does not add intensity to grief for Thomas because the guilty grieve more on account of the penalty than the crime. See Levering, "Israel and the Shape of Thomas Aquinas's Soteriology," p. 80, n. 11.

49. John Paul II, "Audiencia general del 30 de noviembre de 1988," no. 4.

50. John Paul II, *Novo Millennio Ineunte* 26.

51. Adrienne von Speyr, *Rechtfertigung: Die gegenwärtige kontroverstheologische Problematik der Rechtfertigung zwischen der evangelisch-lutherischen und der römisch-katholischen Kirche* (Gütersloh, 1971), p. 306; as quoted in Hans Urs von Balthasar, *Theo-Logic*, vol. 2, *Truth of God*, trans. Adrian J. Walker (San Francisco: Ignatius Press, 2004), p. 352.

52. John Paul II, "Audiencia general del 30 de noviembre de 1988," no. 4.

of the divine unity of Christ than in his reply to the question of whether the Logos was separated from the cadaver when it lay in the tomb.[53]

Thomas offers three powerful objections to the union of the Logos with the dead body. In the first, he submits that divinity must have been separated from the flesh when Christ died since Jesus himself cried out, "My God, my God, why hast thou forsaken me?"[54] This is substantiated by Ambrose of Milan, who reads the words of Psalm 21 (22) on Jesus' lips thus: "The man cried out when about to expire by being severed from the divinity; for since the divinity is immune from death, assuredly death could not be there, except life departed, for the divinity is life."[55] The second objection refers to the previously established position of Thomas that divinity was united to the humanity of Christ through the human soul.[56] Wherefore, if the body and soul were separated, the divine Logos would remain united with the soul and not the body from which death would have separated it.[57] The third objection consists in affirming the life-giving power of God, which, being greater than any soul, could not allow a body with which it was united to taste death.[58]

As Thomas notes in his *sed contra* to the article, all three objections contradict at their core the Cyrillian rule according to which "the attributes of human nature are predicated of the Son of God only by reason of the union."[59] Accordingly, and confirming the logic of *communicatio idiomatum*, Thomas overturns the objections raised as invalid: "what belongs to the body of Christ after death is predicated of the Son of God."[60] The entombed cadaver — maximally different from God's *apatheia* — is nevertheless predicable only by virtue of the hypostatic union. For Thomas, this is basic to the Church's *credo* itself, and thus he justifies it citing the *Symbolum Apostolicum*: "was conceived and born of a Virgin, suffered, died, and was buried."[61] Everything predicated of the Incarnate Son is predi-

---

53. ST III, q. 50, a. 2.

54. ST III, q. 50, a. 2, obj. 1.

55. Ambrose, *De Laudibus Constantini* 15 (PL 20.1413); quoted in ST III, q. 50, a. 2, obj. 1.

56. Cf. ST III, q. 6, a. 1.

57. ST III, q. 50, a. 2, obj. 2.

58. ST III, q. 50, a. 2, obj. 3.

59. ST III, q. 50, a. 2, *sed contra*; cf. III, q. 16, aa. 4-5.

60. ST III, q. 50, a. 2, *sed contra*.

61. Cf. ST III, q. 50, a. 2, *sed contra*: "ea quae sunt humanae naturae, non dicuntur de filio Dei nisi ratione unionis, ut supra habitum est. Sed de filio Dei dicitur id quod convenit corpori Christi post mortem, scilicet esse sepultum, ut patet in symbolo fidei, ubi dicitur

cated of the "one" divine Logos; therefore, "the body of Christ is not separated from the divinity in death."[62] The importance of this invocation of the *credo* of the Church cannot be overplayed. It suggests quite clearly that, for Thomas, the apparent rational absurdity of the union of God maintaining with a cadaver in a tomb notwithstanding, this union is basic to the simple faith of creedal Christianity.[63] Thomas concludes: "as before death Christ's flesh was united personally and hypostatically with the Word of God, it remained so after his death, so that the hypostasis of the Word of God was not different from that of Christ's flesh after death."[64]

In substance, all that Thomas affirms in this article is nothing other than the basic doctrine of the unitary subsistence of the Crucified entailed by the theopaschite dogma of Constantinople II: "He who was crucified in the flesh, our Lord Jesus Christ, is true God, Lord of glory, and one of the Holy Trinity."[65] Through the crucifixion, the paradox of the Incarnate Son is brought to the breaking point — the point of *separatio* — but does not break. This radical sense of Chalcedonian non-dualism (*indivisus, inseparabilis*), across the un-crossable chasm of death, affirms the indissoluble *unio* of the Son across every *maior dissimilitudo* to the point that even the division of sinful humanity can be enfolded into the wider unity of Jesus Christ.[66]

---

quod *filius Dei conceptus est et natus ex virgine, passus, mortuus et sepultus.* Ergo corpus Christi non fuit separatum in morte a divinitate."

62. ST III, q. 50, a. 2, *sed contra.*

63. Cf. CCC 625-626: "Christ's stay in the tomb constitutes the real link between his passible state before Easter and his glorious and risen state today, the same person of the 'Living One' can say, 'I died, and behold I am alive for evermore' (Rev. 1:18). 'God [the Son] did not impede death from separating his soul from his body according to the necessary order of nature, but has reunited them to one another in the Resurrection, so that he himself might be, in his person, the meeting point for death and life, by arresting in himself the decomposition of nature produced by death and so becoming the source of reunion for the separated parts.' (Gregory of Nyssa, *Oratio Catechetica* 16 [PG 45.52d]). Since the 'Author of life' who was killed (cf. Acts 3:15) is the same 'living one [who has] risen' (Luke 24:5-6), the divine person of the Son of God necessarily continued to possess his human soul and body, separated from each other by death."

64. ST III, q. 50, a. 2, *ad* 3.

65. *Anathematismi adversus "tria Capitula,"* canon 10 (DS 432; DEC 1.114-122).

66. Here it is important to clarify that in Thomas the "wider unity" into which Jesus enfolds the world does not include the interior alienation of damnation of the lost. Jesus descends into hell, but he does not descend into the freedom of those who turn away from him, that is into the hell of the lost. Cf. ST III, q. 52, a. 2. It is maybe helpful to think of this in terms of C. S. Lewis's dictum that "the doors of hell are locked on the inside" (*The Problem of Pain* [New York: HarperOne, 2009], p. 130). For Thomas, the descent of Jesus into hell does not coerce the free will of those who have chosen despair over hope (cf. q. 52, a. 2, *ad* 1).

A key text of Thomas here is taken from John of Damascus's *De fide orthodoxa*: even in death, the "one hypostasis was not divided into two hypostases."[67] There is no autonomous particularity, no "thingness" or "thisness" that can be granted to any aspect of the Incarnate Christ, not even to the corpse in the tomb, apart from the Son. The whole incarnate reality of Christ exists and is real only insofar as it subsists in union with the divine hypostasis of the Son. For the Damascene, as for Thomas, the body and soul of Christ receive their subsistence in virtue of that union such that, even when severed by death, they exist only in "the one subsistence of the Word." As the Damascene puts it:

> So much is the one subsistence (μία ὑπόστασις) of the Logos the subsistence of the Logos, so too [it is the one subsistence of the] soul and body. Therefore at no time did either the soul or body have a separate subsistence of their own, apart from that of the Logos, and the subsistence of the Logos is forever one (μία), and at no time two. The subsistence of Christ is always one (μία). For, although the soul was separated from the body locally, hypostatically they remained united through the Logos.[68]

The hypostasis of the Logos so constitutes the ontological infrastructure of Christ's humanity that the separation of the body from the soul at death is truly encompassed by the hypostatic union. Just as the Logos remains united to the cadaver in the tomb, so he remains united to the soul that descends into hell. As Thomas writes in his commentary on the *Symbolum Apostolorum*:

> *He descended into hell.* As we say, the death of Christ lies in the separation of the soul from the body, just as in the death of other human beings. But, the divinity was so indissolubly united to the humanity of Christ that, although body and soul were separated from each other, nonetheless the very divinity was always perfectly present both to the soul and the body. Therefore, the Son of God was both in the tomb with the body and descended into hell with the soul. And thus the holy apostles said: "he descended into hell."[69]

---

67. John of Damascus, *De fide orthodoxa* 3.27 (SC 540.152; PG 94.1097a); as quoted in ST III, q. 50, a. 2, *corpus*.

68. John of Damascus, *De fide orthodoxa* 3.27 (SC 540.154; PG 94.1097b).

69. Thomas Aquinas, *The Sermon-Conferences of St. Thomas Aquinas on the Apostles'*

The simultaneous union of the Logos with both the separated soul in hell and the cadaver in the tomb ensures that, through the Cross, God "withdrew his protection, but maintained the union."[70] Christ can be wounded and shattered, his soul can be plunged into hell and his corpse interred, but the union is maintained because he cannot be separated from the one "to whom He is bound more than to Himself: the Father."[71]

Everything that is declared about the hypostatic union thus serves finally to safeguard the legitimacy of the one indispensable knowledge of Christian religion: "Jesus Christ and him crucified" (1 Cor. 2:2). To this end, Thomas's Christology aims in every way to be theopaschite according to Cyril of Alexandria's Twelve Chapters: "If any man does not confess that the Word of God suffered in the flesh and was crucified in the flesh, let him be anathema."[72] The hypostatic union is the most intimate union of God and creation but it is also the most ample, encompassing the abject cadaver and the abandoned soul in the divine unity of the Son himself.

Creed, trans. Nicholas Ayo, C.S.C. (Notre Dame, IN: University of Notre Dame, 1998), p. 79. Cf. Oakes, *Infinity Dwindled to Infancy*, p. 214.

70. ST III, q. 50, a. 2, *ad* 1.

71. Julián Carrón, Assembly, in *Whoever Is in Christ Is a New Creation: Exercises of the Fraternity of Communion and Liberation*, trans. Sheila Beatty (Rimini: Fraternità di Comunione e Liberazione, 2011), pp. 53-72, at p. 57.

72. ST III, q. 46, a. 12, *corpus*. Cf. Cyril of Alexandria, *Epistula* 17, Third Letter to Nestorius, anathema 12 (DS 263; Lionel R. Wickham, ed. and trans., *Cyril of Alexandria: Select Letters* [Oxford, OUP, 1983], p. 32; PG 77.121d).

CHAPTER 10

Son of Mary

*If Mary no longer finds a place in many theologies ... the reason is
obvious: they have reduced faith to an abstraction. And an abstraction does not need a Mother.*

Joseph Ratzinger

A. Christology and *Haecceitas*

Whatever the judgment of Thomas Aquinas, the *homo assumptus* doctrine
enjoyed prominence within the Latin tradition long after him. It flourished,
moreover, in the sixteenth and seventeenth centuries among theologians
of the so-called Scotist variety.[1]

---

1. Walter Kasper, *Jesus the Christ*, trans. V. Green (London: Burns and Oates, 1976), p.
240. Above all, *homo assumptus* Scotism is linked to the French Franciscan Déodat de Basly,
who argued at the beginning of the twentieth century that Scotus himself defended a version
of the doctrine that Déodat himself used to establish and defend a doctrine of an autonomous human "consciousness" in Christ. On Scotus's doctrine of the hypostatic union and the
Latin mediaeval context of the debate, see Richard Cross, *The Metaphysics of the Incarnation:
Thomas Aquinas to Duns Scotus* (Oxford: OUP, 2002); "The Doctrine of the Hypostatic Union
in the Thought of Duns Scotus" (Ph.D. Thesis, Oxford University, 1991); *John Duns Scotus* (Oxford: OUP, 1999), pp. 113-26; cf. Aaron Riches, "Christology and the 'Scotist Rupture,'" *Theological Research* 1 (2013): 31-63. For more on Scotus's doctrine and "Scotist" Christology, see Maria
Burger, *Personalität im Horizont absoluter Prädestination: Untersuchungen zur Christologie
des Johannes Duns Scotus und ihrer Rezeption in modernen theologischen Ansätzen* (Münster:
Aschendorff, 1994). While Scotus's doctrine of the unity of Christ resonated somewhat with
the Lombardian *homo assumptus* theory, he never directly employed the language of *homo
assumptus* and formed his careful Christological formulations to avoid Nestorian error on
their own terms. See Cross, *The Metaphysics of the Incarnation*, pp. 190-91 and 225.

Writing a generation after Thomas, John Duns Scotus (c. 1266-1308) conceived his Christology in qualified opposition to the Christological doctrine represented by Thomas. Whereas Thomas was concerned to foreclose the heretical dualism he detected in the Lombardian *homo assumptus* doctrine, Scotus was motivated to resolve his own theological perplexity: How does Christ assume a human nature *in atomo* without assuming the ontological conditions of personhood (*naturae rationalis individua substantia*)? Or: how is it that Christ is "fully human" without being a human *suppositum*?

The perplexity Scotus raised and set himself to solve led him to begin his Christology from the difference of *haec natura* in relation to the divine *unitas* of the Logos. It is not that the unity of Christ is of secondary concern to Scotus, very much to the contrary. His Christology, however, aims to fully protect the unity of Christ within his wider metaphysical reconfiguration of difference and particularity.[2] The real dichotomy between Thomas and Scotus lies in two different starting points. Whereas Thomas started from the *unitas* of the humanity of Christ in the *unum suppositum* of the divine Logos, Scotus sought to account first for the integral humanity of *haec natura* in order to establish the tenable conditions of the *unio* of divinity and humanity he yet wanted to maintain within the limits of the traditional Christological doctrine of the *unio personalis*.

In order to answer his perplexity, Scotus performed what Richard Cross has described as "an explicit reification of Christ's human nature."[3] Specifically, by rethinking the metaphysics of individuation, Scotus was able to grant a new autonomy to the individuated human nature of Jesus, such that he could now specify an ontological density of *hic homo* that was not constituted by direct recourse to the *unum suppositum* of the one Lord. Thus, whereas for Thomas, *unio* is constitutive of the difference of Jesus' human nature such that even the cadaver in the tomb only "is" to the extent that it subsists in the *unitas* of the divine Logos, for Scotus the "Word could put off his human nature without anything absolute in it being destroyed."[4] While Thomas held that the hypostatic union is absolutely constitutive of the whole human reality of Jesus, for Scotus the hypostatic union does not itself constitute the reality of *hic homo* in any exceptional

2. On this theme and its consequences, see, *inter alia*, Adrian Pabst, *Metaphysics: The Creation of Hierarchy* (Grand Rapids: Eerdmans, 2012).

3. Cross, *The Metaphysics of the Incarnation*, p. 12.

4. John Duns Scotus, *Quodlibetum* 19, n. 21.

way. Scotus deemed this non-constitution of the human Jesus by the divine Logos necessary in order to uphold the basic integrity of the *in atomo* fact of the assumed human nature.[5] To confirm the patristic axiom according to which "that which is not assumed is not healed,"[6] the assumed human nature of Jesus must, so Scotus thought, conform to the bitterly finite condition of human existence as it is experienced by every other particular human being, which for him meant that it was necessary to maintain the principle of the ontological possibility of Jesus' human nature existing apart from the hypostatic union.

The Scotist concern to adequately account for the individuated human nature of Christ should be understood, moreover, within the reallocation of piety which Scotus was living as a Franciscan friar in the thirteenth century.[7] Infused by Francis of Assisi's spiritual devotion to the poverty and simplicity of the human Christ,[8] Scotus's Christology gives doctrinal expression to this new devotional emphasis and is accordingly less animated by the glory of Christ Pantocrator than by the meager finitude of the particular existence of *hic homo*. In this way, Scotus's doctrine exhibits something of the individual meekness of Jesus reflected in the individual poor among whom he and his brother friars lived and ministered. In this spiritual context, the Scotist perplexity takes on a further meaning: if the humanity of Jesus is not understood as existing in a manner that conforms to the poverty of human existence in every other instance, the real and lowly finitude of the incarnate fact, it would seem, risks being lost.

For these reasons, an instantiation of human nature defined exclusively in terms of the hypostatic union would not suffice. Thus Scotus was led to offer a twofold innovation into the mediaeval theology of his day:[9]

1. He proposed a new conception of "individuation" that does not define individuality either as a material or an accidental feature of being, but

5. John Duns Scotus, *Ordinatio* III, dis. 1, q. 1, n. 6; *Quodlibetum* 19, n. 17. Cf. John of Damascus, *De fide orthodoxa* 3.11 (SC 540.64; PG 94.1024a).

6. Cf. Duns Scotus, *Ordinatio* III, dis. 1, q. 1; *Quodlibetum*, 19 n. 18.

7. On the reallocation of popular piety, see Charles Taylor, *A Secular Age* (Cambridge, MA: Belknap Press, 2007), pp. 90-145.

8. On Francis, see Augustine Thompson, O.P., *Francis of Assisi: A New Biography* (New York: Cornell University Press, 2012).

9. See N. den Bok, M. Bac, A. J. Beck, K. Bom, E. Dekker, G. Labooy, H. Veldhuis and A. Vos, "More Than Just an Individual: Scotus's Concept of Person from the Christological Context of *Lectura* III.1," *Franciscan Studies* 66 (2008): 169-96, here at pp. 170-71.

rather as a quasi-essential aspect, not in the sense of "pertaining to the order of essence" but as a kind of formality (but not a "form"); this aspect of being Scotus called *haecceitas* ("thisness").[10]

2. He sought to demonstrate how an individuated rational nature need not itself be conceived of as a person, but instead could be the nature of another *kind* of person (i.e., a fully individuated nature could be assumed by a person of another nature).[11]

We will address these innovations in turn.

1. Scotus's doctrine of *haecceitas* springs from an epiphany about the uniqueness of individual being, that every "one" is un-repeatable and in this sense directly God-willed. This aspect of Scotist doctrine is perhaps expressed most beautifully by the English Jesuit poet Gerard Manley Hopkins, who celebrated the "original, spare, strange" particularity of being, of *haec particularis* whether "sweet or sour, adazzle or dim."[12] This attention to the un-repeatable quality of individual being entailed for Scotus, in the words of Hans Urs von Balthasar, "a vision that penetrates beyond all law, all Platonic ideas and Aristotelian forms, to the incomparability of just this individuality."[13] It led Scotus to argue that the substance of a nature, its existence, must always include a particularizing component, which he called *haecceitas*.[14] He defines *haecceitas* as that which

10. Duns Scotus, *Ordinatio* II, dis. 3, pt. 1, qq. 1-6. Cf. Conor Cunningham, *Genealogy of Nihilism: Philosophies of Nothing and the Difference of Theology* (London: Routledge, 2001), pp. 20-22.

11. John Duns Scotus, *Lectura* III, dist. 1, q. 1, nn. 35-47.

12. Gerard Manley Hopkins, "Pied Beauty," in W. H. Gardner, ed., *Gerard Manley Hopkins: Poems and Prose* (London: Penguin Books, 1953), pp. 30-31. Hopkins's devotion to Scotus is well known, even if the extent of Scotus's influence is debated. In his poem "Duns Scotus's Oxford" (1879), Hopkins writes of Scotus as the one "who of all men most sways my spirits to peace; / Of realty the rarest-veinèd unraveller; a not / Rivalled insight" (*Gerard Manley Hopkins: Poems and Prose*, p. 40). Hopkins famously recorded in his journal after first reading Scotus: "It may come to nothing or it may be a great mercy of God. But just then when I took in any inscape of the sea or sky I thought of Scotus" (Humphry House and Graham Storey, eds., *Journals and Papers of Gerard Manley Hopkins* [London: OUP, 1959], p. 221). On Hopkins and Scotus, see Hans Urs von Balthasar, *The Glory of the Lord: A Theological Aesthetics*, vol. 3, *Studies in Theological Style: Lay Styles*, trans Andrew Louth et al. (San Francisco: Ignatius Press, 1988), pp. 353-99; Bernadette Waterman Ward, *World As Word: Philosophical Theology in Gerard Manley Hopkins* (Washington, DC: Catholic University of America, 2002), pp. 158-97.

13. Balthasar, *The Glory of the Lord*, vol. 3, *Studies in Theological Style: Lay Styles*, p. 356.

14. See Pabst, *Metaphysics*, pp. 282-86; Cross, *The Metaphysics of the Incarnation*, p. 12.

is not matter or form or the composite insofar as each of these is a "nature," but it is the ultimate reality of the being which is matter or form or which is the composite; so that wherever something is common and nevertheless determinable, even though it involves one real thing, we can still distinguish further several formally distinct realities, of which this formally is not that; and this is formally the entity of singularity and that is formally the entity of a nature. Nor can these two realities ever be two distinct real things, in the way the two realities might be that from which the genus is taken (from which two realities the specific reality is taken), but in the same real thing there are always formally distinct realities (be they in the same real part of the same real whole).[15]

The *haecceitas* of each particular *suppositum*, then, is inseparable from the existence of a given nature (although formally they remain distinct), such that a *suppositum* is no longer simply an individuated universal *forma* of "common nature" (*natura communis*). Natures always exist as *haec natura* and never as "nature-in-general." Thus the nature of a *suppositum* is never purely an individuated universal *forma*; it is *forma* "plus" *haecceitas*. The possession of *haecceitas* is thus not only internal to what it means for a nature to exist in every case; it metaphysically precedes in the order of existence the attribution of *suppositum* to a given nature.

In the case of the Incarnation the Scotist doctrine entails that the human nature of Jesus (*haec natura*) is individuated and possesses its own human haecceity apart from the *suppositum* of the Logos and so outside the hypostatic union. And so the doctrine of *haecceitas* introduces a "third term" between the traditional Chalcedonian distinction between *natura* and *persona-suppositum* (hypostasis). By this new term, nature becomes conceived as actualized in such a way that a human nature can now be conceivably individuated without necessarily being a *persona* / *suppositum*. This allows Scotus, in terms of his own doctrine of the *unio personalis*, to perform

---

15. Duns Scotus, *Ordinatio* II, dis. 3, pars 1, q. 6, n. 188: "non est igitur 'ista entitas' materia vel forma vel compositum, in quantum quodlibet istorum est 'natura,' sed est ultima realitas entis quod est materia vel quod est forma vel quod est compositum; ita quod quodcumque commune, et tamen determinabile, adhic potest distingui (quantumcumque sit una res) in plures realitates formaliter distinctas, quarum haec formaliter non est illa: et haec est formaliter entitas singularitatis, et illa est entitas naturae formaliter. Nec possunt istae duae realitates esse res et res, sicut possunt esse realitas unde accipitur genus et realitas unde accipitur differentia (ex quibus realitas specifica accipitur), sed semper in eodem (sive in parte sive in toto) sunt realitates eiusdem rei, formaliter distinctae."

his "reification" of the human nature of Jesus. But in so doing Scotus shifts the prior ontological density of individuated being, traditionally ascribed to *persona / suppositum*, attributing it now to the *haecceitas* of *haec natura*. Indeed Scotus now calls this *haecceitas* the ultimate positive constituent of existing being (*ponit realitatem qua est* haec, *esse ultimam entitatem positivam*),[16] and thus the ultimate positive content of the human Jesus.

2. By applying this new metaphysical distinction, Scotus hoped to reconceive *haec natura* within the limits of the doctrine of the *unio personalis* of Christ such that he could avoid what he judged the problematic of exceptionalism found in Thomas's single *esse* doctrine on the one hand, while avoiding the specter of Nestorian error on the other. In attributing a fully individuated human nature to Christ apart from the *unio personalis*, he satisfied all the traditional *prima facie* conditions set for what it meant to be a human *persona* (*naturae rationalis individua substantia*), and so, as Scotus was well aware, he skirted dangerously near a "two sons" Christology.[17] In order to avoid both the exceptionalism of the traditional conception of the hypostatic union and the Nestorianism of a "two sons" Christology, Scotus was led to introduce a further innovation, re-conceiving now the concept of *persona*.[18] He did this by rejecting the traditional metaphysically "positive" definition of Boethius in favor of a formal-juridical conception of the person rooted in the "negation doctrine" he inherited from William of Auxerre.[19]

According to Scotus, there are two ways to account for how a human nature becomes a person: (1) either "there is something positive in the nature over and beyond what makes it a nature and individual nature"; or

---

16. Cf. Duns Scotus, *Ordinatio* III, dis. 1, q. 1.

17. Cross, *John Duns Scotus*, p. 118. Cf. Peter Geach, *Logic Matters* (Oxford: Blackwell, 1981), pp. 289-327.

18. Cf. Rowan Williams, "Jesus Christus III: Mittelalter," in Gerhard Müller, ed., *Theologische Realenzyklopädie*, vol. 16 (Berlin: De Gruyter, 1987), pp. 745-59, at pp. 751-52.

19. William of Auxerre, *Summa Aurea* 3.1.3.8. Cf. Cross, *John Duns Scotus*, p. 119. Here, as Richard Cross has shown, in addition to William's "doctrine of negation," Scotus is extending a particular theology of the hypostatic union first articulated by Bonaventure, who conceived the hypostatic union primarily in terms of a relation of "dependence" of the human nature on the Logos of God (cf. Bonaventure, *Commentaria in Quatuor Libros Sententiarum* I, 3.1, *ad* 1). See Cross, "The Doctrine of the Hypostatic Union in the Thought of Duns Scotus," p. 25. On the hypostatic union in Bonaventure, cf. Zachary Hayes, O.F.M., *The Hidden Center: Spirituality and Speculative Christology in St. Bonaventure* (New York: Paulist Press, 1981), pp. 71-90. More generally on the influence of these innovations, see Louis Dupré, *Passage to Modernity: An Essay in the Hermeneutics of Nature and Culture* (New Haven: Yale University Press, 1993), pp. 36-41.

(2) "the ultimate positive entity is that by which it becomes 'this' (*haec*), and beyond this there is only that negation by which it is said to be subsisting as an intellectual nature and as a person."[20] Scotus rejects the first position and develops the second, stipulating that we need to distinguish between actual, potential and dispositional dependence.[21] Scotus insists, moreover, that in the case of a human being, personhood is contingent on being free of actual and dispositional dependence on the Logos, a condition that he labels "ultimate solitude" (*ultima solitudo*).[22]

In the case of Christ, although he is ontologically human in every sense, these two freedoms are negated in him to the effect that he is "one" with regard to the person of the Logos. The difference, then, between an individuated human being and a human person lies in a negation of properties such that *persona* is now simply an individual *natura* with one or more private properties.[23] In summary:

> Scotus claims that it is impossible that a created person is assumed, since then "two persons would be one person" . . . Necessary for being a person is *failing* to be assumed by the Word. Any nature assumed by the Word is *eo ipso* not a person.[24]

The actual and dispositional dependence of *hic homo* on the *persona* of the Logos thus "negates" personhood from Jesus' human nature, while at the same time clearing ontological "space" in order to grant *hic homo* a

---

20. Duns Scotus, *Ordinatio* III, dis. 1, q. 1 (Allan B. Wolter, O.F.M., ed. and trans., "John Duns Scotus on the Primacy and Personality of Christ," in Damian McElrath, *Franciscan Christology: Selected Texts, Translations, and Introductory Essays* [St. Bonaventure, NY: Franciscan Institute of St. Bonaventure University, 1980], p. 177).

21. Duns Scotus, *Ordinatio* III, dis. 1, q. 1 (ed. Wolter, p. 176): "Sed sic distinguendum est inter dependentiam actualem, potentialem, et aptitudinalem."

22. Duns Scotus, *Ordinatio* III, dis. 1, q. 1 (ed. Wolter, p. 180): "Ad personalitatem requiritur ultima solitudo sive negatio dependentiae actualis et aptitudinalis ad personam alterius naturae."

23. Duns Scotus, *Ordinatio* III, dis. 1, q. 1, n. 1; and *Quodlibetum*, 19, n. 19.

24. Cross, *Duns Scotus*, p. 120. Cf. Allan Wolter, "John Duns Scotus," p. 143: "Some claim to see some trace of 'Nestorianism' in this interpretation, yet this does an injustice to Scotus['s] ingenious refutation of this heresy at its very roots, for on his theory it would be a contradistinction pure and simple if one held that a human person was, or even could be, assumed hypostatically. Though Christ's human nature was a *natura personabilis in se*, that potentiality to be a human person could only be actualized if it was not actually assumed, and to assert it was both assumed and not assumed would be to contradict oneself."

new ontological autonomy in relation to the Logos in the sense that the individuation of this nature is now no longer determined directly by the hypostatic union. In this way, Scotus effectively loosened the ontological union between *hic homo* and the hypostasis of the Logos. While he did so, nevertheless, he was careful to ensure, through his new definition of *persona*, that, at least formally, Nestorianism was avoided. But this formal avoidance of Nestorianism reconfigures the hypostatic union such that there are now, in principle, other ontological possibilities for *hic homo* "Jesus" apart from being the one Lord. In other words, the *unio* by which the human Jesus is "one person" with the Logos now in no way constitutes his existence as such, since it must remain in all cases possible, in principle, for the human Jesus to exist without being the divine Logos.

* * *

Scotus, on his own terms, avoided a Nestorian position, but the same cannot be said of later extensions of his doctrine. This was the case especially with certain early-twentieth-century "Scotists," and in particular the French Franciscan Christologists Déodat de Basly and Leon Seiller.[25]

Absorbing Cartesian and post-Renaissance concerns over the status of Jesus' human "subjectivity," Déodat radicalized Scotus's "reification" of Christ's human nature to accommodate a psychological "reification," which for him came to imply something like a parallel human "self" in the God-Man.[26] The *haecceitas* of *hic homo*, as Déodat understood it, legitimized two autonomous "egos" of the Incarnate Christ: a human "I" distinct from the "I" of the Logos, yet "united" to the Logos according to the doctrine of negation. Déodat's extension of Scotus, moreover, was articulated in terms of a self-described *homo assumptus* position, which he wrongly attributed to Scotus. This, coupled with Scotus's notion of Christ's human nature as, in principle, fully individuated apart from its union with the Word, justified for Déodat a reapplication of the patristic doctrine of the *communicatio*

---

25. Cf. F. Ocariz, L. F. Mateo Seco, and J. A. Riestra, *The Mystery of Jesus Christ*, trans. Michael Adams and James Gavigan (Dublin: Four Courts Press, 2004), pp. 120-24; Cross, *The Metaphysics of the Incarnation*, pp. 225-28.

26. See Déodat de Basly, O.M.F., *Scotus Docens ou Duns Scot Enseignant: la Philosophie, la Théologie, la Mystique* (Paris: La France Franciscaine, 1933); "Le Moi de Jésus-Christ," *La France franciscaine* 12 (1929): 125-60; "L'Assumptus Homo," *La France franciscaine* 11 (1928): 265-313; "Inopérantes offensives contre l'Assumptus Homo," *La France franciscaine* 17 (1934): 419-73. Cf. Burger, *Personalität im Horizont absoluter Prädestination*, pp. 166-203.

idiomatum in terms of a parallelism in which it was now possible to apply the doctrine "indirectly," as a *communicatio idiomatum in obliquo.* The fundamental ontological "loosening" of the unity in Christ represented in Déodat was taken up and extended by Seiller, who argued that Jesus had a genuine human "psychological personality."[27] In these terms, in the case of Seiller, we see a distinct move towards a full-blown "two sons" Christology, represented by an internal relation in Christ of two "psychological personalities": one of divinity, the other of humanity. These "psychological personalities" tend to function as two subjective centers existing in parallel and thus predicable as two different "things" in the order of being. Seiller in this way came to a position fully reminiscent of Theodore of Mopsuestia, for whom the divinity and humanity of Christ function not only as discretely predicable subjects, but also as distinct centers of volitional and cognitive activity, two psychological centers that can enter into dialogue, the one with the other.[28] Similarly, for Seiller, the distinction of divinity and humanity in Christ entails a *separatio* for which the two subjective centers represent what is necessarily separable in the order of religious devotion such that, in Christ, "God the Word is the subject adored, in no way the subject adoring... the subject prayed to, in no way the subject praying."[29]

In 1951 the Christological program of Déodat and Seiller met with the censure of the Holy See. With the publication of *Sempiternus Rex,* in a more ample version of the passage invoked already at the beginning of this book, a limit was drawn against the new "Scotist" Christology. Pope Pius declared:

---

27. See Léon Seiller, O.M.F., *L'activité humaine du Christ selon Duns Scot* (Paris: Edit. Franciscaines, 1944); *La psychologie humaine du Christ et l'unité de personne* (Rennes-Paris: Vrin, 1950).

28. Cf. John Behr, *The Case against Diodore and Theodore: Texts and Their Contexts* (Oxford: OUP, 2011), p. 33: "So strong is Theodore's insistence upon this, that he can even create a dialogue, apropos of John 12:30, in which 'the assumed man' speaks of the Word in the third person. This is 'scarcely' simply a rhetorical device, Norris argues, concluding that 'the Man and the Word in Christ are not only two logical subjects of which attributes may be predicated. They are psychological subjects as well, at once distinct and intimately related as two centres of will and activity ... [They] are two intimately related agents bent upon an identical project.'" The quotation is from R. A. Norris, *Manhood and Christ: A Study in the Christology of Theodore of Mopsuestia* (Oxford: Clarendon Press, 1963), and refers to Theodore of Mopsuestia, *In Ioannis Evangelium* 12.30.

29. Seiller, *La psychologie humaine du Christ et l'unité de personne,* p. 17. Cf. Bernard Lonergan, *Collected Works of Bernard Lonergan,* vol. 7, *The Ontological and Psychological Constitution of Christ* (Toronto: University of Toronto Press, 2002), pp. 251-53.

While there is no reason why the humanity of Christ should not be studied more deeply also from a psychological point of view, there are, nevertheless, some who, in their arduous pursuit, desert the ancient teachings more than is right, and make an erroneous use of the authority of the definition of Chalcedon to support their new ideas. These emphasize the state and condition of Christ's human nature to such an extent as to make it seem something existing in its own right, and not as subsisting in the Word itself. But the council of Chalcedon in full accord with that of Ephesus, clearly asserts that both natures are united in "one person and subsistence," and rules out the placing of two individuals in Christ, as if some *homo assumptus*, completely autonomous in itself, is placed by the side of the Word.[30]

Having set this limit against the *homo assumptus* program, Pius XII was nevertheless careful not to reject, in principle, the speculative questions raised by Déodat and Seiller. If the Logos assumed a human nature *in atomo*, as Scotus reminds us, he must have likewise assumed the constituents of what modern people call "human psychology." The error of Déodat and Seiller was in failing to proceed from within the enhypostatic logic of the primacy of the divine *unitas* of the one Lord Jesus. Whatever "human psychology" Jesus may possess, it cannot imply a human "psychology" that operates alongside the *persona divina* as a second subjective center.[31] Whatever human "psychology" can be admitted in Christ, this "psychology," as with the whole humanity of Christ, must be recognized as a reality that "is" only as it subsists in the person of the Logos himself (*in ipsius Verbi persona subsistat*).[32] More than seventy years after the publication of

30. Pope Pius XII, *Sempiternus Rex* 30-31 (DS 3905): "Quamvis nihil prohibeat quominus humanitas Christi, etiam psychologica via ac ratione, altius investigetur, tamen in arduis huius generis studiis non desunt qui plus aequo vetera linquant, ut nova astruant et auctoritate ac definitione Chalcedonensis Concilii perperam utantur, ut a se elucubrata suffulciant. Hi humanae Christi naturae statum et conditionem ita provehunt ut eadem reputari videatur subiectum quoddam sui iuris, quasi in ipsius Verbi persona non subsistat. At Chalcedonense Concilium, Ephesino prorsus congruens, lucide asserit utramque Redemptoris nostri naturam « in unam personam atque subsistentiam » convenire vetatque duo in Christo poni individua, ita ut aliquis « homo assumptus », integrae autonomiae compos, penes Verbum collocetur."

31. Cf. Rowan Williams, "'Person' and 'Personality' in Christology," *Downside Review* 94 (1976): 253-60.

32. To say that this "psychology" exists in Christ is implied already by the doctrine that Christ possesses a fully operational human "will," which implies likewise a fully human

Sempiternus Rex, the Pian limit against *homo assumptus* Christology was reiterated by the Congregation for the Doctrine of the Faith in its "Notification on the Works of Father Jon Sobrino, S.J." (2006),[33] reaffirming that the *homo assumptus* doctrine is "incompatible with the Catholic faith."[34]

The *homo assumptus* tendency delineated by the Congregation in the Christology of Jon Sobrino is of a different kind to that of Déodat and Seiller. Whereas Déodat and Seiller were responding to modern ideas of human subjectivity, Sobrino's *homo assumptus* tendency is rooted in a Christological project imbued with modern ideas of political liberation. Sobrino's dogmatic aim is to recover the human poverty of the historical Jesus in the concrete situation of the "the poor of this world."[35] In order to do this, Sobrino seeks to "progress beyond the '*vere homo*' [of traditional

---

"memory," "imagination" and even "consciousness." Cf. John of Damascus, *De fide orthodoxa* 3.13 (SC 540.76; PG 94.133a). Raising these aspects of "full humanity" is best understood, as Thomas Joseph White, O.P. has shown, through careful and full analogical submission to the dyothelite doctrine of Constantinople III. See Thomas Joseph White, O.P., "Dyothelitism and the Instrumental Human Consciousness of Jesus," *Pro Ecclesia* 17 (2008): 369-422.

33. Congregation for the Doctrine of the Faith, "Notificación sobre las obras del P. Jon Sobrino S.J.," 5 (DS 5107): "En el tenor literal de estas frases, el P. Sobrino refleja la llamada teología del *homo assumptus*, que resulta incompatible con la fe católica, que afirma la unidad de la persona de Jesucristo en las dos naturalezas, divina y humana, según las formulaciones de los Concilios de Éfeso y sobre todo de Calcedonia, que afirma: '. . .enseñamos que hay que confesar a un solo y mismo Hijo y Señor nuestro Jesucristo: perfecto en la divinidad y perfecto en la humanidad; verdaderamente Dios y verdaderamente hombre de alma racional y cuerpo; consustancial con el Padre según la divinidad, y consustancial con nosotros según la humanidad, en todo semejante a nosotros excepto en el pecado (cf. *Heb* 4,15), engendrado del Padre antes de los siglos según la divinidad, y en los últimos días, por nosotros y por nuestra salvación, engendrado de María Virgen, la madre de Dios, según la humanidad; que se ha de reconocer a un solo y mismo Cristo Señor, Hijo unigénito en dos naturalezas, sin confusión, sin cambio, sin división, sin separación'. De igual modo se expresó el Papa Pío XII en la encíclica *Sempiternus Rex*: '. . .el Concilio de Calcedonia, en perfecto acuerdo con el de Éfeso, afirma claramente que una y otra naturaleza de nuestro Redentor concurren «en una sola persona y subsistencia», y prohíbe poner en Cristo dos individuos, de modo que se pusiera junto al Verbo un cierto «hombre asumido», dueño de su total autonomía.'"

34. Congregation for the Doctrine of the Faith, "Notificación sobre las obras del P. Jon Sobrino S.J.," 5 (DS 5107).

35. Jon Sobrino, S.J., *Jesus the Liberator: A Historical-Theological Reading of Jesus of Nazareth*, trans. P. Burns and F. McDonagh (Maryknoll: Orbis, 1993). For an uncritical account of Sobrino's Christology, see Sturla J. Stålsett, *The Crucified and the Crucified: A Study in the Liberation Christology of Jon Sobrino* (Oxford: Peter Lang, 2003); for a short and critical assessment, see Edward T. Oakes, S.J., *Infinity Dwindled to Infancy: A Catholic and Evangelical Christology* (Grand Rapids: Eerdmans, 2011), pp. 356-62.

Christology] . . . to see in Jesus the 'homo *verus*'."[36] As such his quest is animated, on one level, by the legitimate concern of the Scotist perplexity to account more fully for the *in atomo* character of Christ's human nature. His specific concern, however, is to identify the humanity of Jesus with the *in atomo* poverty of the most abject and exposed human beings living in the concrete world of today. In this intention to recover the poverty and existential fragility of "homo *verus*," Sobrino gives voice to Scotus's concern to propose *hic homo* against the exceptionalism of Christ Pantocrator (even while the modern political agenda of Sobrino is of course foreign to Scotus).[37] For Sobrino this concern is linked to his explicit intention to subordinate the person of Jesus to the Kingdom he proclaimed.

Privileging the kingdom preached over the *person* of Jesus is directly connected to the *homo assumptus* priority, which aims to account for *hic homo* in a manner that prescinds from the *person* of the Logos. With the former, the *separatio* is performed at the level of dividing the Mediator from the message he mediates, as if the message were extrinsic to his *person*.[38] Conscious that this program sits rather ill at ease with the magiste-

36. Jon Sobrino, *Christ the Liberator: A View from the Victims*, trans. Paul Burns (Maryknoll: Orbis, 2001), p. 290.

37. Sobrino nowhere to my knowledge invokes Duns Scotus directly, although Leonardo Boff, on whom Sobrino depends in many regards, does make direct use of Scotus: see Boff, *Jesus Christ Liberator: A Critical Christology for Our Time*, trans. Hughes Patrick (Maryknoll: Orbis Books, 1978). Sobrino does, however, propose his program as if in the tradition of Francis of Assisi, whose emphasis on the lowliness of Jesus is identified by Sobrino with the poor and oppressed of this world and the Cross with their contemporary sufferings (see Sobrino, *Jesus the Liberator*, p. 56 and *Christ the Liberator*, pp. 290 and 328; cf. Leonardo Boff, *Francis of Assisi: A Model for Human Liberation*, trans. John W. Diercksmeier [Maryknoll: Orbis, 2006]). Invocations by Boff and Sobrino of Francis of Assisi as if he were a proto "liberation theologian" are a demonstrable distortion of Francis's idea of poverty and his piety *tout court*. For a decisive debunking of this whole approach to Francis, see Thompson, *Francis of Assisi, passim*.

38. Sobrino's concern here is that "when Christ the mediator is made absolute," as happens in traditional ecclesial Christology, "there is no sense of his constitutive relatedness to what is mediated, the Kingdom of God" (Sobrino, *Jesus the Liberator*, p. 16; cf. Oakes, *Infinity Dwindled to Infancy*, p. 360). The problem with this position is that it suggests that Jesus' person and what he taught can be separated, and if this were so, the *vita apostolica* should be animated not so much by *sequela Christi*, but by an activistic compliance with the "rules of the Kingdom" given by a Christ. In this way Sobrino's program would seem to end up accommodating, in the form of "moralism," some version of the Pelagian error John Cassian diagnosed in every *solum homo* Christology, which reconfigures Jesus, no longer as the Savior, but as one who merely gives "an example of good works" (*De Incarnatione Christi contra Nestorium* 1.3 [PL 50.22a-23a]).

rial tradition, Sobrino's dogmatic orientation is not generally sympathetic with the conciliar Christology of the Magisterium from its patristic origins, with its constitutive emphasis on the *unus Dominus*, the *descensus de caelis* and the *pro nobis* of the Cross. Indeed, Sobrino suggests there is something of a gulf between the Christology of the New Testament (which apparently privileges the message of Jesus, his humanity and the kingdom) and that of the conciliar tradition (which apparently privileges the messenger, his divinity and his sacrificial death).[39] This notwithstanding, Sobrino is prepared to acknowledge, after the manner of Karl Rahner's "pure" Chalcedonianism, the unique achievement of the *Definitio fidei*:

> I think it is important for us to feel (if that is an appropriate term) that, given the direction taken by christological thinking in the Greco-Roman world, Chalcedon "hit the mark," that it not only formulated the vision of those who won the debate but also expressed a truth that opened the way to "more."[40]

Chalcedon is conceived of here as an exception: it is not valued for its essential continuity with the conciliar tradition, but for the rupture it apparently represents, by which it is said to "hit the mark" and to have "opened the way to 'more.'" The ultimate advantage of Chalcedon, for Sobrino as for Rahner before him, lies in the symmetry of its formulation, which allows the *inconfusus, immutabilis* side of the *Definitio* to be emphasized against the traditional priority of the one Lord (*indivisus, inseparabilis*).[41] To exemplify how this results in a dualistic prescinding from Cyrillian orthodoxy, the Congregation singled out the following text from Sobrino's book *Jesus the Liberator*:

> From a dogmatic point of view, we have to say, without any reservation, that the Son (the second person of the Trinity) took on the whole reality of Jesus and, although the dogmatic formula never explains the manner of this being affected by the human dimension, the thesis is radical. The Son experienced Jesus' humanity, existence in history, life, destiny, and death.[42]

39. Oakes, *Infinity Dwindled to Infancy*, pp. 358-59.
40. Sobrino, *Christ the Liberator*, p. 295.
41. Sobrino, *Christ the Liberator*, p. 295.
42. Sobrino, *Jesus the Liberator*, p. 242. Cf. Congregation for the Doctrine of the Faith, "Notificación sobre las obras del P. Jon Sobrino S.J.," 5 (DS 5107).

In no uncertain terms Sobrino is here parsing the "human Jesus" and the "divine Son." The former possesses his own "whole reality" apart from the Son, who in a second ontological moment takes on (i.e. becoming united to) the prior "reality of Jesus." The whole fact of the human Jesus then, on this view, exists apart from the *unio personalis* on which he is identified with the second person of the Trinity. If there is something of an echo of Scotus's doctrine of the *haecceitas* of Christ's human nature here, the real problem with Sobrino's formulation lies not in this echo but in how it betrays a deficient doctrine of *communicatio idiomatum*. Herein lies the creeping Nestorian problematic against which the Congregation was moved to act.[43] As Edward Oakes notes, it is not the case that there is no *communicatio idiomatum* in Sobrino's Christology, but rather that it functions in only one direction: "the limited human is predicated of God, but the unlimited divine is not predicated of Jesus."[44] While Nestorius was concerned to safeguard in all cases the divine transcendence of God's impassibility, Sobrino is motivated to protect the limitation of Jesus's human finitude. For Nestorius it was inconceivable that the Cross could be truly predicated of the divine Son; for Sobrino it is impossible that the Logos be truly predicated of the bitterly finite Jesus.

B. *Secundarium Esse* Relecture

According to the traditional doctrine of the hypostatic union — reaffirmed by the Pian limit of 1951 and reiterated by the Congregation in 2006 — the Logos did not assume a human person or the ontological infrastructure of a fully individuated human being, but rather assumed human nature so as to himself constitute the existence of this human being. This is the basic dogmatic entailment of the apostolic proclamation concerning the singularity and identity of the one Lord Jesus Christ, ratified at Nicaea and upheld at the councils of Ephesus, Chalcedon, Constantinople II and Constantinople III. Jesus is not a mere human (*purus homo*),[45] he is *verus Deus et verus homo*; he is exceptional, unrepeatable and unique among all

---

43. Cf. Congregation for the Doctrine of the Faith, "Notificación sobre las obras del P. Jon Sobrino S.J.," 6 (DS 5107).

44. Sobrino, *Christ the Liberator*, p. 223. This is Edward Oakes's point; see *Infinity Dwindled to Infancy*, p. 359.

45. Cf. ST III, q. 1, a. 2, *ad* 2.

other human beings: he is true God from true God, come down from above, incarnated of the Virgin and crucified for us.

But if Jesus is not *purus homo*, if he is so constituted in his human being by the *suppositum* of the Logos so as to not even possess a human *suppositum*, does he then fail on some level to be fully human? Does not a human nature that lacks a *suppositum humanum*, who is therefore not a *persona humana*, decline in some integral sense to be fully human? And more, if his humanity is fully constituted by his being the one Lord, does this not suggest that he must lack the singular poverty of "the bitterly finite character"[46] Rahner rightly wanted to affirm? Herein lies the deep contention of the Scotist perplexity (shared in various ways by Déodat, Seiller, Rahner and Sobrino): the traditional Cyrillian priority of the divine *unitas* of Christ makes of his human existence an ontological exception for which the full infrastructure of being human cannot be credibly substantiated. And thus the Scotist perplexity ultimately questions whether traditional orthodoxy, as expressed by Cyril and in the councils, has yet truly confirmed the patristic axiom according to which "that which is not assumed is not healed."[47]

The Cyrillian response I want now to propose in answer to this perplexity is rooted in Thomas's doctrine of the *secundarium esse*, the quasi-substantial *esse* "that is such only in that it is in ontological union with the Son."[48] As we noted in chapter 6, this *secundarium esse* in no way compromises the doctrine of the *unum esse* of Jesus because it functions according to Cyril's distinction of *en theoria mone*. It is not therefore a doctrine of a parallel existence, but a speculative doctrine of how, in the Incarnation, Christ recapitulates the finitization of created being into his own mode of being the Incarnate Son, receiving himself from human nature *ex Maria*.[49] In other words, the *secundarium esse*, far from being a second *suppositum* (or even a second *esse*, strictly speaking), is rather an affirmation of the real metaphysical constitution of Jesus as a creature before God, who receives

---

46. Karl Rahner, S.J., "Christology Today?" *Theological Investigations*, vol. 17, trans. Margaret Kohl (London: Darton, Longman and Todd, 1981), pp. 24-38, at p. 28.

47. Gregory of Nazianzus, *Epistula* 101 (SC 208.50; PG 37.181c-184a).

48. Thomas G. Weinandy, O.F.M., Cap., "Aquinas: God *IS* Man — The Marvel of the Incarnation," in Thomas G. Weinandy, O.F.M., Cap., Daniel A. Keating and John P. Yocum, eds., *Aquinas on Doctrine: A Critical Introduction* (London: T&T Clark International, 2004), pp. 67-89, here at p. 82.

49. Cf. Martin Bieler, *Befreiung der Freiheit: Zur Theologie der stellvertretenden Sühne* (Freiburg: Herder, 1996), pp. 303-4.

his human nature, and therefore his relation to God as creature, through the humanity he receives from his Mother. In this way, the dogma of Theotokos is crucial to respond to the legitimate basis of the Scotist perplexity concerning the *in atomo* reality of Jesus' human nature.

Insofar as it is truly the Son who is incarnated, we must speak of *unum esse simpliciter*, "on account of the one being of the eternal suppositum."[50] But in the light of the doctrine of Christ's incarnate *persona composita*, elevated to a dogma at Constantinople II, "there is also another being of this suppositum . . . insofar as it became a man in time."[51] In this regard, we speak of Christ's *secundarium esse*, which is not the *esse principale* of his *suppositum*, but is rather the mode according to which the divine Son truly receives his human being from someone concrete: the Theotokos. Herein lies the locus of something like a quasi-haecceitatic human reality: *haec natura* of Jesus, fully individuated and constituted by the *persona* of the Logos, is nevertheless *in atomo* only as a reality received from the Virgin of Nazareth. This means that the *persona* of the Logos truly receives his particular human nature *ex Maria;* indeed he allows his human particularity to be constituted in its specificity by her flesh, by her humanity, by her concrete genealogy and by the history of her people. The Son, in his incarnate nature, is truly a *persona composita;* he is irreducibly both *ex Patre* and *ex Maria*. This is not to say that the Incarnate Son possesses an individuated mode of being discrete from his divine individuality (as Scotus's doctrine tends to imply); rather, it is to say that the particularity of Jesus' human nature is concretely inherited in a way that it cannot be understood solely in reference to his eternal filiation. Hence, as Adrian Walker has suggested, "it is as if Christ had a subordinate human *esse*, but possessed it only in an unceasing, fluid exchange with the Theotokos."[52] Just as the divinity of Christ is only knowable in terms of his concrete filiation from the Father (the term according to which he is *relatio subsistens*),[53] so analogously the Incarnation is only specified by the filiation of Jesus from Mary.

---

50. Thomas Aquinas, *De unione Verbi incarnati*, a. 4, *corpus*.

51. Thomas Aquinas, *De unione Verbi incarnati*, a. 4, *corpus*.

52. Adrian J. Walker, "*Singulariter in spe constituisti me*: on the Christian Attitude towards Death," *Communio* 39 (2012): 351-63, at p. 359, n. 16. Cf. Ferdinand Ulrich, *Leben in der Einheit von Leben und Tod* (Freiburg: Johannes Verlag, 1999).

53. ST I, q. 29, a. 4, *corpus*. The root of this definition already lies in the Nicene orthodoxy, which used the language of οὐσία to designate the unity of the divinity and ὁμοούσιος (*consubstantialis*) to designate the unity of the Son and the Father. "Propter hanc unitatem Pater est totus in Filio, totus in Spiritu Sancto; Filius totus est in Patre, totus in Spiritu Sancto;

In this light, the Thomist doctrine of the *secundarium esse* implies a doctrine of haecceity, not as a formal ontological constituent of *haec natura*, but as a description of the constitution of that nature within the finite field of contingent relationality in which it is incarnated. This field of concrete relationality is enabled by the fluid exchange of the Jesus-Mary relation; it begins at the Annunciation, continues through the Incarnation and is re-incarnated in every mystical encounter with Christ, which can only take place within concrete history as an unrepeatable event of the recognition of a genuine "other," a historical figure with a genealogy who cannot be reduced to an abstraction. Thus the "unceasing, fluid exchange with the Theotokos" that is the haecceitatic reality of the *secundarium esse* is rooted, not only in the fact that Jesus in the Incarnation proceeds *ex Maria*, but also in the fact that she is constitutive within the experience of mystical encounter with Jesus. The particularity of the human Jesus cannot be thought of or accounted for outside the Jesus-Mary relation because the *esse personale* of the divine Son is human only to the extent that he receives himself *ex Maria*. Mary ensures that the humanity of Christ is not an abstraction, since "an abstraction does not need a Mother."[54] Hence:

> The appearance of a truly Marian awareness serves as the touchstone indicating whether or not the christological substance is fully present. Nestorianism involves the fabrication of a Christology from which the nativity and the Mother are removed, a Christology without mariological consequences. Precisely this operation, which surgically removes God so far from man that nativity and maternity — all of corporeality — remain in a different sphere, indicated unambiguously to the Chris-

---

Spiritus Sanctus totus est in Patre, totus in Filio. Nullus alium aut praecedit aeternitate aut excedit magnitudine, aut superat potestate. Aeternum quippe et sine initio est, quod Filius de Patre exstitit; et aeternum ac sine initio est, quod Spiritus Sanctus de Patre Filioque procedit. Pater quidquid est aut habet, non habet ab alio, sed ex se; et est principium sine principio. Filius quidquid est aut habet, habet a Patre, et est principium de principio. Spiritus Sanctus quidquid est aut habet, habet a Patre simul et Filio. Sed Pater et Filius non duo principia Spiritus Sancti, sed unum principium: sicut Pater et Filius et Spiritus Sanctus non tria principia creaturae, sed unum principium" (DS 1331).

54. This is to appropriate to Christology something Joseph Ratzinger said about Mary in terms of ecclesiology; see Joseph Cardinal Ratzinger with Vittorio Messori, *The Ratzinger Report: An Exclusive Interview on the State of the Church*, trans. Salvator Attanasio and Graham Harrison (San Francisco: Ignatius Press, 1986), p. 108: "If Mary no longer finds a place in many theologies and ecclesiologies, the reason is obvious: they have reduced faith to an abstraction. And an abstraction does not need a Mother."

tian consciousness that the discussion no longer concerned In*carn*ation (becoming *flesh*), that the center of Christ's mystery was endangered, if not already destroyed. Thus in Mariology Christology was defended. Far from belittling Christology, it signifies the comprehensive triumph of a confession of faith in Christ which has achieved authenticity.[55]

This authenticity of the human nature of Jesus, then, which simply is its *ex Maria* fact, specifies the enhypostatic logic of the Constantinopolitan dogma of Christ's *persona composita*: "Mary plays a permanent role in Christ's metaphysical constitution qua 'compound hypostasis.'"[56]

In this way, responding to the Scotist perplexity, it is important to acknowledge the legitimacy of the impulse: that the haecceity of the *ex Maria* procession cannot simply be subsumed within the *ex Patre* fact of who the Incarnate Son is. The Incarnate Son is *persona composita*, as Constantinople II designated. This means that the "enhypostatization" of the Son's Incarnate nature cannot be upheld without a Mariological consequence. There can be no indifference in Christology to the carnal womb and personal being that gives the Logos his humanity. Only *ex Maria* can we develop an account of the significance of the particularity of *this* Jewish flesh, *this* birth in time and place, *this* Davidic ancestry out of which *this* "one" is born the Messiah of Israel. This entails because, by the Incarnation, the Logos "has two nativities . . . one from all eternity of the Father, without time and without body; the other in these last days, coming down from heaven and being made flesh of the holy and glorious Mary, Mother of God and always a virgin, and born of her."[57] Or: "in the mystery of Christ the synthetic union (σύνθεσιν ἕνωσις) not only preserves unconfusedly the natures which are united, but also allows no separation."[58]

C. Mary and the Hypostatic Union

If the *ex Maria* filiation of the Incarnate Son so constitutes his *secundarium esse* that she should be understood as playing a metaphysically permanent

---

55. Joseph Ratzinger, *Daughter Zion: Meditations on the Church's Marian Belief,* trans. John M. McDermott, S.J. (San Francisco: Ignatius Press, 1983), p. 35. Italics are Ratzinger's.

56. Walker, "*Singulariter in spe constituisti me,*" p. 359, n. 16.

57. *Anathematismi adversus "tria Capitula,"* canon 2 (DS 422; DEC 1.114).

58. *Anathematismi adversus "tria Capitula,"* canon 4 (DS 424-425; DEC 1.114-115).

role in his incarnate *persona composita*, then Mary, in a sense, supplies not only the fleshy substance that makes Jesus "human," but also the human infrastructure (education, culture, family, etc.) that forms an essential component of the personality of his human being. Recognizing this helps us to see how Mary, as a figure of the mystical body and its personal guarantor, supplies in herself at the origin a human *suppositum* and *persona* that uniquely corresponds with the *homo verus* of her divine Son. And so Mary is in herself the *mystica persona* of humanity united to Christ. This correspondence of Mary and Jesus is expounded in the Thomistic mystical theology of Père Louis Chardon, O.P. (1595-1651).

Chardon's *La Croix de Jésus: où les plus belles vérités de la théologie mystique et de la grâce sanctifiante sont établies* (1647) is one of the great spiritual texts of le grand siècle.[59] In *La Croix de Jésus*, Chardon dedicates himself to propose a theology of mystical union rooted in the subsistence doctrine of the *tertia pars* of Thomas's *Summa*, according to which the human nature in Christ does not subsist in itself, separately, but exists in the hypostasis of the Son.[60] From this starting point, Chardon aims to expound the Christological doctrine of Thomas to ground a mystical theology, both speculative and practical. The precedent in Thomas for this development lies in Thomas's underdeveloped doctrine of the union of the ecclesial body with its head *quasi una persona mystica*.[61]

Taking up the Thomist doctrine of the *una persona mystica* that unites Christ and his mystical body, Chardon explores how the mode of the singular subsistent reality of Jesus in his humanity and divinity is in this way the prime analogate of the unity of human persons in the divine person of the Son. The *unitas* of the hypostatic union produces and constitutes the mystical union of Christians with Christ. This is how Chardon makes the doctrine of mystical union internal to the doctrine of the hypostatic union: the *persona Filii* is incarnated in a fluid relation that both consti-

---

59. Louis Chardon, O.P., *La Croix de Jésus: où les plus belles vérités de la théologie mystique et de la grâce sanctifiante sont établies* (Paris: Cerf, 2004). References to *La Croix de Jésus* give the book number followed by the chapter and paragraph. The translations are my own. On Chardon's mysticism, see Réginald Garrigou-Lagrange, O.P., "Unité de la tradition dominicaine sur les rapports de l'ascétique et de mystique," *Supplément à la Vie Spirituelle* 9 (1923): 1-27; Olivier-Thomas Venard, O.P., *Thomas d'Aquin poète théologien*, vols. 1 & 2 (Geneva: Ad Solem, 2002-2004), vol. 3 (Paris: Cerf, 2010); Jean-Luis Chrétien, *L'intelligence du feu: réponses humaines à une parole de Jésus* (Paris: Bayard, 2003), pp. 170-76.

60. ST III, q. 2. Cf. Thomas Aquinas, *De unione Verbi incarnati*, a. 2.

61. Cf. ST III, q. 48, a. 1, *ad* 1.

tutes and is (paradoxically) constituted by his relation to a mystical "other," the *persona mystica*.

The *persona mystica* of the Church is, in its exemplar and original realization, the person of Mary, and she is therefore key to a proper understanding of Jesus' humanity. The uniqueness of Mary, in the first place, is rooted in the fact that she is "Theotokos," the human being from whom the Son emerged in such a way that she uniquely corresponds to the absolute *verus homo* of the incarnate being. But in order for Mary to be Theotokos, in order for the Son to receive himself from her womb, Mary must be divinely adopted as a child of God. Every honor attributed to Mary thus lies in a prior grace divinely given and mysteriously rooted in the merits of her Son's Cross.[62] This means that Mary cannot be graced to be Theotokos apart from her adoption into the *quasi una persona mystica* of those being deified by the Holy Spirit into union with the Son.

For Chardon, thus, Mary eminently — and in a singularly excellent way — is a "child of God." This means that the fullness of her being and the depth of her union with her Son is rooted in a "double relation" she enjoys with God: she is both a creature of God and the Mother of God.[63] Mary thus constitutes, according to Chardon, an order of grace that is singular: Jesus is God "by nature," the saints are gods "by adoptive participation," while Mary alone is a god "by affinity ... [since] the venerable bonds which render her Christ's Mother touch the very threshold of the divinity."[64] Mary is neither deiform by nature nor merely by adoptive participation;[65] she is the Theotokos who encompasses God in her womb (where he grows and takes her human flesh as his own) and therefore she is the prototype of adoptive filiation.[66] This means that, on account of her unique relation to the Son at his incarnate source, she is the first and exemplary member of his mystical body and therefore the personal representative of mystical union. In her *persona* and *suppositum humanum*, in her mode of being the

---

62. Cf. The Collect for the Feast of the Immaculate Conception: "Deus, qui per Immaculatam Virginis Conceptionem dignum Filio tuo habitaculum praeparasti: quaesumus; [N.B.:] *ut qui ex morte eiusdem Filii tui praevisa, eam ab omni labe praeservasti,* nos quoque mundos eius intercessione ad te pervenire concedas. Per eumdem Dominum nostrum, Iesum Christum."

63. Chardon, *La Croix de Jésus* 1.24.311.

64. Chardon, *La Croix de Jésus* 1.24.318.

65. Chardon, *La Croix de Jésus* 1.24.317; cf. 314-315.

66. Cf. Adrienne von Speyr, *Mary in the Redemption*, trans. Helena M. Tomko (San Francisco: Ignatius Press, 2003), pp. 19-26.

first and perfect receptacle of the divine grace of her Son, the Church is fully present as co-belonging to the Incarnation. Adoptive participation in Christ is in this way made possible by the adopted daughter of God (*fille adoptive*), since the grace of adoptive filiation dwells in its original plenitude in Mary in order that she may conceive the Son in whom we are predestined to be adopted *filii in Filio*.[67]

According to Chardon, thus, for Mary to be both Theotokos and the exemplar of adoptive filiation, the origin of her Son's humanity and the perfect receptacle of divine grace, she must receive a grace that the human Jesus himself did not possess.

The receptivity of Jesus to the grace of filiation is "perfect" because it coincides with his person.[68] This means that he is the source of the deifying grace by which human beings become adopted as children of God. On one level this means that all the fullness of grace resides in Jesus, who is the one source of all grace; but because the grace of filiation coincides with his person — he truly is the natural Son of the Father — the proper effect of the grace of his filiation (adoptive filiation) is eclipsed in him.[69] Natural filiation and adoptive filiation are "incompatible in the same subject."[70] Chardon writes:

> The grace of union, which gives natural filiation, is not contrary to the habitual grace which gives adoptive filiation in all other persons apart from Jesus. The grace of personal union [i.e. hypostatic union], the source of natural filiation and habitual grace, causes adoptive filiation — as an older man causes a younger, as the spring causes a river, as the sun causes a ray of light, and these were perfectly coupled in the holy and sacred humanity of Jesus. Two filiations, however, cannot abide in one [Son] . . . the lesser must give way to the greater.[71]

In Cyrillian fashion, Chardon resists the introduction of any Christological parallelism: Jesus is *unus Filius*, the one Son of the Father. This means that while Jesus is *verus homo*, he is not a subject other than the Son

---

67. Chardon, *La Croix de Jésus* 1.24.321.

68. For an eminently clear manualist account of the Thomist doctrine of the grace of Christ's human nature, see Adolphe Tanquerey, *A Manual of Dogmatic Theology*, 2 vols., trans. J. Byrnes (Rome: Desclee Company, 1959), vol. 2, pp. 37-57.

69. Chardon, *La Croix de Jésus* 1.24.322.

70. Chardon, *La Croix de Jésus* 1.24.323.

71. Chardon, *La Croix de Jésus* 1.24.323.

of God and cannot personally receive the effects and benefits of the grace of the filiation, which naturally belongs to him. The Christological entailment of this fact is expounded, radically, by Chardon: correspondent to the positive declaration of Chalcedonian orthodoxy, that the *una persona* of Jesus is none other than the Logos, there is at the same time a necessarily negative declaration: the *verus homo* (Jesus Christ) is not a *persona humana*. The human Jesus *qua* humanity is therefore "anhypostatic" (in a Barthian sense). But if this anhypostatic fact is fully upheld by Chardon, for him it only makes sense within a wider account of the Incarnation as inclusive of the *communio* of the *persona mystica* of the Church. In this sense, the concrete correlate of the *verus homo* of the Incarnate Son is the *persona mystica* of mystical union, a reality that resides wholly in the Marian principle.

Mary thus comes to play an integral role on the level of *persona*, both in the incarnational event of her Son and the event of mystical union of those being joined to him in his mystical body. The *persona divina* of Christ, in his being *verus homo*, is constituted in relation to her *persona humana* as to a genuine "other." In Cyrillian fashion, Christology requires Mariological specification, beginning from the dogma of the Theotokos.

Mary is thus first in the order of grace after her Son because she is his "other." His grace does not come up against the obstacle of natural filiation, which would possess that grace by nature and not by receptivity.[72] Mary is a *persona humana* and this means that she can truly receive the grace of her Son to become "the first adopted child (*fille*) into the Son's order of grace, just as he is the unique natural Child (*Filius*) of grace."[73] There are thus two exemplar modes of the grace of filiation: one is causal and natural, which belongs uniquely to Jesus; the second is effectual and adoptive, and belongs first to Mary.[74]

The fullness of the grace of Christ therefore includes the *persona* of Mary such that a "pure" *solus Christus* account of the grace of adoptive filiation would be insufficient. And there is something surprising in this realization. As Chardon notes, "One might have expected a 'double image of the Son,' conformable to the 'two abundances of grace' [causal-natural and effectual-adoptive] which were in him."[75] But if this had been the case,

---

72. Chardon, *La Croix de Jésus* 1.24.325.
73. Chardon, *La Croix de Jésus* 1.24.325.
74. Chardon, *La Croix de Jésus* 1.25.326.
75. Chardon, *La Croix de Jésus* 1.25.327.

if the Son had been the singular embodiment of all grace in an exclusive and Christo-monistic manner, this would have been a lesser grace.

Being *unus Filius*, it is more fitting that Christ would withdraw the personal filiation of adoption from his human nature in order to allow the pre-eminence of his *persona divina* to overwhelm his created nature such that his nature would reveal all the fullness of humanity without a second subjective principle of participation. As Chardon writes:

> For in the [hypostatic] order of his grace, he [Jesus] was impressed with the venerable character of the grandeur of being the Son of God by nature; which, without difficulty, was sufficiently powerful to produce a "son" of God by participation.[76]

A "two sons" filiation would have ensured a *solus Christus* Christology without co-being, but this would mean that Jesus could not have been "one and the same" Son, the only begotten of the Father (cf. John 1:14).[77]

Mary's unique personal being is thus required to safeguard the traditional dogma of the one Lord Jesus Christ, both from the dualism that would separate the Son *ex Maria* from the Son *ex Patre* on the one hand, and from a self-enclosed (i.e. Christo-monistic) construal of the salvific act that would foreclose the participative possibility of the *persona mystica* being a co-worker of the Lord (in a Pauline sense). What Chardon helps us to establish, is how the dualism of a "two sons" Christology is in fact internal to the Christo-monism of a reductive *solus Christus* doctrine (and vice versa).[78] If Christ is *unus* — if the two natures are really united in "one and the same" Son — then the human nature of the *unus Filius* includes Marian *communio* from its incarnate origin. Jesus must be the *verus homo*, but he cannot be *vera humana persona*. While "two natures are mutually supported in Jesus Christ," in conformity with Thomas and the dogma of Constantinople II, "the two subsistences proper to those natures cannot

---

76. Chardon, *La Croix de Jésus* 1.25.327.

77. Chardon, *La Croix de Jésus* 1.25.327: "S'il n'a été fils par participation, c'est à cause qu'il y a plus d'honneur d'être Fils par nature. C'est pourquoi nous devons croire que saint Jean se set d'une adresse divine, quand, expriment les deux grâces en Jésus-Christ, à savoir l'incréé, le créé et il fait voir en l'une et en l'autre la seul filiation naturel, lorsqu'il dit: « Nous avons vu sa gloire, la gloire du Fils uniquement engendré du Père »."

78. Again, this is to Christologically confirm the thesis of Conor Cunningham's *Genealogy of Nihilism* on the hidden monism of every dualist reduction.

maintain in unity."[79] Hence: "the human subsistence cedes to the divine, so as not to hinder (*ne point mettre d'empêchement*) but rather to ennoble that nature."[80] The ennoblement of human nature now becomes the *unitas* in which the hypostatic union takes place internally to give way and constitute the *communio* Christ wills to accomplish "with" the *persona mystica* of the Church. In this way, Chardon shows how the doctrine of the hypostatic union involves, at its source, in the person of Mary, the "mystical union" of the Church's subsistence through the grace of filial adoption.[81]

79. Chardon, *La Croix de Jésus* 1.25.329.

80. Chardon, *La Croix de Jésus* 1.25.329. Cf. 1.25.331: "pourvu qu'il ne blessent point les vérités orthodoxes qui leur doivent servir de lumière, qu'on me laisse dire que, de cette incompatibilité de la filiation adoptive en l'âme sacrée de Jésus, il en a tiré le dessein de la donner à sa Mère, afin qu'elle fût la première fille adoptive de la grâce."

81. Chardon, *La Croix de Jésus* 1.25.332: "Deux filiations doivent correspondre à la double grâce de Jésus; il prend l'une, et laisse l'autre à sa mère, avec le privilège de primauté qu'il veut avoir commun avec elle ... contractant avec elle la plus intime et la plus parfait union que Dieu puisse avoir avec une pure créature." Also cf. 1.25.332.

The Communion of Jesus and Mary

CHAPTER 11

The Weight of the Cross

The grace of Mary, the Mother of Jesus, is measured by the Cross.

Louis Chardon

A. The Plenitude of the Cross

For Chardon, the Cross lies at the heart of who the Son truly is. The whole trajectory of Jesus' life, as it is given in all four Gospels, is accordingly informed by the "weight" that leads him to Calvary.[1] Concretely, this "weight" is the weight of the love that unites the Son to the Father. And because the Spirit is the *vinculum amoris* by which he is bound to the Father, it is the same Spirit who urges the Son's descent from heaven to Golgotha. "The Holy Spirit, the bond and loving embrace of the divinity, casts him out of the womb of his eternal filiation."[2] The Spirit incarnates the Son in the womb of Mary, descends upon him at his baptism and at the Transfiguration, and drives him in his mission to achieve the sacrificial sundering that is the glory of the Son of God.[3] The identity of Jesus is firmly fixed by the

1. Louis Chardon, O.P., *La Croix de Jésus: où les plus belles vérités de la théologie mystique et de la grâce sanctifiante sont établies* (Paris: Cerf, 2004), 1.6.66-1.8.104. (As noted above, references to *La Croix de Jésus* give the book number followed by the chapter and paragraph. The translations are my own.)

2. Chardon, *La Croix de Jésus* 1.8.103. Here again, Balthasar has a similar view to Chardon. See Nicholas J. Healy, *The Eschatology of Hans Urs von Balthasar: Being as Communion* (Oxford: OUP, 2005), pp. 137-55.

3. Chardon, *La Croix de Jésus* 1.8.103: "Saint Marc ne dit point que le saint-Esprit lui commande, qu'il le presse, qu'il l'inspire; mais qu'il l'entraîne au désert [cf. Mark 1:12]. En ceci il s'accommode à la disposition de son âme; ainsi qu'il arriva lorsqu'on entendit cette

Spirit in two places: in the bosom of the Father in heaven and on the hard wood of the Cross on earth. He is the Crucified Son of Glory.

Nowhere for Chardon is the crux of the identity of Jesus more starkly realized than in the conversation narrated in the synoptic Gospels that begins with the question of Jesus: "Who do men say that the Son of man is?" and ends with the exhortation to *sequela Christi*: "If any man would come after me, let him deny himself and take up his cross and follow me" (Matt. 16:13-28; cf. Mark 8:27-35 and Luke 9:18-24). Here the necessity of the Cross, which binds the question to the exhortation, binds also the recognition of the identity of Jesus with the company of his followers.[4] Let us turn to this passage and look at it more closely, in order to take our bearings in what is the first and fundamental Christological confession.

To the initial question of Jesus a confused reply is given: "Some say John the Baptist, others say Elijah, and others Jeremiah or one of the prophets" (Matt. 16:14). The multitudes who have encountered Jesus do not know who he is. In the face of this confusion over the true identity of Jesus, the Lord turns to his own disciples, those friends he has chosen, to that company who have lived and ministered with him and presumably know him better than the multitudes. Jesus asks: "But who do you say that I am?" (Matt. 16:15). Peter replies: "You are the Christ, the Son of the living God" (Matt. 16:16).

Peter's confession has been traditionally understood as lying at the very heart of the mystery of faith and of the Petrine office, and so as the bond that unites ecclesial unity with the unity of faith.[5] As the Catechism puts it: "On the rock of this faith confessed by St. Peter, Christ built his Church."[6] But in the first place, the core of what Chardon sees is not the juridical power allocated to Peter or his successors, but rather the mode of faith here clarified, and the form that faith must take. As Jesus responds to Peter:

---

voix de tonnerre qui disait: « Je l'ai glorifié et le glorifierai encore » [John 12:28], où au même moment il se cache, après sa réponse de la Croix, comme s'il était honteux de paraître en la présence des hommes après avoir été déclaré, de la bouche de Dieu, l'image de sa gloire."

4. See Chardon, *La Croix de Jésus* 1.10.114-1.10.127. For a reading more or less convertible with Chardon, see John Behr, *The Mystery of Christ: Life in Death* (Crestwood, NY: Saint Vladimir's Seminary Press, 2006), pp. 21-44, and "The Paschal Foundation of Christian Theology," *St. Vladimir's Theological Quarterly* 45 (2001): 115-36.

5. See Vatican I, *Pastor aeternus* c. 4 (DS 3066), and CCC 881-882. Cf. Hans Urs von Balthasar, *The Office of Peter and the Structure of the Church* (San Francisco: Ignatius Press, 1986).

6. CCC 424.

Blessed are you, Simon Bar-Jona! For flesh and blood has not revealed this to you, but my Father who is in heaven. And I tell you, you are Peter, and on this rock I will build my church, and the powers of death shall not prevail against it. (Matt. 16:17-18)

The first thing and crucial thing: Peter does not provide the answer he gives; he receives it "from above." It is not by "flesh and blood," but by the grace of the Father in heaven that the confession is made. In other words, the protagonist of faith, in declaring who Jesus is, is not Peter, but the Holy Spirit, who comes down from above and reveals the divine filial identity of Jesus. This means that the interrelation of ecclesial unity and the unity of faith are internally bound within the Love, the Spirit, who himself binds (and is) the filial union of Son to the Father. This fact is truly a prologue to the deeper Christological truth of Jesus's identity, and it leads us to a second crucial point of the passage: the triumph over death.

The Church is the mystical reality over which death has no power; but the concrete mode of actualizing this triumph over death involves being radically conformed to the personal identity of Jesus. Hence, in his own exegesis of this passage, Chardon roots the Petrine confession in its wider narrative framework, and specifically in what immediately follows: (1) the confession of Jesus, that he will have to "go to Jerusalem and suffer many things . . . and be killed, and on the third day be raised" (Matt. 16:21); and (2) Jesus' rebuke of Peter — "Get behind me, Satan!" (Matt. 16:23) — in response to Peter's denial of the necessity of Jesus to go to the Cross.

For Chardon, Jesus' foretelling of the suffering and death that will presently befall him lies at the heart of the Petrine confession; the divine sonship of Jesus entails the Paschal Mystery (cf. Luke 24:13-35), which is rooted in the *missio* of the Son given of the Father. Chardon expresses all of this in terms of the "weight" of Jesus' Cross, which weighs on him from his birth, toward which he is compelled to realize the weight of his love (*Pondus meum amor meus*).[7] Precisely this "weight" is the filial bond of the Son to the Father in the *vinculum amoris* of the Holy Spirit, which animates (and is) that eternal union of Love. The Spirit, who binds the Son to the Father, leads the Son in his incarnate life to the severing sacrifice that is the ultimate union of love realized in total self-abandonment: "My Father, if it be possible . . . nevertheless, not as I will, but as thou wilt" (Matt. 26:39). The Spirit, the *unio* of divine love in whom Father and Son are eternally

---

7. Cf. Augustine, *Confessions* 13.9 (LCL 27.390).

"one," leads Jesus in all things: he incarnates the Son by overshadowing the Virgin (cf. Luke 1:35); he rests upon Jesus at his baptism (cf. Matt. 3:17); he drives Jesus into the wilderness to be tempted by the devil (cf. Mark 1:12); he goes before Jesus in all things to lead him to Calvary. In all these matters, according to Chardon, the Holy Spirit "unifies and detaches, consoles and afflicts,"[8] until the Son gives up the same Spirit to the Father in his dying breath: "Father, into thy hands I commit my spirit!" (Luke 23:46; cf. Matt. 27:50). The centrality of the Spirit to the meaning of the Cross is thus crucial for Chardon: the "Spirit is, in a sense, the 'crucifier,' both as the 'bond of love' (in an Augustinian sense) who joins Son to Father and also, because of that, as the dissolution of that bond within the life of the Triune God itself that allows for a costly, because saving, self-offering."[9] That Jesus must "go to Jerusalem and suffer many things" is on account of the Spirit who leads him out of love of the Father, in his resolve to do the Father's will and so to accomplish the mission the Father has given him. The handing over of Jesus to the Spirit is basic to who he is.

Jesus' declaration of the necessity of his cruciform trajectory provokes an outcry from Peter: "God forbid, Lord! This shall never happen to you" (Matt. 16:22). According to Chardon, the reaction of Peter is based precisely in his sense of the impossibility that the one eternally born of the Father could be abandoned to this death (cf. Deut. 21:22-23). But in this presupposition of what it means to be eternally born of the Father, and in his confusion and limitation of what the form of the filial mission of Jesus could be, Peter is not unlike the multitudes, scandalized and perplexed by Jesus. Peter has lived with Jesus, but he still does not know who Jesus is. The confession he received from above, true as it may be, has not helped him understand what is most fundamental: the weight of the Lord's Cross. And so, putting himself between Jesus and the Cross, Peter puts himself between the Son and the Father's will, the *vinculum amoris* that animates Jesus' very being: "God forbid, Lord! This [death] shall never happen to you" (Matt. 16:22). What Peter cannot know is that this death will realize the love of the Father and thereby turn "death inside-out,"[10] trampling down death by death.

According to Chardon, nothing turns the love of Jesus more quickly to

---

8. Chardon, *La Croix de Jésus* 1.5.62.

9. Ephraim Radner, *The End of the Church: A Pneumatology of Christian Division in the West* (Grand Rapids: Eerdmans, 1998), p. 342. Cf. pp. 340-46 for an expert elaboration in a few pages of Chardon's pneumatology, and the best thing written on Chardon in English.

10. John Behr, *Becoming Human: Meditations on Christian Anthropology in Word and Image* (Crestwood, NY: Saint Vladimir's Seminary Press, 2013), p. 49.

anger than that which obstructs his inclination to the Cross.[11] Hence Jesus' rebuke of Peter: "Get behind me, Satan! You are a hindrance to me; for you are not on the side of God, but of men" (Matt. 16:23). As Chardon notes, it is as if Jesus preferred the Cross to the dignity of being the Son of God, as if he preferred his brutal death to his eternal birth. The depth of the mystery of the unity of the incarnate mission in the eternal filiation cannot be unwound without deconstructing the personal unity of the Lord Jesus Christ himself, a unity finally cemented by the *vinculum amoris* of the Son eternally united to the Father. Full of sorrow and joy, the plenitude of Jesus's love is the root scandal of his being and identity: his divine origin *ex Patre* entails the death of the Son *ex Maria*. What was revealed to Peter "from above" concerning the divine filiation of Jesus must now become fixed to the wood of the Cross. And if this was not scandal enough, Jesus finishes his discourse with a simple injunction to his disciples: "If any man would come after me, let him deny himself and take up his cross and follow me" (Matt. 16:24). The *via crucis* is not only the way of the Son; it is the universal sign of discipleship, *sequela Christi*.[12]

The full narrative context of the Petrine confession shows that the filiation *ex Patre* is confirmed and not abrogated by the Cross. To declare that Jesus is "the Christ, the Son of God" is (even if unawares) to declare the Crucified Lord. These two confessions are "one." In the conciliar tradition this is nowhere more succinctly upheld than in the tenth anathema of Constantinople II: "He who was crucified in the flesh, our Lord Jesus Christ, is true God, Lord of glory, and one of the Holy Trinity."[13] This is not all: to truly confess the Lord Jesus is to take up the pattern of his trampling down death by death, his perfect love of the Father, his perfect docility to the prompting of the Spirit. To truly understand who Jesus is, then, is to bear witness to him in a manner that confirms and conforms to the gift he makes of himself on Calvary; it is to partake in the weight of his love and be bound by the Spirit in the same way that the *vinculum amoris* binds the Son to the Father and leads him through the Paschal Mystery. This participation in the Spirit, that conforms the disciple to the Cross, precisely entails that the powers of death cannot prevail against the Church; that is why Tertullian could rightly say that the blood of the martyrs is the seed of Christians.[14] The Church

---

11. Chardon, *La Croix de Jésus* 1.10.114.

12. Cf. the comments on the Petrine confession, the Cross and discipleship in Pope Francis, Homily of the *Missa pro Ecclesia* with the Cardinal electors, 14 March 2013. Also cf. Thomas Aquinas, *De perfectione spiritualis vitae* 10; ST II-II, q. 188, a. 7.

13. *Anathematismi adversus "tria Capitula,"* canon 10 (DS 432; DEC 1.114-122).

14. Tertullian, *Apology* 50.13 (PL 1.603).

lives beyond the horizon of death because she is animated by the Spirit that led Jesus to the Cross, the Spirit Jesus both gave up to the Father on the Cross and sent into the Church through the Paschal Mystery (cf. John 16:7).

Just as the Spirit overshadowed Mary and made possible the hypostatic union in her, now by the Pentecostal outpouring made possible by the Cross, the Spirit overshadows the Church to form in her womb the mystical union of humanity with Christ. By this outpouring of the Spirit, according to Chardon, the Incarnate Son "makes himself the mystical supposit and subsistence" of the Church,[15] such that the Church truly possesses "a subsistence which is not human but divine."[16] The Cyrillian doctrine of the hypostatic union now becomes the prime analogate according to which human beings enter into the mystical union of participation in the divine nature itself (cf. 2 Pet. 1:4). But if this divinization of humanity, for Chardon, analogically conforms to the hypostatic union, it is in all things informed by the pattern of the Spirit's trajectory, the Spirit of adoption who is sent into the heart of the mystical body, the Spirit by whom the human being becomes mystically bound to the distinct pattern of the Son's incarnate life. This means that the Church must be animated and obedient to the same weight that weighed on the Incarnate Christ and led him to Jerusalem.[17] And so the "Spirit's presence in the Church presses always to the moment of perfect holiness and love when Jesus himself touched death alone."[18]

B. A Correlate on Co-redemption

If the incarnate filiation *ex Maria* entails that the Theotokos "plays a permanent role in Christ's metaphysical constitution qua 'compound hypostasis,'"[19] it is also the case that as the first and exemplar embodiment of receptivity to the grace of adoptive filiation, she plays a permanent role of co-belonging to the Cross, and so to the concrete content of the Son's glorification. If Mary is truly the *vera persona humana* correspondent to the *verus homo* of her divine Son, then we would indeed expect a direct association to exist between her personal being as Theotokos and the per-

15. Chardon, *La Croix de Jésus* 1.1.14-15.
16. Chardon, *La Croix de Jésus* 1.1.15.
17. Cf. Chardon, *La Croix de Jésus* 1.3.31.
18. Radner, *The End of the Church*, p. 342.
19. Adrian J. Walker, "*Singulariter in spe constituisti me:* On the Christian Attitude towards Death," *Communio* 39 (2012): 351-63, at p. 359, n. 16.

sonal act of synergistic love she presents at Golgotha. To the same extent that the Incarnation is determined by the Son's *pro nobis*, a "weight" that binds him from the moment of his incarnation in the womb of Mary to the Cross that is the goal of his *missio*, the union of Mary and Jesus must be realized within this "weight," and must be perfected in the Pietà of the Virgin of Anguish, bearing in her arms the Crucified Lord. The Virgin is truly the exemplar of adoptive filiation, the first in the order of grace of the Spirit's adoption of human beings into the *communio* of adoptive filiation, because her being too is centered on the sacrifice of Calvary. As Chardon puts it: "The grace of Mary, the Mother of Jesus, is measured by the Cross."[20]

The mystical union with Christ to which humanity is called in the Church finds its perfect expression in Mary, who, filled with a grace that unites her uniquely to her Son, inhabits and follows the cruciform path of Jesus in an exemplary and singular fashion.[21] This means that Mary too must plunge into the sorrow and suffering of the Paschal Mystery, to which the whole reality of the Son's life drives as of a necessity of his being.[22] The Mother-Son relation is animated thus from its origin:

> her breasts, full of heavenly fecundity, were a fountain of life to her suckling infant . . . but was not her joy transformed into excessive pain when she recalled that he was only changing this milk into his own substance in order one day to pour down his blood from the Cross where all things declared bitter war upon him, without regard for the fact that he was their creator?[23]

The nursing Mother of Sorrow nourishes the child in order to give him to the Cross. In Christ, God conquered as man insofar as he conquers by means of the human nature he receives of Mary. But there is another aspect: the motherly delight of the Theotokos is in each moment a participation in the trajectory of her Son's *pro nobis*, which ever more draws them together in a bond brought to perfection in their union-in-separation at Calvary.[24]

---

20. Chardon, *La Croix de Jésus* 1.24.309.
21. Chardon, *La Croix de Jésus* 1.24.309.
22. Cf. Chardon, *La Croix de Jésus* 1.5.62.
23. Chardon, *La Croix de Jésus* 1.30.407.
24. Here, in a Marian context, Chardon is close to the mystical theme of *La noche oscura*, the "dark night" of Juan de la Cruz, for whom the experience of *diastasis* is a supreme mode of union in divine love. Cf. Reginald Garrigou-Lagrange, O.P., "Unité de la tradition dominicaine sur les rapports de l'ascétique et de mystique," *Supplément à la Vie Spirituelle* 9 (1923): 1-27.

Thus, while Mary constitutes the human nature of her Son, she must also, in turn, be constituted within the *forma* of her Son's *via crucis;* she must be conformed to his self-abandonment, his *sui exinanitio* (cf. Phil. 2:5-11). "Mary belongs to the Cross of Jesus."[25]

Mary belongs to the Cross, in the first place, because of the unique and permanent role she plays in the "metaphysical constitution" of the Incarnate Son, his "compound hypostasis." But for Chardon, Mary belongs to the Cross also because, as the exemplar of adoptive filiation, the personal representative of the mystical body, she must correspond impeccably to the course of *sequela Christi.* These two "belongings" of Mary to the Cross are internal: Mary is in her *persona* the *ecclesia sancta et immaculata,*[26] and this is what allows her to be Theotokos.[27] She realizes in her being the perfect mystical aligning of adoptive filiation with the form of natural filiation lived by her Son.[28]

Mary's union in the Cross is ultimately a union with Christ in perfect love, a love surpassing in excellence that of all others. The contrast of Mary with Peter here is important. She is the sign of union in love with her Son without reservation, without obstacle, and so all the way through the Passion into which the Spirit leads him.

> Mary loved Jesus without any of the imperfections for which the apostles were reproached and without any kind of attachment which is incompatible with the sending of the Holy Spirit . . . But this did not prevent her from suffering on account of this love, which is the principle of sep-

---

25. Chardon, *La Croix de Jésus* 1.26.336; cf. 1.26.338. For this reason Chardon, despite his overwhelming fidelity to Thomistic doctrine in most other cases, tends to imply (if not overtly) a doctrine of the Immaculate Conception, not necessarily along "Scotist" lines, but along the lines of the latter Pian dogma, which emphasizes Mary's Immaculate Conception as grace issuing from the Cross of Jesus. Cf. Chardon, *La Croix de Jésus* 1.26.341, 348; 1.27.354, 367; 1.29.400.

26. Cf. Hans Urs von Balthasar and Adrienne von Speyr, *To the Heart of the Mystery of Redemption* (San Francisco: Ignatius Press, 2010), pp. 45-49.

27. Cf. Pius IX, *Ineffabilis Deus* (DS 2803).

28. Cf. Chardon, *La Croix de Jésus* 1.28.369: "Dieu veut que Marie soit dans le temps la Mère de son Fils ; c'est à condition que le lien de l'affinité très auguste par lequel Jésus lui appartient, sera le fondement d'une grâce qui la séparera d'autant plus de lui. Elle sera sa Mère, non pas afin qu'elle s'enivre des douceurs à ravir de sa présence, pendant qu'il s'afflige d'ennui et qu'il se consume de tristesses ; c'est plutôt afin qu'il soit en son sein un bouquet de myrrhe très amère, et qu'elle lui soit, en la chair qu'elle lui donne et en la nourriture qu'elle lui fournit, une source vivante de déplaisirs. . . . Sa qualité de mère la déprend de son Fils, et son affinité très auguste avec le Verbe incarné est une croix qui crucifie Dieu et Marie."

aration (*principe de séparation*), as it is a greater elevation, purer, holier, more intimately adhering because it is more united to its source.[29]

This "greater elevation" of Mary's love for Christ, purer because so intimately united to the source, yet entails a form of love she must learn. The "principle of separation" as union-in-love entails that she too must advance in her own "pilgrimage of faith," as *Lumen gentium* put it.[30]

Mary's school of experience in the *forma* of her Son's love is signaled already in the prophecy of the sword piercing her soul (cf. Luke 2:35); it is a school of experience in which Jesus himself will teach her. According to Chardon, it is based in her experience of "ever more rigorous separations and most sensible privations."[31] Chardon highlights four events: (1) The encounter of Mary with the lost child Jesus who, found in the Temple, curtly declares that he "must be in my Father's house" (Luke 2:39-52).[32] (2) The rebuke of Mary by Jesus at the marriage-feast at Cana, when he asks, "Woman, what have you to do with me?" (John 2:4).[33] (3) The attempt of Mary to visit Jesus during his ministry when he refuses to receive her, declaring to the crowd that whoever does the will of his Father is his brother, sister and mother (cf. Luke 8:21).[34] And (4) Jesus' response to the woman in the crowd who cries out, "Blessed is the womb that bore you, and the breasts that you sucked," to which he answers, "Blessed rather are those who hear the word of God and keep it!" (Luke 11:27-28).[35] These distancings of Mary from Jesus and by Jesus set Mary on her *via crucis* — her concrete schooling in the nature and meaning of the maternal union she has with her Son, which will be perfected in the abandonment she will suffer at the Cross. Chardon writes:

> These [four] examples of ["ever more rigorous separations"] . . . were not nearly so rigorous as what happened on Calvary, when Jesus was

29. Chardon, *La Croix de Jésus* 1.30.404-405.

30. Cf. *Lumen gentium* 58.

31. Chardon, *La Croix de Jésus* 1.30.409. Chardon's reading of these four events of encounter between Jesus and Mary is deeply resonant with those proposed by Adrienne von Speyr and taken up by Hans Urs von Balthasar. See Adrienne von Speyr, *Handmaid of the Lord*, trans. E. A. Nelson (San Francisco: Ignatius Press, 1985).

32. Chardon, *La Croix de Jésus* 1.30.410.

33. Chardon, *La Croix de Jésus* 1.30.411.

34. Chardon, *La Croix de Jésus* 1.30.413.

35. Chardon, *La Croix de Jésus* 1.30.413.

nearing his death. At the center of this universal desolation full of the horror that had come to afflict his soul, he comports himself towards his grieving Mother with less courtesy, it would seem, than if she were a stranger. He addresses her simply as "Woman."[36]

This deprivation of Mary at the Cross is her martyrdom of "living death" and a "dying life,"[37] a perfect witness to the truth of Christ that conforms to his death, not after the crucifixion but "with" Jesus in his original sacrifice. For Chardon, it perfectly realizes the grace of Mary's maternity.[38] Herein lies the deep paradox of Mary's vocation: what makes her uniquely Theo-tokos among all creatures, finally "separates her from her maternity."[39] Thus she enters with her Son into the dereliction of *sui exinanitio*:

> Though he was in the form of God (*qui cum in forma Dei esset*), [he] did not count equality with God a thing to be grasped, but emptied himself (*ipsum exinanivit*), taking the form of a servant, being born in the like-ness of men. And being found in human form he humbled himself and became obedient unto death, even death on a cross. (Phil. 2:6-8)

Because Jesus must divest himself of the *forma divina*, the Mother must divest herself of divine maternity in order to remain united with her Son.[40] When the Son empties himself unto death, Mary becomes deprived of her child and of the God to whom she gave flesh. Giving her Son and her God to the Cross, Mary becomes dispossessed of the unique privilege of being "Theotokos." Chardon writes:

> It was not due to lack of affection that Jesus addressed her from the Cross as "Woman." Rather it was part of a mysterious plan for a more perfect union . . . in order to render her, like him, separated (*séparée*) from every thought of consolation and to realize a stripping (*désap-propriation*) away of all grandeur, in order to purify and elevate her to what she could be. He separated (*sépare*) her from every possession and property, including her own Son. Thus he deprived (*détache*) her of every relationship, including that which she contracted by her affinity

36. Chardon, *La Croix de Jésus* 1.28.414.
37. Chardon, *La Croix de Jésus* 1.30.419.
38. Chardon, *La Croix de Jésus* 1.28.369.
39. Chardon, *La Croix de Jésus* 1.28.369.
40. Chardon, *La Croix de Jésus* 1.30.416.

with the person of a God. He contributed to despoil (*déprendre*) her of all her honors owed to her by creatures and of all the glory that the creator willed to bestow on her by reason of the excellence of her state, which she occupies in the order of grace.[41]

For the Mary-Jesus *unio* to be perfected, the distancing must be ever greater (*maior dissimilitudo*). Mary must be stripped of her Son not only by physical death but also by a state of divine abandonment in which she can no longer claim to be the "Mother of God."

The personal *maior dissimilitudo* suffered in the ultimate and perfect interpersonal *unio* of Mary and Jesus becomes the key, for Chardon, to understanding the role of the Holy Spirit: "if I do not go away, the Counselor will not come to you; but if I go, I will send him to you" (John 16:7).[42] Chardon writes:

> Jesus was the cause of her dying. She was dead to her august relationship with the heavenly Father, and the Holy Spirit only poured himself forth in her heart in order to bring about in her an agonizing death and new martyrdom, heretofore unknown to man.[43]

This new martyrdom of *unio* in *maior dissimilitudo,* of participation in the death of Jesus to the point of being "one" with him in his abandonment to the Father, is for Chardon "pneumatological" in the fullest sense. Mary, by the overshadowing of the Holy Spirit at the Annunciation (cf. Luke 1:35), is from the beginning prepared to play a permanent role, not merely in her Son's being in a distinct sense, but in the theandric act by which he personally accomplishes and fulfills his incarnate vocation.

The abandonment of Jesus by the Father on the Cross is, for Chardon, a true dilation of the Trinity insofar as the Crucifixion is understood primarily as an abandonment of Jesus by the Holy Spirit, the *vinculum amoris* of Father and Son. The whole "weight" of Jesus' life leading to the Cross is the weight of the Holy Spirit. The Spirit who drove Jesus into the wilderness (cf. Mark 1:12) now drives him to the Cross where he offers himself without blemish "through the Spirit" (cf. Heb. 9:14). The Spirit is the "crucifier," the *unio* that joins Son to Father in his being and in his abandonment. The

---

41. Chardon, *La Croix de Jésus* 1.30.417.
42. Cf. Radner, *The End of the Church*, pp. 340-46.
43. Chardon, *La Croix de Jésus* 1.30.419.

vinculum amoris pours forth in the moment of total *sui exinanitio* in order to realize the living death and dying life that is the Christian vocation perfectly received and lived by Mary in the moment of the Sacrifice of Calvary.

Mary's personal co-being with Jesus exerts, through the Spirit, a *via crucis* that ensures that the Sacrifice of Calvary will be established in terms of an unceasing, fluid exchange of theandric *maior dissimilitudo* between the original martyrdom of the Church and the unique Sacrifice of the Son. To this extent, there can be no argument about co-redemption.[44] As a descriptive term of what actually happened on Calvary, it is a fact. The *verus homo* is the Redeemer, and the Virgin of Nazareth is with him in his unique act of Redemption. The Mother is in *communio* with her Son at the foot of the Cross: she suffers and sorrows with him; she is united with him in mutual abandonment. All of this entails from her exemplary status, her perfect co-being with the Son in the Spirit and her perfect docility to that same Spirit by which her perfect act of *sequela Christi* proceeds.

Because she is the first and exemplary person of adoptive filiation, she is irreducibly *with* the Crucified in his solitary act of redemption. But just as her *persona* does not "add" to his *verus homo*, so Mary's co-redemptive role is not a contribution of something otherwise lacking in the Son's redemptive sacrifice. Her presence, rather, shows that the *unio* of the Incarnate Son included, at its origin, the pneumatological *communio* of Jesus-Mary.

Mary's suffering, then, is both a true participation in the Cross and a contribution of nothing but the "adequate response" of the *ecclesia immaculata*, a response in the Holy Spirit that is itself a grace given in Christ.[45] By the grace that flows backwards from the Cross, Mary gives her own consent, *fiat mihi*, to that on which God himself waits: the immolation of the sacred victim.

> *Vergine madre, figlia del tuo figlio,*
> *umile ed alta più che creatura,*
> *termine fisso d'eterno consiglio.*

---

44. Cf. Josef Seifert, "Mary as Coredemptrix and Mediatrix of All Graces: Philosophical and Personalistic Foundations of a Marian Doctrine," in Mark I. Miravalle, ed., *Mary Coredemptrix, Mediatrix, Advocate: Theological Foundations II: Papal, Pneumatological, Ecumenical* (Santa Barbara: Queenship Publishing, 1997), pp. 149-74.

45. Cf. Hans Urs von Balthasar, "Who Is the Church?," in *Explorations in Theology*, vol. 2, *Spouse of the Word*, trans. A. V. Littledale (San Francisco: Ignatius Press, 1991), pp. 143-93, esp. p. 161.

Conclusion

In 1928, in his *L'Itinéraire philosophique*, Maurice Blondel warned: "If there is a fear of confusing/mixing, there ought to be a greater fear of not uniting enough . . . since, in fact, it is when one does not know how to unite things well that one especially fears confusing/mixing."[1]

On one level this book has been nothing other than a Christological verification of Blondel's judgment, rooted at the heart of Nicene orthodoxy. The hypostatic union of divinity and humanity in Christ is at once the highest union of God and creation, and a perfect confirmation of the *maior dissimilitudo* between created and uncreated nature. In other words, the unity of Christ involves a complete "oneness" that is just the opposite of confusion or mixture: *unio* confirms and perfects *maior dissimilitudo*. Seen in this light, the unity of Christ constitutes and grounds the distinct integrity, not only of his own human nature, but also of human nature as such, whose positive difference from God he reveals in

---

1. M. Blondel, *L'Itinéraire philosophique de Maurice Blondel. Propos recueillis par Frédéric Lefèvre* (Paris: Spes, 1928), pp. 160-61: "Vous l'avez déjà entrevu, l'hétérogénéité de la nature et du surnaturel est telle qu'il n'y a pas de confusion compréhensible pour qui est expressément averti, par un plein enseignement, de ce dont il s'agit; si bien que le problème le plus réel, le plus actuel à poser est l'inverse de celui auquel on se borne le plus souvent: on craint de confondre, il faut craindre de ne pas unir assez, de ne faire du christianisme qu'un surcroît postiche, de ne pas montrer que les barrières et les mortifications très apparentes ne sont en réalité que des moyens très secrets de réaliser une plus béatifiante union; et c'est en effet quand on ne sait pas bien unir qu'on craint surtout de confondre. Si trop souvent aujourd'hui la vie générale de l'humanité se retire du Christianisme, c'est peut-être qu'on a trop souvent déraciné le Christianisme des viscères intimes de l'homme." Cf. Henri de Lubac, S.J., Lettre le 3 avril 1932 à M. Blondel, in *Mémoire sur l'occasion de mes écrits* (Namur: Culture et vérité, 1989), p. 189, where de Lubac takes up these words as constitutive of his theological trajectory.

the *missio* of his descent from heaven. "Christ . . . in the very revelation of the mystery of the Father and of his love, fully reveals man to himself and brings to light his most high calling."[2] To attenuate Christ's divine unity is also to diminish his human difference and with it the mode by which he accomplishes the theandric act that "reveals man to himself." Abstracted from the one Lord Jesus Christ, the Christological meaning and the relation of divinity and humanity is shattered. The resulting fragmentation, realized in every theological program of *separatio*, is nowhere more acutely evident than in the modern so-called "quest for the historical Jesus."

In the Foreword to the first volume of his *Jesus of Nazareth*, Pope Benedict XVI chronicles how, in the field of biblical scholarship, the "gap between 'the historical Jesus' and the 'Christ of Faith' grew wider . . . [until] the two visibly fell apart."[3] The achievement of the "quest for the historical Jesus" was to decisively realize, not the hidden integrity of the merely "human Jesus" obscured behind the *Gestalt* of divine *unio*, but the total disintegration of every coherent account of the human fact it sought to establish.[4] In other words, the modern penchant for *separatio* failed precisely to the extent that it sought to establish a "state and condition of Christ's human nature" existing *sui iuris*, as if it did not derive its whole existence and reality from being "one" with the hypostasis of the Logos.

The theological program of *separatio*, which recoils in every case from the singular starting point of the apostolic witness and of Nicene orthodoxy, has now extended itself detrimentally into the life of the Church. In the realm of Christian culture, self-understanding and piety, modern Christianity accommodates and internalizes with increasingly less resistance the modern-liberal ethos that separates *religio* from *homo*. In broad currents of both modern academic theology and popular Christian culture, the question of God has been effectively expelled from the original question of the human being, such that the human is longer thought of as "homo religiosus," much less an experience of being awaiting its ultimate illumination in Jesus Christ, the God-Man. Under this influence, as Javier Martínez argues,

2. *Gaudium et spes* 22 (DS 4322).
3. Joseph Ratzinger — Pope Benedict XVI, *Jesus of Nazareth*, pt. 1, *From the Baptism in the Jordan to the Transfiguration*, trans. Adrian J. Walker (New York: Doubleday, 2007), p. xi.
4. Ratzinger — Benedict, *Jesus of Nazareth*, pt. 1, p. xii.

"Christian" has come to designate not so much a concrete human experience and endowment that cannot be understood apart from its "particular" categories, but rather now a particular self-enclosed world, [defined in relation to] . . . a humanity *without Christ*, which now becomes the "universal."[5]

But for classical Christological orthodoxy, a humanity "without Christ" is quite simply an "anhypostatic" impossibility. Only the divine Son reveals the truly human. Against the impossibility of being human "without Christ," the recovery of a Cyrillian doctrine of the Incarnation with its accompanying grammar of *communicatio idiomatum*, forged against the perennial temptation to Nestorian dualism, stands forth as a prolegomenon to a Christological humanism, to a theology of the *sequela Christi* after modernity.

* * *

As a work in dogmatic Christology, a thematic study of this sort could have been conducted in different ways. The approach taken here has been broadly genealogical and mystical, even while an attempt has been made to be "systematic" in a basic sense. The central focus throughout has been on the exceptional unity of the Incarnate Son. This union has been described as paradoxical because it involves an ineliminable, yet fruitful, tension: the scandal of the Cross sustained by the hypostatic union.

The indissoluble union of the Incarnate Logos is "stretched out" from the height of the Son's eternal being with the Father to the cold stone on which his cadaver is laid, from the human breast of the Mother to the region of hell in which the crucified soul of Jesus is abandoned. This mystery at the core of all being is not a tidy fact about divinity or humanity; it is the scandal of the Incarnate Son of God. And "none of the rulers of this age understood this; for if they had, they would not have crucified the Lord of glory" (1 Cor. 2:8).

---

5. Francisco Javier Martínez, archbishop of Granada, "Prefacio a la Edición de 2008," in Luigi Giussani, *El Sentido Religioso: Curso Básico de Cristianismo*, vol. 1, trans. José Miguel Oriol (Madrid: Ediciones Encuentro, 2008), pp. 1-6, here at p. 1.

Bibliography

Adams, Marilyn McCord. *Christ and Horrors: The Coherence of Christology.* Cambridge: Cambridge University Press, 2006.

Alexander III. *Cum Christus.* In Heinrich Denzinger, *Enchiridion Symbolorum et Declarationum de Rebus Fidei et Morum,* edited by Peter Hünermann. 43rd ed. San Francisco: Ignatius Press, 2012.

——. *Cum in nostra.* In Heinrich Denzinger, *Enchiridion Symbolorum et Declarationum de Rebus Fidei et Morum,* edited by Peter Hünermann. 43rd ed. San Francisco: Ignatius Press, 2012.

Allen, Pauline, and Bronwen Neil. *Maximus the Confessor and His Companions.* Oxford: Oxford University Press, 2003.

Allen, Pauline, and C. T. R. Hayward. *Severus of Antioch.* Early Church Fathers. London: Routledge, 2004.

Anastos, Milton V. "Nestorius Was Orthodox." *Dumbarton Oaks Papers* 16 (1962): 117-40.

Anatolios, Khaled. *Athanasius.* Early Church Fathers. London: Routledge, 2004.

Armitage, J. M. *A Twofold Solidarity: Leo the Great's Theology of Redemption.* Strathfield: St. Pauls, 2005.

Athanasius of Alexandria. *De decretis Nicaenae synodi.* In *Patrologia Graeca,* edited by Jacques-Paul Migne, vol. 25, cols. 415-476. Paris: Imprimerie Catholique, 1857-1866.

——. *Epistula ad Epictetum.* In *Patrologia Graeca,* edited by Jacques-Paul Migne, vol. 26, cols. 1049-1070. Paris: Imprimerie Catholique, 1857-1866.

——. *Oratio de incarnatione verbi.* In *Patrologia Graeca,* edited by Jacques-Paul Migne, vol. 25, cols. 95-196. Paris: Imprimerie Catholique, 1857-1866.

——. *Orationes adversus Arianos.* In *Patrologia Graeca,* edited by Jacques-Paul Migne, vol. 26, cols. 12-524. Paris: Imprimerie Catholique, 1857-1866.

Augustine of Hippo. *Epistula* 4*. In *Sancti Aureli Augustini opera: Epistolae ex duobus codicibus nuper in lucem prolatae,* edited by Johannes Divjak, pp. 26-29. Vienna: Hoelder-Pichler-Tempsky, 1981.

——. *In Natali Domini, Sermo* 128. In *Patrologia Latina,* edited by Jacques-Paul Migne, vol. 39, cols. 1996-1997. Paris: Vrayet, 1844-1864.

Ayres, Lewis. *Nicaea and Its Legacy: An Approach to Fourth-Century Trinitarian Theology.* Oxford: Oxford University Press, 2004.

Bibliography

Backes, Ignaz. *Die Christologie des heiligen Thomas von Aquin und die griechischen Kirchenväter.* Paderborn: Schöningh, 1931.

Balthasar, Hans Urs von. *Cosmic Liturgy: The Universe according to Maximus the Confessor.* Translated by Brian E. Daley. San Francisco: Ignatius Press, 2003.

———. *The Glory of the Lord: A Theological Aesthetics.* Vol. 3, *Studies in Theological Style: Lay Styles.* Translated by Andrew Louth et al. San Francisco: Ignatius Press, 1988.

———. *Presence and Thought: Essay on the Religious Philosophy of Gregory of Nyssa.* Translated by Mark Sebanc. San Francisco: Ignatius Press, 1995.

———. *Theo-Drama: Theological Dramatic Theory.* Vol. 3, *Dramatis Personae: Persons in Christ.* Translated by Graham Harrison. San Francisco: Ignatius Press, 1992.

———. *Theo-Logic.* Vol. 2, *Truth of God.* Translated by Adrian J. Walker. San Francisco: Ignatius Press, 2004.

———. *The Theology of Karl Barth.* Translated by Edward T. Oakes. San Francisco: Ignatius Press, 1992.

Balthasar, Hans Urs von, and Adrienne von Speyr. *To the Heart of the Mystery of Redemption.* San Francisco: Ignatius Press, 2010.

Barnes, Corey L. *Christ's Two Wills in Scholastic Thought: The Christology of Aquinas and Its Historical Contexts.* Toronto: PIMS, 2012.

Barth, Bernhard. "Ein neues Dokument zur Geschichte der frühscholastischen Christologie." *Theologische Quartalschrift* 100 (1919): 409-26.

Barth, Karl. *Church Dogmatics* I/2. *The Doctrine of the Word of God.* Translated by G. T. Thompson and Harold Knight. Edited by G. W. Bromiley and T. F. Torrance. Edinburgh: T. & T. Clark, 1956.

———. *The Göttingen Dogmatics: Instruction in the Christian Religion.* Translated by G. W. Bromiley. Grand Rapids: Eerdmans, 1991.

———. *The Humanity of God.* Translated by John Newton Thomas. Richmond: John Knox Press, 1960.

Basly, Déodat de. "L'Assumptus Homo." *La France franciscaine* 11 (1928): 265-313.

———. "Inopérantes offensives contre l'Assumptus Homo." *La France franciscaine* 17 (1934): 419-73.

———. "Le Moi de Jésus-Christ." *La France franciscaine* 12 (1929): 125-60.

———. *Scotus Docens ou Duns Scot Enseignant: la Philosophie, la Théologie, la Mystique.* Paris: La France Franciscaine, 1933.

Bathrellos, Demetrios. *The Byzantine Christ: Person, Nature, and Will in the Christology of Saint Maximus the Confessor.* Oxford: Oxford University Press, 2005.

Bauerschmidt, Frederick Christian. *Thomas Aquinas: Faith, Reason, and Following Christ.* Oxford: Oxford University Press, 2013.

Baxter, Anthony. "Chalcedon and the Subject in Christ." *Downside Review* 107 (1989): 1-21.

Beeley, Christopher A. "The Early Christological Controversy: Apollinarius, Diodore, and Gregory Nazianzen." *Vigiliae Christianae* 65 (2011): 1-32.

———. *Gregory of Nazianzus on the Trinity and the Knowledge of God: In Your Light We Shall See Light.* Oxford: Oxford University Press, 2008.

———. *The Unity of Christ: Continuity and Conflict in Patristic Tradition.* New Haven: Yale University Press, 2012.

Behr, John. *Becoming Human: Meditations on Christian Anthropology in Word and Image.* Crestwood, NY: Saint Vladimir's Seminary Press, 2013.

————. *The Case against Diodore and Theodore: Texts and Their Contexts.* Oxford: Oxford University Press, 2011.

————. *The Formation of Christian Theology.* Vol. 1, *The Way to Nicaea.* Crestwood, NY: Saint Vladimir's Seminary Press, 2001.

————. *The Formation of Christian Theology.* Vol. 2, *The Nicene Faith.* Crestwood, NY: Saint Vladimir's Seminary Press, 2004.

————. *The Mystery of Christ: Life in Death.* Crestwood, NY: Saint Vladimir's Seminary Press, 2006.

————. "The Paschal Foundation of Christian Theology." *St. Vladimir's Theological Quarterly* 45 (2001): 115-36.

————. "Severus of Antioch: Eastern and Oriental Perspectives." *St. Nersess Theological Review* 3 (1998): 23-35.

Benedict XVI. *Church Fathers: From Clement of Rome to Augustine.* San Francisco: Ignatius Press, 2008.

————. *God Is Love: Deus Caritas Est.* San Francisco: Ignatius Press, 2006.

Bethune-Baker, J. F. *Nestorius and His Teachings: A Fresh Examination of the Evidence.* Cambridge: Cambridge University Press, 1908.

Bieler, Martin. *Befreiung der Freiheit: Zur Theologie der stellvertretenden Sühne.* Freiburg: Herder, 1996.

Billot, Ludovico. *De Verbo Incarnato: Commentarius in Tertiam Partem S. Thomae.* Prati: Libraria Giachetti, 1912.

Blowers, Paul M. "The Passion of Jesus Christ in Maximus the Confessor: A Reconsideration." *Studia Patristica* 37 (2001): 361-77.

Boethius. *Contra Eutyche et Nestorium.* In *The Theological Tractates and the Consolation of Philosophy,* edited and translated by E. K. Rand, H. F. Stewart, and S. J. Tester. Loeb Classical Library 74. Cambridge, MA: Harvard University Press, 1973.

Bok, N. den, M. Bac, A. J. Beck, K. Bom, E. Dekker, G. Labooy, H. Veldhuis, and A. Vos. "More Than Just an Individual: Scotus's Concept of Person from the Christological Context of *Lectura* III.1." *Franciscan Studies* 66 (2008): 169-96.

Bonino, S.-T., ed. *Saint Thomas au XXe siècle.* Paris: Editions Saint-Paul, 1994.

Bonner, Gerald. "Pelagianism and Augustine." *Augustinian Studies* 23 (1992): 33-51.

Boulnois, M.-O. "Die Eucharistie, Mysterium der Einigung bei Cyrill von Alexandrien: Die Modelle der trinitarischen und christologischen Einigung." *Theologische Quartalschrift* 4 (1998): 294-310.

Bradshaw, David. *Aristotle East and West: Metaphysics and the Division of Christendom.* Cambridge: Cambridge University Press, 2004.

Bro, Bernard. "La notion métaphysique de tout et son application au problème théologique de l'union hypostatique." *Revue Thomiste* 68 (1968): 181-97, 357-80.

Brock, Sebastian. "The Conversations with the Syrian Orthodox under Justinian, 523." *Orientalia Christiana Periodica* 47 (1981): 87-121.

————. *Fire from Heaven: Studies in Syriac Theology and Liturgy.* Aldershot: Ashgate, 2006.

Browning, Robert. *Justinian and Theodora.* London: Thames & Hudson, 1987.

Bulgakov, Sergei. *The Lamb of God.* Translated by Boris Jakim. Grand Rapids: Eerdmans, 2008.

Burger, Maria. *Personalität im Horizont absoluter Prädestination: Untersuchungen zur*

*Christologie des Johannes Duns Scotus und ihrer Rezeption in modernen theolo-
gischen Ansätzen.* Münster: Aschendorff, 1994.

Casiday, Augustine. *Tradition and Theology in St. John Cassian.* Oxford: Oxford University Press, 2007.

Cessario, Romanus. *The Godly Image: Christ and Salvation in Catholic Thought from
Anselm to Aquinas.* Petersham, MA: St. Bede's Publications, 1989.

Chadwick, Henry. *Boethius: The Consolations of Music, Logic, Theology, and Philosophy.*
Oxford: Clarendon Press, 1981.

———. "Eucharist and Christology in the Nestorian Controversy." *Journal of Theological
Studies* 2 (1951): 145-64.

———. "The Exile and Death of Flavian of Constantinople: A Prologue to the Council
of Chalcedon." *Journal of Theological Studies* 6 (1955): 17-34.

Chadwick, Owen. *John Cassian.* Cambridge: Cambridge University Press, 1950.

Chardon, Louis. *La Croix de Jésus: où les plus belles vérités de la théologie mystique et de
la grâce sanctifiante sont établies.* Paris: Cerf, 2004.

Chesnut, Roberta C. *Three Monophysite Christologies: Severus of Antioch, Philoxenus of
Mabbug, and Jacob of Sarug.* Oxford: Oxford University Press, 1985.

———. "The Two Prosopa in Nestorius' Bazaar of Heracleides." *Journal of Theological
Studies* 29 (1978): 392-409.

Chrétien, Jean-Luis. *L'intelligence du feu: réponses humaines à une parole de Jésus.* Paris:
Bayard, 2003.

Clarke, W. Norris. *Explorations in Metaphysics: Being–God–Person.* London: University
of Notre Dame Press, 1994.

Clayton, Paul B. *The Christology of Theodoret of Cyrus: Antiochene Christology from the
Council of Ephesus.* Oxford: Oxford University Press, 2007.

Coakley, Sarah. "'Mingling' in Gregory of Nyssa's Christology: A Reconsideration." In
Who Is Jesus Christ for Us Today? Pathways to Contemporary Christology, edited
by Andreas Schuele and Günter Thomas, pp. 72-84. Louisville: Westminster John
Knox Press, 2009.

———. "What Does Chalcedon Solve and What Does It Not? Some Reflections on
the Status and Meaning of the Chalcedonian 'Definition.'" In *The Incarnation: An
Interdisciplinary Symposium on the Incarnation of the Son of God,* edited by Stephen T. Davis, Daniel Kendall, and Gerald O'Collins, pp. 143-63. Oxford: Oxford
University Press, 2002.

Coakley, Sarah, and Charles M. Stang, eds. *Re-Thinking Dionysius the Areopagite.* Oxford:
Wiley-Blackwell, 2008.

Colish, Marcia. *Peter Lombard.* 2 vols. Leiden: E. J. Brill, 1994.

Concannon, Ellen. "The Eucharist as Source of St. Cyril of Alexandria's Christology."
Pro Ecclesia 18 (2009): 318-36.

Congregation for the Doctrine of the Faith. "Notificación sobre las obras del P. Jon
Sobrino S.J." In Heinrich Denzinger, *Enchiridion Symbolorum et Declarationum de
Rebus Fidei et Morum,* edited by Peter Hünermann, #5107. 43rd ed. San Francisco:
Ignatius Press, 2012.

———. "Notification on the Book *Jesus Symbol of God* by Father Roger Haight, S.J."
In Heinrich Denzinger, *Enchiridion Symbolorum et Declarationum de Rebus Fidei*

et Morum, edited by Peter Hünermann, #5099. 43rd ed. San Francisco: Ignatius Press, 2012.

Cooper, Adam G. *The Body in St. Maximus the Confessor: Holy Flesh, Wholly Deified.* Oxford: Oxford University Press, 2005.

Council of Chalcedon. *The Acts of the Council of Chalcedon: Translated with an Introduction and Notes.* Edited and translated by Richard Price and Micael Gaddis. 3 vols. Manchester: Liverpool University Press, 2005.

———. *Definitio fidei.* In *Decrees of the Ecumenical Councils,* vol. 1, *Nicaea I–Lateran V,* edited by Norman Tanner, pp. 83-87. Washington, DC: Georgetown University Press, 1990.

Council of Constantinople I. Canons. In *Decrees of the Ecumenical Councils,* vol. 1, *Nicaea I–Lateran V,* edited by Norman Tanner, pp. 31-35. Washington, DC: Georgetown University Press, 1990.

Council of Constantinople II. *The Acts of the Council of Constantinople of 553: With Related Texts on the Three Chapters Controversy, Edited and with an Introduction and Notes.* Edited by Richard Price. 2 vols. Liverpool: Liverpool University Press, 2009.

———. *Anathematismi adversus "tria Capitula."* In *Decrees of the Ecumenical Councils,* vol. 1, *Nicaea I–Lateran V,* edited by Norman Tanner, pp. 114-22. Washington, DC: Georgetown University Press, 1990.

Council of Constantinople III. "Condemnation of the Monothelites and of Pope Honorius I." In Heinrich Denzinger, *Enchiridion Symbolorum et Declarationum de Rebus Fidei et Morum,* edited by Peter Hünermann, ##550-52. 43rd ed. San Francisco: Ignatius Press, 2012.

———. *Terminus.* In *Decrees of the Ecumenical Councils,* vol. 1, *Nicaea I–Lateran V,* edited by Norman Tanner, pp. 124-30. Washington, DC: Georgetown University Press, 1990.

Council of Lateran IV. *Constitutions, 2. De errore abbatis Iochim.* In *Decrees of the Ecumenical Councils,* vol. 1, *Nicaea I–Lateran V,* edited by Norman Tanner, pp. 231-33. Washington, DC: Georgetown University Press, 1990.

Council of Vatican II. *Gaudium et spes.* In *Decrees of the Ecumenical Councils,* vol. 2, *Trent–Vatican II,* edited by Norman Tanner, pp. 1069-1135. Washington, DC: Georgetown University Press, 1990.

Cross, Richard. "Aquinas on Nature, Hypostasis, and the Metaphysics of the Incarnation." *Thomist* 60 (1996): 171-202.

———. "The Doctrine of the Hypostatic Union in the Thought of Duns Scotus." Ph.D. diss., Oxford University, 1991.

———. "Individual Natures in the Christology of Leontius of Byzantium." *Journal of Early Christian Studies* 10 (2002): 245-65.

———. *John Duns Scotus.* Oxford: Oxford University Press, 1999.

———. *The Metaphysics of the Incarnation: Thomas Aquinas to Duns Scotus.* Oxford: Oxford University Press, 2002.

Crowley, Paul G. "*Instrumentum divinitatis* in Thomas Aquinas: Recovering the Divinity of Christ." *Theological Studies* 52 (1991): 451-75.

Cunningham, Conor. "Being Recalled: Life as Anamnesis." In *Divine Transcendence and Immanence in the Work of Thomas Aquinas,* edited by Harm Goris, Herwi Rikhof, and Henk Schoot, pp. 59-80. Leuven: Peeters, 2009.

————. *Genealogy of Nihilism: Philosophies of Nothing and the Difference of Theology.* London: Routledge, 2001.

Cyril of Alexandria. *Apologeticus contra Theodoretum pro duodecim capitibus.* In *Patrologia Graeca,* edited by Jacques-Paul Migne, vol. 76, cols. 386-453. Paris: Imprimerie Catholique, 1857-1866.

————. *Epistula* 1. In *Patrologia Graeca,* edited by Jacques-Paul Migne, vol. 77, cols. 9-40. Paris: Imprimerie Catholique, 1857-1866.

————. *Epistula* 11. In *Patrologia Graeca,* edited by Jacques-Paul Migne, vol. 77, cols. 79-99. Paris: Imprimerie Catholique, 1857-1866.

————. *Epistula* 44. To Eulogius. In *Cyril of Alexandria: Select Letters,* edited by Lionel R. Wickham, pp. 62-69. Oxford: Oxford University Press, 1983.

————. *Epistula* 45. First Letter to Succensus. In *Cyril of Alexandria: Select Letters,* edited by Lionel R. Wickham, pp. 70-83. Oxford: Oxford University Press, 1983.

————. *Epistula* 46. Second Letter to Succensus. In *Cyril of Alexandria: Select Letters,* edited by Lionel R. Wickham, pp. 84-93. Oxford: Oxford University Press, 1983.

————. *Epistula* 55. On the Creed. In *Cyril of Alexandria: Select Letters,* edited by Lionel R. Wickham, pp. 94-131. Oxford: Oxford University Press, 1983.

————. *Epistula ad Ioannem Antiochenum de pace.* In *Decrees of the Ecumenical Councils,* edited by Norman Tanner, vol. 1, pp. 70-74. London: Sheed & Ward, 1990.

————. *Epistula altera ad Nestorium.* In *Decrees of the Ecumenical Councils,* edited by Norman Tanner, vol. 1, pp. 40-44. London: Sheed & Ward, 1990.

————. *Epistula tertia ad Nestorium.* In *Decrees of the Ecumenical Councils,* edited by Norman Tanner, vol. 1, pp. 50-61. London: Sheed & Ward, 1990.

————. *Expositio in Joannis Evangelium.* In *Patrologia Graeca,* edited by Jacques-Paul Migne, vols. 73-74. Paris: Imprimerie Catholique, 1857-1866.

————. *In Genesim.* In *Patrologia Graeca,* edited by Jacques-Paul Migne, vol. 69, cols. 13-383. Paris: Imprimerie Catholique, 1857-1866.

————. The Twelve Chapters. In Heinrich Denzinger, *Enchiridion Symbolorum et Declarationum de Rebus Fidei et Morum,* edited by Peter Hünermann, ##252-263. 43rd ed. San Francisco: Ignatius Press, 2012.

Daley, Brian E. "Anhypostasie." In *Dictionnaire critique de Théologie,* edited by J.-Y. Lacoste, pp. 50-51. Paris: PUF, 1998.

————. "Divine Transcendence and Human Transformation: Gregory of Nyssa's Anti-Apollinarian Christology." *Modern Theology* 18 (2002): 497-506.

————. "The Giant's Twin Substances: Ambrose and the Christology of Augustine's 'Contra sermonem Arrianorum.'" In *Augustine: Presbyter factus sum,* vol. 2 of *Collectanea Augustiniana,* edited by Joseph T. Lienhard et al., pp. 477-95. New York: Peter Lang, 1993.

————. *Gregory of Nazianzus.* Early Church Fathers. London: Routledge, 2006.

————. "'Heavenly Man' and 'Eternal Christ': Apollinarius and Gregory of Nyssa on the Personal Identity of the Savior." *Journal of Early Christian Studies* 10 (2002): 469-88.

————. "A Humble Mediator: The Distinctive Elements in St. Augustine's Christology." *Word and Spirit* 9 (1987): 100-117.

————. "Nature and the 'Mode of Union': Late Patristic Models for the Personal Unity of Christ." In *The Incarnation: An Interdisciplinary Symposium on the Incarnation of the Son of God*, edited by Stephen T. Davis, Daniel Kendall, and Gerald O'Collins, pp. 164-96. Oxford: Oxford University Press, 2002.

————. "'A Richer Union': Leontius of Byzantium and the Relationship of Human and Divine in Christ." *Studia Patristica* 24 (1939): 239-65.

Davidson, Ivor J. "'Not My Will but Yours Be Done': The Ontological Dynamics of Incarnational Intention." *International Journal of Systematic Theology* 7 (2005): 178-204.

————. "Reappropriating Patristic Christology: One Doctrine, Two Styles." *Irish Theological Quarterly* 67 (2002): 225-39.

————. "Theologizing the Human Jesus: An Ancient (and Modern) Approach to Christology Reassessed." *International Journal of Systematic Theology* 3 (2001): 129-53.

Davis, Leo D. *The First Seven Ecumenical Councils (325-787): Their History and Theology.* Collegeville, MN: Liturgical Press, 1990.

Davis, Raymond. *The Book of Pontiffs.* 2nd ed. Liverpool: University of Liverpool Press, 2000.

Davis, Stephen T., Daniel Kendall, and Gerald O'Collins, eds. *The Incarnation: An Interdisciplinary Symposium on the Incarnation of the Son of God.* Oxford: Oxford University Press, 2002.

Deloffre, Marie-Hélène. "Introduction to Thomas Aquinas." In *Question disputée: l'union du Verbe incarné (De unione Verbi incarnati),* by Thomas Aquinas, pp. 13-78. Translated and edited by Marie-Hélène Deloffre. Paris: J. Vrin, 2000.

Denys the Areopagite. *Corpus Areopagiticum.* In *Patrologia Graeca,* edited by Jacques-Paul Migne, vol. 3. Paris: Imprimerie Catholique, 1857-1866.

————. *Pseudo-Dionysius: The Complete Works.* Translated by Colm Luibheid. New York: Paulist Press, 1987.

Denzinger, Heinrich. *Enchiridion Symbolorum et Declarationum de Rebus Fidei et Morum: Compendium of Creeds, Definitions and Declarations on Matters of Faith and Morals.* Edited by Peter Hünermann. Latin-English. 43rd ed. San Francisco: Ignatius Press, 2012.

Divjak, J., ed. *Les Lettres de saint Augustine.* Paris: Études Augustiniennes, 1983.

Dix, Gregory. *The Shape of the Liturgy.* New ed. London: Continuum, 2005.

Dondaine, H. F. "Note sur la documentation patristique de Saint Thomas à Paris en 1270." *Revue des science philosophiques et théologiques* 47 (1963): 403-6.

Doucet, Marcel. "La volonté humaine du Christ, spécialement en son agonie: Maxime le Confesseur, interprète de l'Écriture." *Science et Esprit* 37 (1985): 123-59.

Draguet, R. "La christologie d'Eutyches d'apres les actes du synode de Flavien." *Byzantion* 6 (1931): 441-57.

Dunn, Geoffrey D. "Augustine, Cyril of Alexandria, and the Pelagian Controversy." *Augustinian Studies* 37 (2006): 63-88.

Duns Scotus, John. *God and Creatures: The Quodlibetal Questions.* Edited and translated by Allan Wolter and Felix Alluntis. Princeton: Princeton University Press, 1975.

————. *Opera Omnia.* Vatican City: Typis Polyglottis Vaticanis, 1950-.

Dupré, Louis. *Passage to Modernity: An Essay in the Hermeneutics of Nature and Culture.* New Haven: Yale University Press, 1993.

Duquoc, Christian. *Cristología. Ensayo dogmático sobre Jesús de Nazaret el Mesías.* Translated by Alfonso Ortiz. Salamanca: Ediciones Sigueme, 1974.

Ehrman, Bart, ed. *Apostolic Fathers.* Vol. 1, *I Clement, II Clement, Ignatius, Polycarp, Didache.* Loeb Classical Library 24. Cambridge, MA: Harvard University Press, 2003.

Ekonomou, Andrew J. *Byzantine Rome and the Greek Popes: Eastern Influences on Rome and the Papacy from Gregory the Great to Zacharias, A.D. 590-752.* Lanham, MD: Lexington Books, 2007.

Emery, Gilles. *Trinity, Church, and the Human Person: Thomistic Essays.* Naples, FL: Sapientia Press, 2007.

―――. Review of *Question disputée: l'union du Verbe incarné (De unione Verbi incarnati),* by Thomas Aquinas. Translated and edited by Marie-Hélène Deloffre. Paris: J. Vrin, 2000. Also available at *Nova et Vetera: Revue trimestrielle* 75 (2001): 98-101.

Emery, Kent, Jr., and Joseph P. Wawrykow, eds. *Christ among the Medieval Dominicans.* Notre Dame: University of Notre Dame Press, 1998.

Evans, David. *Leontius of Byzantium: An Origenist Christology.* Washington, DC: Dumbarton Oaks, 1970.

Fabro, Cornelio. *Participation et causalité selon s. Thomas d'Aquin.* Paris: Editions Beatrice-Nauwelaerts, 1961.

Fairbairn, Donald. *Grace and Christology in the Early Church.* Oxford: Oxford University Press, 2003.

Feingold, Lawrence. *The Natural Desire to See God according to St. Thomas Aquinas and His Interpreters.* 2nd ed. Naples, FL: Sapientia Press of Ave Maria University, 2010.

Ferrara, Dennis. "'Hypostatized in the Logos': Leontius of Byzantium, Leontius of Jerusalem and the Unfinished Business of the Council of Chalcedon." *Louvain Studies* 22 (1997): 311-27.

Festugière, André-Jean, ed. *Actes du Concile de Chalcédoine.* Geneva: Patrick Cramer, 1983.

Florovsky, Georges. *The Byzantine Fathers of the Sixth to Eighth Century.* In *Collected Works,* translated by Raymond Miller and Anne-Marie Döllinger-Labriolle, vol. 9. Vaduz: Büchervertriebsanstalt, 1987.

―――. "Christological Dogma and Its Terminology." *Greek Orthodox Theological Review* 13 (1968): 190-93.

Frend, W. H. C. *The Rise of the Monophysite Movement.* Cambridge: Cambridge University Press, 1972.

Gaddis, Michael. *There Is No Crime for Those Who Have Christ: Religious Violence in the Christian Roman Empire.* Berkeley: University of California Press, 2005.

Galot, Jean. "Le Christ terrestre et la vision." *Gregorianum* 67 (1986): 429-50.

Garland, Lynda. *Byzantine Empresses: Women and Power in Byzantium, AD 527-1204.* London: Routledge, 1999.

Garrigou-Lagrange, Reginald. *Christ the Savior: A Commentary on the Third Part of St. Thomas' Theological Summa.* Translated by Bede Rose. St. Louis: B. Herder, 1950.

―――. *Grace: Commentary on the Summa Theologica of St. Thomas, I-II, q. 109-114.* Translated by the Dominican Nuns of Corpus Christi Monastery. St Louis: B. Herder, 1952.

―――. "Unité de la tradition dominicaine sur les rapports de l'ascétique et de mystique." *Supplément à la Vie Spirituelle* 9 (1923): 1-27.

Gauthier, R.-A. "Les 'Articuli in quibus frater Thomas melius in Summa quam in Scriptis.'" *Recherches de théologie ancienne et médiévale* 19 (1952): 271-326.

―――. "Introduction historique à S. Thomas d'Aquin." In *Thomas Aquinas, Summa*

Contra Gentiles, translated by R. Bernier and M. Corvez, vol. 1, pp. 7-123. Paris: P. Lethielleux, 1961.

Gavrilyuk, Paul. *The Suffering of the Impassible God: The Dialectics of Patristic Thought.* Oxford: Oxford University Press, 2004.

Geenen, C. G. "En marge du concile de Chalcédoine: Les textes du Quatrième Concile dans les oeuvres de Saint Thomas." *Angelicum* 29 (1952): 43-59.

George, Cardinal Francis. *The Difference God Makes: A Catholic Vision of Faith, Communion, and Culture.* New York: Crossroad, 2009.

Gilson, Étienne. "L'*esse* du Verbe Incarné selon saint Thomas d'Aquin." *Archives d'Histoire Doctrinale et Littéraire du Moyen Age* 35 (1968): 23-37.

Giussani, Luigi. *El Sentido Religioso. Curso Básico de Cristianismo.* Translated by José Miguel Oriol. Vol. 1. Madrid: Ediciones Encuentro, 2008.

Gleede, Benjamin. *The Development of the Term* ἐνυπόστατος *from Origen to John of Damascus.* Leiden: Brill, 2012.

Glorieux, Paul. "L'orthodoxie de III Sentences (d. 6, 7 et 10)." In *Miscellanea lombardiana,* pp. 137-47. Novara: Istituto geografico de Agostini, 1957.

————. "Les Questions Disputées de S. Thomas et leurs suite chronologique." *Recherches de théologie ancienne et médiévale* 4 (1939): 5-33.

Glotin, Édouard. *La Bible du Coeur de Jésus.* Paris: Presse de la Renaissance, 2007.

Gockel, Matthias. "A Dubious Christological Formula? Leontius of Byzantium and the *Anhypostasis-Enhypostasis* Theory." *Journal of Theological Studies* 51 (2000): 515-32.

Golitzin, Alexander. *Et introibo ad altare dei: The Mystagogy of Dionysius the Areopagite.* Thessalonica: Patriarchal Institute of Patristic Studies, 1994.

————. "Hierarchy versus Anarchy? Dionysius Areopagita, Symeon the New Theologian, Nicetas Stethatos, and Their Common Roots in Ascetical Tradition." *St. Vladimir's Theological Quarterly* 38 (1994): 131-79.

————. *Mystagogy: A Monastic Reading of Dionysius Areopagita.* Edited by Bogdan G. Bucur. Kalamazoo, MI: Cistercian Publications, 2013.

————. "'Suddenly, Christ': The Place of Negative Theology in the Mystagogy of Dionysius Areopagite." In *Mystics: Presence and Aporia,* edited by Michael Kessler and Christian Shepherd, pp. 8-37. Chicago: University of Chicago Press, 2003.

Gondreau, Paul. *The Passions of Christ's Soul in the Theology of St. Thomas Aquinas.* Münster: Aschendorff, 2002.

Gore, Charles. "Our Lord's Human Example." *Church Quarterly Review* 16 (1883): 282-313.

Gorman, Michael. "Christ as Composite according to Aquinas." *Traditio* 55 (2000): 143-57.

————. "The Hypostatic Union according to Thomas Aquinas." Ph.D. diss., Boston College, 1997.

Gray, Patrick T. R., ed. *Leontius of Jerusalem: Against the Monophysites; Testimonies of the Saints and Aporiae.* Oxford: Oxford University Press, 2006.

Greer, Rowan A. "The Image of God and the Prosopic Union in Nestorius' Bazaar of Heraclides." In *Lux in Luminae: Essays in Honor of W. Norman Pittenger,* edited by R. A. Norris, pp. 46-61. New York: Seabury, 1966.

————. *Theodore of Mopsuestia: Exegete and Theologian.* London: Faith Press, 1961.

Gregory the Great. *Consideranti mihi.* In Heinrich Denzinger, *Enchiridion Symbolorum et Declarationum de Rebus Fidei et Morum,* edited by Peter Hünermann, #472. 43rd ed. San Francisco: Ignatius Press, 2012.

Gregory of Nazianzus. *Epistula* 101. In *Lettres théologiques.* Sources Chrétiennes, vol. 208. Paris: Cerf, 1974.

————. *Oratio* 21. In *Discours 20-23.* Sources Chrétiennes, vol. 270. Paris: Cerf, 1980.

————. *Oratio* 22. In *Discours 20-23.* Sources Chrétiennes, vol. 270. Paris: Cerf, 1980.

————. *Oratio* 30. In *Discours 27-31: Discours théologiques.* Sources Chrétiennes, vol. 250. Paris: Cerf, 1978.

————. *Oratio* 37. In *Discours 32-37.* Sources Chrétiennes, vol. 318. Paris: Cerf, 1985.

————. *Oratio* 38. In *Discours 38-41.* Sources Chrétiennes, vol. 358. Paris: Cerf, 1990.

————. *Poema dogmatica, De Incarnatione, adversus Apollinarium.* In *Patrologia Graeca,* edited by Jacques-Paul Migne, vol. 34, cols. 465-470. Paris: Imprimerie Catholique, 1857-1866.

————. *De vita sua.* In *Gregory of Nazianzus: Autobiographical Poems,* edited by Caroline White. Cambridge: Cambridge University Press, 1996.

Gregory of Nyssa. *In Christi Resurrectionem.* In *Patrologia Graeca,* edited by Jacques-Paul Migne, vol. 46, cols. 599-689. Paris: Imprimerie Catholique, 1857-1866.

————. *Contra Eunomium.* In *Gregorii Nysseni Opera,* edited by Jaeger Werner, vol. 1. Leiden: Brill, 1952.

————. *Oratio catechetica. Discours catéchétique.* Sources Chrétiennes, vol. 524. Paris: Cerf, 2010.

————. *Orationis Dominicae.* In *Patrologia Graeca,* edited by Jacques-Paul Migne, vol. 44, cols. 1119-1193. Paris: Imprimerie Catholique, 1857-1866.

————. *Ad Theophilum adversus Apollinaristas.* In *Gregorii Nysseni Opera,* edited by Fridericus Mueller, vol. 3, pt. 1. Leiden: Brill, 1958.

Grillmeier, Aloys, S.J. *Christ in Christian Tradition.* Vol. 1, *From the Apostolic Age to Chalcedon (451).* Translated by John Bowden. 2nd rev. ed. London: Mowbray, 1975.

————. *Christ in Christian Tradition.* Vol. 2, *From the Council of Chalcedon (451) to Gregory the Great (590–604).* Pt. 1, *Reception and Contradiction: The Development of the Discussion about Chalcedon from 451 to the Beginning of the Reign of Justinian.* Translated by Pauline Allen and John Cawte. Louisville: Westminster John Knox Press, 1987.

————. *Christ in Christian Tradition.* Vol. 2, *From the Council of Chalcedon (451) to Gregory the Great (590–604).* Pt. 2, *The Church of Constantinople in the Sixth Century.* With Theresia Hainthaler. Translated by Pauline Allen and John Cawte. Louisville: Westminster John Knox Press, 1995.

Grillmeier, A., and H. Bacht, eds. *Das Konzil von Chalkedon. Geschichte und Gegenwart.* Würzburg: Echter-Verlag, 1954.

Guillou, Marie-Joseph le. "Quelques Réflexions sur Constantinople III et la Sotériologie de Maxime." In *Maximus Confessor: Actes du Symposium sur Maxime le Confesseur Fribourg, 2-5 septembre 1980,* edited by Félix Heinzer and Christoph Schönborn. Fribourg: Éditions Universitaires, 1982.

Hackett, W. Chris. "A Fragment of Christology: Feminism as a Moment of Chalcedonian Humanism." *Australian eJournal of Theology* 20 (2013): 1-17.

Haight, Roger, S.J. *The Future of Christology.* London: Continuum, 2005.

————. *Jesus: Symbol of God.* Maryknoll, NY: Orbis, 1999.

BIBLIOGRAPHY

Halleux, André de. "La Définition christologique à Chalcédoine." *Revue théologique de Louvain* 7 (1976): 3-23, 155-70.

———. "La réception du symbole oecuménique de Nicée à Chalcédoine." *Ephemerides Theologicae Lovanienses* 61 (1985): 5-47.

Hanson, R. P. C. *The Search for the Christian Doctrine of God: The Arian Controversy, 318-381.* Edinburgh: T. & T. Clark, 1988.

Häring, Nikolaus M. "The Case of Gilbert de la Porrée, Bishop of Poitiers (1142-1154)." *Mediaeval Studies* 13 (1951): 1-40.

Harkins, Franklin T. "*Homo Assumptus* and St. Victor: Reconsidering the Relationship between Victorine Christology and Peter Lombard's First Opinion." *Thomist* 72 (2008): 595-624.

Hathaway, Ronald F. *Hierarchy and the Definition of Order in the Letters of Pseudo-Dionysius: A Study in the Form and Meaning of the Pseudo-Dionysian Writings.* The Hague: Nijhoff, 1969.

Hauerwas, Stanley. *With the Grain of the Universe: The Church's Witness and Natural Theology.* Grand Rapids: Brazos Press, 2001.

Hayes, Zachary. *The Hidden Center: Spirituality and Speculative Christology in St. Bonaventure.* New York: Paulist Press, 1981.

Healy, Nicholas J. *The Eschatology of Hans Urs von Balthasar: Being as Communion.* Oxford: Oxford University Press, 2005.

Heinzer, Félix, and Christoph Schönborn, eds. *Maximus Confessor: Actes du Symposium sur Maxime le Confesseur Fribourg, 2-5 septembre 1980.* Fribourg: Éditions Universitaires, 1982.

Heppe, Heinrich. *Schriften zur Reformierten Theologie.* Elberfeld: Friderichs, 1860.

Hofer, Andrew. "Dionysian Elements in Thomas Aquinas's Christology: A Case of Authority and Ambiguity of Pseudo-Dionysius." *Thomist* 72 (2008): 409-42.

Honorius I. "*Scripta fraternitatis*" *ad Sergium.* In Heinrich Denzinger, *Enchiridion Symbolorum et Declarationum de Rebus Fidei et Morum,* edited by Peter Hünermann, #487. 43rd ed. San Francisco: Ignatius Press, 2012.

Hopkins, Gerard Manley. "Pied Beauty." In *Gerard Manley Hopkins: Poems and Prose,* edited by W. H. Gardner, pp. 30-31. London: Penguin Books, 1953.

Houselander, Caryll. *This War Is the Passion.* Notre Dame: Ave Maria Press, 2008.

Hugh of St. Victor. *De anima Christi.* In *Patrologia Latina,* edited by Jacques-Paul Migne, vol. 176, cols. 84-856. Paris: Vrayet, 1844-1864.

———. *De Sacramentis fidei Christiane.* In *Patrologia Latina,* edited by Jacques-Paul Migne, vol. 176, cols. 173-618. Paris: Vrayet, 1844-1864.

Hussey, J. M. *The Orthodox Church in the Byzantine Empire.* Oxford: Oxford University Press, 2010.

International Theological Commission. "Select Questions on Christology." In *International Theological Commission: Texts and Documents, 1969-1985,* edited by Michael Sharkey, pp. 185-206. San Francisco: Ignatius Press, 1989.

———. "Theology, Christology, Anthropology." In *International Theological Commission: Texts and Documents, 1969-1985,* edited by Michael Sharkey, pp. 207-23. San Francisco: Ignatius Press, 1989.

Irenaeus of Lyon. *Adversus haereses* 1. *Contre les hérésies, Livre I.* Sources Chrétiennes, vol. 263. Paris: Cerf, 1979.

————. *Adversus haereses 2. Contre les hérésies, Livre II.* Sources Chrétiennes, vols. 293-294. Paris: Cerf, 1982.

————. *Adversus haereses 3. Contre les hérésies, Livre III.* Sources Chrétiennes, vols. 210-211. Paris: Cerf, 1974.

————. *Adversus haereses 4. Contre les hérésies, Livre IV.* Sources Chrétiennes, vol. 100. Paris: Cerf, 1965.

————. *Adversus haereses 5. Contre les hérésies, Livre V.* Sources Chrétiennes, vols. 152-153. Paris: Cerf, 1969.

John Cassian. *De Coenobiorum institutis libri duodecim.* In *Patrologia Latina,* edited by Jacques-Paul Migne, vol. 49, cols. 53-477. Paris: Vrayet, 1844-1864.

————. *De Incarnatione Christi contra Nestorium Haereticum.* In *Patrologia Latina,* edited by Jacques-Paul Migne, vol. 50, cols. 9-372. Paris: Vrayet, 1844-1864.

————. *Vigintiquatuor collationes.* In *Patrologia Latina,* edited by Jacques-Paul Migne, vol. 49, cols. 478-1328. Paris: Vrayet, 1844-1864.

John of Damascus. *Contra Jacobitas.* In *Patrologia Graeca,* edited by Jacques-Paul Migne, vol. 94, cols. 1433-1502. Paris: Imprimerie Catholique, 1857-1866.

————. *De fide orthodoxa. La Foi orthodoxe.* Sources Chrétiennes, vols. 535 and 540. Paris: Cerf, 2010-2011.

John Paul II. "Audiencia general del 30 de noviembre de 1988." Online at: https://w2 .vatican.va/content/john-paul-ii/es/audiences/1988/documents/hf_jp-ii_aud _19881130.html.

————. *Novo Millennio Ineunte.* Apostolic Letter. 2001. Online at: https://w2.vatican.va/ content/john-paul-ii/en/apost_letters/2001/documents/hf_jp-ii_apl_20010106 _novo-millennio-ineunte.html.

————. *Redemptoris missio.* Encyclical Letter. 1990. Online at: http://w2.vatican .va/content/john-paul-ii/en/encyclicals/documents/hf_jp-ii_enc_07121990_ redemptoris-missio.html.

Johnson, Luke Timothy. *The Real Jesus.* San Francisco: Harper, 1997.

Jungmann, J. A. *Die Frohbotschaft und unsere Glaubensverkündigung.* Regensburg: Pustet, 1936.

————. *Die Stellung Christi im liturgischen Gebet.* Münster: Aschendorff, 1925.

Justinian. *Confessio rectae fidei.* In *Patrologia Graeca,* edited by Jacques-Paul Migne, vol. 86, cols. 993-1033. Paris: Imprimerie Catholique, 1857-1866.

Kasper, Walter. *Jesus the Christ.* Translated by V. Green. London: Burns and Oates, 1976.

Keating, Daniel A. *The Appropriation of Divine Life in Cyril of Alexandria.* Oxford: Oxford University Press, 2004.

————. "Divinization in Cyril: The Appropriation of Divine Life." In *The Theology of St. Cyril of Alexandria: A Critical Appreciation,* edited by Thomas G. Weinandy and Daniel A. Keating, pp. 149-86. London: T. & T. Clark, 2003.

Kelly, J. N. D. *Early Christian Doctrines.* Rev. ed. New York: HarperOne, 1978.

Kerr, Fergus, O.P. *After Aquinas: Versions of Thomism.* Oxford: Blackwell, 2002.

————. "Thomistica III." *New Blackfriars* (2004): 628-41.

Kilby, Karen. *A Brief Introduction to Karl Rahner.* London: Crossroad, 2007.

Kötter, Jan-Markus. *Zwischen Kaisern und Aposteln. Das Akakianische Schisma (484-519) als kirchlicher Ordnungskonflikt der Spätantike.* Stuttgart: Franz-Steiner Verlag, 2013.

Krausmüller, Dirk. "Leontius of Jerusalem: A Theologian of the Seventh Century." *Journal of Theological Studies* 52 (2001): 637-57.

Kyle, Richard. "Nestorius: The Partial Rehabilitation of a Heretic." *Journal of the Evangelical Theological Society* 32 (1989): 73-83.

Lang, U. M. "Anhypostatos-Enhypostatos: Church Fathers, Protestant Orthodoxy and Karl Barth." *Journal of Theological Studies* 49 (1998): 630-57.

Lateran Synod (649). Canons. In Heinrich Denzinger, *Enchiridion Symbolorum et Declarationum de Rebus Fidei et Morum*, edited by Peter Hünermann, ##501-522. 43rd ed. San Francisco: Ignatius Press, 2012.

Lauritzen, Frederick. "Pagan Energies in Maximus the Confessor: The Influence of Proclus on *Ad Thomam* 5." *Greek, Roman, and Byzantine Studies* 52 (2012): 226-39.

Lebon, Joseph. *Le monophysisme sévérien: étude historique, littéraire et théologique sur la résistance monophysite au Concile de Chalcédoine jusqu'à la constitution de l'Église jacobite.* Leuven: J. Van Linthout, 1909.

Leo XIII. *Rerum novarum.* Encyclical Letter. 1891. Online at: http://w2.vatican.va/content/leo-xiii/en/encyclicals/documents/hf_l-xiii_enc_15051891_rerum-novarum.html.

Leontius of Byzantium. *Adversus argumenta Severi.* In *Patrologia Graeca,* edited by Jacques-Paul Migne, vol. 86, cols. 1916-1945. Paris: Imprimerie Catholique, 1857-1866.

————. *Contra Nestorianos et Eutychianos.* In *Patrologia Graeca,* edited by Jacques-Paul Migne, vol. 86, cols. 1268-1357. Paris: Imprimerie Catholique, 1857-1866.

Leontius of Jerusalem. *Tractatus contra Nestorianos.* In *Patrologia Graeca,* edited by Jacques-Paul Migne, vol. 86, cols. 1400-1768. Paris: Imprimerie Catholique, 1857-1866. [N.B.: in Migne, wrongly attributed to Leontius of Byzantium.]

Leo the Great. *Epistulae.* In *Patrologia Latina,* edited by Jacques-Paul Migne, vol. 50. Paris: Vrayet, 1844-1864.

————. *Epistula Papae Leonis ad Flavianum.* In *Decrees of the Ecumenical Councils,* edited by Norman Tanner, vol. 1, pp. 77-82. London: Sheed & Ward, 1990.

————. *Sermo 74. "De ascensione Domini II."* In *Patrologia Latina,* edited by Jacques-Paul Migne, vol. 54, cols. 397-400. Paris: Vrayet, 1844-1864.

Leroy, M.-V. "L'union selon l'hypostase d'après saint Thomas d'Aquin." *Revue Thomiste* 74 (1974): 231-39.

Léthel, François-Marie. "La Prière de Jésus a Gethsémani dans la Controverse Monothélite." In *Maximus Confessor: Actes du Symposium sur Maxime le Confesseur Fribourg, 2-5 septembre 1980,* edited by Félix Heinzer and Christoph Schönborn, pp. 207-14. Fribourg: Éditions Universitaires, 1982.

————. *Théologie de l'agonie de Christ: La liberté humaine de fils de Dieu et son importance sotériologique mises en lumière par saint Maxime Confesseur.* Théologie Historique 52. Paris: Éditions Beauchesne, 1979.

Levering, Matthew. *Christ's Fulfillment of Torah and Temple: Salvation according to Thomas Aquinas.* Notre Dame: University of Notre Dame Press, 2002.

————. "Israel and the Shape of Thomas Aquinas's Soteriology." *Thomist* 63 (1999): 65-82.

————. *Scripture and Metaphysics: Aquinas and the Renewal of Trinitarian Theology.* Oxford: Blackwell, 2004.

Liébaert, J. *La doctrine christologique de S. Cyrille d'Alexandrie avant la querelle nestorienne*. Lille: Facultés Catholiques, 1951.

―――. *L'Incarnation, I: Des origines au concile de Chalcédoine*. Paris: Cerf, 1966.

Lietzmann, Hans, ed. *Apollinarius von Laodicea und seine Schule: Texte und Untersuchungen*. Tübingen: Möhr, 1904.

Long, Steven A. *Natura Pura: On the Recovery of Nature in the Doctrine of Grace, Moral Philosophy and Moral Theology*. New York: Fordham University Press, 2010.

Loofs, Friedrich. *Leontius von Byzanz und die gleichnamigen Schriftsteller der griechischen Kirche*. Texte und Untersuchungen 3, edited by Oskar von Gebhardt and Adolf von Harnack. Leipzig: J.C. Hinrich'sche Buchhandlung, 1887.

―――, ed. *Nestoriana: Die Fragmente des Nestorius*. Halle: Niemeyer, 1905.

Loon, Hans van. *The Dyophysite Christology of Cyril of Alexandria*. Leiden: Brill, 2009.

Lossky, Vladimir. *The Mystical Theology of the Eastern Church*. Translated by members of the Fellowship of St. Alban and St. Sergius. Crestwood, NY: Saint Vladimir's Seminary Press, 1976.

Louth, Andrew. *Denys the Areopagite*. London: Continuum, 2001.

―――. *Maximus the Confessor*. Early Church Fathers. London: Routledge, 1996.

―――. *St. John Damascene: Tradition and Originality in Byzantine Theology*. Oxford: Oxford University Press, 2002.

―――. "Why Did the Syrians Reject the Council of Chalcedon?" In *Chalcedon in Context: Church Councils, 400-700*, edited by Richard Price and Mary Whitby, pp. 107-16. Liverpool: Liverpool University Press, 2009.

Lubac, Henri de. *Catholicisme, les aspects sociaux du dogme*. Paris: Cerf, 1947.

Macquarrie, John. *Jesus Christ in Modern Thought*. London: SCM Press, 1990.

Martínez, Javier. "Prefacio a la Edición de 2008." In Luigi Giussani, *El Sentido Religioso. Curso Básico de Cristianismo*, translated by José Miguel Oriol, vol. 1, pp. i-vi. Madrid: Ediciones Encuentro, 2008.

Maximus the Confessor. *Ambiguorum liber sive de variis difficilibus locis SS. Dionysii Areopagitae et Gregorii Theolog*. In *Patrologia Graeca*, edited by Jacques-Paul Migne, vol. 91, cols. 1031-1417. Paris: Imprimerie Catholique, 1857-1866.

―――. *Disputatio cum Pyrrho*. In *Patrologia Graeca*, edited by Jacques-Paul Migne, vol. 91, cols. 288-353. Paris: Imprimerie Catholique, 1857-1866.

―――. *The Disputation with Pyrrhus of Our Father among the Saints Maximus the Confessor*. Translated by Joseph P. Farrell. South Canaan, PA: St. Tikhon's Seminary Press, 1990.

―――. *On the Cosmic Mystery of Jesus Christ*. Translated and edited by Paul M. Blowers and Robert L. Wilken. Crestwood, NY: Saint Vladimir's Seminary Press, 2003.

―――. *Opuscula theologica et polemica*. In *Patrologia Graeca*, edited by Jacques-Paul Migne, vol. 91, cols. 9-286. Paris: Imprimerie Catholique, 1857-1866.

―――. *Ad Thalassium 21*. In *Patrologia Graeca*, edited by Jacques-Paul Migne, vol. 90, cols. 312-317. Paris: Imprimerie Catholique, 1857-1866.

―――. *Ad Thalassium 61*. In *Patrologia Graeca*, edited by Jacques-Paul Migne, vol. 90, cols. 625-645. Paris: Imprimerie Catholique, 1857-1866.

McCormack, Bruce L. *Karl Barth's Critically Realistic Dialectical Theology: Its Genesis and Development, 1909-1936*. Oxford: Oxford University Press, 1995.

McCosker, Philip. "Parsing Paradox, Analysing 'And': Christological Configurations of

Theological Paradox in Some Mystical Theologies." Ph.D. diss., Cambridge University, 2008.

———. Review of *Communicatio idiomatum: lo scambio delle proprietà; storia, status quaestionis e prospettive*, by Grzegorz Strzelczyk. *Modern Theology* 23 (2007): 298-301.

McGuckin, John. "Did Augustine's Christology Depend on Theodore of Mopsuestia?" *Heythrop Journal* 55 (1990): 39-52.

———. *Gregory of Nazianzus: An Intellectual Biography*. Crestwood, NY: Saint Vladimir's Seminary Press, 2001.

———. *Saint Cyril of Alexandria and the Christological Controversy*. Crestwood, NY: Saint Vladimir's Seminary Press, 2004.

———. "The 'Theopaschite Confession' (Text and Historical Context): A Study in the Cyrillian Reinterpretation of Chalcedon." *Journal of Ecclesiastical History* 35 (1984): 239-55.

McLeod, Frederick. *Theodore of Mopsuestia*. Early Church Fathers. London: Routledge, 2008.

Meredith, Anthony. *Gregory of Nyssa*. Early Church Fathers. London: Routledge, 2009.

Meyendorff, John. *Christ in Eastern Christian Thought*. Crestwood, NY: Saint Vladimir's Seminary Press, 1975.

———. *Imperial Unity and Christian Divisions*. Crestwood, NY: Saint Vladimir's Seminary Press, 1989.

Michel, A. "Hypostase: Hypostatique (union)." In *Dictionnaire de théologie catholique*, edited by A. Vacant et al., vol. 7, pp. 369-568. Paris: Letouzey et Ané, 1903-1950.

Milbank, John. "Can a Gift Be Given? Prolegomena to a Future Trinitarian Metaphysic." In *Rethinking Metaphysics*, edited by L. Gregory Jones and Stephen E. Fowl, pp. 119-61. Oxford: Blackwell, 1995.

———. "The Soul of Reciprocity." *Modern Theology* 17 (2001): 335-91, 485-507.

Milbank, John, and Catherine Pickstock. *Truth in Aquinas*. New York: Routledge, 2001.

Morard, Martin. "Thomas d'Aquin lecteur des conciles." *Archivum Franciscanum Historicum* 98 (2005): 211-365.

———. "Une source de Saint Thomas d'Aquin: Le deuxième concile de Constantinople (553)." *Revue des sciences philosophiques et théologiques* 81 (1997): 21-56.

Murphy, F.-X., and Polycarp Sherwood. *Constantinople II et III*. Histoire Des Conciles Oecumeniques 3. Paris: l'Orante, 1973.

Neil, Bronwen. *Leo the Great*. Early Church Fathers. London: Routledge, 2009.

Nestorius. *The Bazaar of Heracleides*. Translated and edited by C. R. Driver and L. Hodgson. Oxford: Clarendon Press, 1925.

———. *Livre d'Héraclide de Damas*. Translated and edited by F. Nau. Paris: Letouzey et Ané, 1910.

———. *Nestoriana: Die Fragmente des Nestorius*. Edited by Friedrich Loofs. Halle: Niemeyer, 1905.

Newman, John Henry. *Parochial and Plain Sermons*. San Francisco: Ignatius Press, 1997.

Nicholas, J. H. "L'unité d'être dans le Christ d'après St. Thomas." *Revue Thomiste* 65 (1965): 229-60.

Nichols, Aidan, O.P. *Byzantine Gospel: Maximus the Confessor in Modern Scholarship*. London: Continuum, 1993.

————. *Rome and the Eastern Churches: A Study in Schism*. San Francisco: Ignatius Press, 2010.

Nielsen, Lauge Olaf. *Theology and Philosophy in the Twelfth Century: A Study of Gilbert Porreta's Thinking and the Theological Expositions of the Doctrine of the Incarnation during the Period 1130-1180*. Leiden: E. J. Brill, 1982.

Norris, R. A. *Manhood and Christ: A Study in the Christology of Theodore of Mopsuestia*. Oxford: Clarendon Press, 1963.

Oakes, Edward T. *Infinity Dwindled to Infancy: A Catholic and Evangelical Christology*. Grand Rapids: Eerdmans, 2011.

Obenaur, Klaus. "Aquinas's De unione verbi incarnati: An Interview with Klaus Obenauer." Online at: http://thomistica.net/news/2011/9/6/aquinas-de-unione -verbi-incarnati-an-interview-with-dr-klaus.html.

————. *Thomas von Aquin: Quaestio disputata "De unione Verbi incarnati."* Stuttgart-Bad Cannstatt: Frommann-Holzboog, 2011.

Ocáriz, F., L. F. Mateo Seco, and J. A. Riestra. *The Mystery of Jesus Christ*. Translated by Michael Adams and James Gavigan. Dublin: Four Courts Press, 2004.

O'Collins, Gerald. *Christology: A Biblical, Historical, and Systematic Study of Jesus*. Oxford: Oxford University Press, 1995.

O'Keefe, John. "Impassible Suffering? Divine Passion and Fifth-Century Christology." *Theological Studies* 58 (1997): 39-60.

O'Neill, Coleman E. Appendix 3: "The Problem of Christ's Human Autonomy." In Thomas Aquinas, *Summa Theologiae*, vol. 50 (III, 16-26): *The One Mediator*. Cambridge: Cambridge University Press, 2006.

Origen of Alexandria. *In Evangelium Ioannis*. In *Patrologia Graeca*, edited by Jacques-Paul Migne, vol. 14, cols. 21-830. Paris: Imprimerie Catholique, 1857-1866.

Ott, Ludwig. "Das Konzil von Chalkedon in der Frühscholastik." In *Das Konzil von Chalkedon: Geschichte und Gegenwart*, edited by A. Grillmeier and H. Bacht, vol. 2. Würzburg: Echter-Verlag, 1953.

Pabst, Adrian. *Metaphysics: The Creation of Hierarchy*. Grand Rapids: Eerdmans, 2012.

Pannenberg, Wolfhart. *Jesus—God and Man*. Translated by Lewis L. Wilkins and Duane A. Priebe. London: SCM Press, 1968.

Pásztori-Kupán, István. *Theodoret of Cyrus*. Early Church Fathers. London: Routledge, 2006.

Patfoort, A. "L'enseignement de Saint Thomas sur l'esse du Christ." In *Problèmes actuels de christologie*, edited by H. Bouëssé and J. J. Latour. Paris: Desclée, 1965.

————. *L'unité d'être dans le Christ d'après S. Thomas: A la croisée de l'ontologie et de la christologie*. Paris: Desclée, 1958.

Pelagius I. *Vas electionis*. In Heinrich Denzinger, *Enchiridion Symbolorum et Declarationum de Rebus Fidei et Morum*, edited by Peter Hünermann, #444. 43rd ed. San Francisco: Ignatius Press, 2012.

Pelikan, Jaroslav. *The Christian Tradition: A History of the Development of Doctrine*. Vol. 1, *The Emergence of the Catholic Tradition (100-600)*. Chicago: University of Chicago Press, 1975.

————. *The Christian Tradition: A History of the Development of Doctrine*. Vol. 2, *The Spirit of Eastern Christendom (600-1700)*. Chicago: University of Chicago Press, 1974.

Perczel, István. "The Christology of Pseudo-Dionysius the Areopagite: The Fourth Letter in Its Indirect and Direct Text Traditions." *Le Muséon* 117 (2004): 409-46.

Peter Lombard. *Libri quatuor Sententiarum.* In *Patrologia Latina,* edited by Jacques-Paul Migne, vol. 192, cols. 519-964. Paris: Vrayet, 1844-1864.

Piret, Pierre. *Le Christ et la Trinité selon Maxime le Confesseur.* Paris: Les Éditions du Cerf, 1983.

Pius X. *Lamentabili Sane Exitu.* Encyclical Letter. 1907. Online at: http://papalencyclicals .net/Pius10/p10lamen.htm.

Pius XII. *Mediator Dei et hominum.* Encyclical Letter. 1947. Online at: http://w2.vatican .va/content/pius-xii/en/encyclicals/documents/hf_p-xii_enc_20111947_mediator -dei.html.

———. *Sempiternus Rex.* Encyclical Letter. 1951. Online at: http://w2.vatican.va/ content/pius-xii/en/encyclicals/documents/hf_p-xii_enc_08091951_sempiternus -rex-christus.html.

Price, Richard. *The Acts of the Council of Constantinople of 553: With Related Texts on the Three Chapters Controversy, Edited and with an Introduction and Notes.* 2 vols. Liverpool: Liverpool University Press, 2009.

Price, Richard, and Michael Gaddis. *The Acts of the Council of Chalcedon: Translated with an Introduction and Notes.* 3 vols. Manchester: Liverpool University Press, 2005.

Price, Richard, and Mary Whitby, eds. *Chalcedon in Context: Church Councils, 400-700.* Liverpool: Liverpool University Press, 2009.

Pusey, Phillip E., ed. *Sancti patris nostri Cyrilli Archiepiscopi Alexandrini in d. Ioannis Evangelium.* Oxford: Clarendon Press, 1872.

Radner, Ephraim. *The End of the Church: A Pneumatology of Christian Division in the West.* Grand Rapids: Eerdmans, 1998.

Rahner, Karl. "Chalkedon—Ende oder Anfang?" In *Das Konzil von Chalkedon,* edited by A. von Grillmeier and H. Bacht, vol. 3, pp. 3-49. Würzburg: Echter Verlag, 1954.

———. *Foundations of Christian Faith: An Introduction to the Idea of Christianity.* Translated by William V. Dych. New York: Seabury Press, 1978.

———. *Karl Rahner in Dialogue: Conversations and Interviews, 1965-1982.* Edited by Paul Imhof and Hubert Biallowons. New York: Crossroad, 1986.

———. *Theological Investigations.* Vol. 1. Translated by Cornelius Ernst. Baltimore: Helicon, 1961.

———. *Theological Investigations.* Vol. 17. Translated by Margaret Kohl. London: Darton, Longman & Todd, 1981. Pp. 24-38.

———. *Theological Investigations.* Vol. 21. Translated by Hugh M. Riley. London: Darton, Longman & Todd, 1988.

Ratzinger, Joseph. *Behold the Pierced One: An Approach to a Spiritual Christology.* Translated by Graham Harrison. San Francisco: Ignatius Press, 1986.

———. *Un Canto Nuevo Para el Señor: La fe en Jesucristo y la liturgia hoy.* Salamanca: Ediciones Sigueme, 1999.

———. *Daughter Zion: Meditations on the Church's Marian Belief.* Translated by John M. McDermott, S.J. San Francisco: Ignatius Press, 1983.

———. *Dogma and Preaching.* Translated by Matthew J. O'Connell. Chicago: Franciscan Herald, 1985.

————. *Eschatology, Death, and Eternal Life.* Translated by Michael Waldstein. 2nd ed. Washington, DC: Catholic University of America Press, 1988.

————. *A New Song for the Lord: Faith in Christ and Liturgy Today.* Translated by Martha M. Matesich. London: Crossroads, 1996.

Ratzinger, Joseph (Pope Benedict XVI). *Jesus of Nazareth.* Pt. 1, *From the Baptism in the Jordan to the Transfiguration.* Translated by Adrian J. Walker. New York: Doubleday, 2007.

————. *Jesus of Nazareth.* Pt. 2, *Holy Week: From the Entrance into Jerusalem to the Resurrection.* Translation provided by the Vatican Secretariat of State. San Francisco: Ignatius Press, 2011.

Ratzinger, Joseph Cardinal, with Vittorio Messori. *The Ratzinger Report: An Exclusive Interview on the State of the Church.* Translated by Salvator Attanasio and Graham Harrison. San Francisco: Ignatius Press, 1986.

Reynolds, Roger E. *Collectio Canonum Casinensis Duodecimi Seculi (Codex Terscriptus): A Derivative of the South-Italian Collection in Five Books; An Implicit Edition with Introductory Study.* Rome: Pontifical Institute of Mediaeval Studies, 2001.

Riches, Aaron. "After Chalcedon: The Oneness of Christ and the Dyothelite Mediation of His Theandric Unity." *Modern Theology* 24 (2008): 199-224.

————. "Christology and Anti-Humanism." *Modern Theology* 29 (2013): 311-37.

————. "Christology and the 'Scotist Rupture.'" *Theological Research* 1 (2013): 31-63.

————. "Theandric Humanism: Constantinople III in the Thought of St. Thomas." *Pro Ecclesia* 23, no. 2 (2014): 195-218.

Riedinger, Rudolf. "Die Lateransynode von 649 und Maximos der Bekenner." In *Maximus Confessor: Actes du Symposium sur Maxime le Confesseur Fribourg, 2-5 septembre 1980,* edited by Félix Heinzer and Christoph Schönborn. Fribourg: Éditions Universitaires, 1982.

Riordan, William. *Divine Light: The Theology of Denys the Areopagite.* San Francisco: Ignatius Press, 2008.

Rogers, Eugene F., Jr. *After the Spirit: A Constructive Pneumatology from Resources Outside the Modern West.* Grand Rapids: Eerdmans, 2005.

————. "The Eclipse of the Spirit in Karl Barth." In *Conversing with Barth,* edited by John McDowell and Michael Higton, pp. 173-90. London: Ashgate, 2004.

Rorem, Paul, and John C. Lamoreaux. "John of Scythopolis on Apollinarian Christology and the Pseudo-Areopagite's True Identity." *Church History* 62 (1993): 469-82.

Rosemann, Philipp W. *Peter Lombard.* Oxford: Oxford University Press, 2004.

Ruello, Francis. *La christologie de Thomas d'Aquin.* Paris: Beauchesne, 1987.

Russell, Norman. *Cyril of Alexandria.* Early Church Fathers. London: Routledge, 2000.

————. *The Doctrine of Deification in the Greek Patristic Tradition.* Oxford: Oxford University Press, 2004.

Salas, Victor, Jr. "Thomas Aquinas on Christ's *Esse:* A Metaphysics of the Incarnation." *Thomist* 70 (2006): 577-603.

Samuel, V. C. "The Christology of Severus of Antioch." *Abba Salama* 4 (1973): 126-90.

————. *The Council of Chalcedon Re-Examined.* New York: Xlibris, 2001.

————. "Further Studies in the Christology of Severus of Antioch." *Ekklesiastikos Pharos* 58 (1976): 270-301.

―――. "One Incarnate Nature of God the Word." *Greek Orthodox Theological Review* 10 (1964/1965): 37-53.

Sharkey, Michael, ed. *International Theological Commission: Texts and Documents, 1969-1985.* San Francisco: Ignatius Press, 1989.

Schindler, David L. "The Embodied Person as Gift and the Cultural Task on America: *Status Quaestionis.*" *Communio: International Catholic Review* 35 (2008): 397-431.

―――. *Heart of the World, Center of the Church:* Communio *Ecclesiology, Liberalism, and Liberation.* Grand Rapids: Eerdmans, 1996.

―――. *Ordering Love: Liberal Societies and the Memory of God.* Grand Rapids: Eerdmans, 2011.

―――. "The Person: Philosophy, Theology, and Receptivity." *Communio* 21 (1994): 172-90.

Schleiermacher, Friedrich. *The Christian Faith.* Translated by H. R. Mackintosh and J. S. Stewart. Edinburgh: T. & T. Clark, 1928.

Schönborn, Christoph von. *God Sent His Son: A Contemporary Christology.* Translated by Henry Taylor. San Francisco: Ignatius Press, 2004.

―――. *Sophrone de Jérusalem: vie monastique et confession dogmatique.* Paris: Beauchesne, 1972.

Schoot, Henk J. M. *Christ the "Name" of God: Thomas Aquinas on Naming Christ.* Leuven: Peeters, 1993.

Seifert, Josef. *Das Leib-Seele-Problem in der gegenwärtigen philosophischen Diskussion.* Darmstadt: Wissenschaftliche Buchgesellschaft, 1979.

―――. "Mary as Coredemptrix and Mediatrix of All Graces: Philosophical and Personalistic Foundations of a Marian Doctrine." In *Mary Coredemptrix, Mediatrix, Advocate: Theological Foundations II; Papal, Pneumatological, Ecumenical,* edited by Mark I. Miravalle, pp. 149-74. Santa Barbara, CA: Queenship Publishing, 1997.

Seiller, Léon. *L'activité humaine du Christ selon Duns Scot.* Paris: Édit. Franciscaines, 1944.

―――. *La psychologie humaine du Christ et l'unité de personne.* Rennes-Paris: Vrin, 1950.

Sellers, R. V. *The Council of Chalcedon: A Historical and Doctrinal Survey.* London: SPCK, 1953.

―――. *Two Ancient Christologies.* London: SPCK, 1940.

Sherwood, Polycarp. *St. Maximus: The Ascetic Life, the Four Centuries on Charity.* Mahwah, NJ: Newman, 1955.

Shults, F. LeRon. "A Dubious Christological Formula: From Leontius of Byzantium to Karl Barth." *Theological Studies* 57 (1996): 431-46.

Siebenrock, Roman A. "Christology." In *The Cambridge Companion to Karl Rahner,* edited by Declan Marmion and Mary E. Hines, pp. 112-27. Cambridge: Cambridge University Press, 2005.

Sobrino, Jon. *Christ the Liberator: A View from the Victims.* Translated by Paul Burns. Maryknoll, NY: Orbis, 2001.

―――. *Jesus the Liberator: A Historical-Theological Reading of Jesus of Nazareth.* Translated by P. Burns and F. McDonagh. Maryknoll, NY: Orbis, 1993.

Speyr, Adrienne von. *Handmaid of the Lord.* Translated by E. A. Nelson. San Francisco: Ignatius Press, 1985.

————. *Mary in the Redemption.* Translated by Helena M. Tomko. San Francisco: Ignatius Press, 2003.

————. *The World of Prayer.* Translated by Graham Harrison. San Francisco: Ignatius Press, 1985.

Stang, Charles M. *Apophasis and Pseudonymity in Dionysius the Areopagite: "No Longer I."* Oxford: Oxford University Press, 2012.

Starowieyski, Marek. "Le title Θεοτόκος avant le concile d'Ephèse." *Studia Patristica* 19 (1989): 236-42.

Strzelczyk, Grzegorz. *Communicatio idiomatum: lo scambio delle proprietà; storia, status quaestionis e prospettive.* Rome: Pontificia Università Gregoriana, 2004.

Sullivan, Francis A. *The Christology of Theodore of Mopsuestia.* Rome: Pontifical Gregorian University Press, 1956.

Takis, Nancy Chalker, ed. *The Divine Liturgy of Our Father among the Saints John Chrysostom: For Sunday Worship.* In Modern English and Greek. 3rd ed. Williamston, MI: New Byzantium Publications, 2010.

Tanner, Kathryn. *God and Creation in Christian Theology: Tyranny or Empowerment?* New York: Basil Blackwell, 1988.

————. *Jesus, Humanity, and the Trinity: A Brief Systematic Theology.* Edinburgh: T. & T. Clark, 2001.

Tanner, Norman. *The Church in Council: Conciliar Movements, Religious Practice, and the Papacy from Nicaea to Vatican II.* London: I. B. Tauris, 2011.

————, ed. *Decrees of the Ecumenical Councils.* 2 vols. Washington, DC: Georgetown University Press, 1990.

Tanquerey, A. D. *A Manual of Dogmatic Theology.* Translated by John J. Byrnes. 2 vols. New York: Desclee Co., 1959.

Thomas Aquinas. *Commentary on the Gospel of John.* Translated by Fabian Larcher and James A. Weisheipl. Edited by Daniel Keating and Matthew Levering. 3 vols. Washington, DC: CUA, 2010.

————. *Compendium of Theology.* Translated by Richard J. Regan. Oxford: Oxford University Press, 2009.

————. *Corpus Thomisticum S. Thomas de Aquino Opera Omnia.* Universitatis Studiorum Navarrensis. 2009. Online at: http://www.corpusthomisticum.org/iopera .html.

————. *Question disputée: l'union du Verbe incarné (De unione Verbi incarnati).* Translated and edited by Marie-Hélène Deloffre. Paris: J. Vrin, 2000.

————. *The Sermon-Conferences of St. Thomas Aquinas on the Apostles' Creed.* Translated by Nicholas Ayo. Notre Dame: University of Notre Dame, 1998.

————. *Summa Contra Gentiles.* Translated by Anton C. Pegis et al. 5 vols. Notre Dame: University of Notre Dame Press, 1975.

————. *The Summa Theologica.* Translated by the Fathers of the English Dominican Province. 5 vols. Westminster, MD: Christian Classics, 1981.

Thompson, Augustine. *Francis of Assisi: A New Biography.* Ithaca, NY: Cornell University Press, 2012.

Thunberg, Lars. *Microcosm and Mediator: The Theological Anthropology of Maximus the Confessor.* 2nd ed. Chicago: Open Court, 1995.

Tillich, Paul. *Systematic Theology*. Vol. 2, *Existence and the Christ*. Chicago: University of Chicago Press, 1957.

Tixeront, Joseph. *Histoire des dogmes dans l'antiquité chrétienne*. 2 vols. Paris: J. Gabalda, 1912.

Torrance, Iain R. *Christology after Chalcedon: Severus of Antioch and Sergius the Monophysite*. Norwich: Canterbury Press, 1988.

Torrell, Jean-Pierre. "La causalité salvifique de la résurrection du Christ selon saint Thomas." *Revue thomiste* 96 (1996): 179-208.

—. "S. Thomas d'Aquin et la science du Christ: une relecture des Questions 9-12 de la *tertia pars* de la *Somme de théologie*." In *Saint Thomas au XXe siècle*, edited by S.-T. Bonino. Paris: Editions Saint-Paul, 1994.

—. *Thomas Aquinas*. Vol. 1, *The Person and His Work*. Translated by Robert Royal. Washington, DC: Catholic University Press, 1996.

—. "Le Thomisme dans le débat christologique contemporain." In *Saint Thomas au XXe siècle*, edited by S.-T. Bonino. Paris: Editions Saint-Paul, 1994.

Trigg, Joseph W. *Origen*. Early Church Fathers. London: Routledge, 1998.

Tschipke, Theophil. *L'humanité du Christ comme instrument de salut de la divinité*. Translated by Philibert Secrétan. Fribourg: Academic Press Fribourg, 2003.

Tsonievsky, Elias. "The Union of the Two Natures in Christ according to the Non-Chalcedonian Churches and Orthodoxy." *Greek Orthodox Theological Review* 13 (1968): 170-80.

Turner, H. E. W. "Nestorius Reconsidered." *Studia Patristica* 13 (1975): 306-21.

Ulrich, Ferdinand. *Leben in der Einheit von Leben und Tod*. Freiburg: Johannes Verlag, 1999.

Venard, Olivier-Thomas. *Thomas d'Aquin poète théologien*. 3 vols. Geneva and Paris: Ad Solem/Cerf, 2002-2010.

Verghese, Paul. "The Monothelite Controversy—A Historical Survey." *Greek Orthodox Theological Review* 13 (1968): 196-208.

Vine, Aubrey R. *An Approach to Christology: An Interpretation and Development of Some Elements in the Metaphysic and Christology of Nestorius*. London: Independent Press, 1948.

Walker, Adrian J. "*Singulariter in spe constituisti me:* On the Christian Attitude towards Death." *Communio* 39 (2012): 351-63.

Wallace-Hadrill, D. S. *Christian Antioch: A Study of Early Christian Thought in the East*. Cambridge: Cambridge University Press, 1982.

Wawrykow, Joseph. "Wisdom in the Christology of Thomas Aquinas." In *Christ among the Medieval Dominicans*, edited by Kent Emery Jr. and Joseph P. Wawrykow, pp. 175-94. Notre Dame: University of Notre Dame Press, 1998.

Wear, Sarah Klitenic, and John Dillon. *Dionysius the Areopagite and the Neoplatonist Tradition: Despoiling the Hellenes*. Aldershot: Ashgate, 2007.

Wéber, É.-H. *Le Christ selon Saint Thomas d'Aquin*. Paris: Desclée, 1988.

Weinandy, Thomas G. "The Apostolic Christology of Ignatius of Antioch: The Road to Chalcedon." In *Trajectories through the New Testament and the Apostolic Fathers*, edited by A. Gregory and C. Tuckett, pp. 71-84. Oxford: Oxford University Press, 2005.

—. "Aquinas: God *IS* Man—the Marvel of the Incarnation." In *Aquinas on Doctrine:*

A Critical Introduction, edited by Thomas G. Weinandy, Daniel A. Keating, and John P. Yocum, pp. 67-89. London: T. & T. Clark International, 2004.

———. *Athanasius: A Theological Introduction*. London: Ashgate, 2007.

———. "The Beatific Vision and the Incarnate Son: Furthering the Discussion." *Thomist* 70 (2006): 605-15.

———. "Cyril and the Mystery of the Incarnation." In *The Theology of Cyril of Alexandria: A Critical Appreciation*, edited by Thomas G. Weinandy and Daniel A. Keating, pp. 23-54. London: T. & T. Clark, 2003.

———. *Does God Change? The Word's Becoming in the Incarnation*. Still River, MA: St. Bede's Publications, 1985.

———. *Does God Suffer?* Edinburgh: T. & T. Clark, 2000.

———. *In the Likeness of Sinful Flesh: An Essay on the Humanity of Christ*. Edinburgh: T. & T. Clark, 1993.

———. "Jesus' Filial Vision of the Father." *Pro Ecclesia* 13 (2004): 189-201.

Weinandy, Thomas G., and Daniel A. Keating, eds. *The Theology of Cyril of Alexandria: A Critical Appreciation*. London: T. & T. Clark, 2003.

Weinandy, Thomas G., Daniel A. Keating, and John P. Yocum, eds. *Aquinas on Doctrine: A Critical Introduction*. London: T. & T. Clark International, 2004.

Weisheipl, James. *Friar Thomas d'Aquino: His Life, Thought, and Works*. New York: Doubleday, 1974.

Welch, Lawrence J. *Christology and Eucharist in the Early Thought of Cyril of Alexandria*. San Francisco: International Scholars Press, 1994.

Welte, B. "'Homoousios hemin.' Gedanken zum Verständnis und zur theologischen Problematik der Kategorien von Chalkedon." In *Das Konzil von Chalkedon*, edited by A. von Grillmeier and H. Bacht, vol. 3, pp. 51-80 Würzburg: Echter Verlag, 1954.

Wesche, Kenneth P. *On the Person of Christ: The Christology of Emperor Justinian*. Crestwood, NY: Saint Vladimir's Seminary Press, 1991.

Wessel, Susan. *Cyril of Alexandria and the Nestorian Controversy: The Making of a Saint and of a Heretic*. Oxford: Oxford University Press, 2004.

———. *Leo the Great and the Spiritual Rebuilding of a Universal Rome*. Leiden: Brill, 2008.

West, J. L. "Aquinas on the Metaphysics of the *Esse* in Christ." *Thomist* 66 (2002): 231-50.

White, Thomas Joseph. "Dyothelitism and the Instrumental Human Consciousness of Jesus." *Pro Ecclesia* 17 (2008): 369-422.

———. "The Voluntary Action of the Earthly Christ and the Necessity of the Beatific Vision." *Thomist* 69 (2005): 497-534.

Wickham, Lionel R., ed. *Cyril of Alexandria: Select Letters*. Oxford: Oxford University Press, 1983.

———. "Pelagianism in the East." In *The Making of Orthodoxy: Essays in Honour of Henry Chadwick*, edited by Rowan Williams, pp. 200-215. Cambridge: Cambridge University Press, 1989.

Wilken, Robert L. "Cyril of Alexandria as Interpreter of the Old Testament." In *The Theology of Cyril of Alexandria: A Critical Appreciation*, edited by Thomas G. Weinandy and Daniel A. Keating, pp. 1-22. London: T. & T. Clark, 2003.

———. "Exegesis and the History of Theology: Reflections on the Adam-Christ Typology in Cyril of Alexandria." *Church History* 35 (1966): 139-56.

————. *The First Thousand Years: A Global History of Christianity.* New Haven: Yale University Press, 2012.

————. *Judaism and the Early Christian Mind: A Study of Cyril of Alexandria's Exegesis and Theology.* New Haven: Yale University Press, 1971.

————. "St. Cyril of Alexandria: Biblical Expositor." *Coptic Church Review* 19 (1998): 30-41.

————. "St. Cyril of Alexandria: The Mystery of Christ in the Bible." *Pro Ecclesia* 4 (1995): 454-78.

————. *The Spirit of Early Christian Thought.* New Haven: Yale University Press, 2003.

Williams, Rowan. *Arius: Heresy and Tradition.* Rev. ed. London: SCM, 2001.

————. "Jesus Christus III: Mittelalter." In *Theologische Realenzyklopädie,* edited by Gerhard Müller, vol. 16, pp. 745-59. Berlin: De Gruyter, 1987.

————, ed. *The Making of Orthodoxy: Essays in Honour of Henry Chadwick.* Cambridge: Cambridge University Press, 1989.

————. "'Person' and 'Personality' in Christology." *Downside Review* 94 (1976): 253-60.

Wippel, John F. *The Metaphysical Thought of Thomas Aquinas: From Finite Being to Uncreated Being.* Washington, DC: Catholic University of America Press, 2000.

Witherington, Ben, III. *The Jesus Quest: The Third Search for the Jew of Nazareth.* Downers Grove, IL: InterVarsity Press, 1995.

Wybrew, Hugh. *The Orthodox Liturgy: The Development of the Eucharistic Liturgy in the Byzantine Rite.* Crestwood, NY: Saint Vladimir's Seminary Press, 1990.

Young, Frances. *From Nicaea to Chalcedon: A Guide to the Literature and Its Background.* London: SCM Press, 1983.

————. "*Theotokos:* Mary and the Pattern of Fall and Reception in the Theology of Cyril of Alexandria." In *The Theology of Cyril of Alexandria: A Critical Appreciation,* edited by Thomas G. Weinandy and Daniel A. Keating, pp. 55-74. London: T. & T. Clark, 2003.

Zambolotsky, N. "The Christology of Severus of Antioch." *Ekklesiastikos Pharos* 58 (1976): 357-86.

Zimmerman, Heinrich. "Das absolute 'Ich bin' in der Redeweise Jesu." *Trierer Theologische Zeitschrift* 69 (1960): 1-20.

Index of Names and Subjects